Complementary Therapies in Context

Health, the Individual, and Integrated Medicine
Revisiting an Aesthetic of Health Care
David Aldridge
ISBN 1 84310 232 3

Spirituality in Health Care Contexts
Edited by Helen Orchard
ISBN 1 85302 969 6

Spiritual Dimensions of Pastoral Care
Practical Theology in a Multidisciplinary Context
Edited by David Willows and John Swinton
ISBN 1 85302 892 4

Complementary Therapies in Context
The Psychology of Healing

Helen Graham

Jessica Kingsley Publishers
London and Philadelphia

First edition, *Time, Energy and Psychology of Healing,* published in 1990 by Jessica Kingsley Publishers.
This edition published in the United Kingdom in 1999 by
Jessica Kingsley Publishers
116 Pentonville Road
London N1 9JB, UK
and
400 Market Street, Suite 400
Philadelphia PA 19106, USA

www.jkp.com

Copyright © 1999 Helen Graham

Prinited digitally since 2004

Library of Congress Cataloging in Publication Data
A CIP catalog record for this book is available from the Library of Congress

British Library Cataloguing in Publication Data
Graham, Helen, 1949–
Complementary therapies in context : the psychology of healing
1.Holistic medicine
I.Title
615.5

ISBN-13 978 1 85302 640 9 pb
ISBN-10 1 85302 640 9 pb

Contents

1

The Case for Complementary Medicine

Idries Shah[1] relates the tale of Mulla Nasrudin who, when asked why he was looking on the ground outside for a key he had lost indoors, replied that there was more light there than inside his house. Although Nasrudin's behaviour seems absurd, it is precisely what most people do when they have a problem. Rather than search within themselves they look outside, often recruiting the services of others, in the hope that they will find the key to a solution. This is nowhere more apparent than in the field of healing, or medicine (from the Latin *medicina*: the art of healing). Perhaps more than any other discipline, it is expected to provide solutions for human problems. In its attempts to do so, the medical profession has tended, like Nasrudin, to look where the light is good, so in Western culture the apparent clarity and systematic investigation of medical science is greatly preferred to the mysterious fumblings of self-cure. Certainly medical science has made some startling and significant discoveries, and yielded important keys to understanding numerous conditions. Therefore the possibility that, like Nasrudin, it has been looking in the wrong place has rarely been considered. Yet despite the advances achieved by medical science, it is becoming clear that throughout the Western world there is a profound crisis in medicine, and a growing disillusionment and dissatisfaction with health care, especially among those who provide it. Put simply, 'medicine isn't right and we know it'.[2]

Doctors

Evidence to support this claim can be found in prestigious medical journals and research reports. These reveal that there is no direct relation between changes in disease patterns and the so-called 'progress' of medicine, and that the environment is the primary determinant of the general health status of any population. So, despite widespread belief to the contrary, the increased life expectancy of modern times is less a triumph for medicine than for improved sanitation, nutrition, housing, working conditions and standards of living, smaller families and other social improvements. Analysis of disease trends reveals that the incidence of most bacterial disease began to fall long before the introduction of sulphonamide drugs and antibiotics. Ninety per cent of the total decline in the combined death rate from scarlet fever, diphtheria, whooping cough and measles after 1900 occurred *before* the advent of these drugs or mass immunisation.[3] Between 1800 and 1947, when Streptomycin was introduced, there had been a 95 per cent decline in mortality from tuberculosis, and decline in mortality from streptococcal infections and pneumonia followed much the same pattern.[4] The decline of cholera, dysentery and typhoid was also largely outside medical control. Advances in agriculture led to the production of more varied and nutritious foods, better diet and increased resistance to infection. Improvements in water purification, pasteurisation of milk, better food hygiene and improved sewage processing also had a significant impact on health. So, the farmer, foodhandler and sewage engineer deserve credit for improved health rather than doctors, whose interventions in disease have been greatly over-emphasised: 'People are healthier today not because they receive all this well-publicised better treatment when ill, but simply because they tend not to become ill in the first place'.[5] Hence the effectiveness of doctors is largely illusory.

Drugs

The impact of drugs on infection is also largely an illusion.[6] While this is not a position most doctors would support, drugs having played an unquestionable role in the control of pneumonia, gonorrhoea, syphilis, malaria and many other conditions, it is nevertheless true to say that they account for only a small proportion of the increase in life expectancy. They also have a very high price in terms of drug-induced illness and dependence. Certainly claims made for drugs have to be carefully evaluated, and the benefits weighed against their dangers, drawbacks and disadvantages, which are considerable.[7,8] The possible dangers of drugs have been highlighted in recent years by scandals surrounding the anti-arthritic drug Opren, chemical contraceptives such as the Dalcon Shield and Depoprovera, the tranquilliser Ativan and the anti-malarial drug, Lariam, and the over-prescription of drugs by doctors.[9] Increasingly attention is being drawn to unwanted side-effects of medicines;[10,11] drug combinations that counteract each other;[12] addictive, mutilating and mutagenic drugs,[13] and those which induce superinfection or contribute to drug-resistant viruses.[14,15] There is growing concern that antibiotics can disrupt immune function, and may be implicated in the increasing incidence of conditions such as candida albicans, childhood developmental disorders and diabetes;[16] and there is evidence to suggest that chronic fatigue syndrome or ME may be triggered by vaccinations.[17] Two thirds of patients receiving drugs in treatment suffer side-effects, in many cases more serious than the problem being treated.[18] In one incident in the USA in 1990 more than 650,000 people aged over 60 were hospitalised after reacting to a drug.[19] An earlier study in Boston which monitored 1900 hospital patients found that one in three suffered adverse drug effects, and that one in 200 died from these – more than the number killed annually on US roads.[20] According to a World Health Congress report in the 1980s, 25 million people have sustained permanent damage from drugs used in psychiatric treatment;[21] and in 1997 it was acknowledged that hundreds of the British armed forces serving in the Gulf War suffered horrifying side effects from drugs given to them as preventative medicine. It is therefore not surprising if 'the first movement away from what Western medicine has to offer starts with a disenchantment or even frank horror of what drugs do to people, mainly because going to the doctor has become synonymous with drugtaking'.[22]

Surgery

If going to the doctor has come to mean taking drugs, then going into hospital has become synonymous with undergoing surgery. Although the emergency medicine of the West is probably the best in the world, the actual amount of life-saving surgery is only a tiny fraction of the total, which is mostly for preventable conditions such as hernias, haemorrhoids or gallstones; and much is avoidable or unnecessary. Indeed, unnecessary surgery has become a standard procedure.[23] This is certainly the case in obstetrics. In practice, pregnancy is treated as 'a nine month self-limiting illness often requiring surgery at the end'.[24] Twenty-five per cent of births in the USA and 20 per cent in Canada are achieved by Caesarian section and the number is rising.[25] Britain appears to be following this trend.[26] At some hospitals the Caesarian rate is one in seven, while elsewhere it is as high as one in five. Few of these operations are justified on health grounds but are performed for medical convenience.[27] Britain is also following the US trend in employing forceps or vacuum extraction.[28] In the USA, where virtually all births occur in hospital, the chance of a baby being born with brain damage or dying during birth, as a result of these procedures, is twice what it is in Holland, where more than half of all births take place within the home. At all levels of obstetric risk, giving birth at home is safer than doing so in hospital. This is largely because the medical technology surrounding hospital childbirth is not as safe as is generally supposed.[29] There is ample evidence that most of the hi-tech forms of care offered during pregnancy and childbirth, including ultrasound scans and foetal monitoring, are unnecessary and potentially dangerous.[30,31] Foetal monitors, for example, have been shown to increase the rate of surgical intervention without a corresponding decrease in neonatal morbidity.[32] Moreover, despite modern surgical techniques and drugs, infection and fever still occur in one in five mothers who undergo Caesarian section, and psychological disturbance is not uncommon.

Medical treatment

It is not only mothers and babies who are at risk from unnecessary surgery and medical procedures. In the 1970s US Department of Health statistics revealed that 7 per cent of all patients suffered compensatable injuries while hospitalised, and that an estimated one in five patients admitted to a typical teaching hospital acquired an *iatrogenic* or doctor-created disease that would not otherwise have occurred. Sometimes this was a relatively trivial matter, although usually requiring special treatment, but one case in 30 led to the patient's death. Half of these incidents resulted from complications of drug therapy, and an alarming one in ten from diagnostic procedures.[33] In a study of 815 consecutive patients at a US university medical centre during the 1980s, 36 per cent were being treated because of health problems created directly or indirectly by medicine itself.[34] Extrapolation of these results to the US population as a whole suggests that over one million people are injured in hospital each year, and that 180,000 die in consequence.[35] Results of the world's first study into hospital safety carried out by the Australian Department of Health, published in 1995, show that one in six people are hospitalised because some medical treatment has gone wrong, and there is a one in six chance of dying or suffering injury while there. The chances of dying in hospital, or suffering some injury while there, is about 16 per cent. Since half the risk is caused by doctors or hospital error, there is an 8 per cent chance of being killed by hospital staff.[36] Some 1.17 million Britons are hospitalised each year as a result of doctor error or a bad reaction to a drug.[37]

> To put the magnitude of the problem in perspective, the entire population of Birmingham is put in a hospital bed every year by medical error. If you live in the US, where about 40,000 people are shot dead every year, you are nevertheless three times more likely to be killed by a doctor than by a gun.[38]

Medical training

Arguably medicine itself has become a major threat to health, with dysfunction, disability and morbidity resulting from its technical interventions rivalling that caused by traffic, work, and even war.[39] Certainly it appears that everyone has their own horror story about those who have suffered desperately from treatment methods, incorrect diagnosis or treatment; those whose records or test results have been lost; or those who have been told 'ten different truths by ten different experts'.[40] Such experiences have led many people to lose confidence in medicine, to question its progress and its emphasis, which is predominantly on 'plumbing'.[41]

> This leaves a vast area that is badly taught, poorly understood and indeed almost ignored by modern Western medicine – the mind, the soul and the spirit. So badly have most doctors been trained in these areas that they can't even recognise the malfunction of the mind, soul or spirit when it stares them in the face, and

even if they did, most of them wouldn't be adequately trained to cope with it. And all of this is in the face of studies that have shown that up to 40% of all patients seen by doctors in the West have nothing physically wrong with them at all.[42]

Certainly, many patients don't need Western medicine *per se*. Some 80 per cent of all conditions currently treated by doctors are self-limiting, or chronic psychological and social problems. There is, in fact, very little relationship between the physician's training and the tasks he or she is required to perform; and this leads to confusion, disappointment and anger in both the general public and members of the medical profession.[43] Pain, for example, is one of the most common symptoms doctors are required to deal with. Yet there is teaching on pain in only 4 of the 21 medical schools in Britain, and even where taught, it is covered in an average of 3.5 *hours* over a five-year medical degree course.[44] Similarly there is little or no training given in psychological and social aspects of illness. The general disregard of social and mental factors in health has been likened to the attitude prevalent in the 1800s when surgeons ridiculed the concept of sepsis and the germ theory of disease and 'persisted in operating in unclean surroundings, sometimes defiantly sharpening their scalpels on the soles of their shoes to show their contempt for the putative power of invisible germs'.[45] Ornstein and Sobel claim that the current ignorance of and insensitivity to the 'invisible' symbolic messages in human interactions between doctor and patient limit the effectiveness of contemporary medicine.[46] Arguably a more fundamental limitation on the effectiveness of medicine is the failure of many doctors to listen to the *spoken* messages of their patients, much less the subtext of these communications, or to give them information about their condition or treatment. Recognition of this fact led Glasgow University to announce in 1987 its intention of following the universities of Manchester and Leicester in examining all future medical students in their ability to communicate with and relate to patients.

Hospitals

The failure of many doctors to respond to patients as human beings and their tendency to view them solely in terms of 'plumbing', by organ or disease only – as 'heart' or 'kidney' cases – to the neglect of their other features, has other important implications which contribute in no small measure to the uncaring and inhumane character of much modern medicine. 'The more we learn about the technical craft of saving physical life, the less we seem to keep in touch with the *human* art of caring about the person'.[47] This is nowhere more evident than within hospitals. Although the word hospital derives from the Latin for 'guest', seldom are such institutions truly hospitable, and they usually give little attention 'to caring and healing as opposed to medicating'.[48] As a result many people feel lost, alone, confused, anonymous and alienated in hospitals. Other shortcomings of modern hospitals include:

> the surprising lack of respect for basic sanitation; the rapidity with which staphylocci and other pathogenic organisms can run through an entire hospital; the extensive and sometimes promiscuous use of X-ray equipment; the seemingly indiscriminate administration of tranquillisers and powerful painkillers, sometimes more for the convenience of hospital staff in managing patients than for therapeutic needs; and the regularity with which hospital routine takes precedence over the rest requirements of the patient.[49]

Hospitals are clearly 'no place for a person who is seriously ill'.[50] Given this, other facts of hospital life, such as shortage of hospital beds, ward closures, long waiting lists, lack of specialist nurses and trained personnel, may be considered something of a mixed blessing.

Medical results

It was reported in November 1997 that hospital waiting lists in Britain were longer than ever before.[51] Advocates of modern medicine typically argue that this, and the other shortcomings of contemporary health care services, are the direct results of under-funding, and that given more medical services, more people would be healthy. Such a view may be unrealistic.

> In many respects people in developed Western societies have reached an age of diminishing returns whereby more and more medical care and more and more medical expenditures will probably contribute only marginally to better health because the increasing medical care and medical approaches were not responsible in the first place for much of it.[52]

Health statistics support such a view. Life expectancy in Sweden has not increased over the last 20 years although its expenditure on health care has multiplied six times; and Scotland, which has a much higher *per capita* health expenditure than England, also has a much higher death rate for most common conditions. Moreover, despite vastly increased expenditure on its National Health Service, death rates in Britain from heart disease have not fallen as they have elsewhere. In fact, infant mortality has increased, immunisation levels are low, and deaths from breast and cervical cancer unnecessarily high.[53] Both Britain and the United States are losing the 'war' on cancer. Rates of cancer have increased by 18 per cent since 1991 and the mortality rate has grown by 9 per cent.[54]

> Asthma, arthritis, diabetes, cancer, virtually all the chronic degenerative diseases known to mankind are thriving, and medicine hasn't affected their incidence one tiny bit. One glance at the statistics shows that, except in the case of getting run

over or needing an emergency caesarian, orthodox Western medicine not only won't cure you but may leave you worse off than you were before.[55]

An increasingly well-informed public is becoming progressively disappointed with the failure of scientific medicine to live up to its promise and fulfil popular expectations. 'Advice like "it's your age" or "you'll have to learn to put up with it" is beginning to wear a bit thin and many people are searching desperately for alternatives which will hold the promise of improved health'.[56] Many nurses are also disillusioned with current approaches to health.[57] Nurses are trained to assess and respond to the person at every level, but in practice this holistic approach is denied within the existing system. A major cause of staff wastage in nursing is the uncaring attitude within the medical profession, its authoritarian, fixed attitudes, and treatment of people as machines.[58,59]

Alternative medicine

The failure of many doctors to respond to patients as human beings accounts for much of the drift towards so-called 'alternative' medicine, which recognises the person's role in maintaining health and overcoming disease, and encourages active participation in treatments that are generally non-invasive and avoid iatrogenicity. Mainstream medicine is accused of having supported the boom of alternative medicine in Switzerland, where it has become increasingly attractive, by neglecting psychosocial factors, such as the doctor–patient relationship, and failing to satisfy other patient needs.[60] In Britain, emphasis on treating the whole person and on taking personal responsibility for maintaining health emerge as two of the most strongly cited reasons for seeking treatments such as acupuncture, osteopathy and homeopathy.[61] Other reasons, in order of importance, are: positive evaluation of alternative treatments; belief in the ineffectiveness of orthodox medicine for particular complaints; concerns about the adverse effects of orthodox treatments; and concerns about communication with doctors. The more personal and holistic approach of non-orthodox medicine is preferred by women in the USA, where most female patients sampled use some form of unorthodox medicine at some time in their lives.[62]

In Australia 48.5 per cent of the population have used at least one non-medically prescribed alternative medicine.[63] In Israel use of unconventional medicine has increased significantly in recent decades by patients suffering from illnesses for which conventional medicine has been ineffective, such as allergies, recurrent upper respiratory tract infections and skin problems.[64] Six per cent of respondents surveyed in one study[65] had visited an alternative practitioner during the previous year, most commonly a homeopath, followed by reflexologists, naturopaths and acupuncturists. The most commonly presented medical condition was pain, particularly back pain, and the reason most often cited for doing so was disappointment with the outcome of conventional treatment. Over 60 per cent of all doctors sampled in the USA, Mexico and southern Israel had referred patients to alternative practitioners, usually at the patient's request, because of the failure of conventional treatments. Referral rates were the same across these locations, despite cross-cultural and health system differences.[66] In Canada, 65 per cent of doctors studied perceived a demand from their patients for alternative methods, mainly for musculo-skeletal problems, chronic pain and illness. They perceived the most effective therapies for chronic pain to be chiropractic, hypnosis and acupuncture. They considered homeopathy and reflexology to be least effective.[67] Eleven per cent of children sampled in a large-scale study in Canada had been treated by alternative practitioners, 84 per cent accounted for by chiropractors, homeopaths, naturopaths or acupuncturists.[68] In Norway 20 per cent of patients with cancer treated in the oncology department of a university hospital, and 20 per cent of patients with non-malignant disorders in general practice, had used or were using non-proven therapies. The therapies most favoured by cancer patients were laying-on-hands and faith healing. 63.4 per cent of general practice patients believed these should be available as a treatment option for cancer patients in Norwegian hospitals.[69]

However, a study of the German population[70] found that people who select alternative therapies do so from deep-seated beliefs in their effectiveness rather than disenchantment with, or bad experiences of, orthodox medicine. A meta-analysis of surveys on alternative medicine[71] found that most physicians regarded it as moderately effective. Young doctors emerged as more enthusiastic about alternative approaches than their older colleagues.

Results of most studies suggest that alternative therapies should be regarded as complementary to rather than in competition with conventional methods. In Israel 39 per cent of patients studied were receiving both orthodox and alternative treatments at the same time.[72] A Canadian study[73] found that 8 per cent of patients consulted an alternative practitioner for the same condition for which they consulted a gastroenterologist. In Canada physicians have been urged to view alternative health care services with an open mind and consider therapeutic options which may be used in addition to conventional medical therapy.[74] Indeed the conclusions drawn from a study of general practitioners in Canada[75] were that undergraduate, graduate clinical, and continuing medical education will be obliged to address alternative therapies in order to provide doctors with up-to-date and relevant information.

A survey conducted in 1980[76] found that in Britain alternative medicine consultations were increasing at the rate of 10–15 per cent per year, and that alternative medicine was growing five times as rapidly as orthodox medicine. More recent surveys suggest that as many as one in seven people are treated by alternative practitioners,[77] and that almost three quarters of the population wish to have better established forms of alternative therapy more widely available on the National Health Service.[78] As regards Britain:

> All the evidence suggests that even if we cannot come up with a firm national statistic to express the present level of usage we can confidently agree with Fulder that non-orthodox medicine represents a 'significant second system apart from conventional medicine'.[79,80]

A similar picture emerges in the USA where the projected growth of alternative medicine into the twenty-first century predicts an 88 per cent increase in supply of alternative medical practitioners by 2010 compared with a growth in the supply of physicians of 16 per cent.[81]

Sharma suggests that:

> By the end of the century usage of non-orthodox medicine of some kind may well be a majority experience. The implication of this is that if orthodox medicine retains its status as the form of medicine authorised by the state in most western countries, it will continue to be 'orthodox' in the narrow political sense but may no longer be 'orthodox' in the cultural sense of being the form in which the public at large has the most confidence and regards as the most legitimate'.[82]

There is clear evidence of a change in attitude among doctors to alternative medicine. In a study of the attitudes to alternative medicine of general practitioners, hospital doctors and medical students in the South West Regional Health Authority in Britain,[83] general practitioners and hospital doctors had similar levels of knowledge. Medical students were least informed but most enthusiastic. Seventy per cent of hospital doctors and 93 per cent of GPs had suggested referral for alternative medicine (acupuncture, chiropractic, homeopathy, naturopathy, osteopathy) at least once, and 12 per cent of hospital doctors and 20 per cent of GPs practised alternative therapies. The majority felt these therapies should be available on the National Health Service and that medical students should receive training about alternative medicine. In the USA a desire for training in alternative medicine was expressed by most family doctors surveyed.[84] Seventy to ninety per cent of family doctors in Maryland and Baltimore considered diet, exercise, behavioural medicine, counselling, psychotherapy and hypnotherapy to be legitimate medical practices. The majority of doctors had referred patients to non-medical practitioners for these therapies, or had used them in their own practices. However, homeopathy, Native American medicine and traditional oriental medicine were not favoured as legitimate medical practices.

Medical models

The above finding highlights the fundamental problem underpinning the current crisis in orthodox Western medicine. Recent explanations for the failure of modern medicine have focused on economic recession, under-funding, government policies, widening economic division, mass unemployment, and failure to tackle smoking, alcohol use and pure nutrition. The focus of advanced industrial societies on disease, as opposed to health, has also been cited as a structural explanation for the long-term crisis in Western medicine.[85] However, the current crisis in health care is not economic or structural but conceptual. Western medicine has built its notions of health and disease around a particular view of the universe. The world view underpinning orthodox Western medicine is generally unquestioned. It is assumed to be correct and the only view possible in the light of modern discoveries and knowledge. Accordingly medicine grounded in the physical sciences is held to be the only way of mediating between people and disease. Alternative views, whether those of earlier epochs or other cultures, and medical approaches derived from them, where recognised at all, tend to be dismissed and even despised as 'primitive', defective, inferior and, although untested, disparaged in practice. The 'alternative' approaches currently finding favour within orthodox medicine are, for the most part, those doctors can perceive as legitimately within the framework of physical treatments, such as chiropractic, osteopathy and naturopathy, or those they can appropriate as part of clinical practice, such as 'medical' acupuncture as opposed to traditional oriental acupuncture. All other approaches tend to be denounced as 'unscientific', not having been objectively evaluated in reputable, randomised, double-blind, placebo-controlled trials.

The position of the medical establishment is clearly stated in the British Medical Association's Report on Alternative Medicine:

> there is one fundamental and consistent strand to the argument which creates a division consistently separating medical orthodoxy from alternative approaches.
>
> This is that the work and approach of the medical profession are based on scientific method... In as much as scientific method lays such firm emphasis on observation, measurement, and reproducibility, historically it has become inevitably and increasingly separated from doctrines embracing superstition, magic and the supernatural. It is important to realise that this separation was (and is) quite independent of therapeutic effectiveness; it seemingly represents a completely different conception of why observable phenomena have the effects they do. It is not necessarily the case that in the early days the evolving science of medicine led immediately to more effective treatment but it was the case that its evolution was in accordance with the definition of natural laws as fundamental as that of gravity. An all-embracing and internally consistent theory of medical

science was the result, with direct and logical consequences for success in therapeutics.

Thus, herein lies the first and most important difficulty that orthodox medical science has with alternative approaches. So many of them do not base their rationale on any theory with natural laws as we now understand them. It is simply not possible, to take one simple example, for orthodox scientists to accept that a medicine so dilute that it may contain not so much as one molecule of the remedy in a given dose can have any pharmacological action. In addition there is a related problem: the rationales of the various forms of alternative therapy differ widely one from another, and there is little or no consistency of concept or practice between their various approaches... About the only aspect of these therapies which is common to all is that they are not based on orthodox scientific principles; in other respects, with a few minor exceptions, they differ totally.[86]

However, medicine is not based on science, but on faith.[87] Medicine is 'a belief system so fixed, so inherent, that any truth to the contrary' is 'dismissed as virtual blasphemy'.[88]

The fact is that medicine is *not* a science, or even an art. Many of your doctor's arsenal of treatments don't work – indeed, have never been proven to work, let alone to be safe. It is a false science, built upon conjuring tricks, supposition and blind preconception, whose so-called scientific method is a vast amount of stumbling in the dark.[89]

Eighty per cent of medical procedures now used have never been properly tested,[90] and treatments such as lobotomy and electric shock therapy continue to be used, despite any kind of convincing explanation and serious and disabling side-effects, because some patients appear to derive benefit from them.

Doctors believe so fervently in the power of their tools that they are willing to suspend all reasonable scepticism about current and new medical treatments – so long as these treatments fit in with orthodox medical practice. Most doctors and researchers act on the assumption of *a priori* benefit, whether or not a given remedy has actually been proven ... Even if studies have been done demonstrating that a treatment is ineffective or even downright dangerous, so powerful is this faith that these results often get ignored.[91]

Moreover, medical 'science' is based on a totally outmoded scientific model of the universe which is no longer tenable, a model that was fundamentally flawed from the outset, but is now inappropriate to the world we live in. While the physical sciences have recognised this and have attempted since the early years of the twentieth century to revise their model, medicine has ignored these developments, with the result that it is left with a set of guiding beliefs 'as antiquated as are body humors, bloodletting and leeching'.[92]

Modern medicine has learned to look to the hard sciences as models, hoping to embody the precision and exactness demonstrated most notably by classical physics. Believing we have actually found that precision, we in medicine refuse to listen to the message that has come from physics for over half a century; that the exactness never existed.[93]

The fundamental crisis in modern medicine, and one which urgently needs to be addressed, is not finance, politics or organisation, but that of perception – the way in which the universe and man's place in it are viewed. It comes as something of a shock to those who hold the views of the medical establishment to realise that the world view which has emerged from the physical sciences in the West in the twentieth century is not only radically different to that on which contemporary medicine is based, but is also strikingly similar to those of ancient and oriental traditions (dismissed in the BMA report as so much superstition and magic). Furthermore, the apparently disparate approaches can be integrated within this common framework. Such an awareness casts 'alternative' (i.e. non-scientific) approaches to healing in a very different light.

Complementary medicine

Ironically, therefore, if modern medicine is to be in the vanguard of scientific progress rather than consigned to its fringe, the medical profession, together with those striving to understand the growing appeal and acceptance of alternative approaches to healing, has to recognise that these approaches are in fact *complementary* to any scientific medicine worthy of the name, and need to be given full and serious consideration. His Royal Highness the Prince of Wales in a written letter of 29 June 1983 urged the BMA, of which he is president, to do precisely this:

> Sophistication is only skin deep, and when it comes to healing people, it seems to me that account has to be taken of sometimes long neglected complementary methods of healing which, in the right hands, can bring considerable relief, if not hope, to an increasing number of people.[94]

What follows is an account of complementary methods of healing. In Part I (Chapters 2 to 5) similarities in the approaches to healing of ancient Eastern and Western cultures will be examined and discussed in relation to each other and to the similarities in cosmology or world view underpinning these approaches and those which have emerged within contemporary science over recent years. It is argued that these approaches are rooted in the same world view, and can be integrated with each other by way of one of the most fundamental concepts of modern physics, Einstein's General Theory of Relativity. This not only explains the large-scale structure of the universe but also shows the way in which time and energy are intrinsically related as different aspects of the same material phenomena.

In Parts II and III: complementary therapies are examined within this integrative framework as either 'timely interventions' (Part II: Chapters 6–10), which achieve their effects by modification of the time sense, or as 'energy medicine' (Part III: Chapters 11–13) – 'energetic treatments' which work to modify subtle energies. It is argued that these therapies are intrinsically reciprocal. In effect, time therapies modify energy, energetic treatments modify the time sense; and both have important implications for 'material' or physical health and well-being. It is concluded that understanding time, energy and the relationship between them constitutes the psychology of healing, which is the proper context for the evaluation of complementary therapies.

Part I

PERSPECTIVES ON HEALING

2

Ancient Perspectives on Healing

Ancient wisdom

It might be supposed that the world view of early man was shrouded in mystery and that without modern-day understanding of mundane phenomena such as the weather or seasonal and diurnal change the world was a magical and awesome place. However, there are indications in ancient mythology and in various teachings that have been passed down through history, such as the *Huang Ti Nei Ching* (The Yellow Emperor's Treatise on Internal Medicine *c.* 770–467 BC), that early man was inherently attuned to nature, and that he instinctively and collectively understood and lived in accordance with its fundamental forces. This wisdom was not a function of intellect or reasoning but rather of an intuitive grasping of the truth of things, a seeing into them. This instinctive apperception of reality, which has been described as 'our inherent attunement with the magical',[1] is evident in ancient Greek mythology, whose characters do not act on the basis of conscious plans, reasons and motives but automatically in accordance with the promptings of the 'gods'.[2] This aspect of the ancient mind, which appears to be a feature of pre-literate cultures, has largely been lost by mankind during the course of intellectual evolution as the parts of the brain specialised for language and language-related functions have evolved and eclipsed those parts of the brain more specialised for non-verbal, intuitive processes. Consequently it is impossible for modern man to understand the ancients or the universe they inhabited.

Colegrave[3] insists that this loss is unrecoverable but others such as Blavatsky,[4] Besant,[5] Freedom Long,[6] Gurdjieff,[7] Ashe,[8] Drury,[9,10] Butler,[11] and Scott[12] argue that this ancient wisdom, although fragmented and obscured, has never fully disappeared but has been passed down the ages in various traditions, many of them secret. It 'runs like an underground river emerging now and then into the light of day, then disappearing again beneath the surface'.[13]

Certainly the ancient mythology and history of many cultures supports the latter proposition. Within the West this ancient wisdom has surfaced in a number of magical orders and fraternities including the Order of the Golden Dawn, The Order of Temple, the Albigensians, Brethren of the Golden and Rosy Cross, the Illuminati, Magnetists, Theosophists and Kabbalists, whose aim is the realisation of the truth of the world through the development of insight and intuition. These traditions assert that man's vision of the universe is blinkered by conventional reality, or certain learned ways of perceiving, which confine his awareness to what is immediately apparent. They maintain that a far greater hidden or *occult* reality exists beyond normal awareness and ordinary comprehension: an infinite, ever-changing, expanding, indivisible and ultimately indescribable universe of harmonious relationships and interrelationships of which man is part, and which can only be perceived by those so attuned. These individuals with insight into the true nature of the universe and its mysteries are variously referred to as visionaries, seers, clairvoyants or mystics – a term derived from the Greek *muo*, meaning to close or complete. Mystics are therefore persons with a complete picture of reality, or cosmic vision. Mysticism refers to an experience of, or belief in, a reality surpassing normal human understanding or experience which is fundamental to life.

Mysticism

Throughout history and all parts of the world, mysticism is characterised by certain beliefs: the concept of a timeless reality beyond and utterly different from the world of ordinary appearance, knowledge of which comes by way of revelation, sudden insight or intuition 'certain beyond the possibility of doubt'; and awareness of the unity and indivisibility of all things.[14] Magic can be considered applied mysticism in as much as mystic vision, awareness and sensitivity enable the individual to penetrate and understand the secrets of the universe, together with man's nature and destiny, and to work with universal forces accordingly to produce desired effects at will. Those able to do so, often using spells, incantations, invocations and certain rituals, are variously known as magicians, sorcerers, or shamans.

Shamanism

The term *shaman* was introduced to the West in the seventeenth century by Russians who first encountered the Tungus of Siberia. The life of these tribes centred on an individual known as the *shaman*, *saman* or *haman* to whom various powers were attributed, including mastery of natural lore, healing the sick, telepathy, clairvoyance, divination of the future, dream interpretation, mastery of fire, rain making and communication with spirits. This person was not simply a practitioner of magic and medicine believed to cure and perform miracles, but also a priest, mystic and poet. In many tribes the shaman co-existed alongside other priests, magicians and healers but nevertheless remained the dominating figure by virtue of the fact that he or she alone was the master of ecstasy, a trance-like or out-of-the-body state, during which the soul was believed to leave the body and ascend into the sky or descend into the underworld in order to help members of the community in various different ways:

> For instance, the shaman may journey for the purpose of diagnosing or treating illnesses; for divination or prophecy; for acquisition of power through interaction with spirits, power animals, guardians or other spiritual entities; for establishing guides or teachers in non-ordinary reality from whom the shaman may solicit advice on tribal or individual problems; or for contact with the spirits of the dead.[15]

The ability to journey in non-ordinary reality is the defining characteristic which distinguishes the shaman from other magicians and medicine peoples of primitive societies.[16] Whereas the latter work basically in ordinary reality, the shaman 'journeys and works in another reality while in a substantially altered state of consciousness'.[17] By so doing the shaman plays an essential role in the community, combating not only disease but demons and the power of evil.

> In a general way, it can be said that shamanism defends life, health, fertility and the world of 'light', against death, diseases, sterility, disaster, and the world of 'darkness'.[18]

These powers are critical to communal life and human survival, helping people to maintain the necessary delicate balance 'between the world of pragmatic necessities and the more subtle world of spirits; acting as an intermediary between these worlds'.[19]

In its strict sense shamanism is pre-eminently a religious phenomenon of Siberia and central Asia, although it is not confined to those regions. Similar magico-religious phenomena have been described and documented in North America, Polynesia and elsewhere, and are still found throughout the world. Among the best documented by anthropologists are those of the Australian Aborigines, who until the late eighteenth century, when Australia was colonised by West Europeans, had been totally isolated from the rest of humanity for tens of thousands of years, and were still living in a Stone Age culture. There are also contemporary descriptions of such practices in Polynesia,[20,21] Tibet,[22] India,[23] Australasia and Indonesia,[24] North America and the Arctic,[25-27] Central America;[28-35] Africa and Australia,[36,37] Japan,[38] China[39] and Oceania.[40,41] Archaeological evidence, together with studies[42,43] which suggest that shamanism was influential within ancient Celtic cultures, confirm that shamanism is very ancient (many thousands of years old), widespread and remarkably similar throughout the world.

The spiritual vision of the shaman

In order to understand how the shaman acts as a go-between in the different worlds it is necessary to recognise the importance of the concept of the soul or spirit. In primitive societies the soul was conceived as 'permeating on earth, in the air and on water, in all diverse forms assumed by persons and objects, one and the same essential reality; both one and multiple, both material and spiritual'.[44] This all-pervading quality unified man and nature and the present with the eternal because it was believed that the core of each person, his real self, belonged to the spiritual sphere, coming from a pre-existing world of spirits, descending from spirit ancestors, and returning after death to its spirit home. The spiritual and sacred were not divorced from the natural world and the material body, however, because the material world was itself impregnated with spiritual qualities. The spirit realm therefore permeated all time and space and endowed the world with life and meaning.

Accordingly, the shaman perceives the soul or essence of man as integral to an infinite and eternal universe in which no part is separate from any other, all phenomena being an expression of an underlying unity, and man as a replica of it. The essential nature of man is to live in harmony with the universe, and the aim and purpose of human life is to preserve the soul and maintain its integrity, harmony and balance. Failure to do so is disastrous as it renders life pointless. It is the shaman's role to defend the integrity of the community by keeping man in touch with his soul, nurturing and protecting it and restoring it to those individuals who have lost sight of or contact with it. This process is generally conceived as a quest in which the shaman journeys through the underworld. It can be understood, however, as a journey through the landscapes of the unconscious mind.

In most archaic traditions the soul is regarded as the animating principle or force that gives shape and structure to human life, influencing, directing and regulating it, albeit functioning below conscious awareness. Its processes are to a great extent unknown to the conscious mind, communicating with it only by way of feelings, intuitions, dreams and imagery. This hidden, inner world has been commented on by poets and philosophers throughout history. It is the province of religion, and also occultism, which is concerned with the development of methods for accessing this hidden realm and applying the knowledge acquired thereby. Mastery of methods for divining the inner world is traditionally the aim and purpose of shamanism. The shaman's essential role in the community depends above all on the ability to 'see' what is invisible to others and to provide direct and reliable information from this hidden or occult domain, for it falls to him or her to guard and defend the 'soul' of the community, whose 'form' and destiny he or she alone can 'see', albeit in the mind's eye.[45] Hence shamans 'all seem to be able to see through the filters of culture, language and sense systems to other aspects of the real world – to non-ordinary reality'.[46]

This insight is achieved by withdrawing consciousness from the everyday world and shifting it towards the inner world, which is accessed, explored and interpreted by way of images. By provoking powerful imagery in themselves and others, shamans commune with the energies of the unconscious mind, and characterise them in various ways as human or animal spirits. These are cultivated as 'inner guides' to help them explore the inner world of others. Various techniques which have the effect of transferring consciousness from the outer sensory world to the inner are used, including sensory and sleep deprivation, fatigue, fasting, and breath control. Hallucinatory and stimulant drugs, drumming, dancing, rhythmic movement, chanting, incantation and other rituals may also be used to intensify perception, intuition and imagination in preparation for what, in the manner of the native American Indians, might be termed a *vision quest*: 'a journey which is visually a fact-finding mission aimed at discovering the cause of sickness, injury, drought, famine and so on. It is essentially a 'dream of knowledge'.[47] All of these shamanic techniques essentially put the shaman beyond ordinary conscious processes, and thus out of his or her mind in the normal sense, and in contact with what might be thought of as living energies conveying information and ideas. Applying this knowledge in the mundane world constitutes the science or knowledge on which the practices of shamanism, including healing or medicine, are based.

Shamanic healing

For the shaman, healing is a spiritual rather than a physical issue, disease being considered to originate and gain its meaning from the spirit. The purpose of life is spiritual development and the maintenance of oneself in harmony or balance with all things. The aim of shamanic healing is primarily to preserve and nurture the soul, and restore its balance.

Whereas in the modern sense illness is viewed as an external agent entering the body, something to be destroyed or protected against, in the shamanic system it is loss of personal power that allowed the intrusion in the first place. All shamanic treatment therefore emphasises augmenting the personal power of the sick person and is only secondarily concerned with counteracting the power of illness-producing agents, which are seen to constitute a threat to health only when a person's protective mantle develops a weakness. Accordingly the shaman does not work exclusively in the context of disease. In tribal societies where shamanism has flourished the practice of healing overlaps with all aspects of secular and sacred life.[48]

Shamanic ecstasy

Ecstasy is the central and characteristic feature of shamanism.[49] Indeed shamanism has been defined as 'archaic techniques of ecstasy'.[50] Analysis of shamanic practices in 42 cultures[51] has suggested that shamanic ecstasy is a specific altered state of consciousness or trance. This has been termed the shamanic state of consciousness or SSC.[52] Achterberg[53] identifies it with the 'clairvoyant reality' described by LeShan[54] as a timeless reality, a unified whole experienced by both mystics and healers, where neither time nor space can prevent information exchange. Shamans can control the trance dimension, entering into this altered state of consciousness or expanded awareness at will so as to access and explore knowledge, insights and information from ordinarily inaccessible realms of the cosmos, and awaking from it 'with conscious memory of the journey to the gods or ancestral spirits, and full knowledge of magical cures and healing procedures'.[55]

According to some traditions, shamans also have the ability to generate and control internal heat: 'Every real shaman has to feel an illumination in his body, in the inside of his head or in his brain, something that gleams like fire, that gives him power to see even with closed eyes into the darkness, into the hidden things or into the future, or into another man'.[56]

As an élite with access to knowledge inaccessible to others, shamans exercised, and still exercise, a powerful influence on religious ideology, mythology and rituals worldwide, and on the practices of healing. However, their magico-spiritual practices have always existed alongside more mechanical and technological forms of medicine, so typically in shamanic cultures a healing hierarchy exists with specialists in physical manipulation and prescription succeeded by diagnostic specialists, then by those who use their imagination to intervene with the supernatural.

The shamanic tradition of healing in Western culture

Although the origins of Western medicine are shrouded in mythology, shamanic practices and healing hierarchies are nonetheless discernible.

Medicine in Ancient Egypt

According to Homer, the Egyptians were more skilled in healing than any other people, and pictographs and hieroglyphics at ancient temples such as Kom Ombo bear witness to the sophistication of their healing arts. Their medicine was rooted in the magical vision of a harmoniously interrelated universe suffused with the divine. Man was viewed as a microcosm of the macrocosm and expected to reflect its order and harmony. This was achieved through a balancing of subtle energies: cosmic 'uranian' forces and subterranean 'telluric' forces.

Uranian forces were seen as an expression of God and symbolised as light radiating from the sun, or *Ra*, which is broken down into rays corresponding to the colour spectrum, each ray manifesting a different facet of the divine and influencing different qualities of life. The most important aim of life was for man to realise the light and thereby the divine; to become 'enlightened' by opening up to the light, channelling and distributing it, and merging it with earth energies. These telluric forces were characterised as spontaneous upward movement and symbolised by a rearing serpent. Those who had successfully raised this latent serpent energy to merge with the uranian forces are depicted in Egyptian art with a snake emerging from their forehead, which was thought to be the seat of divine consciousness. In so far as man achieved this union, he was the mediator of heaven and earth, and the aim of magic[57] was to produce this connection thereby 'bringing down the light', transferring and reflecting its power.

The secrets of this ancient wisdom were passed on only to the highest order of priests for sole use in the service of man and his spiritual development. Magic and religion were thus inextricably linked with each other and with medicine, which was sacerdotal, although essentially practical, catering for the whole person in soul, mind and body.[58]

The vital energies were thought to be absorbed and regulated by a finer etheric or spiritual 'body' which enveloped the physical body, so the temple priests sought to direct these forces by passing their hands over the body, and are often depicted thus in bas relief. The priests also recognised the therapeutic effects of colour and employed variously coloured sanctuaries in treatment. They also recognised the relationship of colour to other vibrational forms, and understood that rhythm – 'the expression of movement in life and the pulse of everything that exists'[59] – carries with it the potential for creating harmony and healing, or disintegration and destruction. The laws of rhythm were among the most closely guarded secrets, passed from father to son and master to pupil by secret oral tradition. Rhythmical invocations and incantations, music and movement all played a substantial part in the rites of magic, religion and healing.

In addition to the temple priests there were healers of various grades. Those who could tap into and direct natural forces were at the highest level and bone-setters were at the lowest. Dream interpretation was of great importance in healing and those healers with the ability to provoke and interpret dreams in both diagnosis and treatment were the most highly prized.

The first known Egyptian physician, represented as Thoth (known by the Greeks as Hermes Trimegistus), was the god of wisdom, medicine and the moon. The mystery schools of the ancient world (ancient occult traditions) that were handed down by the shamans of prehistory and used in the training of the physician/priests originated from him. The most renowned healer, Imhotep, born *c.* 3000 BC, clearly displays the shamanic origins of Egyptian medicine, being a master of magic, poetry, divination, herbal lore and rainmaking. On his death he was elevated first to the status of a demi-god and then, circa 525 BC, to that of a full deity of medicine, being designated the son of Ptah, the god of healing. In his name the traditions of healing were passed down and found their way into classical Greek culture.

Medicine in Ancient Greece

The aim of the Greeks until the sixth century BC was *physis* – the attempt to perceive the essential nature of all things – and the word from which the term 'physics' derives.[60] It was synonymous with mysticism and its practical applications consistent with magic. All knowledge concerned understanding the meaning and purpose of natural phenomena and living in accordance with the natural order. The concept of harmony was of central importance to the Greeks, as was the related concept of measure.

Maintaining a sense of proportion or 'right measure' was vital because all things have measure. This was viewed not as an overt feature of phenomena but as a deeper hidden harmony which was deemed to lie in the ratio of its inner proportions to one another and the whole. To understand this ratio, and so have the measure of a thing, was a form of insight into its essential nature or harmony. This was of particular importance in human affairs because, as Protagoras observed, by virtue of his perception and insight, man is the measure of all things. Accordingly, man was seen as the most significant subject of enquiry, and the main focus of study was his conscious or mental life.

According to Plato, this could best be described in terms of pairs of opposite features, and the balance or harmony between them constituted the soul, essence or *psyche*: literally a moving force. *Psychology,* the study of the soul and its development, was essential in maintaining the proper balance or sense of proportion. Virtue, or harmony, consisted not in accentuating the positive but in maintaining a dynamic balance between opposites. When the soul lost its right proportions or went beyond its proper measure, it lost its overall balance, becoming unbalanced and fragmented (the literal meaning of *ratio*). It cracked up, becoming irrational – the personal consequences of which were dramatically depicted in Greek theatre.

Human problems were seen as disharmony or dis-ease, as soul sickness – literally, *psychopathology* – and as fundamentally spiritual in nature. Physical disorders were largely regarded as symptomatic of this fundamental disharmony. Treatment was therefore directed to the cure of the soul, or *psychotherapy,* through the restoration of its balance and harmony. Accordingly, man had to be attuned to, and in harmony with, both spiritual and physical realities to be healthy, or whole.

The legacy of this idea is found in the terms 'health' and 'healing' which originate in the German *heilen*, meaning whole. This is closely related to the Old English words *hael* (whole) and *haelen* (heal), from which the English *hale* (as in the phrase 'hale and hearty') and the Welsh *hoil* derive. These terms are very similar to the German *heilig* and the Old English *halig*, meaning holy. Etymologically, therefore, to be healthy is to be whole or holy, which clearly embraces both spiritual and physical features, and not merely the latter.

Such a distinction would have been meaningless to the early Greeks who didn't have a word for matter since they saw all forms of existence as manifestations of the physis and endowed with life and spirituality.[61] All things were deemed to be comprised of gods and spirits, and the universe was deemed to be a kind of organism sustained by *pneuma* or cosmic breath, in much the same way as the human body is sustained by air. Until the sixth century BC gods and spirits were central to all thinking about the universe, so healing was essentially a spiritual phenomena associated with these deities.

Three gods were seen as principally responsible for healing: Apollo, healer to the gods, who with his arrows, the rays of the sun, brought not only healing but also pestilence and death; his sister Artemis, on the one hand helper to women in childbirth, and on the other the goddess of death; and Pallas, also known as Athena, goddess of wisdom and practical skills, and patron of eyesight. In the Homeric tradition this healing trinity is compounded by the myth of Asclepios, the son of Apollo and King of Thessally, who with his wife Epione, the soother of pain, created a dynasty of healers. His heroic sons, Machaon and Podilirius, were military surgeons; and Telesporos brought about completion of the healing process, while his daughters Hygiea and Panacea were respectively the dispenser of health and the friendly goddess of the sick. Panacea had knowledge of medicines to treat disease, and Hygiea advocated living in harmony with nature in order to avoid illness.

It is in the cult of Asclepios (known by the Romans as Aesculapius) that similarities with Egyptian medicine can most clearly be seen. Like Imhotep, Asclepios has uncertain origins. There appears to have been a mortal physician of that name revered as the founder of medicine who on his death became first a demi-god then a full deity. The follower of the latter, Asclepiads, or the Sons of Asclepios, constituted the temple priests. Like their Egyptian counterparts, they worshipped the symbol of the rising sun. Moreover, Asclepios was typically depicted with the *caduceus*, or rustic staff, around which is curled a serpent representing earth energy. This later became the emblem of the Hippocratic school of medicine, and subsequently of Western medicine. Like the Egyptians, the Asclepiads also made use of dreams in diagnosis and treatment and therapeutic use of music and movement. Galen, the physician to Marcus Aurelius, who like Hippocrates and Aristotle was trained in the Asclepian tradition, used colour in treatment and recognised the power of the imagination in sickness and health. He believed that dreams frequently provide clinically important diagnostic information.

By the fifth century BC the cult of Asclepios had spread widely, but the most revered of the healing deities was Hygeia who can be thought of as the goddess of preventative medicine. She was concerned with the promotion of health and personified the wisdom that one can be healthy by understanding how to live in harmony with oneself and the environment. The tradition which grew up in the name of Hygeia focused on special diets, baths, ablutions, exercise, dance and various methods such as listening to music, and attending theatre, which was seen as instrumental in maintaining health and effecting cure. Both comedy and tragedy were regarded as highly therapeutic, the former because it provoked laughter, and the latter because evocations of pity and fear evoke *katharsis*: emotional purging and purification.

The Hippocratic tradition of medicine

Hippocrates, who subsequently established a medical school on the island of Kos which flourished at the end of the fifth century BC, is commonly regarded as the father of medicine. He integrated medicine into the universal laws of nature as they were then conceived, thereby unifying medicine and philosophy.

Hippocrates viewed health in terms of harmony or the equivalence of basic elements, and adaptation to context. He saw disease as imbalance in the constituent elements of earth, fire, water and air, which he associated with the qualities of coldness, heat, wetness and dryness. These were represented in the body by four bodily fluids or humours: black bile, or melancholy; yellow bile, or choler: blood; and phlegm, which arose in various bodily organs, and were affected by thoughts, feelings, emotions and behaviours, climate, polluted water, over- and under-activity, lack of sunlight and other environmental factors. As the proper balance of humours constituted health, healing involved restoring equilibrium within these fluid essences by regulation of psychological and environmental variables, and lifestyle.

Like the shaman, the Hippocratic physician was a diviner of natural signs and an expert in natural lore. He used all his senses to measure and define the environment, taking account of its position in relation to the stars, sunrise and wind direction, the conditions of soil and water, and the weather. Students of medicine were required to study the effects of natural cycles such as the seasons on health. Like the shaman, the physician recognised the wholeness of things and didn't look at disease as an isolated phenomenon. This principle is embodied in the Hippocratic doctrine: *There is one common flow, one common breathing; all things are in sympathy.*

So too is the idea of a life force inherent in all living organisms, which Hippocrates recognised as nature's healing power – the *vix medicatrix naturae*. He placed great emphasis on this, insisting that the healing process is only designed to assist the body's own self-healing, providing assistance to the natural forces by creating the most favourable conditions for such a process. Accordingly the physician was the servant of nature. Physicians trained in the Hippocratic tradition did not try to cure patients without educating them in the nature, origin and development of their illness. They clearly saw their role as that of helping nature heal herself: restoring the balance disturbed by disease but not interfering with nature. The physician was a therapist – literally, an attendant (from the Greek *therapeia*: attendance) to the healing process.

There is little doubt that Hippocratic philosophy was inspired by mystical vision. It is therefore somewhat ironic that Hippocrates is regarded as the father of modern medicine because in the main his views were diametrically opposed to much modern medical theory and practice. However, in the Hippocratic tradition there emerges for the first time the awareness that health and illness are natural biological phenomena rather than the work of gods and spirits, that they are the reactions of an organism to its environment, lifestyle and other factors, and can be influenced by therapeutic procedures and by wise management of one's life. As such it represents a break with the magico-religious tradition of ancient medicine, healing by rational methods of treatment rather than the magical cures of the temple. Under its influence health became the ideal of culture.

Galenism

The humoral doctrine of Hippocratic medicine was subsequently systematised and codified by the Greek physician Galen *c.* 1 AD. He attributed varieties of human temperament to different admixtures of the humours and described four personality types, each associated with the dominance of one of the humours. Too much black bile produced a tendency to depression and melancholia, while dominance of yellow bile produced a choleric, bad-tempered, bitter character. The phlegmatic personality resulting from excess phlegm was characteristically apathetic; and the sanguine type produced by the dominance of blood was cheerful and ruddy. Accordingly emotional aspects of personality – depression, hostility, apathy and optimism – were considered to be directly linked to health.

The theory of humours was included in the many technical treatises written by Galen which formed the basis of a system of medicine known as Galenism that dominated the Western world throughout the Middle Ages.

The influence of Pythagoras

However, the sixth century BC was something of a turning point in history. It was a period when 'rational thought was emerging from the mythological dream world',[62] a period when the mystic vision of the ancients became fragmented, obscured and virtually lost to Western civilisation. This was largely because of Pythagoras 'whose influence on the human race was probably greater than that of any single man before or after him'.[63]

Ironically Pythagorean philosophy is the perfect embodiment of the mystic view of the universe. It integrates science, religion, mathematics, music and medicine in 'an inspired, luminous synthesis'.[64] It was also epoch-making; the discovery that the pitch of a note depends on the length of the string that produces it, and that concordant intervals in the scale are produced by simple numerical ratios (2:1 octave; 3:2 fifth; 4:3 fourth; etc.) reduced the ancient concept of harmony to mathematics. It was the first successful reduction of quality to quantity, and the first step towards the mathematicization of human experience – and therefore the beginnings of science.[65]

Pythagorean mathematics were to prove the greatest single influence on Western thought because mathematics are the chief source of belief in external and exact truth and an intelligible world.[66] The exactness of geometry, which is not matched in the real world, suggests that all exact reasoning applies to ideal as opposed to sensible objects, and when taken further, to the belief that the objects of thought are more real than those of sense perception. It therefore raises the status of intellect and reduces that of the senses, intuition and feeling, which is quite contrary to mysticism. Nevertheless Pythagoreans didn't live in 'a divided house of faith and reason'. They were aware that the symbols of mythology and mathematics were different aspects of the same reality, and this unitary awareness was reflected in their healing. But not for long, because the concept of measure or ratio soon lost its mystical significance.

It has been surmised[67] that this concept became routinised and habitual as it began to be learned by mechanical conformity to teaching rather than acquired intuitively through the development of insight. Ratio came to be conceptualised as that point on a line which divides it into segments such that the smaller is to the larger as the larger is to the whole. This measure or ratio, known as the Golden Mean or Section, came to be imposed by rule – that is, as an objective 'out there' fact or absolute truth about reality rather than some intuitive feeling about the inner essence of a thing. Thereafter, measure came to denote mainly a process of comparison with some arbitrary external standard, and, as such, it was passed down by the Greeks via the Romans to all Western civilisation. The only sense in which its original meaning is retained is in the notion of 'getting the measure' of a person, thing or situation.

Consequently Western civilisation came to view knowledge as essentially linear – as meaning objective 'out there' fact or objective reality – and such facts as constituting the only valid knowledge of the world. This idea had enormous implications for all subsequent thinking. From this same concept the West derives its notion of time – the idea of a linear sequence from the past, through the present to the future. Such a concept carries with it the idea of progress – that given enough time man will discover everything and discern all possible truth.

From the concepts of measure or ratio Western science also derives its emphasis on measurement, standardisation, rationality and reason, all of which involve dissection and analysis. Western man came to believe in an orderly linear universe that he could in time explore rationally, that is, through reason, by reducing it to its constituent parts, a bit at a time. Dissection and analysis have since come to characterise Western civilisation and its science: 'We are good at it, so good we often forget to put the pieces back together again'.[68]

The Greeks thus made a profound and lasting contribution to the development of Western thought. The first evidence of dissection came with the Eleatic school in the fifth century BC.[69] Parminides of Elea opposed Heraclitus who, consistent with the times, believed in a world of perpetual change or becoming: a continual flow, symbolised for him by fire. He regarded all static being as based on deception. He attributed all the changes in the world to the dynamic and cyclic interplay of opposites, any pair of which constitute a unity. Any experience or values believed to be contrary and distinct were regarded simply as aspects of the same thing. Consistent with this law of opposition based on complementary factors – *enantiodromia* – he believed that man should have knowledge of the whole of things.

Atomism

Parminides challenged Heraclitus by claiming that the basic universal principle was unique and invariable, and that all apparent change was sensory illusion. This led to the notion of an indestructible substance as the subject of varying properties. This substance, matter, was made of several basic constituents – passive, dead particles moving in a void. The smallest individual units were termed atoms (*atom* being Greek for indivisible). The movement of atoms was unexplained but assumed to be spiritual in origin. Hence 'atomists' drew a clear distinction between spirit and matter and this eventually led philosophy to turn its attention away from the material to the spiritual and ethical.

The creation of God

Initially the Eliatic school assumed a divine unifying principle standing above all gods and men, but this devolved into a personal God, standing above and directing the world. God was external to or other than man, and as such a fact or truth, the Ultimate Fact or Truth, and the very embodiment of Western thought. Were it not for the Greek concept of an external world revealed to the intellect but not the senses, the notion of God as it is known in the West might not have existed.[70] However the existence of this concept had importance consequences. It led to the projection of man's personal powers onto God, and resulted in man's alienation from himself and separation from his most valuable potentials.[71] This is the very antithesis of magic.

The magician's belief in his or her ability to alter consciousness at will and so commune with and influence the forces of nature is a challenge to the omnipotence of God. Consequently practices which emphasised the development of human powers and potentials were systematically eradicated in Western culture. As bodies of knowledge became framed within the dominant religious tradition, sources of ancient wisdom were eclipsed. Hence by the end of the classical period in Greek history several developments in thinking had occurred which were to have profound implications for subsequent Western thought – influences that overshadowed the instinctive wisdom of early man on which ancient systems of healing were based. Nevertheless, statues of the Asclepian family, the caduceus symbol, and the Hippocratic Oath have all persisted through the ages and serve as a reminder of it.

Medicine in the Middle Ages

By the end of the classical period in Greece the scientific world view of antiquity had been systematised by Aristotle. In the thirteenth century Thomas Aquinas combined this system with Christian ethics to establish the scientific framework that remained largely unquestioned and unaltered until the Middle Ages. Accordingly, science was rooted in a view of the universe that rested on the authority of the Church. Man was seen as the centre of God's creation, and earth as the centre of the heavens. The pursuit of reason was maintained and progress in knowledge was rapid. The aim of science remained wisdom: understanding the natural order and living in accordance with it. This was tantamount to accepting man's powerlessness in the face of God. Ultimate knowledge was His preserve, and knowing too much constituted sin. All visionary movements were therefore suspect, so during the Middle Ages the Cathars, Albigenses, Bogomils, Freemasons, Rosicrucians and Kabbalists were intensely persecuted by the Church. It was also largely because of the influence of the Church that there was no serious study or practice of medicine. Folk medicine prevailed, preserved largely by secret oral tradition, healing rites being regarded as mysteries to be shared only with initiates. Consequently most healing practices can only be deduced from documents relating to witch trials, reflecting the fact that in the Anglo-Saxon world healing was largely the province of wise women or witches.[72]

Witchcraft

In the ancient world women were generally believed to hold the secrets of life within their very being. During the Middle Ages those with superior knowledge were known as witches. Arguably, they were the most advanced scientists of the period.[73] Many of their practices were clearly shamanic in origin, most notably their 'flight' on broomsticks, which more properly can be thought of as flights of fantasy or imagination, and their use of spells. They were wholly shamanic in their regard for the unity of all things and in their attempts to use the forces of nature for healing.

Paracelsus (1493–1541) was one of the most enduring influences in the development of medicine. He pioneered the use of specific treatments to remedy particular diseases and introduced into the *Materia Medica* chemical compounds such as mercury and antimony, distilled essences of herbs, and opium. His writings, when published in the second part of the sixteenth century, influenced the courts of Europe and continued to exert an influence until the nineteenth century.[74] As the originator of some of the most effective drugs in the Victorian pharmacopoeia, he is credited with laying the foundations of modern chemistry and chemotherapy. He attributed his understanding of the laws and practices of medicine and the role of the healer to conversations with wise women. Certainly his thinking rested on an 'interpenetrative holistic cosmology'.[75] His ideals of bringing all things into perfect harmony were diffused at all levels of medical practice. Yet the wise women, whose wisdom he drew upon, were purged relentlessly by the Church as purveyors of magic and heretics, with dire consequences for medicine:

> The advent of Christianity affected the practice of medicine in such a way that some scholars blame it for bringing about the darkest days in health care. The pagans (Greeks, Egyptians and Romans) had elevated the art of healing to a height it would not see again for centuries. As Christianity spread its own gospel, all that was pagan, including the pagan practice of medicine, had to fall by the wayside. The theory advanced by the Church was that disease was caused by Satan, not by the pagan spirits, therefore pagan medicine could have no role in its exorcism. In other words, the Church expunged the exquisite surgical and herbal skills of the Greeks from the roster of available treatments and substituted instead frequently brutal practices such as mortifying the flesh. This brought the practice of medicine to an all time low.[76]

Mind, matter and medicine

During the sixteenth century Paracelsus challenged the medical orthodoxy by calling for the complete abandonment of Galenism. While his own system of healing had been based on observation and experience, Galen's doctrine discouraged empirical observation. It 'never led to a systematic collection of the observed relationships between lifestyle, thought patterns, emotions and illness. Eventually, as centuries went on without empirical measurement of the humours, the doctrine became dogmatic, and what had been an early holistic paradigm became stagnant, encouraging principally speculation on the nature and consequences of the hypothetical humours in place of the further development of knowledge and practice'.[77] Because of his contribution towards overthrowing Galenic medicine, it is not inappropriate that Paracelsus has been called the 'Luther of medicine'.[78]

Another orthodoxy to come into question at that time was the Church. Copernicus (1473–1543) challenged the biblical notion of the earth as the centre of the universe by suggesting that the planets circled the sun. This effectively removed the earth from its geometrical pre-eminence and made it difficult to attribute to man the cosmic significance assigned to him in Christian theology. The discovery of the laws of planetary motion by Kepler (1571–1630) created a new astronomy which further challenged the old view of the universe, which was finally discredited when Galileo (1564–1642) demonstrated that the earth revolves around the sun.

Until this time the aim of science had been to understand and live in harmony with nature. This was altered entirely by Francis Bacon (1561–1626) who introduced the idea that man was something apart from nature and could use science to gain mastery over it. This view was essentially anti-theological because it encouraged man to sequester powers formerly attributed to God. It brought science and religion into conflict and created a schism between the physical and spiritual realms.

Descartes (1596–1650) advanced this fundamental separation by proposing two discrete realms in nature: mind and matter. This created a split between mind and body that enabled scientists to treat matter as inert and completely distinct from themselves, and led to the belief that the world could be described objectively; that is, in terms of material objects that existed independently of human observers. As a result objectivity became the ideal of science.

A clockwork universe

The material world of objects was thought to be assembled like a huge machine or cosmic clock, operated by impersonal mechanical laws that could be explained in terms of the arrangement and movement of its parts, and described using simple mathematics. Descartes' world view was thus mechanistic and materialistic but also analytic and reductionist in that he viewed complex wholes as understandable in terms of their constituent parts. He extended this mechanistic model to living organisms, likening animals to clocks composed of wheels, cogs and springs; and he later extended this analogy to man. He wrote: 'all the functions which I attribute to this machine... occur naturally... solely by the disposition of its organs not less than the movements of a clock'.[79] To Descartes the human body was a machine, part of a perfect cosmic machine, governed in principle at least by mathematical laws. This view of the body as a mindless machine has governed Western medicine since the seventeenth century.

Isaac Newton (1643–1727) subsequently formulated the mathematical laws or mechanics which were thought to operate the cosmic machine and to give rise to all changes observable in the physical world. The stage on which all physical phenomena took place in the Newtonian universe is the three-dimensional space of classical Euclidian geometry.[80] It is an absolute space, independent of the material objects it contains, always at rest, immovable, constant and unchangeable. All changes in the physical world were described in terms of a separate dimension called time, which is also absolute, unconnected with the material world, and flows uniformly in linear sequence from the past, through the present, to the future. These notions of space and time were to become so deeply rooted in the minds of Western philosophers and scientists that they were taken as unquestionable properties of nature.

Within this absolute space and absolute time moved particles that Newton conceived as small solid indestructible objects of which matter was made. Such a view was similar to that of the Greek atomists. The main difference was that Newton provided a precise description of the force acting between these particles, which he termed gravity. This was seen by Newton as rigidly connected with the bodies it acted on and as acting instantaneously over distance. Both the particles and the forces between them were viewed as having been created and set in motion by God at the beginning of time. All physical events were thus reduced in Newtonian mechanics to the motion of material points in space caused by their mutual attraction. In order to express the effect of this force on mass points in precise mathematical terms, Newton developed differential calculus, and the resulting equations of motion form the basis of classical mechanics. The success of the latter in explaining the motion of the moon and planets encouraged the clockwork view of the universe and inspired the invention of mechanisms that imitated these realities. Laplace (1748–1827) subsequently went further than either Descartes or Newton in assuming that similar mechanical laws governed all things, including human beings.

The divorce of psychology and medicine

By the nineteenth century the scientific view of the universe was mechanistic, reductionist and deterministic. Everything occurring in the cosmic machine was considered to have a definite cause and to give rise to a definite effect, so that the future of any part could be predicted if its state at any time was known in sufficient detail. This view of the universe subsequently guided scientific endeavour in the West for over two hundred years. It brought into question the very existence of

God, the creator of the cosmic machine, as it became increasingly doubtful whether the universe had any beginning in time.

> So long as the universe had a beginning we could suppose it had a creator. But if the universe is really completely self-contained, having no boundary or edge, it would have neither beginning or end; it would simply be. What place then for a creator? [81]

As science made belief in the creator increasingly difficult, so the Divine gradually disappeared from the scientific world view, with the result that in the nineteenth century Nietzsche could justifiably declare God 'dead' in the sense that traditional meanings and values had been negated and physical science had become the ultimate authority in Western culture. This had profound implications because, for the first time in the history of healing, psychology was distilled out from medicine.

During the seventeenth century *physis* with the addition of a 'c' had turned into a 'hard' science – physics – the science of physical matter. With its emphasis on rigour, clarity and objectivity it became the standard for all sciences. This had major consequences for psychology. Descartes had not identified mind with matter, believing that the former could be studied introspectively, by looking inwards. However, as all knowledge or science had, by his own dicta, to comprise that about which there could be no doubt, that is, to be agreed on as objective physical reality or fact by independent observers, this effectively ruled out the mind as a scientific area of study. This left psychology in a dilemma because adopting scientific method and the total objectivity it implies precludes from study human experience, senses, feelings, and consciousness. If it was to be seen as science, as a valid and respectable body of knowledge, psychology had to abandon its traditional subject matter. With scant regard for the absurdity of the situation, its traditional concerns were all jettisoned. Instead, psychology began to focus solely on objective physical aspects of human functioning, that is, behaviour. Adopting a suitably clockwork metaphor, it set itself the task of finding out how human beings 'tick', without any reference to mind, much less the soul or spirit. It concerned itself with the brain, which as a physical entity is legitimately part of the cosmic machine. The resulting neglect of the mind–body link, when viewed against the history of medicine, is quite aberrant since 'in traditional tribal and in Western practice from its beginning in the work of Hippocrates the need to operate through the patient's mind has always been recognised'.[82]

Mindless medicine

The effect on medicine of this negation of mind was devastating. 'As humanity began its preparations for the new world view that would encompass the scientific method, all that was irrational, and all that was intuitive was subject to being purged. Women's science and women's medicine were prime targets'.[83] Yet it was not purely femaleness that was so blatantly challenged. It was rather that the qualities traditionally associated with women posed a threat to the scientific world view. Intuition, feelings, non-rational thoughts, holism, nurturance and imagination simply had no place in the thought mode of a universe made of cogs and wheels. 'The ebb and ultimate dissolution of women's influence on medicine and science were pivotal in directing healing away from the classic womanly virtues… all seen as threats and impediments to progress of the new scientific order'.[84] Its substitute was 'linear medicine',[85] which focused on probing, detecting, isolating, controlling and usually destroying the 'problem', which was seen as an invasion, defect or aberration quite separate from the person.

This medical 'progress' had other implications:

> The hope of bringing to medicine the perfection Copernicus had given to astronomy dates from the time of Galileo. Descartes traced the coordinates for the implementation of the project. His definition effectively turned the human body into a clockwork and placed a distance not only between body and soul but also between the patient's complaint and the physician's eye. Within this mechanical framework pain turned into a red light and sickness into mechanical trouble. A new kind of taxonomy of diseases became possible. As minerals and plants could be classified, so diseases could be isolated and put in their place by the doctor-taxidermist. The logical framework for a new purpose in medicine had been laid. Sickness was placed in the centre of the medical system, a sickness subjected to (a) operational verification by measurement (b) clinical study of measurement and (c) evaluation according to engineering norms.[86]

The use of physical measurement prepared for the belief in the real existence of diseases and their autonomy from the perception of both doctor and patient. This led to a tendency for disease to be spoken of as a thing and not as part of the total life process. In this way the person became separated from the sickness, and doctors' interest shifted from the sick to the sickness. Hospitals became laboratories for the study of disease processes rather than institutions for the care of the sick, and nearly all talk about health actually became about disease, a focus which is essentially negative.

Modern mechanistic medicine

Consistent with the reductionist, deterministic orientation of modern medicine the thrust of medical scientists throughout the twentieth century has been to understand disease processes at the molecular level on the assumption that for any disease it will eventually be possible to locate the misbehaving molecule.[87] In the meantime, consistent with its mechanistic orientation, medicine has settled for repairing, removing or replacing those parts it cannot as yet more successfully engineer. With the approach of the twenty-first century the mechanics of medicine are increasingly evident in various developments in spare part surgery, the mechanisation of childbirth and engineering of every kind: genetic, biochemical, neurological and structural.

The New Age

While during the twentieth century psychology and medicine have both been struggling to conform to the mechanistic model of nineteenth century physics, physics has long since abandoned this paradigm as outmoded and inappropriate since investigations of the subatomic realm in the early years of the twentieth century completely undermined the Cartesian/Newtonian notion of a clockwork universe. Every basic tenet of the older Newtonian view of how the world behaves has been abandoned in our century in favour of a radically new model.[87]

Moreover:

the New Physics soon revealed more than simply a better model of the physical world. Physicists began to realise that their discoveries demanded a radical reformulation of the most fundamental aspects of reality. They learned to approach their subject in totally unexpected and novel ways that seemed to turn common sense on its head and find closer accord with mysticism than materialism.[88]

3

Modern Perspectives on Healing

In an industrial age wedded to the machine, the mechanistic model of classical Newtonian physics 'offered a deceivingly simple epistemology for addressing questions of great complexity that had puzzled philosophers since antiquity'.[1] Its certainty promoted a sense of security about the universe and man's place within it. This was completely undermined when, as a result of discoveries in the first three decades of the twentieth century, understanding of the universe shifted from the mechanistic, deterministic and certain, to the organic, relativistic and uncertain.

> Two separate developments – that of relativity theory and atomic physics – shattered all the principal concepts of the Newtonian world view: the notion of absolute space and time, the elementary solid particles, the strictly causal nature of physical phenomena, and the ideal of an objective description of nature. None of these could be extended to the new domains into which physics was now penetrating.[2]

The Special Theory of Relativity

The first major blow to the Newtonian world view was a series of papers published in 1905 by Albert Einstein. The third of these, 'The Special Theory of Relativity', radically altered traditional concepts of space and time, and thereby the very foundations of Newtonian physics.

According to this theory space is not three dimensional and time is not a separate entity. Both are intimately connected, forming a four-dimensional continuum of 'space-time'. Therefore one cannot speak of time without space, and vice versa, and this has startling implications. In Newtonian physics it was always assumed that rods in motion and at rest are the same length. In relativity theory this is not so. The length of an object depends on its motion relative to the observer and changes with the velocity of that motion. The change is such that the object contracts in the direction of its motion. Hence a rod has its maximum length in a frame of reference when at rest, and becomes shorter with increasing velocity relative to the observer.

It is important to realise that it makes no sense to ask which is the 'real' length of an object, just as it makes no sense in everyday life to ask for the real length of somebody's shadow. The shadow is a projection of points in three dimensional space on a two dimensional plane and its length will be different for different angles of projection. Similarly the length of a moving object is the projection of points in four dimensional space-time onto a three dimensional space and its length is different in different frames of reference.[3]

What is true for length is also true for intervals. They also depend on the frame of reference of the observer, but contrary to spatial distances they become longer as the velocity relative to the observer increases. This means that clocks in motion, whether mechanical, atomic or human (i.e. heartbeat), run slower; so time slows down. This time-dislocation effect has the apparently bizarre implication enshrined in the celebrated 'twins effect', according to which one twin brother on a round trip into outer space would, on his return to earth after ten years, be younger than his twin on earth because in space he would have experienced only one year as his heartbeat, blood flow, and brain waves would slow during the journey from the point of view of the man on the earth. The cosmonaut wouldn't notice anything unusual until his return to earth, when his brother would seem much older. This paradox, however unbelievable, is well tested in physics.

Although these effects are normally not noticeable because they are too small at ordinary speeds, they are easily measurable and demonstrable using rapidly moving atomic clocks, capable of measuring billionths of a second precisely, or subatomic particles with known decay rates. In 1971 two physicists, Hafele and Keating, tested the time dilation effect by flying clocks around the earth in high speed jets, and found a shift of 59 billionths of a second. Greater accuracy is achieved by accelerating subatomic particles, and in 1978 at CERN (Conseil Européen pour la Recherche Nucleaire, Geneva) accelerated muons were found to stretch their time scale in excess of 20 times. These effects only seem strange because the four-dimensional world cannot be experienced by human senses, only its three-dimensional images.

On a more mundane level, to a person travelling at speed on a train through a railway station the railway clock runs slightly slower from his frame of reference, relative to that of a porter on a platform, although in compensation the platform appears slightly shorter. The mutual distortions of space and time can be regarded as a conversion of space, which shrinks, into time, which stretches. Therefore in relativity theory all measurements involving space and time lose their absolute significance.

Whereas previously time was regarded as absolute, fixed, universal and independent of material bodies or observers, in relativity theory it is seen as dynamical, able to stretch, shrink, warp and even stop altogether. Moreover, clock rates, rather than being absolute, are relative to the state of motion and gravitational situation of the observer. Space and time thus become merely elements of the language used by an observer to describe his environment, and they will be used by each observer in a different way.

Without direct sensory experience it is difficult to conceive of or describe four-dimensional space-time. To do so requires a four dimensional picture or map covering the whole span of time, as well as the whole region of space. These space-time diagrams are four-dimensional patterns in space-time representing a network of interrelated events that have no definite direction of time attached to them. Consequently there is no 'before' or 'after' in the processes they picture and no linear relationship of cause or effect, unless direction is imposed on the picture by the 'map' being read in a certain direction, such as from bottom to top. All events are interconnected but the connections are not causal in the Newtonian sense. The ordering of events will be different depending on how a person accesses the 'map' or picture, so there is no universal flow of time as in the Newtonian model. Different observers will order events differently (i.e. take a different slice of the picture) if they move with different velocities relative to the observed events. Two events that are seen as occurring simultaneously by one observer may occur in different temporal sequence for other observers.

One casualty of this 'elastic' time is the division of time into past, present and future. In relativity theory everyone carries around their own personal time, locked to his or her state of motion, so the concept of *the* time – a universal and absolute standard of public time – is an illusion. What people mean by 'now' depends on how they are moving. As Einstein observed, you have to accept the idea that subjective time, with its emphasis on the now, has no objective meaning. Furthermore if there is no universal *now*, then in some sense the past and future exist and are equally real in the present. Accordingly, events are simply *there* in space-time and do not *happen*. The apparent 'flow' of time is illusory. What moves, it would seem, is not time but the human mind.

This reality can be described mathematically, but in ordinary language words refer to conventional notions of time, so descriptions that employ them are highly problematic. Consequently it is difficult to deal with these concepts linguistically or intuitively. 'Relativity has taught us that our common notions of reality are limited to our ordinary experience of the physical world and have to be abandoned whenever we extend this experience'.[4]

So basic are the concepts of space and time to the description of natural phenomena that a radical departure from the conventional view of them as demanded by relativity theory entails a modification of the whole framework used to *describe* the universe. Moreover, as the unification of space and time necessarily unifies other apparently unrelated features, it demands a fundamental modification of the way in which the universe is perceived.

The General Theory of Relativity

In 1915 Einstein extended the Special Theory of Relativity to include gravity. In the resulting 'General Theory of Relativity', which describes gravity and the large-scale structure of the universe, he proposed that the effect of gravity is to make space-time curved. This curvature is caused by the gravitational fields of massive bodies. The degree of curvature depends on the mass of the objects, and because in relativity theory space and time cannot be separated, the curvature caused by gravity cannot be limited to three-dimensional space but must extend into four-dimensional space-time. The distortions caused by gravity in curved space-time mean that Euclidian geometry is no longer valid, as its two-dimensional geometry cannot be applied on the surface of a sphere. Lengths of time intervals are also similarly distorted by the presence of matter. Time doesn't flow at the same rate in all parts of the universe as in flat space-time because as curvature varies from place to place according to the distribution of massive bodies, so does the flow of time.

> The idea that time affects matter is familiar to everyone who has ever seen a field in erosion or watched himself grow older, but the possibility that there may be reciprocal action, in which matter affects time is revolutionary. It means that nothing happens without effect and that whatever happens all of us are touched by it because we live in the continuum of spacetime.[5]

The General Theory of Relativity completely abolishes the concepts of absolute space and time. Not only are these measurements involving space and time relative, but also, as the whole structure of space-time depends on the distribution of matter in the universe, the concept of empty space loses its meaning. Moreover the upheaval in our understanding of the universe demanded by relativity theory doesn't stop here.

Time and energy

A fundamental postulate of relativity theory is that the laws of science should be the same for all freely moving observers, irrespective of their speed. So all observers should measure light as travelling at the same speed no matter how fast they are moving. The implications of this simple idea are dramatic. One of the best known is Einstein's equation $E=mc^2$ (where E is energy, m mass and c the speed of light), which initially concerned the properties of bodies moving at or close to the speed of light. It is the mathematical embodiment of the statement that mass and energy are equivalent – that mass has energy and energy has mass – and that the energy that an object has owing to its movement will add to its mass. According to this formulation any distinction between energy and mass has to be abandoned. Mass and energy are simply different manifestations of the same thing, mass being a bound form of energy. Mass is no longer associated with a material substance and is not seen as consisting of any basic 'stuff' but as bundles or 'quanta' of energy.

Energy, however, is associated with activity, and with processes, and this implies that the nature of matter is intrinsically dynamic. So matter can no longer be pictured as in the Newtonian view as composed of units, whether tiny billiard balls or grains of sand. Such images are inappropriate because not only do they represent the constituents of matter as separate, but they are also static three dimensional images. Subatomic particles must be conceived as four-dimensional entities in space-time. Their forces have to be understood dynamically as forms in space and time, as dynamic patterns of activity which have both a spatial and a temporal aspect. The former makes them appear as objects with a certain mass, and the latter makes them appear as processes involving the equivalent energy. As they are different aspects of the same space-time reality, the being of matter and its activity cannot be separated.

The equivalence of mass and energy has since been verified innumerable times by physicists and has forced fundamental modifications of existing notions about matter. These are embodied in Quantum Theory and its mathematical formulation Quantum Mechanics, which set out the laws of the subatomic realm as they were mapped out by a number of physicists in the early twentieth century.

The Quantum description of reality

Newtonian physics is based on the concept of solid material bodies moving in empty space. This idea is so deeply ingrained in Western thought that it is extremely difficult to imagine a physical reality where it does not apply. Yet this is precisely what twentieth century physics obliges us to do. Moreover, not only is the concept of matter drastically altered, but also the concept of force, which is now seen to have a common origin in dynamic energy patterns continually changing into each other, so that it unifies concepts formerly held to be distinct.

When Rutherford split the atom in 1909 it became clear that atoms are nothing like the solid objects conceived by Newton but are vast regions of empty space in which extremely small particles – electrons – move around the nucleus, bound to it by electric forces. The distinction between matter and empty space finally had to be abandoned when it became evident that particles can come into being spontaneously out of the void, and vanish into it again; 'the vacuum is far from empty. On the contrary, it contains an unlimited number of particles which come into being and vanish without end'.[6]

Subsequent investigations into the subatomic realm produced more astonishing discoveries.

The high energy scattering experiments of past decades have shown us the dynamic and ever-changing nature of the particle world in the most striking way. Matter has appeared in these experiments as completely mutable. All particles can be transmuted into all other particles; they can be created from energy and can vanish into energy. In this world classical concepts like 'elementary particle', 'material substance' or 'isolated object' have lost their meaning; the whole universe appears as a dynamic web of inseparable energy patterns.[7]

It was found that subatomic particles make discontinuous jumps, so-called 'quantum leaps' – from one orbit to another without leaving any trace of their path. They have no meaningful trajectory but an abrupt and unpredictable motion. So at the subatomic level, matter doesn't exist with certainty at definite places, nor do subatomic events occur at definite times and in definite ways. Rather, matter shows 'tendencies to exist' and subatomic events show 'tendencies to occur'. These tendencies are expressed mathematically as probabilities which take the form of waves. These are not three-dimensional waves like those of sound or water but abstract probabilities. Hence particles can at the same time be waves depending on the way in which they are observed. Consequently subatomic events can never be predicted with certainty, only the likelihood of their happening. Such a view completely overturns common sense, and Einstein preferred the common-sense view that electrons really exist in a definite place and with a definite trajectory. He maintained that any ambiguity or uncertainty encountered in the observation of atoms is the result of imprecision in the measuring instruments used. However, the 'common sense' view favoured by Einstein was subsequently shown to be false.

The Uncertainty Principle

Heisenberg established that there are limits beyond which the processes of nature cannot be measured accurately at the time they are occurring – limits beyond which there can be no certainty, and which are not imposed by the inexactness of measuring devices or the extremely small size of the entities being measured, but by nature itself. This is because all attempts to observe the electron alter it. Indeed the atom 'only materialises when you look at it'.[8] Heisenberg's Uncertainty Principle therefore holds that reality is not only *not* independent of the observer but is shaped by the observer. The observer is not only necessary to observe the properties of subatomic phenomena but also to bring certain of these about:

> My conscious decision about how to observe, say, an electron will determine the electron's properties to some extent. If I ask it a particle question it will give me a particle answer; if I ask it a wave question it will give me a wave answer. The electron does not *have* objective properties independent of mind.[9]

The implications of this are that 'we can never speak about nature without at the same time speaking about ourselves.'[10]

In dispensing entirely with the notion of a fixed, observable reality, the Uncertainty Principle signified the end of a model of the universe that could be completely predictable. 'One certainly cannot predict future events exactly if one cannot even measure the present state of the universe precisely!'[11] It follows from this that the ideal of measurable objectivity in science is quite unfounded.

Yet again the implications of this seem bizarre because: 'the concrete matter of daily experience dissolves into a maelstrom of fleeting ghostly images'.[12] Indeed, as Niels Böhr indicates, those who aren't shocked by Quantum Theory have not understood it.

Many people fail to acknowledge the full implications of this quantum weirdness because they regard it merely as theoretical speculation. Yet, despite its bizarre implications, Quantum Theory is primarily a practical branch of physics which has yielded the laser, the electron microscope, the transistor, the superconductor, nuclear power, and the basis of modern chemistry and biology.

> At a stroke it explained chemical bonding, the structure of the atom and nucleus, the conduction of electricity, the mechanical and thermal properties of solids, the stiffness of collapsed stars and a host of other important physical phenomena... In short the Quantum Theory is in its everyday application a very down to earth subject with a vast body of supporting evidence, not only from commercial gadgetry, but also from careful and delicate scientific experiments.[13]

Moreover, Quantum Theory must give the same predictions as classical Newtonian physics in spite of being on a very different conceptual basis.[14] Böhr saw this relationship between the two as a deep truth, 'the correspondence principle'. Clearly Quantum Theory must agree with Newtonian physics when applied to large or heavy systems, that is, in what is known as the 'classical limit' – the realm of daily experience. Newton's theory is therefore still used for practical purposes, not merely because in the situations that we normally deal with, the differences between its predictions and those of Quantum Theory are very small, but also because it has the advantage of being much simpler to work with. Nevertheless, Quantum Theory:

> projects the 'irrational' aspects of subatomic phenomena squarely into the macroscopic domain. It says not only do events in the realm of the very small behave in ways which are utterly different from our common sense view of the world at large, but also events in the world at large, the world of freeways and sports cars, behave in ways which are utterly different from our common sense view of them.[15]

The New Physics

The 'New Physics' arising from twentieth century descriptions of the subatomic realm presents a totally different world view from that portrayed by Newton. It can be characterised as organic, holistic and ecological in as much as that it suggests a basic oneness of the universe, whose apparently separate parts are connected in an intimate and immediate way.

> Parts are seen in immediate connection in which their dynamical relationships depend in an irreducible way on the state of the whole system... Thus, one is led to a new notion of unbroken wholeness which denies the classical idea of analyzability of the world into separately existing parts.[16]

The New Physics highlights the inadequacy of mechanistic notions of order, or the way in which the world is thought to be arranged. The mechanistic order of Newton may be described as *explicate* in that each of its elements lies only in its own regions of space and time and outside the regions appertaining to other things. It is in this sense that events are conceived of as separate and independent, and understandable in terms of regular arrangement of objects as in rows or events in sequence. The undivided wholeness implied by the New Physics, in which all parts of the universe, including the observer and his instruments, merge and unite in one interdependent totality demands a new concept of order. Physicist David Bohm proposed such a concept by suggesting that the universe is holographic.

A holographic universe

Each part of a hologram contains information about the whole and if the hologram is broken into pieces each piece will reconstruct the whole image. This means that the hologram cannot be understood in terms of mechanistic explicate order. It has to be understood in terms of a total order contained *implicitly* in each region of time and space. (Here 'implicit' – from the verb *to implicate*, meaning 'to fold inwards' – is used in the sense that each region contains a total structure enfolded within it.) Examples of this *implicate* order are demonstrable in the laboratory, but the value of the hologram is that it focuses attention on this new concept of order in a clearly perceptible way.

Nevertheless, the hologram is a static record of this order, whereas the order itself is conveyed in a complex movement of electromagnetic fields in the form of light waves, which Bohm termed *holomovement* – or life energy. It is an unbroken and undivided totality from which particular aspects such as light and sound or electrons may be abstracted but are essentially inseparable. This holomovement, which in its totality cannot be limited in any specifiable way, nor bound by any particular measure, is undefinable and immeasurable. Thus Bohm's theory is essentially that *what is* is movement, and that the explicate order – the world of manifest reality – is a secondary derivation from the primary order of the universe. Hard reality is an abstraction from the 'blur' of basic reality, a notion long held by mystics and sages: 'Life and all that lives is conceived in the mist and not in the crystal. And who knows but a crystal is a mist in decay'.[17]

In describing a holographic universe, Bohm, like the mystics of antiquity, is depicting a world in which what appears to be stable, tangible and 'out there' is not really there at all, but is an illusion, a magic show – what the Hindu describe as *maya*.

Such a view has also been advanced by neuroscientist Karl Pribram[18] who, in attempting to account for the way in which memory appears to be distributed throughout the brain rather than localised in any one part, proposed that information is enfolded over the whole brain in much the same way as in a hologram. Having proposed this holographic model of the brain, he then pursued the notion formerly advanced by psychologists of the Gestalt School, that the world 'out there' is isomorphic with brain processes, that they both exhibit the same form. By so doing he reached the conclusion that the world is a hologram, apparently unaware that Bohm had done likewise. He went on to suggest that reality is not what is perceived by the eyes, and that the brain may act as a lens, transforming mathematically the blur of primary reality into hard reality. Without these mathematics we would possibly know a world organised in the frequency domain, a world without space and time, such as that described by mystics throughout history. Hence it may be that 'what is essential is invisible to the eye'.[19]

Nevertheless, the problem for the physicist and neuroscientist is to account for 'normal' perception of mundane 'explicate' reality, that which Hindu mystics term *avidja* or a 'not-seeing'. Bohm suggested that we learn to see the world in certain ways. We do not necessarily notice the primary order because we are habituated to the primary order which is emphasised in thought and language, both of which are predominantly linear and sequential. Indeed, both linguistic and cognitive development result from objects being named and pointed out. In this way they emerge as discrete entities from a diffuse, homogenous background, and it is in this way that a child learns about its world. Western culture as a whole is habituated to the rational, the logical, the linear and sequential and to a description of a manifest, explicate reality. As a result the ability to 'think straight' is highly valued and there is a tendency to feel that primary experience is of this order.

Another possible explanation suggested by Bohm is that the contents of memory focus attention on what is static and fragmented in the manner of a hologram, with the result that the more subtle and transitory features of the unbroken flow 'tend to pale into such seeming insignificance that one is at best only dimly conscious of them'.[20]

Mystical and magical traditions emphasise that true seeing or direction perception of reality can be achieved by developing insight – literally a looking inwards – which might be thought of as an enfoldment. This is consistent with the holographic notion that the world is enfolded within each of its parts. Accordingly, the truth of the universe – ultimate truth – lies within the person.

Just as the mystics of old held that this reality could be accessed by various means, so a number of modern scientists have suggested likewise. Some[21,22] propose that certain drugs, notably psychedelics such as those traditionally used in shamanic ritual, prevent one from 'thinking straight', thereby circumventing the 'reducing valve of ordinary consciousness',[23] enabling direct perception of the holographic universe described by Bohm and Pribram.

Transformation Theory

Bohm's holographic theory finds support in the Transformation Theory advanced by the chemist Ilya Prigogine, for which he was awarded the Nobel Prize in 1977.[24] This suggests the means of unfolding from the implicate order, and thus the way it is manifested in time and space. It also establishes the connectedness of living and non-living forms, and so bridges the critical gap between living systems and the apparently lifeless universe in which they arise.

Prigogine's theory concerns dissipative structures – that is, all living things and some non-living things such as certain chemical reactions, which maintain their form by a continuing dissipation of energy. As such they constitute a flowing wholeness which is highly complex and always in process. The greater its complexity, the more energy the structure requires to maintain its coherence. This produces the paradoxical situation that the greater its coherence, the greater its instability. Prigogine suggested that this instability is the key to transformation because the dissipation of energy creates the potential for sudden reordering.

> The continuous movement of energy through the system results in fluctuations. If they are minor the system damps them and they do not alter its structural integrity. But if they reach a critical size they 'perturb' the system. They increase the number of novel interactions within it. They shake it up. The elements of the old pattern come into contact with each other in new ways and make new connections. The parts reorganize into a new whole'.[25]

Accordingly, nature has the potential to create new forms by allowing a shake-up of old forms, and it is this capacity which is the key to growth. Put another way, flexibility creates growth. It is the key to creativity. Structures insulated from disturbance are protected from change and become stagnant, never evolving towards a more complex form. This is as true for forms of knowledge or science as for any other system, and suggests that paradigm shifts are essential for the development of thought. Only through the chaos they introduce can order emerge.

Such a view is fully consistent with that of the ancients, as is the central tenet of Prigogine's theory, that the meaning of the whole is traceable to the behaviour of its parts, which reverberate throughout the entire system. Here again there are parallels with the views of mysticism, which Prigogine has acknowledged and repeatedly drawn attention to (see Chapter 4 for further discussion).

Transformation in ancient approaches to healing

The insights provided by Transformation Theory are far from new. In ancient Greece theatre was recognised and valued as therapy because of its power to 'shake up' or perturb. The Greeks believed that the evocation of unsettling emotions such as fear and pity by tragedy caused a profound change to take place, an emotional purging, which Aristotle termed 'catharsis'.

> The assumption is that the emotional stresses within us, often subconscious, and the moral contradictions too, likely to be equally deeply buried, need to be relieved and resolved. By losing our everyday awareness of ourselves and by identifying with the actors – themselves divested of self in the drama's heightened world – we expose ourselves to the full force of their sufferings and sins as we may never be able to own, and this effects relief... Aristotle thought that to witness tragedy in a theatre is one of the ways in which human beings can be purged of stress and inner conflict. Our own pity and fear draws us towards a point of balance, and from this comes a sense of health and therefore pleasure.
>
> The Greeks believed that life was to be enjoyed, but they also knew its pain and terrors and their own vulnerability to its dark and irrational forces. Tragedy was a means to contain and express the paradox, but it was also an end in itself, the creation of something for the living even out of death.[26]

The Greeks also understood that laughter could possess and purge an audience, and comedy was used widely as therapy several thousand years before its healing effects were pointed to in the twentieth century.[27-32]

Parallels between modern science and ancient mysticism

In the light of the many similarities between the insights of modern science and ancient wisdom, mysticism cannot be dismissed as trivial or as a mere anthropological curiosity. Rather, it has to be admitted into any scientific framework that purports to a complete understanding of reality. Indeed it is now recognised that the New Physics, and to some extent modern chemistry, restates, albeit in the language of mathematics, the mystical descriptions of reality common to ancient traditions throughout the world, and still emphasised within Eastern culture.

Striking parallels between the discoveries of modern physics and Eastern mysticism have been identified and discussed.[33-36] These parallels have also been recognised by many of the most distinguished physicists of the twentieth century, including Nobel prize winners Heisenberg, Schrödinger and Böhr. Indeed when Bohr was knighted for his achievements, he chose as his coat of arms the symbol of traditional Chinese thought because of the consistency of the ancient Chinese world view and that of the most advanced physics.

This has forced acknowledgment, in some quarters at least, that if the basic world view of the East is fundamentally correct, or at least, consistent with the present state of scientific knowledge in the West, then other aspects of Eastern thought which derive from this perspective, such as that relating to medicine and healing, may possibly also be more appropriate. For many people this idea is difficult to accept because they have been conditioned to believe that Western science is qualitatively supreme among all other forms of knowing, and that 'all others are either primitive or false, or unsuccessful attempts to gain our level'.[36]

For precisely this reason, many physicists reared in the Western tradition were shocked by comparisons between the descriptions of physics and mysticism, but they have increasingly come to accept that mysticism provides a consistent and relevant philosophical background to Western science, which unifies and harmonises scientific discoveries and man's spiritual aims and beliefs. In so doing they have come to appreciate that it is not so much a matter of choosing between alternative views, but more of embracing what is complementary among them:

> Science is the tool of the Western mind, and with it one can open more doors than with bare hands. It is part and parcel of our understanding, and obscures our insight only when it claims that the understanding it conveys is the only kind there is.[37]

Medicine and modern thought

Unfortunately Western medical science has been less willing to accept this position. Indeed the institution of medicine itself reflects this resistance to external challenges by adhering steadfastly to an outmoded model of how the world behaves and almost totally ignoring the insights of modern physics. The result is that modern Western medicine finds itself with 'a set of guiding beliefs that are as antiquated as are body humors, leeching and bleeding'.[38] Notions of life, death, health and disease in Western culture rest solidly on seventeenth century scientific principles, and its medicine has resisted any redefinition of these notions and is still governed by mechanistic thinking.

The body is viewed as a machine in good or bad repair; disease or disability is seen as a thing or entity to be treated by elimination of symptoms, primarily with drugs and surgery, after diagnosis that relies on quantitative 'factual' information. Psychological factors, where acknowledged at all, are regarded as of secondary importance, and so-called 'psychosomatic illness' is treated by the separate specialism of psychiatry. All treatment is viewed as a matter for professionals, who are emotionally neutral authority figures, responsible for patients who are passive and dependent. Twentieth century descriptions of reality demand a radical re-examination of these principles and practices. 'To refuse to face its consequences is to favour dogma over evolving knowledge'.[39]

A fundamental problem facing contemporary medicine is that of reconciling ordinary descriptions of bodies, health and disease with the idea that the universe and everything in it is an inseparable entity. Clearly 'separateness of bodies, and absolute distinctions between health and disease cannot be maintained in a context of quantum wholeness'.[40] While this does not mean that these notions cannot be abstracted as apparently discrete features of reality and spoken of as aspects of the world in just the way that physicists speak of the wave and particle features of electrons, it does mean that the underlying unbroken wholeness of all manifestations of the entire universe has to be acknowledged. The principles of relatedness, oneness and unity have to be addressed, rather than fragmentation and isolation.

The radical reformulation of reality provided by modern physics is profoundly unsettling to those attached to the old scientific model because it demands a fundamental re-examination of the principles and practices of medicine. However such crises are a precondition for the emergence of a new perspective because it is only as a result of these changes that scientific understanding develops. Without some shaking of their foundations, as indicated in Transformation Theory, systems of knowledge cannot evolve and progress. Hence the history of science is characterised by such shifts. The implications for medicine of continuing to resist the challenge they offer are considerable because 'flawed images of the body lead to flawed therapies for the body'.[41]

New Biology

The so-called 'New Biology' is consistent with the new understanding of reality. It emphasises the unitary ontological nature of a material world in which the biological and social are 'neither separable, nor antithetical, nor alternatives; but complementary'.[42]

Awareness of this interrelatedness and complementarity means that organisms or the environment can no longer be considered in isolation from each other.

> Just as there is no organism without an environment, there is no environment without an organism. Neither organism nor environment is a closed system, each is open to the other. There is a variety of ways in which the organism is the determinant of its own milieu.[43]

Hence there is no universal physical fact of nature whose effect on or even relevance to an organism is 'not in part a consequence of the nature of the organism itself'.[44]

This New Biology calls for a radical reappraisal of our thinking about 'being in the world' and has important implications for medical science. When translated into practice these new conceptions of reality require bodies, health and disease to be viewed as dynamic processes rather than discrete entities, which need to be understood in terms of patterns of relationships within the organism and its environment, rather than in terms of separate parts. Health and illness need to be viewed in relation to the wholeness or integration of these processes, rather than in terms of symptoms, or the lack of them. Accordingly mind has to be regarded as a primary factor in health and illness and therefore so-called 'psychosomatic' illness becomes a matter for all health care professionals, who are themselves therapeutic partners in the healing process rather than 'external' to it. Essentially the new description of reality demands, as did Hippocrates, that physicians understand the whole of things.

The physics of health

If the entire universe can be understood as an inseparable entity the total order of which is contained implicitly in each of its parts, as proposed in holographic theory, this means that information about the whole is everywhere at once. This being so, the organism has wisdom concerning all the body in each of its parts. This resolves some puzzling body–brain paradoxes such as 'phantom limb' sensations, because if the brain is a hologram it is unnecessary to have a leg in order for the brain to process information relating to the leg. It is sufficient to have once had a leg or even to have thought about having a leg. Either way 'leg' storage patterns are established which give rise to sensation in an amputated limb, and some control over what the brain perceives as movement.[45]

This has potentially important implications for diagnosis and treatment. First, it suggests that qualitative information, including the patient's subjective experience and intuition, together with that of the medical practitioner, needs to be considered as the primary data in diagnosis, with quantitative methods as an adjunct. Second, it suggests that the mind can, through the generation of imagery, effect physical processes; and it also raises the possibility that diagnosis and treatment can be effected by way of any given part. The latter has long been claimed by traditional and oriental systems of healing and those such as iridology and radionics which are currently accorded little validity or status. Indeed, all of these principles are fundamental to ancient and oriental systems which traditionally employ intuition and imagination in healing, and regard the healer and patient as equals in the healing process.

Perturbation, immunity and health

Viewed within the framework of Transformation Theory, disease, especially major illness, is clearly a perturbation. Accordingly it is a means whereby the system can, in Prigogine's terms, 'escape' to a higher level of organisation or integration, and thus to greater wholeness and health. Perturbation is therefore bound up in shifts towards physiological complexity.

In fact, the tenets of Transformation Theory are already invoked in many health care methodologies including orthodox medical practice. Immunisation, for example, involves inducing a mini-disease just sufficient to stimulate the body to produce protective antibodies, thereby 'producing an evolution toward biological complexity through intentionally perturbing the immune system'.[46]

Immune function relies upon perturbation of the body's integration. If it never occurred the body would be defenceless because necessary mechanisms would not evolve. This is the case in children born with immune deficiency, who because they are unable to respond to perturbations from outside cannot escape to a higher degree of immune complexity and usually succumb to overwhelming infections in early life.[46]

> Clearly, processes of perturbation and health form a complementary whole. Yet orthodox medicine frequently moves *against* perturbation rather than *with* it, 'battering the perceived threats with a constantly changing array of injections, pills and surgery', and trying 'to avoid external challenges to our health; failing that we struggle to resist them using any means at hand'.[47]

Perhaps unsurprisingly, antibiotic, antibacterial and anti-viral treatments often prove to be counterproductive. Not only do they prevent development of the immune system by denying it the possibility of challenge, but also by perturbing viruses and bacteria they may actually contribute to the development of super-resistant strains.

Preventative medicine

Clearly general medical practice needs to be re-examined in the light of these factors. Health strategies need to incorporate flexibility as a primary goal because the ability to react effectively to challenges to the body–mind integration is a fundamental requirement of health. The interval between illness also becomes crucial because it is here that a person can sabotage the body's ability to react to perturbations by negative habits such as smoking, over-eating, fatigue and negative attitudes.

> Seen from this perspective the 'real' medicine is what we do between illness-events. All of the techniques which we relegate to the second-class status of preventative medicine are of critical importance, for they help determine the body's capacity to successfully reorder itself to a higher degree of complexity when actually challenged by disease processes. Conversely, the traditional approach of medicine and surgery should be viewed as a second-line of defence. These methods should be viewed as a last resort, as a supplement to the body's wisdom. Too often they are used as an effort to shield the body from physical

onslaught – as in the condemnable practice of prescribing antibiotics for the common cold, or using tranquillisers for the commonplace anxieties of daily living. For most assaults to its integrity the body needs no shielding. In any event, our efforts of this type result less frequently in *protecting* the body than in *meddling* in its affairs and frustrating its wisdom.[48]

Undeniably perturbation does not always end in reorganisation but in death, and so sometimes a second line of defence is required. Nevertheless insufficient attention is given to approaches which complement the wisdom of the body, working with perturbations rather than against them. This is the fundamental principle of homeopathy and contemporary 'humanistic' psychotherapies which, rather than opposing a problem, facilitate confrontation with it as the solution.

Transformation and mental health

Prigogine's theory that order and organisation can arise spontaneously out of disorder and chaos through a process of self-organisation helps to account for the transformative effects claimed for psychotherapy in which typically there is 'shake-up' of existing assumptions and perceptions.

An individual reliving a traumatic incident in a state of highly focused inward attention perturbs the pattern of that specific old memory. This triggers a reorganization – a new dissipative structure.[49]

It also lends support to the view advanced by the psychiatrist R.D. Laing[50] that mental illness or 'dis-order' frequently enables reintegration of the personal self rather than merely disintegration, and so often represents a breakthrough rather than a breakdown.

Long before Transformation Theory had been confirmed empirically, an Israeli research chemist, Aaron Katchalsky, had identified the brain as an example of a dissipative structure.[51] His untimely death prevented further research on how this might apply to investigations of the human brain and consciousness. Such research might explain the transformative power of altered states of consciousness, imaginative processes, psychological therapies and the ancient and oriental healing systems which seem fully consistent with the new description of reality, and to enshrine its principles. It would seem therefore that there is nothing to be lost and a great deal to be gained from examination of the fundamental assumptions on which these systems are based:

The universe has been known by exceptional, deeply conscious human beings for thousands of years. It is the duty of science to acknowledge this.[52]

4

Eastern Perspectives on Healing

The astigmatism in Western medical science would appear to conform with 'Fort's Theorem',[1] named after the philosopher Charles Fort, which holds that if you encounter data which lie outside an area that you have defined for yourself as containing the only possible data, you will either fail to see it altogether, or else will plausibly discredit it in terms of your own prior assumptions. This is particularly evident in Western attitudes towards Eastern ideas. When looked at from 'the incurably externalistic standpoint'[2] of the Western intellect, the practical importance of Eastern ideas is difficult to comprehend, with the result that they have been classified as mere philosophical and ethnological curiosities and nothing more. Yet,

> As it now begins to appear, data for resolving the West's scientific impasse was available in the East all along but the East's culture and philosophy, both ancient and modern, was consistently assumed to be either puerile or defective, or both. The knowledge of the East was not tried and found wanting. It was assumed to be inferior and not tried.[3]

Eastern philosophy

Eastern perspectives on the universe are based on a philosophical tradition quite different from that of the West. The distortions introduced into the mystic tradition of ancient times by classical Greek civilisation are not present, at least to the same extent, in cultures that largely lack its influence. Consequently the thinking in most Eastern cultures remains close to its mystical origins. In their traditions there is a strong intuition of the space-time nature of reality, and a different rhythm to life. The awareness that space and time are inseparably linked with each other and other aspects of the universe is stressed again and again, as are the concepts of change and movement, or energy, which may be one of the reasons why Eastern thought in general corresponds much better with modern scientific thought than does that of most Greek philosophy.

The interpenetration of space and time is most clearly expressed in Indian thought:

> The Indian mind is imbued with the sense of the relativity of all things and enterprises in the world and rigorously resists the yes or no, black or white tendencies of much modern Western thought. Greek natural philosophy was on the whole essentially static and largely based on geometrical considerations. Its influence on Western thought may well be one reason why in the West we have great conceptual difficulties with the relativistic models of modern physics.[4]

Indian thought

Whereas in Western culture the universe is seen as composed of parts distinctly separate from each other – nature, man, animals, birds, trees, plants, minerals and so on – having been created as such by God in the beginning of time, the thinkers of ancient India regarded the idea of such separateness as erroneous. They considered there to be a connection among all these phenomena, a unity which pervades the whole universe, including God. This one great, impersonal, absolute power, an immutable, ultimate and essentially indescribable reality that pervades and transcends all things, unifying all the apparent differences of the phenomenal world – known as *Brahman* – is the first principle from which all things derive, by which all are supported, and into which they eventually disappear. All phenomenal existence is viewed as transitory, impermanent and in the process of change, a ceaseless cycle of beginning and ending which in the sacred writing of India, Sanskrit, is termed *samsara*, literally meaning 'a going around in circles'. Just as man is subject to cycles of birth and rebirth, the universe itself is thought to go through cycles of dissolution and recreation spanning vast periods of time. This process is held to be indivisible and irreducible. Therefore all reduction into objective facts and forms constitutes illusion, or *maya*.

A frequent metaphor for Brahman is 'ocean,'[5] which denotes inexhaustible potentiality. Like Brahman, the greater part of the ocean is never visible or known, and the rising and disappearing waves represent the ephemeral lives of myriads of living creatures that come into existence for a while and then are reabsorbed into it.

Etymologically, the word 'Brahman' denotes an entity whose greatness, powers and expansion cannot be measured.[6] Thus, reason, rationality, objectivity, analysis and dissection, with their implicit notions of measurement so esteemed in the West, are seen as *avidja*, or ignorance which is not so much a not-knowing as a not-seeing of the reality of the world. They are the very antithesis of knowledge or philosophy (*darsana* in Sanskrit, or 'seeing'), the aim of which is understanding the unity of all things, or Natural Law.

Vedanta, the philosophy expounded in the earliest scriptures of the Hindu (originally the Persian word for Indian), comprises all the various sects that exist in India. It derives from the Vedas, ancient teachings or knowledge (from the Sanskrit *vid:* to know), and is a practical philosophy rather than a mere intellectual understanding, in which reality must be directly known and this knowledge applied in daily life. Vedanta teaches that life has no other purpose than learning to know ourselves for what we really are – a manifestation of Brahman, the Ultimate Reality.

Essentially, the teaching of Vedanta is that man can, by personal effort and the use of inner knowledge, attain union with the divine while on earth. Its aim is to harmonise all. This is possible because Ultimate Reality, or Brahman, and the individual soul (*atman*), though seemingly apart, are, in actuality, one, as is conveyed in the teaching: *The real is one. It is the mind which makes it appear many.* This illusion, *maya*, disappears when knowledge of Brahman is attained. Understanding maya – the illusory nature of reality – is therefore of key importance. The 'three strands which constitute the rope of maya with which men become bound to the phenomenal world'[7] are termed *gunas*, and symbolised in the Indian 'trick' in which a rope appears to observers to be a snake. The gunas, known as Sattva, Rajas and Tamas, are held to be present in various degrees in all phenomena, including mind, intellect and ego.

Rajas is characterised by energy and manifests in ceaseless activity. It creates attachment and suffering. Tamas, which manifests in inactivity, dullness, inadvertence and stupidity, is the mother of illusion and represents the veiling power of maya. Sattva, which manifests as spiritual qualities, strikes a balance between the opposing characteristics of Rajas and Tamas. Although these gunas are present in all things, one sometimes preponderates and sometimes another. According to Vedanta, when these three gunas are in balance the universe remains in a state of non-manifestation, or dissolution; and when this equilibrium is disturbed through a preponderance of any one guna, the creation of the material universe occurs.

The first element to evolve at the beginning of a cycle is *akasha*, often incorrectly translated as ether, space or sky. It is the intangible material substance that pervades the whole universe, filling all space between worlds and molecules. It is the substance from which all else is formed. Often referred to as *prana* or breath, it is seen as the primal life-giving force, and thought of as a subtle biological conductor in the body.

Gradually four other elements become manifest: air, fire, water and earth, but these are not the elements perceived by the sense organs. Initially subtle, they become more gross through a process of combination, and from the gross and subtle elements emerge physical objects, the body, mind, intellect, mind-stuff and ego. Vedanta speaks of five elements only because from the standpoint of sense perception there are only five elemental features in the universe: sound, touch, form, taste and smell.

After these material forms are projected through maya, the material cause of the universe, Brahman, the pure intelligence or efficient cause of the universe, enters as life and consciousness and animates them. Divinity thereby pervades all things and this belief forms the basis of Indian morality. Prana is material and immaterial, endowed with intelligence and likened to the spirit. The flow of this psychic energy is the totality of the entire self, and the equivalent of vitality.

According to Hindu tradition, cosmic energy is distributed down through the body to the base of the spine, where it mixes with dense, dormant earth energy represented by the coiled serpent, *Kundalini*. This symbolises the stored energy or potential of the organism. It is seen as the task of the individual to mix, balance and refine these energies, and direct them upwards. The ascent occurs along two major pathways or *nadis*, the *Ida* on the left, and *Pingala* on the right, which criss-cross around the central *Shushumna*. This is represented symbolically as twin serpents coiling upwards around a central staff (cf. the caduceus). As the ascent occurs, the various energies are blended and transmuted, creating a variety of experiences and profound changes in awareness.[8,9] The ultimate goal is not only to raise the energy vertically but also to appropriately open and balance the energy in flowing harmony through the total body/mind/soul system. It is directed to achieving a state of harmony, wholeness or holiness, and oneness with the Ultimate Reality, synonymous with health. In this sense Indian culture is concerned with health and healing, which are essentially spiritual in nature.

Self-belief

Vedanta recognises that the human mind is incapable of imagining the Ultimate Reality with which it seeks union and that it turns towards the highest it can conceive, either a God or gods with attributes that are projections of human virtues, or God-like men or exemplars, such as Ramakrishnan, who strengthen and purify by example. The dynamic unity of the universe, for example, is personified in the God Shiva, the cosmic dancer, who sustains the manifold phenomena of the universe, unifying by immersing them in his rhythm, and making them partake in the cosmic dance. Such deities are worshipped in the hope that through devotion the worshipper can become like them.

Vedanta doesn't condemn cults of this kind, but reminds the worshipper that the god or exemplar must not come between them and the knowledge that they are both essential projections of the same Ultimate Reality, and that in worshipping those in whom eternal nature is revealed, they are revering their own divine nature which is more or less obscured. Vedanta has thus sustained and interrelated many cults of gods and divine incarnations. As a result Hinduism is often seen as polytheistic, but this is not the case, rather that there is one truth, called by many names.[10] Essentially, 'Vedanta teaches men to have faith in themselves first',[11] and this is reflected in traditional Indian medicine, Ayurveda.

Ayurveda

The tradition of Ayurveda, the grandfather of all holistic health systems, is some 3000 years old. Until the formation of the British Empire, when Western medicine overtook India, it was dominant on the Indian subcontinent. Since 1945, when India gained independence, there has been a remarkable upsurgeance of interest in this system and many colleges and universities now offer training in this discipline. According to some estimates[12] approximately 80 per cent of India's population rely on Ayurvedic remedies, supplemented to some extent by modern medicines.

Ayurveda, and its offshoot Unani, which is dominant in Pakistan, have become known in the West only relatively recently through its practice within immigrant Asian communities, but in 1980 the World Health Organisation suggested that its principles should be widely known as they could help to integrate complementary and modern medicine.

Ayurveda is Sanskrit for 'the science of life', and is a section in the last four Vedas, the *Atharva Veda*, written about 1200 BC. Although its early history is obscure it contains magical spells and charms to cope with a wide range of natural and supernatural conditions, suggesting origins in early magic. Moreover, as ancient India had no writing, all its teachings were memorised and handed down by the highest caste, the Brahmins, in characteristic occult tradition.

The first school of medicine as such was established at Banaras in 500 BC, and here in 5 and 6 BC respectively the main texts *Susruta Samhita* and *Charaka Samhita* were written. Together they constitute a comprehensive system of medicine which is essentially cosmological, for, as in all traditional systems, health is considered a balance between constituent qualities and energies of man and the universe. Fundamental to it is the idea that man must be regarded as a whole, with no separation of his mind, body or soul. Only one third of the system is concerned with disease. It is mainly concerned with health and providing a guide to living. As such it is an excellent system of preventative medicine and balanced living.

Healing in Ayurveda is based on the premise that balance can be achieved through the *tridosha* or *tridhatu*, which differentiates into three elemental energies, *kapha, pitta, vata* or *vayu*. Kaphic energy is associated with air and is concerned with growth and nutrition, or anabolism. Pitta energy is associated with fire and relates to digestion or catabolism. Vata or vayu is associated with water and concerned with the nervous system, mind and the distribution of psychic energy. It also controls and regulates the other two elements, which come under the general heading of metabolism. Vata, which reflects the psychosomatic component of Ayurveda, is therefore central to health and healing.

All areas of human functioning are located in one or other of these *doshas* or cosmic forces, each of which has two aspects, *purusha* – the material side of man and his conscious state – and his essence, *prakriti*, the unmanifest self, subconscious or spirit. These dynamic processes are intimately connected and move together. The interplay of these forces is described in terms of 25 fundamental qualities or *gunas*. These are enduring qualities consistent throughout nature and the source of all the characteristics of worldly phenomena. The degree to which the gunas associated with a particular dosha prevail over the others determines the nature of a person or thing, and people are thought to be constitutionally of one predominant type or another.

From the Ayurvedic standpoint the body's systems exist to balance the gunas and achieve dynamic equilibrium of the doshas. Illness is viewed as imbalance, and so healing relies upon accurate diagnosis of constitutional type, which is achieved in part by observation of the person's attitudes and behaviour. More fundamentally it relies on the intuition of the practitioner:

> When an Ayurvedic doctor looks at you he sees signs of the three doshas everywhere, but he cannot literally see the doshas themselves. Doshas are invisible. They govern the physical processes in your body without being quite physical themselves. We have called them 'metabolic principles', a term which is quite abstract. Yet the doshas are concrete enough to be moved around, increased, and decreased: they can get 'stuck' in tissues and displaced to parts of the body where they don't belong – so they are on the borderline of being physical. Lying as they do in the gap between mind and body, they resemble nothing that exists in our Western scientific framework. Vata, Pitta and Kapha only come into clear focus once you begin to view yourself within an Ayurvedic perspective'.[13]

Once a person's constitutional type has been established the physician recommends certain foods, minerals and specific remedies. This is a logical process since the gunas required to promote balance are identifiable in all things. The three doshas are 'located' in every cell of the body but are also considered to be concentrated at major sites around the body. Each dosha has a primary location, or seat, which serves as a focal point for treatment. So, for example, the condition commonly known as asthma is one in which the Ayurvedic physician would note a dominance of air (kapha). Accordingly he would prescribe a diet that excludes vayu foods such as rice and spices, and would use a remedy that would stimulate the other two elements.[14] (The complexity of Indian curries owes partly to the necessity of balancing various components such as water-generating coriander with heat-producing chilli.[15])

Diagnosis and prescription is no simple matter, given that Siddha, the Tamil language version of Ayurveda, recognises 4492 different sicknesses, and all remedies need to be prepared with regard to the patient's individual susceptibilities, seasonal and climatic variations, and other environmental considerations. Here again close similarities can be seen between the Ayurvedic and Hippocratic traditions, which have prompted some commentators to suggest that at some point Pythagoras was influenced by Indian philosophy. It is more likely, however, that these similarities arise from their common origin in the mystical, shamanic traditions of the ancient world.

Access to prakriti, or the spirit, is by way of five doshas or essence types. The energy system and the five fundamental powers of nature – space, air, fire, water and earth – are seen as intrinsically related, and all bodies as different combinations of these natural elements, arising out of the absolute substance prakriti. In human bodies these elements combine in special ways to become transformed into seven tissue types or *dhatus*. Excess, under-use or abuse of any of these is considered an important cause of imbalance or 'unmeasured' being, and consequently ill health. Alienation of man from his natural environment is seen as the loss of the natural relationship between the senses and the elemental powers of nature at both the individual and social levels. In this way modern man has 'taken leave of his senses'. He needs to return not only to his senses but to right measures, knowledge of which is present in the human heart:

> They come most readily to mind when it is still and quiet, in the full awareness of the senses working in the moment. Then discrimination is seen to act by itself and the right measures become clear and the right actions needed can be undertaken with confidence.[16]

In this Indian concept of measure one finds, yet again, close similarities with the ancient Greek tradition. The view of the physician–patient relationship is also similar. Ayurveda has always been based on positive interaction between physician and patient. The principle of self-help is fundamental to Ayurveda.

> An understanding of the need to strive for spiritual self development is taken for granted and in this respect the physician combines the role of spiritual guide. The patient understands that his obligation is to direct himself towards purity... This is marked contrast to the relationship between a Western doctor and his patient, who is the passive recipient of the practitioner's treatment, often ignoring his obligation to strive for his own fundamental physical well-being.[17]

A great deal of research in Ayurveda is carried out and published in the *Journal of Research in Indian Medicine*, although this is little known in the West. Fulder[18] indicates that when he was investigating Ayurveda in India he was shown remedies that induce muscle regeneration, which, until relatively recently, was not considered possible in Western medicine. Some ancient traditional practices of Ayurveda such as vaccination, anaesthesia by inhalation and dietetics have only been practised in the West for the last hundred years or so. However, over the past decade, Ayurveda has become better known and popularised in the West, largely through the best-selling books of Deepak Chopra.[19,20]

Yoga

One of the practices of Ayurveda already well known in the West – albeit only in the twentieth century – is yoga. This is not, as some Westerners suppose, merely a system of physical exercise 'that requires a pupil to contort his limbs into the weirdest and most intricate positions which only ballet dancers, acrobats and the limbless can achieve'.[21] This belief has gained currency because of certain practices which are concerned with physical fitness. Yoga is much more than a combination of physical and breathing exercises. It is a complete philosophy and self-help system which embraces the whole person in their physical, mental and spiritual aspects.

The word 'yoga' derives from the Sanskrit *yuj* meaning to join or yoke, and it signifies the yoking or union of the individual with the Ultimate Reality. It is essentially a spiritual discipline, a means of attaining the highest aims of Vedanta and the Hindu tradition. It is 'the most eloquent expression of the Indian mind and at the same time the instrument continually used to produce this peculiar attitude of mind'.[22] The practice of yoga is a training that unifies the parts of the body with the whole of mind and spirit. Without this understanding its practice is both unthinkable and ineffectual, so the Western mind makes it impossible at the outset for the intentions of yoga to be realised in any adequate way; 'The Indian can forget neither the body nor the mind, while the European is always forgetting either one or the other'.[23]

There are many different forms of yoga. *Hatha* yoga is concerned with integration through strength, and with bringing the body and its vital energies to the peak of health and efficiency through physical and breathing exercises. *Jnana* yoga involves deep study of and meditation on sacred texts. *Bhakti* yoga is concerned with intense devotion to a chosen deity, or *isvara*. *Karma* yoga is directed to integration through right action and good works. *Raja* yoga aims to control the subconscious mind. *Mantra* yoga is based on the inherent power of sound and vibration as revealed by ancient seers. Its aim is to alter ordinary consciousness by rhythmical repetition of divine names or phrases known as *mantras*. *Laya* yoga is concerned with arousing cosmic energies so as to enable the individual to merge with Ultimate Reality. It helps the adept to gain mastery over his senses rather than remaining enslaved by them. Like Laya yoga, *Kundalini* yoga is concerned with arousing cosmic energy. Kundalini is a type of *shakti*, or divine cosmic energy, that exists in every living thing and signifies unlimited potential. It is conceived as the female creative energy, symbolised as a serpent curled half-asleep at the base of the spine. The aim of Kundalini yoga is to raise this energy upwards through the body, generating intense heat and various psychic effects,[24] primarily through meditation and imagery. As such, Kundalini is consistent with the shamanic practice of generating heat. The raising of the serpent can be seen as a metaphor to enable description of a movement of energy that cannot be expressed clearly in any other way. Like Kundalini yoga, *Tantra* is also a refinement of ancient shamanic practices.[25] It endeavours to overcome the distractions of the world that stand between the individual and Ultimate Reality, by using them to destroy the desire for new experience. Erotic practices conducted in a strictly ritual manner are intended to enable the adept to utilise the immense power of sexuality in order to overcome every vestige of desire. The aim of tantra is a kind of 'eternal orgasm': a union with Ultimate Reality that transcends the duality of self and other. In the West, and to a lesser extent in India, its methods are frequently misunderstood as giving rise to unbridled sexuality and libertinism.

All forms of yoga are developments of the Upanishads, that portion of the Vedas dating from 1500 BC devoted to philosophy. Its original formulation is obscure, but Patanjali is held by most authorities to have been responsible for collating the original teachings just prior to the time of Christ, although virtually nothing is known of him, and his true identity has not been ascertained. Nevertheless, the *Yogasutra*, in which the metaphysical and doctrinal aspects of yoga are expounded, is attributed to him. Patanjali's *Aratamsahasutra* clearly suggests a holographic understanding of the universe:

> It is said that in the sky of Indra is a set of pearls so arranged that when you look at one pearl you see all the other pearls reflected in it. Whenever you enter one part of the net you set a bell ringing which reverberates from every part of the net, from every part of reality.[26]

The yoga of Patanjali consists of eight parts and is known as *ashtanga* yoga, or the yoga with eight limbs. These are *yama*: abstention from evil thought and deed; *niyama*: daily observances such as purity, austerity, contentment, study of the scriptures and devotion; *asana*: posture; *pranamaya*: regulation and control of breathing; *pratyahara*: subjugation of the mind; *dhyana*: steady unbroken concentration, or deep contemplation; and *samadhi*: ecstatic union or integration with Ultimate Reality.

When Westerners speak of yoga they are usually referring only to Hatha yoga, yet this was never intended to be pursued in isolation from the other forms. Its function is to prepare for concentrating the powers of the mind, or meditation, which is held to be the only way to know Ultimate Reality. Only by overcoming physical obstacles can the yogin commence the inner journey towards integration or union, which is the aim of yoga. Furthermore, Westerners typically regard Hatha yoga as merely a system of physical exercises and breathing techniques. Yet Hatha yoga includes practices of internal and external hygiene largely unknown in the West and a branch of yoga, *Anna* yoga or the yoga of food, governs diet and nutrition.[27] These practices, and many more, are all intended as a preparation for meditation. It is technically quite incorrect, therefore, to describe anyone performing several postures or asanas efficiently as practising yoga, just as it is inaccurate to describe mere concentration as yoga.[28]

Meditation

All Eastern traditions share a common emphasis on meditation, which is said to be a state in which the true self is known. From a psychological point of view it can be thought of as a modification of the process of attention, an introversion or drawing inwards away from the ephemera of the external manifest world to that of the inner self. The thoughts, images and experiences with which the mind normally identifies fade away so that one cease to think 'I am this or that' but simply 'I am'. When the sense of self is relinquished the person is said to be in a state of pure being or consciousness in which he feels unified with the whole of life and creation. This state, known in the Hindu tradition as *samadhi* or still mind, can be likened to a state of inner mental silence, a void or no-thingness, in which experience as it is usually known ceases.

Buddhism

Westerners appear to take the view that Buddhism is a characteristic Indian religion, and while it is true that Buddhism emerges from Hinduism as a dominant philosophy of the Indian subcontinent, there are nevertheless relatively few Buddhists in India. In time, the tradition of Buddhism in India was reabsorbed back into the all-embracing Hinduism from which it sprang, but it became and remained the dominant influence in vast regions of Asia, Burma, Cambodia, China, Japan, Korea, Laos, Mongolia, Sri Lanka, Thailand, Tibet and Vietnam, 'where it has had an almost incalculable effect on art, literature and ways of life'.[29]

Buddhism is an evolving tradition extending over two and a half millennia. No other philosophical tradition has existed in such disparate cultures as a major influence for so long. Over 50 per cent of the world's population live in areas where Buddhism has at some time been the dominant philosophical force.

Buddhism originated around the sixth century BC in the teachings of the Indian sage, Siddhartha Gautama, the Buddha or Awakened One, so called because he had 'woken up' to the true nature of reality and knew the basic truths of the universe. The cardinal principles expounded by the Buddha are held by his followers to be fundamental truths which explain the human condition. He asserted that the individual lives in process or continuous motion, *samsara*, and so life is experienced as change or flux. The impersonal law operating within this process and governing growth and development is termed *karma*, the law of causation, or cause and effect. The doctrine of karma holds that everything performed during life has moral significance and will influence the fate of the individual in subsequent incarnations. Consequently all living beings exist under conditions they have inherited by virtue of their past deeds. This Cosmic Law shapes all deeds on Earth, but without eliminating human free will, because man can decide his actions, and therefore his karma.

To Westerners, karma often appears to suggest a deterministic view of man as activated by uncontrollable, external forces, and to justify a resigned attitude to life. Such a view is a misrepresentation of karma. In the teachings of Buddha the mind has a dual aspect. One aspect creates its own bondage and suffering by its attachment to and apparent inability to grow beyond the appearance of things. Buddha viewed this as a form of ignorance or not seeing, *avidja*, which reflects the human tendency to obscure and veil the true nature of the universe. The other aspect of mind has the potential to transform karma into the pursuit of wisdom and enlightenment, implicit in which is the ability for transcendence which frees the individual from all desires and needs. When the mind is turned inwards it is the cause of release and freedom, but when turned outwards it is the cause of bondage. The outer aspect of mind is identified with ego or rational mind, and its attachment to power and possessions is likened to a monkey that plays tricks on man by creating illusion or maya. The inner aspect of mind is identified with essence or authentic being. For the individual, freedom from the endless cycle of existence, symbolised by a circle or wheel, lies in looking inwards. Buddhism therefore focuses on the self-liberating power of the introverted mind.

This self-awareness or self-perception is literally insight, and emphasis is placed upon its development through meditation and the abandonment of ego, because in Buddhism, the perfect man has no self or ego but fuses with the Ultimate Reality or unity of the universe which is indivisible, timeless and formless. Its aim is attainment of one's centre, a point of balance or harmony, a still point from which the infinite in all things is perceived. Achievement of this state constitutes perfect health or holiness. Hence Buddhism addresses itself to healing the human condition.

The Buddhist concept of suffering

The essence of Buddhist teaching is deliverance from suffering through maximal development of consciousness. One of Buddha's most penetrating insights was the understanding of the role of sorrow, suffering or *dukka* in human experience. This is intimately connected with the concept of impermanence or *anicca* which is a consequence of living in process. Buddha observed that sorrow is experienced because of the impermanence of things, or change, whether physical, psychological or emotional, man's awareness of it, and its consequences – illness, ageing, disease, death, loss, changing relationships and separation. He recognised that change is stressful and produces anxiety and fear, and that man's hunger for security and permanence, represented as resistance to change, are manifestations of suffering. So too is clinging to the ego, and our deep-seated fear of losing our identity or sense of self. Man defends himself against change by clinging to the familiar and the habitual, which gives a false sense of security. Nevertheless, irrespective of man's intolerance of it, change is intrinsic to the human condition. So, the human condition is the cause of sorrow.

Buddha saw the possibility of transformation through acceptance of change, which requires attention to and confrontation with the very anxieties it generates. This is achieved in primarily by meditation, which in 'switching off' ordinary consciousness allows unconscious contents to present themselves, and also by adherence to a code of conduct – a way of achieving balance between the extremes of self-indulgence and asceticism.[30] The basic formula for deliverance from suffering is as follows. First see clearly what is wrong. Next decide to be cured. Then act. Speak to aim at being cured. Your livelihood must not conflict with your therapy. Therapy must go forward at the 'staying speed': the critical velocity that can be sustained. Learn how to contemplate with the deep mind.[31] The same procedure can also be stated more succinctly in a list of simple steps: right seeing; right purpose; right conduct; right speech; right means of livelihood, or vocation; right effort; right kind of awareness, or mind control; and right concentration or meditation.

Nevertheless, Buddhism does not encourage a solemn view of life. On the contrary, the Buddha, who saw the cosmic 'joke' or truth of the whole universe, rather than the illusory and fragmented mind the rational mind tricks us into perceiving, personifies the Eastern belief in the wholesome nature of humour, which according to Hindu sages 'joins our split' parts and 'glues our fragments into one whole'.[32] 'When we discover that we create our own sense of unfulfilment, and maintain it only through constant effort, we may well burst out laughing!'[33] Hence the Buddha is traditionally depicted laughing.

Buddhist meditation and medicine

In Buddhism, as in the Hindu tradition, all forms of mental and physical hygiene are a preparation for meditation, which is the means by which the individual realises his true nature. The techniques of what is known as the Theravada School of Buddhism has two stages: *satipatthana*, in which the mind is controlled, or trained to see things as they are, without emotion or thought of the self; and *satpatthana*, transcendence of the mind, which involves concentration, and commences with the practice of attention and the attempt to bring the mind under wilful control, in the manner of a training a dog to come to heel and stay there.[34] Only when this is achieved is a person thought to be in a fit state to start meditation. Exercises in self-control may involve focus on external objects, or on internal features such as breathing or the emotions. Potential subjects are endless.

The third stage, known variously as *vipassana*, *satori* or *samadhi*, is an utterly impersonal awareness of the essence of the subject under observation such that the observer becomes the essence of the thing observed. This is a state of no-mind, void of all particulars. Only when the truths of the Theravada School have been assimilated can the individual grasp the expanded and deeper truths of the Mahayana School.

These different schools have arisen because as Buddhism spread from India it found different forms of expression. So, schools of Buddhism in various cultures differ from each other. There have been two major schools of Buddhist teaching almost from the beginning. The Theravada or School of Elders is the Buddhism of Burma, Thailand, Kampuchea, Laos, Sri Lanka, Vietnam, Bangladesh and India. The majority sect, the Mahayana or Large Vehicle, spread north and east from India to Tibet, Mongolia, the Himalayas, parts of China and Russia, Japan and Korea. In general, the former is more austere and strict and the latter more flexible and permissive. Consequently in countries where Mahayana has flourished a wider diversity of practices has arisen. Nevertheless this diversity rests on a basic unity that exists in spite of many denominational differences in interpretation and practice.[35]

Tibetan Buddhism and medicine

Tibetan Buddhism is part of the Mahayana school and includes a third force, *Vajrayana* or Tantric Buddhism, known as the diamond vehicle because it is many faceted.

In Tibetan Buddhism ego is viewed as a limitation of human reality and as such not only a mental and spiritual problem but also a physical one. This is because holding on to a rigid self-image, struggling to censor and manipulate experience to meet its demands, is hard work involving physical tension and pain.[36] So Tibetan Buddhism promotes a series of exercises in relaxation to deal with life's anxieties. The Tibetan approach to healing therefore reflects the belief that optimum well-being is a relaxed, balanced, open state. Human illness, however minor, is seen as a cosmic event.

> As a body man is a microscopic but faithful reflection of the macroscopic reality in which he is embedded and which preserves and nourishes him every second of his life; as a mind, he is a ripple on the surface of a great ocean of consciousness. Health is the proper relationship between the microcosm which is man and the macrocosm which is the universe. Disease is a disruption of this relationship.[37]

The aim of Tibetan medicine is to restore harmony and balance. Healing is essentially spiritual and the leading physicians are *lamas* or monks. However, although Tibetans have developed a complex system of medicine with elaborate techniques and a sophisticated pharmacology, it has never resembled its Western counterpart.

There are three levels of medical practice within the Tibetan system: the 'gentle' methods, which include simple practices such as giving medicines or applying salves to the skin; the 'stronger' methods, such as bloodletting and lancing abscesses; and the 'violent' methods, including removal of foreign objects and cauterisation of wounds. Wherever possible the gentler methods are used. Although developed to a fairly high level and practised for several centuries, surgery was abandoned for unknown reasons, possibly because permanent nerve and vein damage may make meditation difficult and therefore physical self-control and self-healing impossible.

Diagnosis and care in traditional Tibetan medicine also operate on several levels. Emotional, physical, spiritual and ecological aspects of the disorder are considered. The physician always looks into the life situation of the patient and may diagnose disease as some expression of disturbance in the psycho-social environment such as bereavement, personal misfortune or sudden change in routine. Emotional nourishment may be the prescribed remedy for such conditions. Tibetan medicine thus anticipated contemporary attention to stress and life-change by several thousands of years.

In most cases extensive physiological diagnosis is also conducted. The doctor examines the body, takes the pulse, analyses urine, faeces, sleep and eating patterns. Where medicines are called for, herbs, flowers, fruit, roots, honey and minerals are used as infusions, poultices and vapours. The patient is always an active participant in cure, rather than a passive participant:

> The feeling tone of the healing experience is extremely important, perhaps more important than the specifics of medical practice. A certain caring and trust has to be present and mutually experienced.[38]

Compassion is the supreme virtue of the medical practitioner, but the state of mind of the patient is equally important. The optimum emotional state for healing includes such qualities as compassion for the self, awareness or mindfulness, a realistic understanding of karma in illness, cheerfulness, optimism, and a basic confidence in the naturalness of the healing process. (A full discussion of Tibetan medicine can be found in the writings of Yeshe Donden, personal physician to the Dalai Lama,[39,40] and elsewhere.[41,42])

Zen Buddhism

Buddhism reached China in, or some time before, the first century AD and from its introduction one form was unique in purpose and method. It focused on meditation or *Djana* in Sanskrit, and the Chinese version of this, *Chu'an* was subsequently rendered as *zen* when passed on via Korea to Japan. The character of zen has largely been influenced by its cross-cultural evolution. It is, in essence, a unique blend of Indian mysticism and Chinese naturalism sieved through the rather special net of Japanese character.[43]

> If the foundations of the building called Buddhism are best seen in the Theravada school, and the Mahayana schools may be viewed as so many rooms on the first floor, then the zen school is the top storey, above which there are nor more, nor any roof to the building which at this level is utterly open to the sky.[44]

Zen is based on specific Buddhist teachings, specifically, 'Look within, thou art the Buddha'. Accordingly, it emphasises the development of insight through meditation. Its aim is enlightenment, the realisation of the Ultimate Reality which is beyond words and reasoning. Zen denies that understanding of the universe can be achieved by conceptual thought or ever fully communicated, but it can best be accessed and expressed through wordless activities. Wisdom is derived from intuitive awareness or insightful understanding achieved by close attention to the performance of mundane activities. For the student of the Rinzai School of zen, brought to Japan in 1191 by the Japanese monk Ersai, the path to enlightenment may involve archery; judo; *kendo* (fencing); *ikebana* (flower arranging); the ceremonial preparation of tea; gardening; *haiku*, the Japanese 17-syllable poem; and calligraphy. All are used as ways to the One.

In the Soto School of zen, introduced by the monk Dogen, intuitive insight is achieved primarily by *zazen*, or seated meditation, which is directed to riddles or *koans* that defy reason and rational analysis, their aim being complete destruction of the rational intellect.

Although the aim of zen and its basic approach is stated in Buddhism, it and all Japanese culture were profoundly influenced by Chinese philosophy and thought. Indeed the priests who were the indigenous physicians of ancient Japan had been completely displaced by Chinese medicine by the ninth century BC, and, according to a Book Of Laws published in 702 BC, medicine and education were already regulated along Chinese lines.

Taoism

China has two classic philosophies, Taoism and Confucianism, which are said to represent the two sides of Chinese character, the mystical and practical respectively. Both teach trust in human beings and in humanity; express belief in man's intuitive wisdom, which only needs awakening to serve as his support and guide; maintain a strong case for being present-centred; and are concerned with the Tao, which in the pre-Confucian world was implicitly and explicitly a symbol for the ideas of men.

The concept of Tao is one of the oldest and certainly the most fundamental in all Chinese thought from its emergence out of prehistoric myths up until the twentieth century.[45] The ancient concept of Tao is implicit in every system of

Chinese thought. 'The Chinese have always recognised a magical link between man and the landscape, viewing the world and themselves as part of a sacred metabolic system.'[46] In the Chinese view, the cosmos is an organic unit which spontaneously, out of itself, evolved the manifest and unmanifest worlds. The cosmic source, without beginning or end, is the Tao or Dao, which is roughly translated in English as 'the Way'.

The character for Tao, composed of a foot and a head, suggests the idea of walking and thinking, of knowing the correct path and following it. In combining the idea of 'foot' and 'head' it personifies wholeness, from 'head to foot', as it were, and since the head is often equated with Heaven and the foot with Earth, it also implies cosmic wholeness.[47] The Tao is at once the primal principle of the universe and the way to achieve personal realisation of it.

The most important principle of the Tao relates to consciousness, which is expressed in analogies to light. Tao is symbolised by white light, and the *Hui Ming Ching* – the Book of Consciousness and Light – contains instructions as to the way of producing light within the self.

Taoism, or the Teachings of the Way, was formally expounded in the doctrines of Lao Tzu in about 6000 BC and later expanded by Chuang Tsu. Other than the *Tao Te Ching* or Book of Changes, which forms the basis of classical Taoism and is attributed to both Lao Tzu and Chung Tsu, there is no other authentic text.

At the centre of Taoist thinking is the concept of *chi, ch'i* or *qi* (*ki* as it is known in Japan) which is translated inaccurately as gas or ether, and refers to the vital energy or breath that animates the cosmos. It inflates the earth, moves wind and water (*feng* and *shui*) and breathes life in plants and animals. It pulses throughout the cosmos, motivating all things. It was first described by Emperor Fu Hsi around 2900 BC and likened to dragon veins running in invisible lines from sky to earth[48] – a similar notion to the concept of energy found in ancient Egypt. The movement of this energy between two poles or extremes known as *yin* and *yang* is the activating force of all phenomena (and comparable with Platonic conceptions of energy). Everything has chi, but the rate and quality of this movement or vibration between the two poles yin and yang vary in different phenomena, giving rise to their distinctive character.

Yin and yang are tendencies in the movement of energy. Yin, which literally means 'dark side',[49] is the term used for the tendency towards expansion, or centrifugality emanating from the planet Earth, and is associated with sedation, passivity and negative force, and characterised as feminine. Earth energy is thus *yin chi.* Yang, or the 'sunny side', is the tendency towards contraction or centripetality, energy acting on the planet Earth from beyond. It is symbolised as the force of Heaven, associated with activity and positive energy, and characterised as masculine. *Yang chi* is cosmic energy.

When the contracting force reaches its limit, it changes direction and begins to expand, and vice versa. At the extremes, therefore, it changes into its opposite, and it is this constant flux between extremes that can be observed in all things from the smallest molecule to the pulsation of the galaxies. It is the rhythm of life and can be perceived within the human body in the movement of the heart and lungs and in the peristaltic waves of the intestines. Often the transition from yin to yang, or vice versa, takes place in a spirallic manner. This is discernible in the spirallic formation of the human embryo, and in the structure of muscle and bone. The movement is typically characterised as like two fishes (see Figure 1), a symbol which implies the dynamic principle of constant movement, but also the unity of opposites.

Figure 1

'The yin-yang principle is not therefore what we would ordinarily call a dualism, but rather an explicit duality expressing an implicit unity.'[50] Indeed, Taoism asserts that although man's experience of the world is characterised by continual movement or change, there is within this change a pattern that is non-random and has a kind of structural unity, constancy or fixity. This is the Ultimate Reality or background against which the two opposite but complimentary yin-yang forces are reconciled, and as such it gives coherence, continuity and unity to all things. This unity or One was identified by Lao Tzu as the indivisible, inaudible and unfathomable Tao. 'It is the same One, past and present; it embraces form and formless alike, being as well as non-being. The One is therefore a unification of duality and multiplicity.'[51] It is eternally without action, yet there is nothing it does not do. By doing nothing (*wu-wei*) and saying nothing (*puh-yeh*) the condition of equilibrium or balance (*hu-wu*) is achieved. Wu-wei is having effect without acting, a state of being rather than doing.

Similarities between Chinese and Indian thought and modern physics

The Tao is similar to Ultimate Reality or Brahman in Indian thought, and its vehicle for subtle energies, chi, is similar to prana. There are also clear parallels between the concepts of chi and prana and the central concepts of modern physics. Western sinologists typically have considerable difficulty in translating chi[52] because they are largely prisoners of a dualistic conception of the world that divides reality into matter and spirit, space and form. Within the Newtonian tradition where matter is viewed as a concrete phenomenon which forms the building blocks of the material world, there is no place for a concept that describes both matter and space simultaneously. Yet this is precisely the case with chi and prana, which in some circumstances become form and in others remain space:

> If material force (chi) integrates, its visibility becomes effective and physical form appears. If material force does not integrate, its visibility is not effective, and there is no physical form.[53]

This view is similar to that enshrined in Heisenberg's Uncertainty Principle. The concepts of chi and prana appear to be an intuitive recognition of this reality long before there were scientific instruments with which to observe it.

Principles underlying Chinese concepts of health and illness

According to Taoism, as in Hinduism, within any situation a particular balance may be discerned between the yin and yang energies which comprise the unity. In nature this balance is deemed to be correct, but in human affairs it is influenced by individual choice and volition. The person is therefore the mediator of these two great powers, the centre of his own universe, and is seen as needing to maintain a balance between its forces physically, mentally and emotionally.

Man is thus seen as infused with the powers of the universe – as a microscopic image of the macrocosm, and like the cosmos as a whole, the body is seen as being in a state of continual, multiple and interdependent fluctuations whose patterns are described in terms of the flow of chi. This cosmological view is central to the *Tao Te Ching* which teaches that the task of the sage is to create a conscious harmony between himself and the cosmos. Being infused with all the powers of the universe, man necessarily must look to himself for wisdom rather than to some external source. The aim of finding one's centre and balancing these forces is achieved by looking inwards, or insight. The more off-centre or unbalanced the individual, the more dangerous the opposing forces become, because at the extremes they become antagonistic and destructive. Complete awareness, wakefulness or mindfulness transcends and dissolves all extremes promoting wholeness or health. Inner development is a precondition of health, and when healthy a person resonates with the vibrations of their environment, so that their chi is in harmony with that of their surroundings. All physical and emotional illness is seen as resulting from imbalance in the flow of chi. Oriental medicine therefore aims at maximising the harmonious flow of chi in the body and balancing yin and yang.

Chinese medicine

Traditional Chinese medicine was founded around 2900 BC by the half-mythical Fu Hsi who first described chi and the two complementary principles of the universe, yin and yang. His successor, Huang Ti (c. 2600 BC) introduced into medicine the principles of ancient natural philosophy which regarded the human being as an image of the cosmos. Conversations between Huang Ti and his minister Ch'i Po form the content of the *Nei Ching*, variously known as the Theory of Internal Diseases, or the Yellow Emperor's Classic (or Treatise) on Internal Medicine, based on an oral tradition thousands of years old still in use today.

According to the principles established in the Nei Ching, there are definite pathways of chi in the body, known as *ching mo* or meridians, associated with different bodily functions or organs. Chi flows along these in much the same way as blood and lymph circulate through the body, keeping the organism alive, and its obstruction gives rise to ill health. Treatment focuses on normalising energy flow and restoring the balance of yin and yang. It requires understanding of a number of energy cycles, principally the *Shen Cycle*, or the Cycle of the Spirit.

The Shen cycle

In Chinese thought the symbol of the Tao is represented as a circle containing yin and yang and all opposites (see Figure 1). The clockwise flow of this circle forms the Shen or Spirit Cycle. Healthy people are viewed as flowing with the Tao, through the Shen and other cycles, whereas unhealthy people are seen to resist and fight this natural flow. The natural flow of the Shen Cycle is linked to five seasons: summer, late summer, autumn, winter and spring, each associated with five elements: fire, earth, metal, water and wood. Each of these elements also has various other associations or correspondences: a colour, climate, direction, sound, odour, taste, power, life aspect, time of day, emotion, bodily organs, sense organs, and a secretion. So, for example, fire is associated with summer, heat, the colour red, the time interval 11am–3pm, and a southerly direction. Its associated odour is scorched and its taste bitter. Associated with joyful emotion, its sound is laughter. It is related to the organs and functions of the heart, small intestine and triple heater (for which there is no Western counterpart), circulation and sexuality. Its sense organ is the tongue and its secretion perspiration. Each element also corresponds with specific meats, fruits, vegetables, and grains.

Implicit in the Shen cycle is another cycle, the K'o, the cycle of mastery or control. It is associated with emotions, thoughts and behaviour. Mastery of these involves understanding the K'o, and the fundamental principle of opposites.

Emotions arise in pairs of opposites: empathy and fear; joy and sorrow; anger and sympathy; and each of these can be controlled by the opposite. Hence joy is the antidote to sorrow. The emotions determine thoughts and behaviours because normally a person's emotions dictate his or her response in a given situation. These emotions also affect particular elements and organs, and thereby physical health.

When emotion is too intense or prolonged, disease may ensue. It can be discerned initially as distortion of energy balance within the individual, and eventually in distortion of the organs or functions themselves. Conversely, if an organ becomes diseased there is corresponding imbalance in the emotion associated with that organ. All disease is therefore considered psychosomatic in as much as that it affects both mind and body. Excess anger allows energy to rise up in stiff shoulders, headache, tinnitus and sinusitis. The Chinese regard prolonged or unresolved anger leading to resignation, resentment, frustration, or bitterness as probably the most destructive to health – a view now echoed by many practitioners of Western medicine – and as particularly damaging to the liver. Fear predominantly affects the water element, the kidneys and bladder. A sudden fright may affect the kidneys or heart but chronic anxiety is considered to permeate a person's entire system and be more damaging. Worry and over-concentration are held to damage the spleen, grief the lungs. At the heart of the Chinese system of medicine is the realisation that imbalance of an individual's emotions inevitably leads to imbalance of physical functioning.

Understanding of the Shen and K'o cycles and their correspondences and associations forms the basis of diagnosis in Chinese medicine, which is both complex and subtle. The medical practitioner uses all of these, including colour, sound of the voice, predominant emotion, and smell, to diagnose imbalance, predisposition to imbalance, its type and extent. In addition the practitioner takes the pulses and enquires into the person's dreams.

In the Chinese system there are 12 major bodily organs: the heart, small intestine, bladder, kidneys, the heart protector (responsible for circulation and sex), the triple heater (responsible for heat regulation), gall bladder, liver, lungs, colon, stomach, and spleen/pancreas. Each of these organs has a pulse. According to the theory drafted by the physician Pien Ch'io in the sixth or fifth century BC, the state of energy flow along the meridians associated with each organ can be assessed by pulses, six on each wrist, which can be felt on the forearm, just above the wrist. Energy imbalance and the state of various systems in the body are indicated by the pulses and can be estimated before any signs or symptoms are apparent.

According to this theory all the major meridians course not only throughout the head and torso but also through the limbs and have their respective terminals or 'well points' located next to the bottom corners of the finger and toe nails.

These are very important because it is here that chi is believed to enter and leave the meridians. The energy level at these points is said to reflect accurately the condition of the entire meridian, and in the case of acute illness, treatment at these sites is held to have immediately beneficial effects.

The condition of the spine is also important because in Chinese medicine the Governor Vessel meridian, which is one of the most influential, is said to flow along this path. (The all-important *Shushumna* nadi of the Hindu tradition, through which the tremendously powerful Kundalini energy flows, would appear to correspond to this meridian.)

There are many other ways of diagnosing meridian functioning. One involves pressing the well points and noting skin colour. When on light pressure the skin appears white or cold, chi energy is held to be deficient. Chi is normal when the skin is warm and red in response to pressure. When pressure results in pain, chi is excessive, whereas if pain only develops with deep pressure chi may be deficient.

The half moon of the finger and toe nails may also show the state of the associated meridian. If no moon is apparent this is indicative of chronically deficient energy flow, and excessively small nails suggest long-term deficiency of chi in corresponding meridians. A nail showing normal pink colour indicates a healthy meridian. Vertical wrinkles in certain nails indicate a deficiency in their blood supply, and consequently deficient meridian flow, whereas ridges or bumps reflect deficient blood supply through the whole body, as do nails that are excessively pale or white.

A further way of checking meridian function is by noting the way in which the fingers form when contracted into a fist and opened out again. Fingers which feel or appear weak show weakness in the associated meridians. Deficient energy is also reflected in peeling skin at the well points, and excessive flow in skin rashes.[54]

Imbalances can also be revealed in dreams by the predominance or absence of a particular element or correspondences of that element. So dreams associated with the element fire might involve flames, fires, burning, searching for fire, coldness, the smell of burning and such like.

Treatment in Chinese medicine

In traditional Chinese medicine one practitioner treats the whole person. There are no psychotherapists or psychiatrists. Treatment may involve dietary changes, herbs, mantra therapy, lessons in the Way of life, acupuncture, or moxibustion.

Acupuncture

At various intervals along the meridians there occur sensitive points, known as *Zjen Jin* in China and *tsubo* in Japan. Stimulation of these points is thought to exert an influence on the body organ related to the meridian on which the point lies. By giving treatment on one or more of these carefully selected sites, the skilled practitioner re-establishes normal energy flow and health. Different forms of therapy employ these sites. The best known in the West is acupuncture in which fine gold, silver or stainless steel needles are inserted into these points and stimulated manually or electrically.

Acupressure, the application of manual pressure to the acupuncture points is also used in treatment. It is usually understood as a practice of activating the acupuncture points through heavy finger pressure. **Shen Tao Acupressure** is a form which uses subtle fingertip pressure. **Buqi** uses many different manual techniques including finger vibration to activate chi, and also spontaneous movement, physical and mental exercises.

Moxibustion, whereby *moxa*, the dried leaves of the plant *Artemis vulgaris* or mugwort, are formed into a small cone and ignited over an acupuncture point, may also be used to supplement energy available at a particular site. Remedial massage, respiration therapy and various herbal treatments are also used to redirect and normalise energy flow as is **T'ai Chi Chuan**, a system of physical and meditation exercises designed to promote the flow of chi through the body. This is widely used both in therapy and as a form of preventative medicine. **Qi Gong**, meaning 'energy exercise', also combines physical exercises and meditation to remove energy blockages and harmonise the different parts of the body. It works on the principle that for any one part of the person to be healthy the whole must be healthy; mind, body and spirit together.

Japanese medicine

Japanese medicine corresponds very closely to that of China. Acupuncture is widely used as is Shiatsu – meaning finger pressure in Japanese. It originates in massage techniques dating back over two thousand years but was first developed as a special therapy by Toru Nami Koshi, who established the Shiatsu Institute in 1925.[55] Shiatsu was recognised as a therapy in its own right by the Japanese government in the mid twentieth century and over the past 25 years has spread to the West.

Various styles of shiatsu are practiced; zen, macrobiotic, healing, Namikoshi and hara. All share the common aims of relaxation, improvement of blood and lymphatic flow, alleviation of aches and pains, and heightening of bodily awareness. The client is treated at ground level on a firm pad by a practitioner who uses his or her body weight to apply varying degrees of touch, from gentle contact to firm pressure, by way of the thumbs, fingers, elbows, and even the feet. Single points are stimulated by pressure, rubbing, stroking, tapping or vibration. There may also be some manipulation of limbs. Typically treatment involves the whole body.

Anma, the precursor of Shiatsu, is found in Japan and the Far East. It is a generic term for the use of the hands on certain points of the body to promote healing and well-being. It embraces several different forms collectively referred to as the Anma Arts, including daily massage, pressure, kneading and stretching. **Do-in** and **Ge Jo** are forms of self-healing and first aid widely practised in Japan. They involve self-stimulation of areas by pressure, friction, and percussion; and breathing techniques.

A form of Japanese therapy becoming widely known in the West is **Reiki** (Japanese for 'universal life energy'). It was developed as a method of healing during the nineteenth century by a Japanese monk Dr Mikao Usui, who claimed to have found in ancient Buddhist scriptures the 'Key', or formula, for healing. He discovered how to use its symbols intuitively through intensive meditation upon them. His system of healing involves channelling and balancing energy within oneself and interpersonally by way of these symbols and the laying on of hands. It emphasises the importance of creating a trusting, loving environment in which healing can take place.

Similarities among oriental healing traditions

Clear similarities can be identified in the healing traditions of China and Japan and those of India and Tibet. They are, despite differences in terminology, essentially the same.[56] The correspondence is not exact owing to the different cultural contexts in which they arose but it is nonetheless clear that they deal with the same fundamental reality. They all recognise the universe as a subtle energy system which is reflected within the human body. The channels for subtle energy in the body, nadis and meridians correspond quite closely. These correspondences have been mapped using descriptions in the Upanishads, traditional Chinese medical texts, and clinical practice.[57] Similar energy systems appear to have been discovered by masseurs who noted a series of flows while feeling for reactions in the body during massage, and also by Taoists and yogins who recognised the channels of vital energy intuitively and extra-sensorily during meditation, and developed treatment systems accordingly.

The nadi and meridian theories were brought into contact with each other some 2500 years ago in Nepal and Tibet,[58] and communication and mutual supplementation appears to have occurred quite easily owing to their similarity. At about this time, the Shen and H'o cycles emerged in Chinese thought. These departed from the traditional yin-yang dualism by dividing all aspects of the universe into five elements and the body into three regions, physical, emotional and spiritual, each controlled by a different energy system. These ideas are essentially the same as those found in the Indian concept of prana dividing into five winds of vayus, and the body into four regions. Although the number of divisions differs the basic concept is much the same.

A further similarity is that the person is seen as inextricably part of the environment. In the Chinese system disease is interpreted as originating in man or the environment. Internal causes are mostly viewed as emotional. Therefore, as in Indian medicine, disease is fundamentally psychosomatic in origin. External causes of disease are largely associated with climate, but also trauma and poisoning. Diagnosis in both systems relies on an assessment of all the features of the patient: appearance, facial colour, sound of the voice, body odour, skin quality and texture, appearance of the tongue, the iris and the pulses, disposition; and environmental factors such as climate.

The role of Chinese physicians, like their Indian counterparts, is to prevent disease and recognise pre-disease conditions, and to treat disease according to the patient's needs rather than their symptoms. Tradition has it that Chinese physicians were only paid while their patients remained in health, and this is reflected in the proverb, 'the superior doctor prevents illness; the mediocre doctor imminent illness; the inferior doctor treats actual illness'.

One of the apparent differences between Chinese and Indian medicine is their application. In the former, knowledge about the flow of chi is used to identify which points along the meridians should be stimulated. In Ayurveda, the flow of prana is regulated and the condition of the nadis affected by way of yoga postures, breathing exercises, meditation and other self-help remedies. However, Chinese culture has its own systems of movement therapy in T'ai Chi Chu'an and Qi Gong, which like yoga regulate the flow of subtle energy by conditioning the channels. The conditioning of meridians is important because they function as the intermediary between the physical, emotional and spiritual bodies of the individual. When energy is prevented from flowing smoothly too much may accumulate in some parts of the bodies and too little in others. When such a condition persists, illness on all three levels will follow. The proper stimulation of the meridians harmonises the functions of the three bodies and produces a person who is healthy in the holistic sense of the word.

Common themes in Eastern traditions

Several common themes can be identified in the traditions of the East. They are holistic in recognising the interrelatedness of all things; relativistic, focusing on the illusory nature of time and form; and they all share an awareness of subtle energies within the universe. Man is viewed as imbued with these universal forces and as manifesting them on three levels: physical, emotional and spiritual. The traditions of the East all aim at achieving balance of these forces within man, and between man and the environment. This integration or wholeness is synonymous with holiness and health. Typically, therefore, Eastern traditions are characterised as religious or philosophical. However, 'the psychological window is the best one from which to view the traditional wisdom of the East'.[59] Hence, Ornstein[60,61] refers to the 'traditional esoteric psychologies of the East', and Tart[62] to its 'spiritual psychologies'.

In the West, psychology is generally thought to have little part in the promotion of health and disease. Mind and matter still occupy largely distinct realms. In the East there is no separation into body and mind, nor between the individual and the universe; they are all intimately related in a dynamic manner. Human beings are viewed essentially as dynamic processes rather than material entities, not analysable into separate parts, and closely linked to the environment. Health is characterised as the harmony of fluid movement, as balance, and all approaches to healing treat the whole person, not only the relation of body and mind, but also of this whole to its entire context. Eastern approaches are therefore organic and ecological. All forms of healing are concerned with insightful awareness into universal energies and how they are being utilised for good or ill. They all involve the person in the entire healing process because they all emphasise the need for greater attention on the part of the individual to the pattern of life.

Emphasis is laid on direct immediate experience of the universe through breathing, postural adjustment, ritual movement, dance or meditation. The aims of the healer are to help the person towards reordering of his world view, and the realisation that he is in process, rather than static, part of a whole rather than an isolated entity, and to assist him in getting in touch with his being and situation through the awareness of internal and external relationships, thereby achieving health, balance and tranquillity. Common to all Eastern traditions is the notion that it is the capacity for being 'shaken up' or reordered which is the key to health. Prigogine's idea that new order is created by perturbation[63] resonates with that of Buddha who, in recognising the possibility of transformation through acceptance of change, saw man's clinging to the habitual as a defence against impermanence and a barrier to growth. Similarly the idea of creating order by perturbation is paralleled in numerous ways in the traditional wisdom of the Orient, and reflected in certain practices such as the zen master striking his pupil, thereby enabling him to 'see' the truth of a paradoxical koan. Indeed, 'if we look deeply into such ways of life, we do not find either philosophy or religion as these are understood in the West, we find something more nearly resembling psychotherapy'.[64]

5

Western Perspectives on Healing

With the displacement of religion by science during the nineteenth century, medicine in the West became progressively secularised and the spiritual components of disease obscured, and then ignored. Emphasis within medicine shifted entirely onto the physical aspects of disease as medicine became exclusively concerned with the body. Disease whose origin could not be attributed to the physical body was incorporated into the framework of physical science by the simple expedient of converting soul or psyche into mind, and then into brain function, or dismissing it altogether.

> The materialistic prejudice explains away the psyche as a merely epiphenomenal by-product of organic processes in the brain. Accordingly any psychic disturbance must be an organic or physical disorder which is undiscoverable only because of the insufficiency of our actual diagnostic means.[1]

Therefore, 'either the body is ill or there is nothing wrong with it'.[2] Psychopathology, formerly sickness of the soul, came to be seen as mental illness – a concept which enables human problems to be treated as if part of medical science and in accordance with its principles.[3] Psychotherapy also came within the remit of the 'brain sciences'. Furthermore, 'the modern belief in the primacy of physical explanations... led to a psychology without a psyche'.[4] So, by the early twentieth century, psychology, which since its origins in ancient Greece had been concerned with the study of the soul, had become a science lacking its main subject matter.

One implication for medicine of this shift was that doctors became heir to a 'medical ministry'[5] for which they had no specialised expertise. It fell to them to wrestle with the task of reconciling the spiritual or psychical with the material and medical – a venture doomed to failure, given that Western science paid no attention to these hopes and aspirations, living its intellectual life unconcerned with spiritual and religious convictions.[6] Indeed rather than effect a reconciliation it resulted in an even greater schism between the pioneers of modern psychotherapy, Sigmund Freud and Carl Gustav Jung.

Sigmund Freud

Freud (1856–1939) is generally credited as being the founder of modern psychotherapy. More properly he can be thought of as the pioneer of psychological medicine because everything embraced in his approach originated in medical science. Freudian psychotherapy 'bears the unmistakable imprint of the physician's consulting room – a fact which is evident not only in its terminology but also its framework of theory'.[7] It is also discernible in its most distinctive feature, the analyst's couch.

Freudian theory and psychotherapy abound with postulates which the physician has taken over from natural science. This is unsurprising since Freud was very much a man of his time,[8] and like other nineteenth century physicians, he saw science as the ultimate authority. He was a self-proclaimed enemy of religion, which he viewed as an illusion preventing man from reaching maturity and independence. He described it as a universal obsessional neurosis.[9] He also had a horror of the occult, by which[10] he meant virtually everything that philosophy, religion and the emerging field of parapsychology had contributed to an understanding of the psyche. Freud wished to establish psychotherapy as a scientific discipline fully consistent with the thinking of the time. So he used the basic concepts of nineteenth century physics in his descriptions of psychological phenomena, and subsequently 'made unjustified and mistaken claims to have established psychology on foundations similar to those of any other science, such as physics'.[11] In so doing Freud fooled himself and many of his followers, but in the process he developed 'a model of consciousness which dispensed with spiritual aspirations and made them disreputable'.[12] The emergence of a soul-less psychology can therefore be attributed in good measure to his influence.

Freud developed a theory in which mind is conceived as like a machine, composed of various components, the *id, ego* and *superego*, each driven and regulated by various forces, whose integrity is maintained by various mechanisms which defend it against breakdown – the so-called 'defence mechanisms'. The whole system is fuelled by a basic energy or *libido* (literally: to pour) that flows through the psyche and empowers or drives it. Freud equated this with sexual energy and saw it as originating in bodily processes.

Changes in the psychic apparatus were thought to result from movements of energy from one region to another, while actions were thought to be accompanied by discharge of energy. Freud held that this energy existed in two forms, mobile and bound. He regarded the former as characteristic of unconscious mental processes and as chaotic and unstructured, and the latter as structured, organised and characteristic of conscious mental processes. He believed that unconscious (id) impulses, ideas and emotions strive energetically to become conscious but are prevented from doing so by the restraining forces of the ego. Freud conceived of the id as the dark, inaccessible, largely negative and timeless part of the personality. Known primarily through the images of dreams and fantasy, it is 'a cauldron of seething excitations',[13] instinctual urges and untamed passions, constantly striving to be satisfied. The 'sensible' and reasonable ego tries to control the id, defending conscious awareness from these feelings by various means including repression, denial and projection. At the same time it also tries to meet the demands of the superego, that is, the values and standards internalised by each individual from parents and society as a whole, and to reconcile its demands with those of the id. The ego mediates between these internal and external pressures, and strives to unify the processes of the psyche. When this fails, neurosis or disorder occurs. The psychotherapist is rather like an engineer who can look into this complex psychic machinery and identify its problems through careful analysis of its workings, and in principle at least, set it working again. Freud termed this process psychoanalysis. It was essentially a diagnostic technique, with the therapist trying to find out how the person 'ticks', just as an engineer might.

Freud thus conceived of the mind as a structure at war with itself, a concept not dissimilar to that found in Indian thought. Moreover, just as the latter advocates a looking inwards so as to gain freedom from the bondage of the conscious mind or ego, Freud advocated a cleansing of the mind, or catharsis, by looking inward with the aim of achieving the desirable ego state, a balance between the id and the superego. The early stages of this process consisted in putting a person in touch with the hinterland of his or her mind, in a way described as meditation or contemplation by Eastern traditions. In so doing Freud's role as a therapist was little different from that of the shaman. The methods he employed were remarkably similar, involving as they did evocations and interpretations of imagination as revealed in hypnosis, fantasy, word associations, memories, and especially dreams, which Freud considered to be of central importance, declaring them 'the royal road to the unconscious'. In so far as Freudian psychotherapy 'aims at an artificial introversion for the purpose of making conscious the unconscious components of the subject,'[14] it can be likened to the practices of yoga, tantra[15] and traditional magic.

Psychoanalysis as science

Freud would have been horrified by any comparison of his approach with occult practices. Acceptance of psychoanalysis by the medical profession crucially depended on its being consistent with the scientific thinking of the times, and he was determined to ensure that it was. Just as Newton established absolute Euclidian space as the frame of reference in which material objects are extended and located, so Freud established psychological space as a frame of reference for the structures of the 'mental apparatus' – the id, ego and superego, which were seen as some kind of internal objects, the interactions of which explained human nature.[16] Accordingly spatial metaphors such as 'depth psychology', 'deep unconscious' and 'subconscious' are prominent throughout Freudian theory. Although Freud described these structures as abstractions, and resisted attempts to associate them with specific structures and functions of the brain, they nevertheless had all the properties of material objects:

> No two of them could occupy the same place, and thus any portion of the psychological apparatus could expand only by displacing other parts. As in Newtonian mechanics, the psychological objects were characterised by their extension, position and motion.[17]

The dynamic aspect of Freudian psychotherapy, like that of Newtonian physics, consists of describing how the material objects interact with each other through forces that are essentially different from 'matter'. These forces, the most fundamental of which are the instinctual drives, notably sexual drive or libido – have definite directions and can reinforce or inhibit each other. 'Thus in the Freudian system the mechanisms and machineries of the mind are all driven by forces modeled after classical mechanics'.[18]

A characteristic aspect of Newtonian mechanics is the principle that forces come in pairs, so for every active force there is an equal reactive force of opposite direction. Freud also adopted this principle, calling the active and reactive forces drives and defences respectively. Hence libido is paired with *destrudo* and *eros* with *thanatos*, and as in Newtonian mechanics they are described in terms of their effects. However, the intrinsic nature of these forces is not investigated, and so, just as the force of gravity in Newton's theory is problematic and controversial, so too is the nature of libido in Freudian theory. Moreover, as in Newtonian mechanics, the Freudian model is rigorously deterministic, with every psychological event giving rise to a definite effect, and the whole psychological state being uniquely determined by biology and events in early childhood.

In Freud's view, understanding the dynamics of the unconscious was essential to the therapeutic process. The role of the therapist was essentially reduction and analysis, hence Freud's adoption of the term 'psychoanalysis' for the therapist's attempt to understand the workings of the mind-machine in terms of its elements. To Freud, unfulfilled repressed desires, conflicts between the demands of the id and the superego, and the preponderance of various ego 'defence mechanisms', give rise to pathological or neurotic symptoms and may culminate in mental illness. The analyst concentrates on identifying obstacles to the direct expression of primary forces, and in so doing simply 'brings into action the civil war that is latent and leaves it at that'.[19] Psychoanalysis is therefore principally a method of diagnosis, rather than treatment, and, to the extent that the analyst can eliminate obstacles to the expression of primary forces, is concerned with symptom alleviation. As such, it clearly reflects the disease model of Western medicine wherein health is the absence of disease or pathological symptoms.

Consistent with the Western medical model, the methods of psychoanalysis are cold and impersonal. Freud advised his followers to cultivate the scientific ideal of objectivity and to be 'cold as surgeons' in their explorations of the mind. He assumed that observation of patients during analysis could take place 'objectively' with minimal interaction between analysts and patients, and insisted that there should be no physical interventions of any kind. Freudian psychotherapy thus reflects the mind–body division characteristic of medicine, and neglects the body just as emphatically as medical treatment neglects the mind.

Carl Gustav Jung

During the early years of the twentieth century Freud attracted a substantial following within the medical profession throughout Europe. One of his most influential supporters was the Swiss psychiatrist Carl Gustav Jung, initially a close collaborator. He shared many of Freud's views on the nature of the unconscious mind, the significance of dreams and other imaginative processes, but Jung became increasingly critical of Freud's approach. He attributed the gulf between them to a difference in philosophical background, claiming that while he was steeped in philosophy, Freud had no philosophical training.[20] However, 'ideologically they were always, in fact, poles apart'.[21] Progressively Jung came to view Freud's psychology as not that of the healthy mind but as a one-sided generalisation from features relevant only to neurotic states of mind. He preferred to look at man in the light of what is healthy, sound and positive rather than in terms of the negativity which he believed coloured everything written by Freud.

Contrasts in their approach are discernible at many levels, but the major difference between then is Jung's espousal of the magico-religious tradition. It was Freud's determination to make psychoanalysis 'an unshakeable bulwark against the black tide of mud',[22] which is how he described occultism, that struck irrevocably at the heart of their friendship. His denial of all things spiritual or psychical was to Jung an absurdity, and an irony, given that in certain respects Freud's methods were very similar to those of the occult traditions he so despised. Jung insisted that 'man has, everywhere and always, spontaneously developed religious forms of expression, and the human psyche from time immemorial has been shot through with religious feelings and ideas. Whoever cannot see this aspect of the human psyche is blind, and whoever chooses to explain it away or to enlighten it away has no sense of reality'.[23] He considered that until the religious dimension of man is given proper consideration the problem of the psyche cannot be approached and that the religious dimension is therefore essential to any system of psychology which purports to study man. He insisted that 'a religious attitude is an element in psychic life whose importance can hardly be overrated'.[24] He claimed that he had not seen one patient over 35 years of age whose problem in the last resort was not that of finding a religious outlook on life. It is safe to say that every one of them fell ill because he had lost that which living religions of every age have given their followers, and none of them has been really treated who did not regain his religious outlook – this of course has nothing whatever to do with a particular creed or membership of a church.[25]

By 'religious outlook' Jung is referring to a sense of meaning or purpose in life. He considered that a truly religious attitude presupposes a healthy mind and that all healing is essentially a spiritual problem. Accordingly the central thrust of his psychotherapy can be understood and described, in his terms, as modern man's search for his soul.[26] His philosophy was that it does not take much searching out: 'It is only not there where a nearsighted mind seeks it'.[27] Jungian psychotherapy is, therefore, essentially a vision quest. Indeed, like the shamanism it echoes, Jungian therapy is a *heilsweg* in the twofold sense of the German word: a way of healing and a way of salvation.[28] It has curative power and can release psychic disturbances but can also lead the individual to 'salvation' (knowledge and fulfilment of his true self). It is a method of both medical treatment and self-education, and of value to the sick and healthy alike.

Jung's central theoretical concerns were to map out both the structure and dynamics of the psyche, and to understand its totality as it relates to the wider environment. He conceived of the psyche as a self-regulating system comprising two opposing but complementary spheres, the conscious and unconscious. He did not consider the latter an individual feature but collective and common, not merely to the whole of humanity but the entire cosmos. Just as physical bodies bear within their structure the marks of their evolutionary development from the lower kingdoms of nature, so, in Jung's view, the mind shows a similar line of ascent. Hence Jung has been described[29] as the Darwin of psychology.

Jungian psychology

The structure of the psyche

According to Jung, the structure of the psyche comprises a personal unconscious beneath the conscious mind consisting of ideas, emotions and memories which have been pushed below the threshold of conscious awareness because of the individual's refusal to acknowledge them. These complexes tend to break away from the general unity and become independent or dissociated. Deeper within this level is the collective unconscious which is not individual but universal, and whose contents and modes of behaviour are more or less the same in all individuals. Here reside the primordial or archaic energies which Jung termed archetypes. These are patterns of life energy which have become impressed on the psyche during the course of its evolution, thereby reflecting the life experiences of man and his predecessors, which are shared with all humanity, past and present.

As such these patterns of psychic activity are unconscious and unknowable directly but may be interpreted as images. 'Comprehensive pictures' of the qualitative aspects of these energies are provided by the symbols of visual imagery. These symbols are mediators between different worlds of experience, and transformers of energy.[30] 'The hidden order which surrounds us cannot be perceived by logic alone and we must pass over to the ships of symbolism to ride through the waters of the soul'.[31] Hence symbolism, literally that which brings together (from the Greek *sumballein* meaning 'to throw together'), is the traditional language of the mystic, magician and poet. The energy patterns of the unconscious can be pictured and depicted in various ways, and personified as gods, goddesses, kings, warriors, angels and so on. Archetypal images which recur throughout fairy tales, mythology, magical and mystery traditions are therefore, according to Jung, essentially metaphors for primordial experience.

> The phrase 'representations collective' which Lévy-Bruhl uses to denote the symbolic figures of the primitive view of the world, could easily be applied to unconscious contents as well, since we are actually dealing with the same thing. Primitive tribal lore treats of archetypes that are modified in a particular way. To be sure, these archetypes are no longer the contents of the unconscious, but have already been changed into conscious formulas that are taught according to tradition, generally in the form of esoteric teaching. This last is a typical mode of expression for the transmission of collective events originally derived from the unconscious.[32]

This accords with Jaynes' view of the ancient mind as revealed in the characters of ancient Greek mythology: 'They have no conscious minds such as we say we have, and certainly no introspections',[33] but act automatically in accordance with the promptings of 'gods'.

However, as Jung indicates:

> Another well-known expression of the archetype is myth and fable. But here we are also dealing with conscious and specifically moulded forms that have been handed on, relatively unchanged, through long periods of time. It is thus only indirectly that the concept of the archetype fits the representations collective, for it properly designates the psychic content that has as yet been subjected to no conscious treatment and so represents an immediate, psychic actuality.[34]

As, according to Jung, the unconscious can only be known indirectly through images and symbols encountered in dreams, fantasies and visions, study of these can provide insight into the energies acting deep within the psyche.

> The psyche consists essentially of images. It is a series of images in the truest sense, not an accidental juxtaposition or sequence but a structure that is throughout full of meaning and purpose; it is a picturing of vital activities and just as the material of the body that is ready for life has a need of the psyche in order to be capable of

life, so the psyche presupposes the living bodies in order that its images may live.[35]

Jung recognised the reciprocity of mind (implicit in which is the spirit) and body, and the spirit–mind–body unity as a dynamic life process. He also realised that imagery is a vehicle for perceiving and experiencing this process, and that because the energies they picture are living and alive, images are similarly active and alive, and can be interacted with. He advocated exploration of these energies by way of a process which he termed **active imagination.**

The dynamics of the psyche

Jung conceived of the dynamics of the psyche in terms of psychic energy or the life force, for which he adopted Freud's term libido. In the manner of Hippocrates, he viewed this as play between pairs of complementary features, each of which is opposite in content and energic intensity. However, in the total system the quality of energy is constant and only its distribution variable. Jung's law of conservation of energy and the Platonic concept of the soul as 'that which moves itself' are thus similar. From this law it follows that energy can be displaced, flowing from one member of a pair to its opposite, and can also be transferred from one to another by a direct act of will, in which case its mode of operation and manifestation are transformed. Displacement of energy occurs only when there is a gradient of intensity, or difference in potential, expressed psychologically by the pairs of opposites; that is, when they are unbalanced. Hence blocking of libido causes neurotic symptoms and complexes and leads to breakdown in any pair of opposites when one side is 'emptied'.

Energy lost by consciousness in this process passes into the unconscious and activates its contents which then embark on a life of their own and erupt into consciousness, often provoking disturbances, neuroses, and psychoses. Like Freud, Jung regarded neurosis as a state of being at war with oneself, but unlike Freud he did not see this as negative. He maintained that neuroses tend towards something positive. They shake people out of their apathy and can trigger the struggle for whole personality and health. In this sense, Jung saw order and organisation arising spontaneously out of disorder and chaos, in a way similar to Prigogine[36] and Eastern traditions of thought. Indeed thinking of the 'self' as a dissipative structure helps to account for many of the effects he claimed for therapy.

According to Jung, the flow of psychic energy has direction, which is distinguishable as progressive or regressive movement in temporal succession. The former takes its direction from the conscious mind, and the latter from the unconscious when the former fails. Similarities between Jungian psychodynamics and Chinese concepts of yin and yang are therefore discernible. There are also similarities between Jung's concept of libido and the Indian idea of Kundalini.[37]

Another important quality of energy is that it moves not only forward and back but inward and outward. The specific form in which energy manifests in the psyche is the image, which is raised up by the formations of imagination, or creative fantasy, from the material of the collective unconscious. Creative action of the psyche transforms unconscious content into such images and intuitions as appear in dreams, visions, and fantasies. Thus when normal conscious energy is turned inwards it proceeds to work on the material of the unconscious. When we 'concentrate on a mental picture, it begins to stir, the image becomes enriched by details, it moves and develops... and so when we concentrate on inner pictures and when we are careful not to interrupt the natural flow of events, our consciousness will produce a series which makes a complete story'.[38] This enables the person to identify and integrate this material into consciousness and to become more whole or healthy. Jung saw the use of active imagination as a training for switching off conscious thought, thereby giving a chance for unconscious content to emerge. He regarded this as important because as long as unconscious information is not understood it keeps intruding as symptoms into consciousness. Therefore, the overwhelming of the conscious by the unconscious is more likely when the latter is repressed. Clearly, in active imagination it is possible to see similarities with meditation in content, practice and aim.

From the Jungian perspective, the aim of psychological development is integration or wholeness. The conscious and unconscious have to be worked on simultaneously in order that the parts of the self which are neglected or dissociated can be rediscovered and reintegrated. Jung also recognised that as the self has a dual aspect and can be oriented inwardly or outwardly (as in Indian thought), the reality of both these inner and outer worlds have to be reconciled. He conceived of therapy as a journey along a path of personal development towards integration, or perfect health, a process he termed **individuation,** and which he acknowledged as an unattainable ideal. The process results in 'an integration or completeness of the individual, who in this way approaches wholeness, but not perfection'.[39] Implicitly, he drew attention to an important principle: that health should be conceived not as a state, but as a process of becoming healthy. More explicitly, he stated that the 'goal is only important as an ideal; the essential thing is the opus which leads to a goal; that is the goal of a lifetime'.[40] The process of individuation is therefore a lifetime's task which is never completed: a 'journey upon which the individual hopefully embarks towards a destination at which he never arrives'.[41]

The conscious attitude accompanying individuation is essentially one of acceptance, of ceasing to do violence to one's own nature by repressing or over-developing any particular aspect. Jung described it as 'waiting upon God'.[42]

In this respect the principle of balance at the centre of all Eastern healing traditions is evident in Jungian psychology, as is the conviction that healing is a spiritual journey and a religious experience.

In describing the process of individuation, the reconciliation of opposites, Jung drew attention to the importance of the symbolic healing process. 'He recognised that man, the symbolic animal, could resolve even the deepest divisions within him, upon the symbolic plane; and he invented a technique of psychotherapy by which this could be accomplished'.[43]

Jungian therapy

Jungian psychotherapy is known as 'analytical psychology'. Jung described it, somewhat paradoxically, as both analytical and complex, in contrast to the reductive method of Freudian psychoanalysis. While the latter was concerned only with the identification and exploration of the component elements of the psyche, Jung was concerned with analysing the elements and reshaping the whole. Jung's methods can more appropriately be described as spagyric,[44] a term which means the equivalent of analysis-synthesis, and which derives from the Greek terms *span*, meaning to separate, and *ageiren*: to assemble.

Jungian therapy essentially comprises various techniques for deliberately mobilising active imagination. This consists of suspension of the critical faculty, allowing emotions, fantasies and waking dream images to emerge from the unconscious, and confronting them as though they are objectively present. In this way the person actively interacts with these energies, albeit within the imagination, through 'the spontaneous experiencing, envisioning and speaking of the configurations of existence as psychic presences';[45] that is, by personifying them as images and entering into discourse with them. It is not merely looking passively at images as though projected on a screen, but rather more like a play in which dialogue goes back and forth between the personified image which has been produced spontaneously, and the self which produced it. In this way information and understanding can be gained about the dynamics of the psyche. If inner images are merely looked at nothing happens and it is necessary to enter into the process by way of personal interactions, so 'an alert, wakeful confrontation with the contents of the unconscious is... the very essence of active imagination'.[46] It is also the essence of shamanism.

According to Jung, what the doctor does is less a question of treatment than of developing the creative possibilities latent within the patient. Techniques for encouraging these creative possibilities include painting and drawing fantasies and dreams, meditation upon mandalas, poetry, modelling, sculpture and dance. Much emphasis is laid on the interpretation of these imaginary products, not by the therapist as in the Freudian tradition, but by the patient in collaboration with the therapist. Indeed Jung perceived the therapist as a fellow traveller on the journey of self-realisation indicating that 'the doctor is effective only when he himself is affected... When the doctor wears his personality like a coat of armour he has no effect'.[47] He redefined the doctor–patient relationship in such a way as to make it more like that between master and disciple in the Eastern tradition. He emphasised that 'the relationship between physician and patient remains personal within the frame of the impersonal professional treatment'.[48] So, in the Jungian approach, the human quality of the doctor is crucial. Furthermore, in his view, no one can enlighten others while remaining in the dark about himself. The first stage in healing is for the physician to heal himself, applying to himself the system he prescribes for others.

Dreams are of particular importance in Jungian therapy because Jung regarded the dream as 'specifically the utterance of the unconscious'.[49] However, he disagreed with Freud's claim that the dream is a facade behind which meaning lies hidden, 'a meaning already known but maliciously, so to speak, withheld from consciousness'.[50] For Jung the dream harbours no intent to deceive, but expresses something as best it can, although the dreamer may fail to recognise this through self-deception or lack of insight. He helped people to understand their dream images without the application of rules, theory and dogma. He claimed he knew of no technique that might fathom these inner processes other than paying close attention to them, amplifying and committing the images to memory through sculpture and art.

Jungian therapy as magic

Jung's therapeutic approach has many parallels with various ancient and oriental traditions which attempt to lead man to self-realisation and share the common aim of achieving a point of balance or becoming centred. Indeed Jung was profoundly influenced by, and drew heavily upon them in both theory and practice. However, there are differences. Active imagination is not programmed but is completely individualistic. The therapist does not take the role of guide but merely initiates the process after which the individual undertakes the work alone, becoming independent of the therapist.[51] In this respect, Jung's therapy has parallels with the magical tradition, especially alchemy.

Alchemists considered inorganic matter as alive rather than dead and requiring investigation through the establishment of a relationship with it rather than by technical manipulation. They sought to establish this relationship through dreams, meditation and disciplined fantasy (*phantasia in vera phantastica*), a process very similar to Jung's active imagination, which they described symbolically. Jung realised that the alchemists were imaging the symbolic transformation of the psyche and that they had a deep understanding of the process of psychological growth and healing he called individuation.

What the true alchemists were working on in their retorts and crucibles was the contents of their own unconscious which they projected onto the unknown chemistry of matter. The lead which they were converting into gold, was the darkness of the unknown inner world which, through the alchemical opus, they transformed into the divine light of the Self, the gold of their divine nature.[52]

Jung therefore devoted much of his life's work to interpreting the alchemical process in the contemporary language of psychology, thereby providing access to the Western magical tradition of inner transformation.

The occultist W.E. Butler considered Jung the greatest magician of the modern age, because, as he pointed out,[53] the aim of the genuine magician is realisation of the true self and thus the truth of the world which is masked by the earthly personality. Certainly the concept of the personality (from the Greek persona, meaning mask) as a mask of the soul is central to Jungian psychology. Jungian therapy embodies two of the most central principles of magic expressed in the maxims gnothi se auton: know thyself (the inscription over the entrance to the Temple of the Oracle at Delphi in Ancient Greece); and solve et coagula: dissolve and reform. Like magic it operates on the non-verbal level of pictures and images, accessing the subconscious mind or collective unconscious, referred to in magic and by Jung[54] as the 'treasure house of eternal images', through the archaic images of its rituals and symbols, and thereby producing changes in consciousness as the psychic energy which evokes the unconscious is reinforced by primordial forces emanating from spaceless and timeless regions. The resurrection of the 'deeper self' results in regeneration and reconstitution of the personal self.

Jung's system involves several methods whereby this resurgence can be effected, just as magic involves various forms of training directed towards this end. In magic, symbolic images are chosen and used by the magician to build up the mental atmosphere which will evoke the deeper levels of the mind where archaic images and energies reside. These tend to group around definite nuclei or centres, similar to those which Jung termed 'archetypes'. Evocation of and interaction with archetypal imagery is a central feature of Jungian therapy, and in this respect Jungian methods most closely resemble those of shamans. Drury[55] suggests that the collective unconscious described by Jung is the terrain of the shaman's venture inwards. It is the underworld where the shaman interacts and communes with living energies, personified as human or animal spirits, which, in exactly the same manner as Jungian archetypes, act as guides to the inner world of the self and others. Jungian therapy, therefore, is very clearly within the shamanic tradition of imaginative medicine, and many of the therapeutic approaches he inspired have pronounced shamanic aspects. However, Jungian methods differ from those of the shaman because Jung did not prescribe the images to be contemplated, or intervene in any way to guide the process of active imagination.

Nor did he have a monopoly on the interpretation of dreams, as the patient participated fully in the process.[56]

It was Jung's advocacy of both magic and religion which led to the breach in his association with Freud. However, influenced by Jung, numerous scholars from various disciplines have further highlighted the links between mythology and consciousness.[57-63] Moreover, Jung's contribution was considerable, influencing the practice of psychotherapy during the twentieth century quite appreciably, especially in Europe.

Similarities between Jungian psychology and modern physics

Many of the differences between Freudian and Jungian psychology parallel those between Newtonian and modern physics, and thus between mechanistic, reductionist paradigms on the one hand, and holistic, organic ones on the other. Jung's psychology is naturalistic, rather than mechanistic, as is reflected in his statement that 'if you think along the lines of nature then you think properly'.[64]

> In Jung's psychology everything is dynamic, subject to change; only the most important perspectives, only the basic principles are unalterable. The rest, like the psyche itself, is subject to the Heraclitan principle that 'everything flows'... The undogmatic character of Jung's ideas prevents them from forming a closed system and leaves the way open for continuous new development and differentiation.[65]

Whereas the Freudian system is fixed, rigorously deterministic, causal and dogmatic, the Jungian system is fluid, relativistic and finalistic in the sense that it is always concerned with the totality of the whole psyche. There are clear parallels between it and modern physics. Jung views all processes as energetic. Just as in modern physics there can be no direct perception of the subatomic realm, only inference of the existence of waves and particles from their effects, so the unconscious can only be known indirectly through images and symbols encountered in dreams, fantasies and visions. For Jung the psyche is not confined to space and time. He insisted that only ignorance denies this fact, and that when the psyche is not under obligation to live in time and space, as in dreams and fantasy, it is not subject to these laws. Jung's space-time awareness is also apparent in his concept of synchronicity, the acausal connecting principle, whereby all the experiences of humanity and all events are linked through coincidence in time rather than sequentially or causally. He saw a web of relationships throughout the universe, a fundamental unity of all phenomena. In developing his concept of synchronicity,[66] he worked in collaboration with the Nobel prize-winning physicist Wolfgang Pauli. He recognised that sooner or later nuclear physics and psychology would have to draw together because from different directions they mapped out the same reality, or transcendent territory. He believed that eventually they would arrive at an agreement between physical and psychological concepts and achieve thereby a mind–body, spirit–matter synthesis. Therefore, if 'there is no Einstein of the mind',[67] clearly Jung comes very close to it. Yet his psychological theory was dismissed as 'mere' mysticism rather than science by most psychologists of the time who were apparently unaware that physical scientists had already moved into precisely that realm.

The psychology of Wilhelm Reich

Another 'visionary' was the Austrian psychoanalyst Wilhelm Reich (1897–1957), whose attempt to synthesise psychology and physics led to derision and his social humiliation. As a young man and student of Freud, he contributed significantly to the development of psychoanalysis and was considered a probable successor to Freud as leader of the psychoanalytic movement. However, he became increasingly interested in aspects of human nature which have traditionally been regarded as within the domain of mysticism, and his unorthodox interests and views eventually led to his expulsion from the psychoanalytic school.

All Reich's ideas originated in Freud's theory of psychic energy, or libido. Reich proposed that this sexual energy is constantly built up in the body and needs release. This is the function of orgasm, and if this natural reflex is inhibited for any reason stasis of the energy sets in, giving rise to all kinds of neurotic response. Release of the blocked energy through re-establishment of orgasm is the aim of Reichian therapy since this is held to establish the natural flow of energy and eliminate neurosis.

For Reich this

> life energy is the vitality of our being; when we are moved, this is what moves. Emotions are e-motions; movements out; but they are not just in our minds but in our bodies, in the charge of energy that build up and with luck discharges; in the flooding of hormones, the surge of bodily fluids and electrical potential, expanding from deep within us towards the surface, or retreating into the caves of the abdomen or flowing through and out via head and hands and legs and pelvis, shifting form easily between muscular or electrical tension, fluid, sound, movement, sensation, emotion.[68]

Reich recognised that when energy cannot flow freely in the body it sets up a chronic imbalance in tissues or organs which allows infection of functional disorder to become established. He also realised that organisms do not react simply physically or psychologically. Individuals do not only defend themselves psychologically against emotional trauma, pain and hurt but also physically by contracting various muscles. Emotion that would otherwise be expressed spontaneously is literally held in the muscles, so emotional blocks are also physical blockages. He termed this defensive behaviour pattern 'muscle armouring' and observed that if these tensions are maintained over time they become structural components of our character – in other words, they characterise individuals. These character structures, as Reich termed them, are reflected in posture and in our entire behaviour, and often set up patterns of dysfunction and disease. Accordingly emotional and psychological ways of relating to the world are reflected physically in the body, and vice versa, so for Reich character is as much physical as psychological in nature, as are the defence mechanisms and neurotic patterns that Freud described. In Reichian terms, the neurotic is literally a rigid, tense person. Reichian *character analysis* was directed towards identifying and eliminating the muscle armouring so that the energy blocked there could be released and physical and psychological functioning could be normalised.

For Reich the person is united in its response to various influences, and so it makes no sense to separate mind and body in treatment. He treated neurotic symptoms in their psychic and somatic manifestations at the same time. In his view appropriate manipulation of the musculature rendered the patient incapable of sustaining his defences against the spontaneous expression of emotion, and released it. He became convinced that as emotional problems had physical manifestations they could be addressed by way of physical techniques, breathing exercises and massage. He termed his new therapeutic technique 'vegetotherapy'. It involved a direct physical encounter between him and his patients, and

> did away with the psychoanalytic taboo of never touching a patient, substituting physical attack by the therapist on the muscular attitudes (armouring) in the patient: thus the therapist treats the patient not only from the characterological point of view, but also physically by provoking in him a sharp contraction of the musculature in order to make the patient aware of those contractions which have become chronic. The relaxation of bound-up energy in the musculature in whatever part of the body would often be accompanied by recall of the trauma which has led to the contraction or neurotic symptom in the first place.[69]

Reich also noticed that tense people inhibit their intake of oxygen, so those with psychological problems tend to breathe shallowly and shallow breathing eventually becomes a habit. Neurotics characteristically breathe less deeply than others. Reich insisted that the first step in overcoming nervous tensions is to learn to breathe deeply using the chest, stomach and solar plexus. He instituted breathing exercises as part of therapy and found that as a result many of his patients felt more vital and alive, and experienced a oneness with nature, a mystical harmony which some personified as 'God'. Reich came to believe that he had discovered a biological energy, or bioenergy, which pervades the universe and is the active force responsible for man's longing for orgastic and mystical union with God. Thus in his search for the biological foundation of the Freudian concept of libido he claimed to have discovered the life force, which he called orgone energy and described as blue in colour. The basis of Reich's approach was therefore

> a tremendous vision of the streaming of energy in the cosmos, the galaxies, the oceans, the weather – and in our own bodies. He saw it as the same energy, following the same patterns, the same dance. Although Reich condemned 'mysticism' – by which he meant flight from bodily reality – his own vision is in the best sense truly a mystical one.[70]

Orgone energy, as conceived by Reich, was not merely a biological energy but energy endowed with a spiritual quality, since an essential part of the subjective experience of orgasm is longing to reach beyond oneself to merge with that beyond. As such, Reich considered it to be functionally equivalent with love. In Reich's view, love is the life force which literally makes the world go round, permeating the universe and sustaining all life forms. It is the basic principle of health in all living creatures and lack of it is the cause of disease.

Reich tried to demonstrate the efficacy of orgone energy in the treatment of psychosomatic disease and cancer, which he believed to be caused by energy blockage. The devitalised tissues, he claimed, began to degenerate and form T-bacilli which produce cancer. He claimed that orgone energy could be collected in orgone accumulators and used in the treatment of various disorders. The sale of these orgone boxes eventually led to his imprisonment for alleged fraud, and he died in prison in 1957.

Reich's claim that the life force or orgone energy is synonymous with breath is paralleled in both the Indian and Chinese traditions, where it is known as prana and chi respectively, and in the ancient traditions of many cultures, including those of the West. In Arabic, *rih* or wind is etymologically similar to *ruh* meaning soul, and the Latin words *animus*: spirit and *anima*: soul are similar to the Greek *anaemos*, or wind. The Greek word *pneuma* or wind, also means breath and was used to refer to the cosmic life force. The aims of vegetotherapy are also very similar to those of many oriental traditions, notably Tantra, which is concerned with the raising of Kundalini energy through ritualised sexual practices. In fact, Reich admitted[71] to having been impressed by the principles of Buddhism. It is perhaps not surprising, therefore, that in certain respects his ideas about the body resemble those found in Tibetan Buddhism. Reich's character analysis led him to view character itself as a disorder: a hardening of the fluid human reality into a fixed and limiting pattern of behaviour. He regarded it as both a physical and a mental problem, the body merely expressing the mind's rigidity, and developing character armour as a defence against the fearful uncertainty of life, and inevitably, against feeling.

It is also possible to discern similarities between Reich's later work and shamanic practices. Reich believed that orgone energy could be accumulated and directed to affect natural processes other than healing. He claimed to have demonstrated rainmaking in this way, which lent support to his opponents, who viewed him as a 'quack' suffering from a paranoid delusional system.[72] At best, Reich was seen within the scientific community as a mystic, attempting to express in scientific terms what mystics such as Wordsworth and Blake had conveyed in poetry, and dismissed as fanciful and pathetic. Nevertheless, Reich attracted a number of enthusiastic supporters, and his influence on various approaches to healing has proved to be considerable, and largely under-estimated (see Chapter 12).

Behaviourism

The hostility towards Reich, which led eventually to his incarceration and death in prison, needs to be understood in context. In trying to gain acceptance as a bona fide scientific discipline, psychology had been trying to distance itself from the 'irrational' aspects of its subject matter since the early years of the twentieth century. Accordingly Reich and his followers were a source of profound embarrassment. Psychology had reconciled the apparent incompatibility of science and the psyche by denying the existence of the latter and conceiving of man solely in terms of his objective behaviour. This 'behaviourism' viewed man as a complex machine responding to various environmental stimuli by way of conditioned or learned reflexes. Its basic principle was that complex phenomena could be reduced to combinations of simple stimulus-response patterns, and these were seen as adequate explanation for all human endeavour, including art, religion and science. The attempt to understand man in terms of 'slot machine mechanics'[73] implied a rigorous causal relationship which would allow psychology to predict the response for any given stimulus. The 'mindless' approach of behaviourism was seen as more consistent with the aims and methods of science, and it overtook the psychologies of Freud and Jung, and subsequently dominated the discipline for most of the first half of the century. It reached its peak of ascendency during the 1950s, at the very height of the machine age.

Ironically, at precisely the time that psychology was attempting to claim with certainty the predictability of human beings, physics was demonstrating the uncertainty and unpredictability of the electron. Moreover, psychology was denying the existence of mind when physics was highlighting its importance. Nevertheless, psychotherapy was substituted with **behaviour therapy,** which viewed psychological disorders as learned maladaptive behaviour patterns. Its goal was to rectify deviant behaviour patterns and restore the individual to normal functioning. It was essentially negative and conservative in approach, and both simplistic and demeaning in the image of man it projected, for irrespective of whether man is viewed literally as a machine, or metaphorically, as if one, the net result is that he is reduced to something less than human. In extinguishing man's essence, his psyche, behaviourism had obliterated his very humanity. It had effectively murdered the man it claimed to study,[74] apparently without remorse, as is reflected in the statement : 'To man *qua* man we readily say good riddance'.[75]

Humanistic psychology

However, 'Man does not stand forever his nullification',[76] and during the 1950s a growing number of psychologists, especially in the USA, refused to view man as a machine, enslaved by environmental contingencies and his past. They attempted a fully human alternative to the mechanistic view of man prevalent within Western culture. Their concerns, focusing as they did on the individual as a perceiver and interpreter of himself and his world and a determiner of his own behaviour, represented a return to fundamental questions regarding the nature of the human self, soul or psyche, and its development, and reinstated these as legitimate questions for psychology. What came to be known as 'humanistic psychology' addressed itself to spiritual human concerns, and with devising new methods with which to study the significant problems of man, rather than the relatively trivial problems that fitted the allegedly 'scientific' method of enquiry. These methods included a number of different therapies, all of which directed attention to subjective experience, feelings, impressions, dreams, fantasy, personal responsibility and choice, volition, personal powers and potentials. There was no one figure around whom this effort was organised, but Abraham Maslow is generally acknowledged as being of central importance.

Abraham Maslow

Maslow was for many years a professor of psychology, but he criticised psychology for its emphasis on determinism and its concomitant neglect of the human. Like Jung, he was opposed to generalisation from the 'mentally ill' to man as a whole, arguing that psychology should properly be concerned with the study of health, which he viewed as the fulfilment of a five-level hierarchy of need culminating in self-actualisation. He based his theory on the assumption of man's intrinsic good nature, which he viewed as an essentially biological feature, partly general to the species, and partly individual and unique. He conceived of the inner nature or self as possessing a dynamic for growth and actualisation but as weak rather than strong, and easily frustrated, denied or suppressed. Like Freud and Jung, he saw self denial or suppression of the self as the major cause of illness and distress, and much of it arising from man's fear of and defence against his capacities, potentialities, creativeness and goodness. Like them, he viewed man as at war with himself in so far as that he was engaged in a struggle against his own greatness. According to Maslow, man effectively turns his back on himself out of fear of doing otherwise, and is thereby constrained into outmoded and ineffectual action which generates a state of being which he termed 'the psychopathology of the average'.[77] In contrast, he viewed health as equivalent to self-actualisation, which is characterised by enhanced perception of reality; increased acceptance of oneself, others and nature; increased spontaneity, creativity and autonomy; and ability for mystical experiences. He regarded the latter as evidence of man's ability to transcend personal experience to reach some ultimate experience or reality. Therefore in Maslow's humanistic psychology there are echoes of Jungian psychology and the ancient and oriental traditions. His model of health is also strikingly similar to that which is central to homeopathic medicine.

Similarities between humanistic psychology and the homeopathic model of healing

Reibel[78] points to numerous parallels between humanistic psychology and homeopathy, pioneered in the nineteenth century by Dr Samuel Hahnemann, a physician whose approach to treatment was closely allied to that of Hippocrates and Paracelsus. Hahnemann used the term 'vital force' to describe the balancing mechanism within each living organism which promotes, or at least protects, health. He claimed that this vital force, comparable with Hippocrates' *vix medicatrix naturae*, is stimulated by internal and external factors to build up a counteractive reaction. The result of the interaction between the vital force and the conditions that set it in motion produces various symptoms in the body revealing that an imbalance has occurred. Disease is thus a product of stress and failure of the body's own attempt to heal it, whereas health is the maintenance of the vital force or inner nature of the organism itself. Any treatment or healing must deal with the whole organism in both its objective and subjective aspects, taking into account the individual's perception and interpretation of his or her symptoms and individual features. Therapy consists not in opposing a problem, as in conventional medicine, but in using the problem as its solution, that is, by using a natural substance which in its raw state can produce similar effects to those of the illness, hence the homeopathic axiom: *like cures like*.

> The apparency of anything can be annulled by the creation of a perfect duplicate. The homeopathic physician seeks to create a perfect duplicate of the patient's illness by selecting a medicine whose properties produce an artificial illness that exactly mimics the patient's illness.[79]

The aim of treatment is to establish a total pattern of symptoms that mirrors the whole patient, and is a reflection of his or her overall pattern of adjustment. However, the therapeutic relationship is of particular importance in homeopathy:

> The encounter between a patient and a homeopath is an intimate interaction for both... The prescriber... is not merely a passive observer protected behind a wall of objectivity. Each patient engages the homeopath in a deep and meaningful

way... When homeopathy is practised with this degree of involvement it stimulates growth in the homeopath just as it does for the patient.[80]

In both theory and practice, humanistic psychology parallels homeopathy, not only in sharing its view of the conditions in which the vital force flourishes, but also in recognising that solutions to problems can be facilitated by reflection of their symptoms. This insight is central to the therapeutic approach advocated by Carl Rogers.

Person-centred therapy

Carl Rogers, a distinguished professor of psychology and former President of the American Psychological Association, held views broadly similar to those of Maslow, but drew particular attention to the dynamic features of the self, its tendency to expand, extend, grow and develop. He believed that this tendency exists in every individual and awaits only the proper conditions to be realised and expressed, or actualised. For Rogers, this **self-actualisation** is synonymous with health, wholeness or integration, and he considered therapy as a process wherein the individual has the opportunity to integrate and actualise the self. He viewed the central process of therapy as facilitation of the individual's experience of becoming a more autonomous, spontaneous person. Neverthless, while insisting that the potential for self-actualisation resides within the person, Rogers claimed that the conditions for facilitating its development lie in the relationship between the person and the therapist, and come about through a close, emotionally warm and understanding relationship, in which the individual is free from threat and evaluation and has the freedom to be fully him or herself.

The type of therapeutic relationship Rogers sought to provide has three particularly significant qualities. The first is the authenticity, or genuineness, of the therapist. For this to be achieved, the therapist must be aware of his or her feelings in so far as is possible, and be able to express them where appropriate rather than present any facade. The second quality required by the therapist is his or her unconditional positive regard for a person; that is, the ability to respect and care for an individual, irrespective of his or her condition, behaviour, attitudes and feelings. The third necessary quality is empathic understanding, or genuine listening: the therapist's continuing desire to understand the feelings and personal meanings that the other person is experiencing. Rogers argued that within such a relationship there is an implicit freedom to explore oneself at both the conscious and unconscious levels, and that under such conditions a person moves from fear and defence of inner feelings, to encouragement and acceptance of them; from being out of touch with feelings, to greater awareness of them; from living life by the introjected values of others, to living by those experienced by him or herself in the present; from distrust of spontaneous aspects of the self, to trust in them; and towards greater freedom and more responsible choices. Essentially, Rogerian therapy ideally affords a situation in which a person learns to be free, and as such it is an educational process. In theory and practice, it is largely a restatement of Jungian principles, and likewise it has close parallels with ancient and oriental traditions in its conceptions of health and the role of the therapist in its promotion.

Rogers' concept of therapy accords with the origin of the word in the Greek *therapeia*, meaning attendance or service. Rogers emphasised that attending to a person is not about doing anything to or for them, but is simply about *being*. In his view, simply being attentive, caring, open and genuine, is therapeutic and brings about positive changes that move a person in the direction of wholeness and health. In this respect the Rogerian concept is very similar to that of Eastern traditions, and quite alien to the West, with its obsessive concern for performance, and especially to Western men – the majority of therapists – who are especially conditioned to *doing*. Jourard,[81] who investigated Rogerian principles in practice, observed a considerable dread of passivity among therapists. He suggested that it constitutes a threat to masculine identity, and also, no doubt, to the work ethic. As a result they are frequently attracted to 'manly' active therapeutic techniques that make them feel that *they* are doing something to make their clients well. This technical behaviour often impresses clients, but in so far as it is a manipulation of them by the therapist, rather than an open, spontaneous response to them, it may provoke vigorous defences. This is no less true of attempts to 'do' things to put people at their ease, such as offering cigarettes or coffee, or effecting certain postures and mannerisms. Jourard observed that the 'professional manner' assumed by many people in the presence of clients or patients is an attempt to manipulate them to their own advantage. Despite appearances to the contrary, these therapists are attending primarily to themselves rather than others.

To attend or reach out to others (from *attendere*: to reach out) it is necessary first to put aside any barriers which might be in the way. Professional roles and personal mannerisms are one kind of barrier. Others include one's thoughts, problems, beliefs, prejudices, preconceptions, fantasies and concerns. In other words, the various aspects of one's self or ego. Unless these can be overcome, despite all attempts to attend to others one succeeds only in attending to oneself. Implicit in the Rogerian approach is the notion of the therapist putting aside ego, albeit temporarily. This parallels Eastern and magical concepts of the master as egoless, a condition often likened to a mirror which reflects but does not hold reality, and so reveals it in a non-selective way. This principle is central to the Rogerian concept of reflection, whereby, to the extent that the therapist can put aside or suspend the ego, the client is effectively talking to him or herself, as if speaking into a mirror and, in so doing, is confronting features of him or herself, possibly for the first time. These new insights can then be used for personal growth and change. Accordingly, the Rogerian therapist reflects the content and manner of a person's attempts to communicate as faithfully as possible, without the distortions that arise from his or her own hunches, speculations, theories, experiences and ideas on life; and without being directed to any specific content. Rogers claimed that confronted with such sustained reflection, persons attend more to themselves and come to see themselves more clearly. Their awareness progresses from the general to the specific; from the superficial to the deep; from thoughts to feelings; and from the abstract to the concrete. This same progression also results from meditational practices which traditionally aim to develop attention to the self and achieve insight.

However, the concept of reflection has a limiting feature – the nature of the 'mirror' of which it is a property. A non-human mirror is non-selective in the sense that it is not directed to any particular feature of the reality it reflects. Ideally the mirror-like individual is non-selective, but most therapists have not attained such a state, and never will. They tend to be highly selective in the features of the client they reflect. So, rather than being 'non-directive', as Rogers claimed, his approach is in practice highly selective. It focuses largely on words and to a great extent ignores the whole range of non-verbal expression and communication. Arguably the approach is also somewhat superficial, accepting at 'face value' the truth of what is said and facilitating a potentially misleading view of the person. The therapist may need to be rather more like a magnifying glass than a mirror, bringing certain features into sharp focus and thereby promoting insight into the various modes of a person's being, and integration of formerly disowned and unrecognised features of the self. Such an approach was advocated by Frederick (Fritz) Perls. His **Gestalt therapy** has striking similarities with ancient and Eastern traditions, notably zen, not only in its focus on one-pointed awareness, which is an aim it shares with meditational practices, but also in emphasising the importance of 'the whole of things' to health.

The Gestalt therapy of Fritz Perls

Perls viewed the individual organism as existing within an environmental field in which all parts are interdependent, so that change in any one part affects all other parts: 'The individual is inevitably at every moment a part of some field which includes both him and his environment'.[82] The nature of the relationship between the individual and the environment is therefore of key importance, determining its 'being' in the world. Perls' view, like that of Rogers, is essentially holistic and integrative, and emphasises **self-actualisation** – the 'becoming of what one is' – which Perls viewed as an inborn goal of all living things. He argued that this fundamental need for self-actualisation can only occur through integration of the various parts of the self because it is in this way that the self emerges as a unified figure or *Gestalt* against its environmental field. Only then, when the self is clearly defined and located in relation to others and the world, does it become possible for the individual to fulfil his potential because this integrated self, like any unified force field, is more likely to utilise its potential to act. Perls' concept of self-actualisation is implicitly energetic and dynamic. Such a process requires constant monitoring of the self and redefinition of its boundaries, because the *gestalten* of the environmental field, rather than being static and fixed, are dynamic and ever-changing as the demands of the self, others and the environment alter.

The satisfaction of these needs, which is equivalent to psychological health, is something of a balancing act, maintained by a kind of homeostasis or self-regulating process whose fundamental requirement is awareness of the immediate situation. The aware individual is able to perceive changes in existing gestalten or configurations and act accordingly to create new patterns, thereby restoring the equilibrium between the self and its surroundings. In Perls' approach, as in ancient and oriental traditions, balance and harmony are central features. Like Maslow, Perls attributed much of the difficulty in achieving the figure/ground discrimination necessary for Gestalt formation to society. He saw the problem residing largely in the prescription of one central enduring role to the individual, who is consequently obliged to suppress, disown, or project outside himself, all those features that are inconsistent with the maintenance of that role. This denial of self invariably results in a progressive fragmentation of the person and a difficulty in establishing boundaries between self, others and the external world. The person cannot satisfy his needs because he is unaware of them, and such confusion may ultimately lead to complete breakdown of a physical or psychological nature. Perls viewed neurosis as the inability to perceive boundaries clearly, with the result that the individual experiences the world as encroaching and characteristically responds with fear, anxiety, avoidance tendencies and elaborate defences, all aimed at avoiding this intrusion. Moreover, being unable to define personal boundaries, the neurotic typically manipulates the environment for support in various ways, rather than utilising his personal potential. The individual is therefore unable to satisfy his needs and remains in a state of disequilibrium which might justifiably be thought of as 'unbalanced'.

Gestalt therapy, like zen and other oriental traditions, emphasises change. It is not concerned with explanations or interpretations of past history, or speculations about and planning for the future. Like Buddhism, it emphasises living life rather than meaning, and urges its followers to give up explanations and rationalisations and to get on with the matter at hand. Its anti-intellectualism is embodied in Perls' directive 'lose your mind and come to your senses'. Like Buddhism, Gestalt therapy is also present-centred. For Perls' 'now' covers all that exists:

> The now is the present, is the phenomenon, is what you are aware of, is that moment in which you carry your so-called memories, and your so-called anticipations with you. Whether you remember or anticipate, you do it now.[83]

Accordingly the past and the future exist in the present. Implicitly Perls is speaking of a timeless reality, and in this respect his world view is similar to those of both ancient and oriental traditions, and modern physics.

He recognised this similarity:

> Our scientific attitude has changed. We don't look to the world any more in terms of cause and effect: we look upon the world as a continual ongoing process. We are back to Heraclitus, to the pre-Socratic idea that everything is in flux. We have made in science the transit from linearity and causality to thinking or process, from the why to the how.[84]

Hence he described Gestalt therapy as being

> like a koan – those zen questions which seem to be insoluble. The koan is: Nothing exists except the here and now... These are the two legs upon which Gestalt Therapy walks; the now and how.[85]

By focusing on this koan, Gestalt therapy, like zen, aims to promote insight and integration, and thus transformation. However, the major difference between psychotherapy and zen, or other forms of Buddhism, is that unlike the latter, psychotherapy does not deal with people who are ready to make any sacrifices for the sake of truth, like zen monks, but very often with the most stubborn of people.[86] The tasks of psychotherapy are much more varied, and the phases of the process much more contradictory than is the case in zen. Perls recognised this and used many different methods whereby integration might be achieved. In this respect Gestalt therapy is similar to Tibetan Buddhism, which employs strategies such as bodywork and visualisation. Perls believed that individuals can assimilate projected and disowned features of the self by role playing, and many of the methods he used with the aim of heightening perception, awareness and emotion were of an essentially theatrical nature. In this respect Gestalt therapy is reminiscent of Greek theatre. Working with his clients 'centre-stage', as it were, in front of an audience, Perls required them to play all the parts of the drama themselves, either by acting each role (including the 'props') in turn, or in the form of dialogues between these elements, whether animate or inanimate. For this purpose he developed the famous 'empty chair' method in which a person projects into a vacant chair any element of the drama in order to confront it. The 'occupant' of the chair might be an aspect of the self typically unexpressed in a given situation – the repressed self, which Perls labelled the 'underdog'– or other aspects of the personality, or real or imagined persons, creatures or objects – in fact, anything that the client or therapist wishes it to be. By bringing these features into the open and confronting them in this way, the person may be able to identify and integrate the diffuse parts of the self, distinguish them from other features of the environment, and thus achieve a clear figure/ground discrimination, or individual Gestalt. In this way, Perls worked with clients on their unresolved conflict situations, interpersonal relationships, thoughts and fantasies. He also used this method in working with dreams, which he regarded as 'existential messengers' because of their potential importance to individual self-awareness.

In his emphasis on dreams and other aspects of his approach, Perls reflects not only the practices of the ancient Greeks but also shamanic practice in general. As in these healing traditions, his is a system which relies heavily on the imagination, and the therapist in shaman-like fashion facilitates access to and interpretation of this terrain. The therapist is, like the shaman, also a 'showman', commanding centre-stage in the dramatic enactment of psychic events. Like Jung, and shamans throughout history before him, Perls recognised that dreams form a self-contained whole, or dramatic action, which can be broken down into elements like those of a Greek play. These can be developed through a process of amplification using images and associations so that their content is broadened and enriched, their interrelationships recognised and their messages understood. Whereas Perls restricted the process of amplification to images provided by client, therapist and members of the audience, Jung amplified dream content with the symbolic imagery of fairy tales, mythology and the like, in the belief that they illuminated the universal aspect of human concerns. However, they both recognised the dream as a statement, uninfluenced by consciousness, which expresses the dreamer's inner truth or reality, and that the manifest dream content is not, as Freud insisted, a facade.

Gestalt therapy is one of the most powerful therapies to emerge in the twentieth century, and it was one of the most influential forces in the development of humanistic psychology, and what became known as the human potential movement.[87]

The human potential movement

During the 1960s, Maslow, Rogers and Perls found a particularly receptive setting for their ideas on the West coast of the USA. They were invited to the Esalen Institute in California where the development of human potential and the promotion of qualitative changes in being were emphasised. Here too, exponents of many disciplines from Eastern and Western cultures such as yoga, meditation, the martial arts, dance, bodywork and various forms of healing, were invited to exchange and develop their views with religious and spiritual leaders, philosophers, artists, physicists, and psychologists in seminars, workshops and residential programmes, first opened to the public in 1966. This interchange yielded many different approaches to, and techniques for the development of human potential in general, and healing in particular. Approaches derived from oriental philosophies and religions, or esoteric traditions, were frequently grafted on to the more familiar psychological approaches of the West, particularly those employed in psychotherapy; and vice versa. Out of this curious synthesis emerged numerous new-style therapies, and various ancient and esoteric ones resurfaced. Hence parallels can be identified between them in both concepts and practice. Elsewhere within Western culture, as travel and other developments opened up the East, more people came into more contact with its traditions, and this often served to put them in touch with formerly hidden and obscure sources of similar wisdom in their own cultures. Awareness of the similarities prompted further examination of both, because as Jung observed:

> When an idea is the expression of psychic experience which bears fruit in regions as far separated and as free from historical relation as East and West, then we must look into these matters closely. For such ideas represent forces that are beyond logical justification and moral sanction.[88]

Perspectives: A Synthesis

The ancient, modern, Eastern and Western perspectives on 'life, the universe and everything' presented in the foregoing chapters appear to be one and the same – quite literally. They are all holistic, all parts of the universe being seen as interrelated and inseparable, with no distinction between mind and matter, body, soul or spirit. They all recognise the pre-eminence of mind, consciousness and the subjective, and emphasise the psychological and spiritual rather than the physical and material. They share a space-time intuition, an awareness of subtle energies, and their role in health and disease. All reinforce the Hippocratic wisdom that healers should have knowledge of 'the whole of things'.

Increasing recognition of the 'whole of things' in the West has led to advocacy of holistic medicine – a term whose exact meaning remains elusive. It is an umbrella term which has come to embrace many different approaches and methods, ranging from dietetics and homeopathy to crystal therapy and spiritual healing. Properly, however, as LeShan[1] observes, there is no such thing as an holistic technique or modality, only an holistic attitude – a concern to promote the understanding that all levels of a person's being: physical, psychological, emotional, spiritual, social and ecological, are of equal importance in the prevention of disease and the search for health; and that the potentials for promoting health and overcoming illness reside within the person. He suggests that the remarkable rise in this 'new' medical model, which appears to offer an alternative to conventional reductionist approaches, owes a great deal to the lack of concern for the whole person in orthodox medicine, and the growing awareness that technology alone is not enough.

In fact, many of the approaches now seizing the public imagination, such as homeopathy and osteopathy, have long existed alongside orthodox treatments, while new or unfamiliar ways of promoting health are constantly appearing, or reappearing, and gaining publicity. Cousins pointed to two dozen or more schools or approaches of varying validity, not all of them compatible and some of them competitive, crowding the centre of the holistic stage: 'Some conferences on holistic health seem more like congeries of exhibits and separate theories than the occasion for articulating a cohesive philosophy'.[2] In so doing, he highlighted troubling contradictions within holistic medicine – a movement based on the concept of wholeness becoming progressively fragmented and divisive, with many of its proponents dogmatically and narrowly advocating their approach as the 'only' one. As he suggested, the parts seem to be at odds with a movement based on an integrated approach to health. Moreover, the movement has tended to take on the character of the least workable and reputable of the contending parts.

Certainly, many of the methods which attract paying customers to holistic medicine have not persuaded the medical establishment of their acceptability. While many are serious and complex methodologies, 'some of the specific techniques are the sheerest kookiness... and may be dismissed without further investigation'.[3] Cousins saw this as a continuing difficulty, because 'it is difficult to think of a unifying principle that can bring these together'.[4]

The position adopted here, and elaborated in the chapters to follow, is that there is such a principle, which not only brings together the many disparate approaches of complementary medicine, but also reveals no conflict between the apparently silly or irrational and the sensible or rational, enabling both to be seen as fully consistent with the principles of modern science and understandable in terms of the related principles of time and energy. The premise developed is that all forms of healing can be understood as either modifications of the time sense or of energy; factors which are inextricably linked with each other and material being, as stated in Einstein's formulation $E = mc^2$. What are referred to as 'timely interventions', therapies that promote relaxation, modify the individual's relationship to time and by so doing facilitate greater mobilisation or utilisation of energy; whereas energetic treatments work directly with subtle energies in and around the individual, and by so doing indirectly influence the individual's experience of time by producing relaxation. Modification of either one of these factors has an effect on matter, or physical being, as these are all inextricably related.

Accordingly schools of thought that are currently based on seemingly incommensurate world views may well turn out to be closer than seems apparent at present.[5]

PART II

TIMELY INTERVENTIONS

In the West, time is often spoken of as the great healer, but its significance in the creation and treatment of illness and in the maintenance of health has largely gone unrecognised and remains little understood, as are those apparently diverse techniques, such as meditation, biofeedback, hypnosis, auto-suggestion, autogenic training, relaxation and visualisation, common to which is the modification of the individual's relationship with time. This section addresses these issues.

6

Time and Illness

It is commonly said that 'time is of the essence'. The phrase is generally taken to mean that time is essential, vitally important, absolutely necessary, a matter of urgency, and a property of the external world of objective reality. This view pervades Western culture and is largely unquestioned. Yet the phrase has quite different connotations when viewed etymologically. From this perspective, time is an intrinsic feature of being, a property of the soul, psyche or essence (from the Latin *essentia*), and has very different implications for the way we live our lives.

Absolute linear time

A basic assumption of Western culture is that time is absolute; a fact; a feature of external 'out there' reality existing independently of human consciousness. Such a belief derives from the linear mode of thinking that Western civilisation inherited from the ancient Greeks. Accordingly, time, symbolised by a straight line, is seen as composed of a rigid, fixed succession proceeding in one direction from the past, through the present, to the future, and irreversible. As such it is finite, limited and static. It has a beginning and an end, making everything seem 'once and for all'. It is also tangible; 'It is spoken of as being saved, spent, wasted, lost, made up, accelerated, slowed, crawling and running out'.[1] Although imposed, learned and arbitrary, it tends to be regarded as though it is built into the universe. Such a view pervades Western culture to such an extent that it is difficult to conceive of any other concept of time. Yet quite different concepts of time exist, and have existed since antiquity.

Cyclic or cosmic time

Conceptions of time in the ancient world derived from the awareness of periodicities in nature. The laws of nature are those of the curve, the circle and endless repetition.[2] Observation of natural cycles such as the succession of day and night, the seasons, the phases of the moon, the ebb and flow of tides, gave rise to the idea of time as a cyclic phenomenon. Primitive notions of time mirrored the cyclic aspect of the world. So, for example, the ancient Egyptians are thought to have derived their calendar from observations of the arrival of the Nile floods at Cairo. The Greeks also largely followed the cyclic tradition. Pythagoras and Plato both taught the doctrine of the eternal return, *anakuklosis*, according to which time progresses in a circle or in an indefinite series of cycles, in the course of which the same reality is made, unmade and remade in succession. Not only is the same sum of existence preserved, with nothing being lost or created, but the same situations are reproduced as they have been in previous cycles, and will be in subsequent cycles *ad infinitum*. No event is unique, occurring once and for all, but occurred, occurs and recurs perpetually. The same entities appear and reappear at every turn of the cycle because cyclic time is self-contained, making the transient subject to the law of recurrence. This diminishes the power of death and places emphasis on the cosmic rather than the individual.

In ancient India the awareness of cosmic cycles was elaborately developed into a philosophy of continual metamorphosis. A complete cycle was thought to comprise 12,000 years, each ending in dissolution from which creation proceeds. To the Hindu, therefore, the universal world and the social order are eternal and not temporal, and personal life is but a sample of a succession of lives endlessly repeated. Perpetual rebirth or reincarnation makes any quantitative view of a particular period meaningless: 'Life, infinitely cycled, makes history less significant and an individual's biography is merely a transient moment in the process'.[3] The Hindu thus live in a time domain characterised by a changeless sense of ever becoming. Consequently India has never produced a written history.

In early China naturalists and philosophers also observed the evolutionary transformations of living organisms, and some 16 centuries before Darwin they expressed an evolutionary naturalism which embodied a succession of phylogenetic unfolding rather than a single linear train of evolution. These early concepts of time led to remarkably sophisticated theories that included accurate perception of astronomical changes, views on the nature of fossils, and explanations of the unity of vast time cycles in the development and history of each man. The Tao Te Ching gives an estimate of phases in the evolution of life covering approximately 130,000 years. Similarly, in Japan the concept of transience of the physical world led to the intuitive awareness that time is not an absolute or objective feature but a process – the change of nature.

These cultures all accepted the notion of biological rhythmicity connecting human life with natural or cosmic cycles, and held that these cosmic rhythms manifest order, harmony and balance. This is reflected in their shared conception of time as a turning, as the principle of revolution, renewal, change and movement, variously symbolised as a sphere or wheel. This naturally implies the metaphysical concept of the centre, eye or heart, found in most Eastern traditions; the point from which all force emanates and returns, the place where opposing forces come to rest in perfect equilibrium; where the pull and tension of opposites are finally resolved; from where the infinite in all things can be perceived.

In these early cultures man didn't have the irreversibility of time to contend with. He lived in an eternal present containing everything that ever happened or is likely to. 'If we take eternity to mean not infinite temporal durations but timelessness, then eternal life belongs to those who live in the present'.[4] This feature of primitive consciousness is common to mystics, modern physicists who recognise the space-time nature of reality, and peoples such as the Hopi Indians whose language contains no words referring to time. Such a concept is largely incomprehensible to modern Western man, for whom time 'presents itself as a precarious and evanescent duration, leading irremediably to death'.[5]

Time in the modern world

In the era when the Chinese were calculating astronomical periods of millions of years, Western notions of time were, by contrast, primitive. The linear concept of time dictated that time must have a beginning and an end. As late as the seventeenth century, many Europeans believed in Archbishop Ussher's calculation of the date of creation of the universe as 6 October 4004 BC. The idea that time had to begin with some significant event is still found in 'Big Bang' and other theories of the origin of the universe.[6] This simple linearity dictated much of Western thought, custom and philosophy; 'It encouraged a self-centred concept of our place in the universe, our hustling individualities and our philosophy of cause and effect':[7] notions which have been instrumental in the development of Western science.

However, linear time runs contrary to the laws of nature, cutting across them, and with the development of the pendulum clock in the seventeenth century, man became less observant of cyclical processes in nature. 'He needed nature less in a world of clocks',[8] and some three hundred years later life is so dominated by clocks that most people have not only become largely unconscious of cycles in nature, but also inured to cycles within themselves. They no longer eat when hungry, and sleep when tired, but follow the dictates of the clock. Clock watching is so important to the modern Western way of life that we hasten to teach children to do so. By the end of childhood most children can tell the time, and are also aware that time tells on them. This curious reciprocity was highlighted by the development in the 1980s of a 'watch' with a holographic eye on its face which appeared to look back when looked at by the wearer, thereby reinforcing the idea that not only must we always have an eye on the time, but it also always has its eye on us.

Indeed, in Western culture the passage of time is inextricably linked with the awareness of ageing and death. Hence the watch can be viewed as a symbol of death.[9] 'Using a watch we watch. We watch time and are fixated by it, dominated by it'.[10] Watching as we do, we are acutely aware of time passing, and with it those things we associate with our past: our youth, looks, unblemished complexions and hair. We are always looking over our shoulders to see what we were or could have been, and so we inevitably tend to hold on to the past rather than the present, and we fear change. Buddha's insight into the human condition highlighted this reluctance to accept change, and by implication identified time as a major cause of suffering and distress. Certainly, 'we can destroy ourselves through the creation of illness by perceiving time in a linear one-way flow'.[11] Many illnesses – perhaps most – may be caused, either wholly or in part, by our perception of time. Dossey[12] believes it is possible to eradicate certain illnesses and become healthier by experiencing time as cosmic or non-linear, where past, present, and future merge into a timeless stillness. He claims to have observed patients heal themselves through gaining a new understanding of time.

Understanding time

Time is not a single concept. The time of the physicist is not that of the poet. The time of the calendar is no help in knowing when to cook potatoes, although it can tell us when to plant them. The 'time of my life' is not the same thing as the time to arrive at a party. The football official's 'time out' is not the same as three-quarter waltz time. The time of the mystic is not that of the scientific investigator.[13]

We wander through varied sorts of time each day, giving little or no thought to the matter, discarding one concept of time in favour of another whenever it is convenient to do so. Yet ordinarily we maintain the illusion that time is a single concept, a phenomenon needing no explanation. Most psychologists considering time have taken for granted the existence of a real time, external of our construction of it, which is linear.[14] Such an assumption is at the root of the scientific model psychologists adopted at the beginning of the century, and it has adversely influenced research and led to a great deal of confusion. If correct, then human beings should possess a real sense of time identified with the clock, just as they have a visual sense that emanates from a special organ of perception. However, in analysing the experience of time, one can point neither to an organ of consciousness such as an eye, nor to a physical continuum such as the wavelength of light for study by objective methods. There is no immediate physical or physiological point of departure for a scientific analysis of time experience; no process in the external world which directly gives rise to time experience; nor anything immediately discernible outside ourselves which can apprehend any special 'time stimuli'. Even a little reflection reveals that the clock is not a receiver but a special definer of time.[15] Yet some researchers continue to overlook this lack of a time organ and try to approach temporal experience as if there were a special time sense. While this is a useful convention in ordinary conversation, it seriously impedes understanding of the time experience.

Temporal experience

The most commonly held idea of how time is experienced is that it flows like a liquid. However, even those who share this view are likely to disagree as to the rate of flow. For some people time is sluggish and viscous, and for others it may be fast, moving like rushing water. Moreover, within the same individual the flow of time is not constant, but a variable, changing experience. This can be seen throughout the lifespan. A week has little meaning for a three-year-old child, and the interval between one Christmas and another is seemingly endless for eight- or nine-year-olds. Piaget[16] found that in young children a sense of *vitesse-mouvement*, or rhythmical frequency, appears before they develop a sense of time. Like early man, therefore, they appear to live in an eternal present characterised by an awareness of rhythmic cycles. Until the age of about eight, time is generally experienced as being very expanded and as passing slowly. For very young children each day is its own universe, and they don't appear to have any sense of ordering events. However, a concept of linear time is acquired with age, and years seem to pass more quickly, or to shorten, even though some of their constituent hours, days and weeks may appear infinite. This experience of some time intervals passing more quickly than others constitutes the normal experience of time. It is affected by many variables other than age, such as personality and social class. It is also related to memory.[17] Intervals are judged as relatively longer when their contents are recalled than when they are not. The more difficult it is to remember this information the longer intervals appear to be. The more information has to be coded in an abbreviated manner the longer intervals appear to be, which is why a dull, disorganised speech which is difficult to code seems to last much longer than one that is well-structured and organised. It may be, therefore, that children experience an expanded time sense before they have learned how to code or reduce information. Coding also seems to affect a person's experience of time even after the event. Summarised thus in the mind, a holiday experienced as long and crowded with activities, shrinks to a short interval in the long and familiar pattern of life.

If the experience of time is related to memory, the way we remember is related to the way we think. In the West thinking is linear and reductive. It lends itself to coding. So the time sense is shorter and there is a sense of urgency which is lacking in the East, where different cognitive, and temporal attitudes prevail. The content of time intervals is also a major determinant of how they are experienced. Most people recognise that when they have little interest in or liking for an activity, time seems to drag. Yet when they are engaged in pleasant activity, time flies... or at least it appears to. That it does so, is an illusion.

Time and relativity

An Eastern parable tells of two monks arguing about a flapping banner. One insisted the banner was moving, not the wind; the other that the wind was moving, not the banner. A third monk, passing by, pointed out that neither the wind nor the banner were moving, only their minds. The awareness that it is the mind that moves is central to most thinking about time in the East, and a similar awareness is at the heart of modern physics. Relativity theory reminds us that reality cannot be known directly but is constructed by way of sensory impressions. Hence there is no outward reality, only individualistic and relativistic constructions of it. As Einstein observed, if a man sits with a beautiful woman, two hours seems like two minutes. Whereas if he sits on a hot stove for two minutes, it seems like two hours. That's relativity.

The implications of relativity theory, since confirmed empirically, are that ordinary common sense notions of time are incorrect. Rather than being dependent on some external reality independent of the senses, time is bound up with them; it is part of us, not 'out there'. There is no absolute reality, no external world to consult, so we must look inwards for our understanding of time and its relationship to health and illness.

Time, health and illness

The sense of time has a major effect on health and on the development and course of specific illness. Evidence comes from research on coronary heart disease.[18] This was prompted by the chance remark of an upholsterer, repairing chairs in the day room of a heart unit in a US hospital. He noted that they were only worn on the front edges, as if their occupants had been sitting in tense expectation.[19] This matched the cardiologists' observations of their patients and subsequently, after years of research, they developed a detailed profile of two personality types, A and B, claiming that the former characterises coronary heart patients. These individuals are typically engaged in a relatively chronic and excessive struggle to obtain a usually unlimited number of things from their environment in the shortest period of time, or against the opposing efforts of others in the same environment. They are ambitious, acquisitive, preoccupied with deadlines so they have a continual sense of urgency, and are often highly successful. They are also easily aroused to hostility and are fiercely impatient, even when at leisure. Time is the enemy they are always 'up against'. They never have enough of it. Time exerts constant pressure, leaving them frustrated, nervous, hostile, and even more firmly determined to step up their output. They usually attempt to do too much, too quickly, and expect immediate results. They are constantly rushing to meet deadlines and keep appointments and are often late for both; or they make excessive demands on themselves, working day and night to achieve their aims. They tend to hurry and panic, to leave tasks unfinished or give insufficient attention to them, or to put them off until later. As a result they tend to build up a backlog of undone or uncompleted tasks, and so cannot make time for leisure activities and holidays, or feel guilty if they do. These traits are relatively enduring and consistent over the lifespan.[20,21] By contrast, Type B individuals are more easy-going and relaxed They are unhurried and leisurely in their approach to life, generally well-organised and efficient, and set realistic goals and deadlines. As a result they tend to meet schedules and keep appointments. They are also able to take time for other people, whether family, friends or work colleagues, and to make time for their interests, leisure activities and holidays, and to enjoy themselves. Time is 'on their side' in that they make it work for, rather than against, them. Type B persons are not necessarily less ambitious than Type A individuals and they are just as likely to be successful, but they are largely free of the frantic sense of urgency that characterises Type A individuals, except perhaps when it is warranted. They also tend to be healthier. Type A persons tend to die earlier than Type B individuals, and often suddenly. Indeed for Type A individuals deadlines are often just that – deadly. This is because the time sense of these people is translated into physical behaviours such as brisk body movements, fist clenching during normal conversation, explosive and hurried speech, upper chest breathing, muscle tension, and concomitant physiological effects, such as high blood pressure, elevation of certain blood hormones such as adrenaline, norepinephrine, insulin, growth hormone and hydrocortisone; increased respiratory rate, and activity of the sweat glands. These are all characteristic symptoms of stress and reflect the fact that the Type A person is constantly at full stretch, or stressed.

Time and stress

The word 'stress' is thought to derive from the Latin *stringere*: to draw tight.[22] As such it is similar in meaning to the word 'anxiety', which derives from the Latin *angoustia*: narrowness. Both accurately describe the reactions of an organism to stimulation or change, which involve tension or tightening of the muscles of the body and narrowing of the organs of the throat and chest. These are features of the approach or avoidance tendencies known as 'fight or flight'[23,24] responses. Irrespective of whether an individual confronts or flees from a situation, the same bodily changes occur. Muscle tension prepares the body for action. The tightening of the throat and chest produces more shallow and rapid breathing in order to supply oxygen to the muscles. The level of certain hormones, notably adrenaline which releases stored sugars into the blood, rises, to provide sufficient energy for speedy action. Another hormone, norepinephrine, which increases heart rate and blood pressure, is produced causing blood to be pumped quickly to the muscles; as is cortisol which helps the body prepare for vigorus activity. Fats and cholesterol are released into the blood together with chemicals to make the blood clot more easily in the event of injury. In order to cool the body, perspiration increases. Meanwhile, all processes not immediately necessary to survival are suspended. Salivation and digestion slow down as extra blood is directed to the muscles and the brain. These changes are experienced as stiffness in various parts of the body, especially the neck and back; tightness in the neck, which may feel like a lump in the throat, and in the chest; heart pounding; fluttering stomach; sweating and a dry mouth. After the crisis the body quickly returns to normal.

During human evolution these responses served important survival needs, as they still do when prompt action is required to avoid injury or death. As such they are healthy. However, these responses are often triggered by any situation that requires adjustment and they can become habitual. If triggered repeatedly in response to non-threatening situations they are unhealthy because the body then remains in a continually reactive state, which may become chronic. Muscles stay tense; pulse rate and blood pressure remain elevated; high levels of sugars, fats, cholesterol, hormones and other chemicals persist in the blood; and the digestive processes are inactivated. Over times this state of dis-ease leads to the wear and tear of various body organs and inevitably takes its toll on health. It may result in cardiovascular problems, stroke, heart attack, kidney failure, gastro-intestinal disorders, diabetes and much else. It can, and all too frequently does, prove deadly. In order to understand how life-threatening conditions can occur it is necessary to examine only one feature of the stress reaction – raised blood pressure or hypertension.

Hypertension

Sustained high blood pressure is a very dangerous condition in which the blood vessels throughout the body are made smaller and smaller by constant contraction of the smooth muscles in their walls. Once it develops it will continue throughout adulthood unless treated. The disease itself causes no physical discomfort and may remain undetected until a person develops symptoms or becomes ill. By this time substantial damage may have been caused. One of the long-term effects is widespread cardiovascular disease. Since the blood volume in the system remains constant some vessels carry blood under greater pressure than they would if there were no constriction of blood vessels. As a result the pressure on the vessel walls is greatly increased, and if sustained cause then to weaken and tear. When this occurs cholesterol plaques are formed to repair the damage. If there is an excessive number of these plaques, the vessels become narrower and narrower, creating further pressure and possibly leading to further tears. Pressure also increases because these plaques cause the arteries to harden and become less flexible. Plaques can also become easily detached from the arterial walls and cause further blockage in the blood supply to the heart muscles or create a dangerous situation in which clots are likely to form.

Heart failure

Raised blood pressure also affects the heart directly as it must work harder to pump blood throughout the body under increased resistance. The left ventricle of the heart is frequently adversely affected. It becomes larger and may become abnormally distended when cardiovascular disease is advanced. Ultimately its functioning deteriorates and signs of heart failure appear.

Arteriosclerosis, coronary heart disease and cerebral stroke

The condition in which cholesterol deposits accumulate in the arteries is known as arteriosclerosis and in the developed world it claims more lives annually than any other disease. As the cholesterol plaques decay and die, they can rupture. When this occurs the circulating blood reaching it begins to clot. If the plaque area is large, a dangerously large clot can form and this is the cause of most heart attacks and cerebral strokes, which occur when normal circulation to the heart or brain respectively is cut off. Death in these cases is often sudden. Even if their effects are not fatal, clots may cause tissue to degenerate in the kidneys and may also give rise to ulcers and gangrene in the legs.

Heart attack

Arteriosclerosis is also the usual cause of heart attack, or myocardial infarction, and most frequently affects the left coronary artery. When this artery narrows, the possibility of a blood clot becoming trapped and blocking the constricted vessel increases. If such a blockage occurs, the flow of blood to the heart is arrested and prevents functioning. The areas of the heart starved of blood die, never to recover, and depending on the size and location of the dead tissue, or infarct, death might ensue. If the infarct is detected and treated quickly the person may survive with slight to severely impaired heart function.

Congestive heart failure

Blockage of the coronary arteries also causes congestive heart failure. Here the entire left ventricle of the heart becomes increasingly weak owing to the blood and oxygen starvation resulting from narrowed arteries, and blood accumulates in the lungs. Excessive blood in the lungs results in shortness of breath and eventually failure of the right ventricle, which leads to swelling of the liver and the limbs.

Hypertension also affects other major organs, notably the brain and kidneys.

Brain damage

In addition to the temporary or permanent brain damage that results from cerebral stroke which hypertension causes by way of arteriosclerosis, the brain is also affected directly through brain haemorrhage caused by blood vessels bursting under pressure.

Renal disease

The kidneys usually control blood pressure, but when diseased by hypertension they raise blood pressure further. Normally if blood pressure decreases to low levels, the kidneys' adrenal glands secrete hormones to increase it. They can be thought of as sensors that monitor and maintain adequate blood pressure. However, if arteriosclerosis develops in the blood vessels of the kidneys, these shrink and become blocked. This leads to low blood pressure to the kidneys, which respond by secreting hormones and raising blood pressure in the body. A vicious cycle is established because raising the blood pressure leads to further arteriosclerosis and further blocks blood flow to the kidneys, resulting in further increases in blood pressure. Some of the excess hormones that the adrenal glands release can also interfere with the functioning of the immune system.

Immuno-suppression

The immune system consists of more than a dozen different kinds of white blood cells concentrated in the spleen, thymus gland and lymph nodes which circulate the entire body through the blood and lymphatic system. They are divided into two types: the B-cells, which produce chemicals that neutralise toxins made by disease-inducing organisms and help the body mobilise its own defences; and the T-cells and their helpers – killer cells that destroy invading bacteria and viruses. Both are controlled by the brain, either directly through hormones in the blood stream or indirectly through the nerves and neurochemicals. In emergency situations the primary action of the adrenal hormones is to suppress the work of the immune system. Immunity is placed on hold while the body's energies are used to fight immediate crises. When stress reactions are prolonged so too is immuno-suppression. Hence what is in the short term an adaptive response can eventually become the cause of every conceivable disease involving the immune system. However the massive changes sustained during periods of prolonged stress go far beyond immune activity to affect every gland in the body and the processes involved in the reproduction, growth, integrity and well-being of the body at the cellular level. Unsurprisingly 75 per cent of all illness is estimated to be stress-related.[25]

Stress-related disease

In addition to the conditions identified above, stress has been cited as a major factor in migraine and tension headaches, ulcers, gastro-intestinal conditions, asthmas, chronic backache, arthritis, allergies, hyperthyroidism, vertigo, and diabetes;[26] pruritis, constipation, menstrual difficulties and tuberculosis;[27] and in autoimmune disease such as rheumatoid arthritis, endocrine problems and multiple sclerosis.[28] Dermatologists have identified stress as a factor in skin disorders such as eczema, dermatitis, psoriasis, and hair loss in women; and it is also implicated in health-related behaviours such as smoking, drinking, eating disorders and drug abuse which frequently have negative health consequences. The link between stress and cancer is also well established.[29–38]

Awareness that the ways individuals relate to and experience time are key factors in the stress they suffer has led to stress-related diseases being referred to as 'time' or hurry sickness.[39]

Time sickness

Time sickness is often a feature of the normal response to serious illness because, when ill, temporal factors begin to influence perceptions more profoundly; 'Serious diseases… force us to confront the end, the final state, the forever'.[40] The more severe the illness the greater is the likelihood that the sufferer will be reminded of his mortality and the possibility that his or her 'time is up'. So, one of the first questions usually asked by patients is 'How much time have I got?'. Relatives also want answers to this question. This sense that time is running out may have a significant effect on the subsequent course of illness. Time sickness, expressed as fear of death, seems to present an increased risk in the acute phrase following a heart attack. Intensely anxious patients admitted to a coronary care unit following an acute heart attack have been found to survive in fewer numbers than those who appear calm.[41] This is because the physiological correlates of acute anxiety can produce electrical instability in the heart causing it to fibrillate or beat in a rapid, chaotic manner resulting in death. It would seem, therefore, that time-related anxiety can kill; time sickness can be fatal.[42]

In terminal illness time sickness may hasten death. It may be associated with panic, anxiety, depression and resignation. Dossey[43] suggests that this 'coping style' is itself malignant and should be dealt with as promptly as the physical components of disease. Yet doctors typically focus on physical aspects of disease and ignore the time strategy of the sick person, although their diagnosis frequently engages it directly, possibly to the worst effect. 'The physician's habitual prognosis of how much time a patient has is a terrible mistake. It is a self-fulfilling prophecy'.[44] Not only do some sick people 'destroy themselves in response to an invitation originating from others to stop living',[45] but also those who have reached the time or age at which they are expected to die, assisted in the project by the expectations of others that they will not be around too long. Hence the practice of doctors giving patients a specific survival time has been widely condemned and is advised against within the medical profession.[46]

Time and pain

Pain is often a feature of serious or chronic illness, and is generally experienced as unpleasant. Like other unpleasant experience it affects the experience of time, making time intervals seem longer. Certain drugs, including marijuana, LSD, DMT and opiates, have the opposite effect on time perception. Opiates have a particularly devastating effect. Heroin or diamorphine 'kills' time,[47] and under its influence a person experiences a timeless, painless state. Indeed it is one of the most powerful analgesic or painkillers known and is widely used in medicine, especially in the treatment of terminally ill cancer patients. Without realising it, therefore, doctors routinely modify their patients' perception of time because almost every substance used to treat severe pain does precisely this.[48]

However, any device or technique that changes the perception and experience of time can be used as an analgesic. On receiving a diagnosis of cancer many people take up fishing.[49] Like many hobbies and leisure activities, it helps 'kill time'. When engaged in these 'pastimes' a change in the flow of time is often experienced. As people become absorbed in them they step 'out of time'. Many sportspersons and musicians describe the experience of time 'standing still' as a feature of their activities. Athletes also commonly describe 'crossing the pain barrier' and experiencing a pain-free tranquil state, or a 'high'.[50] Indeed there is abundant evident that certain activities, and concomitant mental states, can evoke actual changes in brain physiology to alter pain perception. Endorphins and enkephalins, natural opiate-like pain-killing substances in the body, can be triggered not only by various physical sports and exercises, but also by other activities that promote absorption, such as music.[51] Such absorption annuls the psychological experience of time in that events which are sequentially changing do not appear to 'happen' in the usual linear sense; they simply are.[52] These events have not stopped moving, because they never 'moved' in the first place. What stops moving, is the mind. Anything that stills the mind brings about this shift in time perception and may be used to modify stress and susceptibility to disease, assist recovery from illness and coping in terminal illness, and to treat pain. Accordingly all forms of meditation, biofeedback, hypnosis, auto-hypnosis, auto-suggestion, autogenic training, relaxation techniques, and visualisation, which bring about a shift in time perception and experience can be regarded as 'timely interventions' with numerous applications to healing. These approaches and their applications to healing are discussed in the following chapters.

7

Meditation and Biofeedback

Our constricted view of time can be likened to a man travelling on a train. From the window he cannot see very far ahead, and his view of a bridge the train is approaching is limited. He can see part of the bridge as the train nears, get a better view during the crossing, and only a little of it again when it is behind him. However, if he were positioned a mile from the track he could see the whole bridge. From such a standpoint – looking in on the scene rather than out upon it – he can see the full picture.[1] Similarly from the introverted perspective of meditation, one can see the whole of things, and realise that the linearity of time is an illusion.

Meditation is 'a family of techniques which have in common a conscious attempt to focus attention in a non-analytical way and an attempt not to dwell on discursive ruminating thought'.[2] This amounts to an attempt to still the mind, to shift from the active 'doing' mode to a passive 'letting things be', and is a state in which experience as it is usually known ceases. In Buddhism this is described as a void; in Hinduism as *samadhi*, or still mind; and in Taoism as *tso wang*: sitting with no thoughts. It crucially involves an introversion: a shift of attention from the external world to the inner. Western culture is characteristically extrovert in attitude and preoccupied with action or 'doing', direction and control. Consequently the passive, receptive, introverted attitude necessary for meditation – and non-doing, is generally regarded as foreign and alien. Yet meditation has been practised in the West for many centuries. As early as 4000 BC it was part of Egyptian religious ceremony, and in the Old Testament[3] we are told that 'Isaac went out to meditate in the field at eventide'.

The Western tradition of meditation

Christianity

Early Christians were urged by Paul to meditate,[4] and meditative practices of early Christian monks were very similar to those of Hinduism and Buddhism. The 'Jesus Prayer', known as Hesychasm, after a fifth century teacher Hesychius of Jerusalem, fulfils Paul's injunction to pray always.[5] The prayer, whose aim is a state of no-mindness, rest or quiet is still rehearsed during every activity by Trappist monks. This constant remembrance of God, and verbal or silent repetition of prayer or scriptural passages, is similar to the practices of Bhakti yoga, while constant repetition of phrases such as *Kyrie Eleison* can be likened to the Eastern use of mantras.

The Roman Catholic Church has articulated a psychology of meditational experience or contemplation in which the conscious exercise of attention to specific content such as Christ, the Virgin Mary or saints, leads to a spontaneous flow of experience to which the person becomes a receptive onlooker, and in the extreme leads to loss of the feeling of separateness as the person attains union with the object of contemplation.[6] Within Christianity there is also the tradition of silent prayer which, like that of contentless meditation, is not directed to any specific content but to becoming more open to and aware of one's experience. The Brotherhood of Friends, or Quakers, emphasise this 'waiting' and 'listening' to inner experience.

Judaism

Kabbala, meaning 'that which is received', is an ancient Jewish mystical tradition dating back to the first century BC based on an esoteric interpretation of the Old Testament. Its practices train students to enter into a state of higher consciousness in which they are more attuned to the divine, and are no longer enslaved by the body and conditioning. To achieve this the individual must observe the workings of the *Yesod*, ordinary mind or ego, so as to see through self-delusion and bring into awareness the unconscious forces that shape personal thoughts and actions. Central to this awareness is attainment of a state of clarity called *tiferet*, which involves one-pointed focus on a single subject or *kavanah*.

Methods for altering consciousness include specific body postures, breathing exercises, solitary contemplation, fasting and meditative exercises. The latter take three forms: visual symbols and chants that help in focusing attention; focus on individual emotional traits until each one disappears; and the use of sound, including various hymns and chants. Meditation is viewed as the doorway to transcendent consciousness, leading to union with the divine, the *Devekuth*. One of the books of the Kabbala, the *Zohar* or Book of Splendour, affirms sexual activity as a method of achieving illumination, but emphasises that action must be coupled with contemplation for salvation to be achieved.

Despite these traditions, or perhaps through ignorance of their existence, most Westerners appear to regard meditation as a somewhat strange oriental practice. This view is largely reinforced, and to some extent justified, in the cults that have grown up in the West around certain Eastern traditions in recent years.

Eastern traditions of meditation

Hindu meditation

Although the aim of meditation is common to all Eastern traditions the means vary with different schools of thought. There are many forms of meditation within Hinduism but the most widely practiced is *bhakti*, or spiritual devotion, the aim of which is one-pointed concentration on an *ishta* or devotional object, such as a deity or divine being. This is achieved by *kirtan*: chanting or singing; and *japa*: silent or spoken repetition of the ishta's name, which is frequently accompanied by the telling of the beads of a *mala*, or rosary. This practice is central to the International Society for Krishna Consciousness founded by His Divine Grace A.C. Bhaktivedanta Swami Pradhupada. Since the 1960s Westerners have become familiar with its *Hare Krishna* chant, popularised by former Beatle George Harrison.

Tantric meditation

The tantric tradition, common to both Hinduism and Buddhism, aims at alteration of consciousness by arousing normally latent energies. It offers a wide variety of techniques for transcending sense consciousness, including *mantra*: the repetition of sounds; *shabd*: concentration on supersubtle inner sounds; *yantra*: visualisation of objects such as mandalas; *asanas*: postures; *pranayama*: concentration on the subtle energies of the body; and *maithuna*: controlled sexual intercourse during which a person achieves detachment and converts sexual energy into higher forms through the repetition of mantras. In attempting to transcend earthly desires it breaks with various taboos and is widely misunderstood by those who adopt a superficial view of it. A modern version of tantra which uses traditional practices is *Siddha yoga*, taught by Swami Muktananda. Its aim, *shaktipat*, is distributing psychic energy, symbolised as a serpent. However, perhaps the best known proponent of tantra in the West is the controversial Osho, formerly known as the Bhagwan Shree Rajneesh, who gained a cult following in Europe and America during the 1970s and 1980s, and equally forceful opposition. Rajneesh first gained notoriety in his native India, where his apparent encouragement of sexual practices attracted thousands of young Westerners to his ashram at Poona, and led to charges of libertinism and debauchery in the Western press. Hindu traditionalists were also opposed to his secularisation, modernisation and Westernisation of ancient practices. The hallmark of Osho's approach is its eclecticism. Nevertheless while he drew on the wisdom of many ancient traditions and also the findings of contemporary psychology, closer scrutiny reveals that his teachings are firmly in the mainstream of the tantric tradition, and concerned primarily with transcending attachment to physical needs and the world. Osho recognised that people differ in their needs and he addressed himself primarily to those of modern man. He therefore advocated many different meditation techniques, some of which derive from psychotherapeutic approaches such as Gestalt therapy. He attempted to show that mundane activities such as brushing the teeth or jogging can be the basis for meditation, and that heightened awareness can be achieved in everyday contexts. He acknowledged that the attitude of non-doing is largely alien to the Western mind and that as a result Westerners generally find it difficult to meditate. He prescribed methods suited to the West which are active and dynamic, employing movement, dance, music and chaotic breathing, in addition to more passive methods.

Irrespective of the method used, the fundamentals of meditation remain the same: relaxation, watchfulness and a non-judgemental attitude. Rather than concentrating, as is commonly supposed, meditation involves relaxing the mind, without any attempt to take control, and watching in a relaxed state of awareness whatever is going on, without interfering. It is a simple but profound state of watching and accepting what is, without judging it 'good' or 'bad'.

Transcendental meditation

Another traditional form of Hindu meditation packaged for a modern Western audience is Transcendental Meditation, or TM. Brought to the West in 1958 by the Maharishi Mahesh Yogi, it attracted public attention and a huge worldwide following during the 1960s when embraced by the Beatles. However, TM has outlasted the trappings of kaftans and beads and is currently practised by millions of people worldwide.[7] It is a classic Hindu mantra meditation:[8] a modern restatement of the basic teaching of Sankaracharya's eighth century Advait School of Vedanta. Thus, although not stated as such, the aim of TM is samadhi, or union with Brahman. Indeed, the Maharishi downplays the orthodox nature of TM, stripping much of the religious element and dogma from his teachings, avoiding Sanskrit terminology, and using scientific findings to validate meditation in a sceptical culture.[9] So, although it is claimed as unique, TM is in the mainstream of Jnana practices which sees duality as the main cause of suffering and aims at one-pointedness or transcendent consciousness. This is achieved by control of attention, which involves turning it inwards towards subtle levels of thought until the source of the thought is reached. Maharishi[10] depicts the finer levels of one-pointedness as increasingly blissful and sublime, and describes the increasing 'charm' as the mind enters progressively more subtle realms. The technique for achieving one-pointedness commences with repetition of a single word or mantra for 20 minutes twice daily while seated with eyes closed. Much emphasis is laid on the tailoring of the mantra to the individual. 'There is a mystique about the specialness of each person's mantra and teachers admonish newcomers never to reveal theirs to anyone or even speak it aloud. But meditators are sometimes chagrined to learn people who fall into general categories of age, education and so on are given the same mantra'.[11] In TM meditators are taught effortless passive concentration, being told to bring the mind gently back to the mantra whenever it wanders. The next stage is the infusion of transcendent consciousness into waking, sleeping and dreaming states by alternating ordinary activities with periods of meditation. This achieves what is termed 'cosmic consciousness' and the means to achieve these higher states are given to meditators over the course of several years practice and service to the TM movement and never divulged to others.

Zen

Little was known of zen in the West before 1927 when the first volume of Suzuki's *Essays in Zen Buddhism*[12] was published. During the 1950s it was promoted by Jack Kerouac, Allen Ginsberg and other writers of the so-called 'beat period', and during the 1960s in the writings of various zen practitioners. During the 1970s it was popularised, notably by Pirsig[13] and a cult developed around it. This 'pop zen' was dismissed as a 'distortion of the fundamental philosophy, flawed by crude oversimplifications and vulgarised by the young'.[14] Nevertheless, despite these simplifications, zen is difficult for Westerners to understand, because they are 'troubled with an itch to interfere in others' lives and the self-governance of the universe; to put right what they consider wrong, and find it hard to accept zen, which is the universe, and its workings'.[15] Its methods of meditation, *zazen* or seated meditation, or ritual activities such as flower arranging, are also difficult for Westerners to comprehend or master. Zazen, although simpler in form than the Rinzai rituals, is in fact so subtle that only a genuine mystical practice prevents it deteriorating into just sitting, in which nothing happens, and which over hours and days can be very stressful and painful.[16]

Sufi

Sufi is the mystic tradition of Islam, and it became more widely known through the teachings of Gurdjieff, who gained a considerable following in the West during the 1920s and subsequently. Sufi has close affinities with the Bhakti tradition of Hinduism, and some Sufi chants have much in common with mantra yoga. The main form of Sufi meditation is *zikr* or *dhikr*, the underlying principle of which is constant remembrance of God, most usually by way of repetitive chants. Perhaps the best known is *La ilaha illa*: 'there is no God but God', which is enhanced by circular dancing whereby ecstasy or out-of-the body consciousness is achieved. This 'whirling' meditation is characteristic of ascetic Muslim monks or Dervishes. Drawing on this tradition, Gurdjieff prescribed repetitive movement, dancing, breathing exercises and remembrance of actions as a means of transcending ordinary consciousness. A similar tradition underlies the breathing and movement exercises known as *zhikr*, a feature of **Arica,** a therapeutic system developed by Oscar Ichazo, which aims at achieving mind/body balance through a system of psychocalisthenics.

Contemporary meditation practices in the West

Many forms of meditation are now widely practised in the West. According to a Gallup Poll published in *Newsweek* magazine in September 1976, there were no less than five million Americans practicing yoga, six million meditating regularly and some two million deeply involved in oriental religions. However, these practices, which were widely and wrongly regarded as confined to the young, also attracted 'much middle-aged and geriatric disfavour'.[17] A major objection to meditation is that it produces introversion, which in the West is largely synonymous with shyness and frequently carries the connotation of weakness. It is generally regarded as an undesirable trait which produces withdrawn and other-worldly people who gradually lose touch with reality. Not uncommonly it is associated with madness. Confusion in both lay and medical circles about the characteristics of mysticism and mental disorder prompted an attempt at clarification by the US Group for the Advancement of Psychiatry in 1977. The group indicated that the resemblance between the mystic and the schizophrenic is only superficial, the retreat of the former into the inner world being deliberate rather than obligatory, and partial rather than complete. Nevertheless the group confessed to doubts and difficulties about the absolute distinction between mysticism and mental disorder. The conclusion reached was that 'from one point of view all mystical experiences may be regarded as symptoms of mental disturbance, and from another they may be regarded as attempts at adaptation' (Editorial Practitioner 1977). The group acknowledged that the 'comfort and satiation of the consumer society may create a need for non-material satisfaction, and the material advances of science and technology a desire for experience that transcends the rational'. The psychiatrist R.D. Laing blamed technological and scientific progress for much madness precisely because it had cut people off from their inner experience. 'I shall restate a frequently reiterated assertion about modern man, that, in gaining control of the outer world, we have largely lost touch with the inner world. We have become strangers to our own experience, we are alienated from ourselves.'[18] Certainly it is not necessary to have a mystical rationale in order to practise meditation and reconnect with the inner world of experience. Nevertheless suspicion about meditation continues, often reinforced by misunderstanding of so-called altered states of consciousness which are suggestive of psychosis or mental disturbance, and frequently associated with the use of illicit drugs. As Le Shan points out, however, in an altered state of consciousness you view the world as if it were put together in a different fashion from the way you normally view it. This by no means implies that you are insane or are deluding yourself. Einsteinian physics is a statement that the world is put together and 'works' in a different way than is believed in a commonsense view or by the older 'classical' physicists. No-one would call an Einsteinian physicist insane because of his views. The physicist would say he was using a 'different metaphysical system', a different explanation of reality. The mystic would say he is in 'an altered state of consciousness'. The only difference between the two is that the physicist is describing, analysing intellectually and examining the implications of this other view of reality, the mystic is perceiving and reacting to it. The first is talking about something; the second is living it.[19]

Nevertheless, Perls was critical of the catatonic-like withdrawal and interference with the spontaneous flow of life that can result from meditation. Similarly spiritual leaders have criticised cross-legged posturing, claiming that it may be an investment in 'precious encapsulated practices'[20] rather than directed to whole being. Osho observed that by attempting 'to practice' meditation it merely becomes another 'doing'.

The same charges can be levelled against any spiritual practice, or psychotherapy, where what occurs in the therapist's office is somehow of a different order from the rest of a person's life. Nevertheless,

> these are serious objections. The primary problem seems to be that people who engage in practices designed to produce personal growth tend to split these practices off from the rest of life. True growth must take place in ordinary living'.[21]

The cross-legged posture commonly associated with meditation is not a necessary feature. Zazen, or seated meditation, is far from easy to achieve and may be counterproductive in that it can lead to drowsiness. Walking meditation (*kinhin*) is frequently employed, as is *fukanzazeng*, or meditation in a reclining position,[22] and standing meditation is currently gaining in popularity. In the *Book of Tantra* there are 112 meditations, many of which involve movement, and some, as in the Japanese tradition, focus on mundane activities.

Most of the criticisms of meditation reflect misconceptions about what it involves. Nevertheless, many people persist in the belief that meditation requires intense concentration and is very difficult. This is not altogether surprising given that the *Visuddhimaggia*, the classical Buddhist text which describes the way in which the meditator trains his attention, begins with a description of an advanced altered state of consciousness which is quite rare and is never experienced by most meditators. In so doing, it neglects the more ordinary experiences in the initial stages of meditation, such as mind-wandering and the tension between concentration on the object of meditation and ordinary thought. It also prescribes the attainment of purity as a prerequisite of meditation.

TM has done much to change many of the ideas held in the West about meditation by demonstrating that anyone can meditate, irrespective of lifestyle or disposition; emphasising that the 'good life' proceeds from meditation, rather than being a prerequisite of it; and that it involves no renunciation of worldly affairs and need only be practised for 20 minutes twice daily.

Much of the confusion that arises in the West is because the term 'concentration' has connotations of focusing the rational mind or intellect, and is synonymous with study. However, absorption in a task is perhaps nearer to the Eastern concept of the term. Osho insisted that meditation is not concentration, which is antithetical to the aims of meditation in that it involves the self concentrating on an object which is concentrated on. This constitutes a duality of consciousness and results in tiredness and exhaustion because such a willed act is hard work. By contrast, in meditation there is no duality, no observer and no observed, because the subject and object of concentration are experienced as one. Meditation involves a letting go of the individual self and absorption in what one is: part of the totality. It is a state of no will; of inaction, or non-doing, which if forced or effortful is doomed. In that it is letting go – of notions of the self or ego and its limitations; of the illusion of separateness; of what one believes or would like oneself to be – it is equivalent to relaxation. Such a view is emphasised by Maharishi, who claims that 'life in cosmic consciousness is tensionless'.[23] Moreover in promoting wholeness or holiness it is synonymous with healing and medicine.

Meditation as medicine

Osho claimed that meditation is medicine. His claims are not unfounded. The Latin root of the word meditation – *mederi* – means to heal, and since the 1930s there has been abundant evidence that meditation as practiced by yogis and adepts of zen confers a number of health benefits. In 1935 the French cardiologist, Thérèse Brosse, recorded measures of heart rate control in Indian yogis during meditation indicative of an advanced voluntary capacity to regulate autonomic functions, including metabolic rate. Subsequent research[24] established that during meditation the oxygen consumption of zen monks decreased by 20 per cent, and their carbon dioxide output also decreased, indicating a slowing of metabolism. A study of the Indian yogi, Swami Ramananada[25] reported a similar finding. Such studies strongly suggested that advanced meditators could produce these effects through control of the autonomic nervous system, which is normally considered to be beyond voluntary control. This was confirmed by investigations conducted within the Voluntary Controls Program at the Menninger Foundation of the yogi Swami Rama. He demonstrated his ability to stop his heart from pumping blood by putting it into 'atrial flutter', and afterwards gave a lecture on how this feat was achieved. In another demonstration, he controlled vascular activity in two areas of his hand less than two inches apart, making one area hotter and the other simultaneously colder, and producing a temperature difference of 10 degrees Fahrenheit without at any time moving his hands.[26] Voluntary control of the autonomic nervous system, control of pain, bleeding and healing were also demonstrated in the laboratories of the Menninger Foundation. They were also demonstrated in the laboratories of the Langley Porter Neuropsychiatric Institute by Jack Schwarz, who inserted a large diameter, unsterilised knitting needle completely through his left bicep without any change in his recorded heart rate or skin temperature, or indicating stress of any kind. He too was able to explain how this was possible, insisting that 'the abilities that I demonstrated in the experiments are within everyone's reach, and achievable by way of creative meditation'.[27]

During the 1950s and 1960s, research was facilitated by the development of sophisticated recording devices, notably the electroencephalograph or EEG, which detects the electrical rhythms generated by the brain. These occur in four principal groups, each of which can be approximately correlated with a particular brain activity or state of awareness, as follows: *beta*: frequency 13–30 Hz (cycles per second) – the normal waking rhythm of the brain; alpha: 8–13 Hz – which has little meaning on its own, but which in conjunction with other rhythms appears to be a building block of other levels of awareness; *theta*: 4–7 Hz – which occurs with physiological relaxation and indicates a calming down or emptying of the mind; and *delta*: 0.5–4 Hz – which is the rhythm of sleep but is found in many persons in response to new ideas and in some people engaged in paranormal activities.

Explorations with the EEG showed that meditation produces changes in brain wave activity.[28-31] During meditation, yogis demonstrated an abundance of alpha activity, and also theta which predominates in deep relaxation with eyes closed, and were not distracted by external stimuli such as strong light, loud noises, being burned with hot glass tubing, or vibrations from a tuning fork. This suggests an association between brain wave regulation and the ability to establish autonomic control. (Shamanic techniques are also known to lead to EEG changes similar to those found in meditation.) It was also found that when practising meditation and showing prominent alpha activity, yogis showed an increased pain threshold to cold water and could keep a hand submerged at 4 degrees centigrade for 45–55 minutes without experiencing discomfort.[32]

Intensive investigations of adepts of Soto zen[33] found that during seated meditation with eyes half open there was a predominance of alpha wave activity that persisted when the eyes were open. In kinhin, or walking meditation, where alpha might be expected to cease owing to physical activity and more rapid breathing, zen priests showed remarkably reduced breathing rates and high emission of alpha waves. Moreover their physiological and mental states were unaltered from zazen.[34]

During meditation skin resistance to an electric current increases, indicating greater relaxation. The pattern of physiological alteration occurring during meditation is characterised by an extreme slowing of respiration to between four and six breaths per minute; a more than 70 per cent increase in the electrical resistance of the skin; a predominance of alpha wave activity in the brain; and a slowing of the heart rate from 72 to 24 beats per minute, which is suggestive of a state of deep relaxation.[35] Indeed meditation is more refreshing than sleep,[36] and after commencing regular meditation subjects report needing less sleep than formerly.[37]

Psychological effects of meditation include greater psychological stability;[38] greater autonomic stability;[39] lower anxiety;[40,41] internal locus of control and sense of being effective in the world rather than a passive victim of circumstance.[42] Effects of zen meditation include life changes such as greater intimacy with and reduced fear of other people; increased energy; greater relaxation, less susceptibility to depression; and greater awareness of diet, exercise and posture leading to abstinence from smoking, drinking and drugs.[43] A substantial reduction in the use of alcohol, cigarettes and coffee has generally been found among meditators,[44] and dietary changes such as eating less meat. Meditators also report more positive mood states, regular daily routines, and a lower incidence of somatic complaints such as headaches, colds and insomnia.[45] Meditation has proved successful in the treatment of asthma,[46] hypertension;[47–49] and phobias.[50]

Yoga has also been shown to have positive therapeutic benefits in the treatment of both psychosomatic and organic disorders, notably in the management of hypertension,[51–53] where it has been shown to have beneficial effects similar to the tranquilliser diazepam. It has also proved effective in the treatment of venous and lymphatic insufficiency, peripheral artery disease, chronic bronchitis, emphysema, and sinusitis.[54]

During the 1970s it was recognised that the diversity of meditative practices led to a wide variety of response. Consequently much research was conducted on Transcendental Meditation, not only because it was practised by millions but also because its well-standardised procedures enabled large-scale studies to be conducted under reasonably well-controlled conditions. As a result TM has been subjected to more scientific investigation than any other form of meditation with results reported in several hundred published research papers. This research confirmed earlier research findings that during meditation there is a reduction in metabolic rate indicated by: a decreased rate and volume of respiration; decreased elimination of carbon monoxide; a low level of arterial blood pressure; decline in blood lactate level; increase in skin resistance; slowing of heart rate; and intensification of alpha waves in the brain.[55,56] Arterial blood pressure was found to remain at a rather low level throughout meditation, and there was a slight increase in blood acidity. Blood lactate level (an indication of metabolism in the absence of free oxygen) declined sharply, nearly four times faster than in people resting normally in a supine position or in subjects during the premeditation period. The reason for the fall in blood lactate remains uncertain but it is clear that it may have beneficial effects. People with anxiety neurosis show a large rise in blood lactate level when placed under stress. Experimental infusions of lactate can bring on anxiety attacks in such people and even produce anxiety symptoms in normal subjects.[57] Hypertensive persons also typically show higher blood pressure, and low lactate in meditators is associated with low blood pressure. 'All in all, it is reasonable to hypothesise that the low level of lactate found in subjects during and after TM may be responsible in part for the meditators' thoroughly relaxed state'.[58]

Other measures confirm the picture of meditation as a highly relaxed but wakeful condition. These changes bear little resemblance to those which occur during sleep or hypnosis. **Hypnosis** produces no noticeable metabolic changes, and during sleep oxygen levels decrease appreciably only after several hours. During sleep concentration of carbon dioxide in the blood increases significantly, indicating a reduction in respiration, and while skin resistance commonly increases in sleep the rate and amount of the increase are on a much smaller scale than in TM. EEG patterns of sleep are also different from those of TM, consisting predominantly of high voltage activity of slow waves at 12–14 cycles per second (cps) and a mixture of low voltage waves at various frequencies – a pattern which does not occur in meditation. The EEG patterns of hypnosis have no resemblance to those of the meditative state. The pattern of changes observed suggest that meditation generates an integrated response, hypometabolic state or reflex, mediated by the central nervous system apparently opposite to the 'fight or flight' arousal response associated with stress, which mobilises a set of physiological reactions including increased blood pressure, heart rate, blood flow, oxygen consumption and muscle tension. This hypometabolic state is characterised by quiescence rather than hyperactivation.

The evidence leaves little doubt that meditation is relaxing and is an effective antidote to anxiety.[59–65] Awareness of the possible therapeutic benefits has led to the application of TM in the treatment of stress, and stress-related conditions.[66] There are indications that it may confer long-term health benefits;[67,68] and that it is possible to develop a habitual low arousal state.[69] However it is not unique in this respect and many studies have shown no difference between meditation and other forms of relaxation.[70–72] The matter remains unresolved, however, as at least one study has found meditation more effective than relaxation techniques in effecting changes in anxiety states.[73]

Other therapeutic benefits have been claimed for TM. Negative personality traits such as depression and neuroticism have been found to change significantly in a positive direction, and anxiety to be significantly reduced as a result of TM.[74] Significant improvements in self-concept have also been reported.[75,76] Other benefits consistent with the aims of both psychotherapy and psychosomatic medicine have been claimed for TM, including greater self-actualisation[77-79] and increased inner locus of control.[80] A meta-analysis involving 50 experimental studies with a total of 9700 subjects and 400 outcome findings concluded that in both clinical and academic settings TM produced a moderate effect outcome.[81]

However, it has been claimed[82] that certain psychological and personality characteristics are associated with those disposed towards TM, and as these people tend to be the subjects in scientific studies of TM this has to be accounted for in any evaluation of its therapeutic efficacy. While adherents of TM are usually reasonably well integrated they tend to be bothered by neurotic guilt, anxiety and phobias. Several authors[83-85] have reported that those attracted to meditation are significantly more anxious and neurotic than the normal population in the first place. Also up to 50 per cent of young people tend to drop out of TM in the first six months so it tends to be older people who keep meditating and the benefits experienced may be due to their high expectations. These factors need to be explored further before any definitive statements can be made about the effects of TM. Nevertheless, research using highly motivated persons does suggest that psychological and physical benefits can result from TM.

Clinically standardised meditation

Although TM offers advantages over other methods of meditation as a subject for research, its clinical applications are limited by its very nature. Although the parent body, the International Meditation Society, asserts that the practice is non-religious, several incongruities remain.[86] There is also ambiguity in the way TM is presented.

Although the TM movement claims it does not involve any kind of philosophical belief, membership of any group, or religious commitment, being a completely mechanical technique which has the effect of producing settled consciousness and concomitant physiological changes, the TM organisation acts to recruit members with the aim of establishing an 'enlightened' international community which favours peace and other objectives. Accordingly, to tell initiates that TM does not involve 'any kind of philosophical belief' is misleading. The TM movement is also a political movement striving to achieve an 'enlightened' populace, and under the banner of the Natural Law Party puts forward parliamentary candidates in Britain. Other features of TM raise questions as to its applicability to clinical research and practice, notably that its induction and details of practice are secret, and no research findings regarding TM can be published without permission from the International Meditation Society. This violates a basic ethical principle of science which is that knowledge is public and available for testing. Consequently, Patricia Carrington, a psychologist at Princeton, USA has developed a modified and secularised TM technique, clinically standardised meditation, or CSM, which she claims is a centring technique, abstracted from traditional meditation. This method and its variants are widely and increasingly used in clinical practice. Like TM, it involves the mental repetition of a mantra, and shares an emphasis on 'letting go' – or detachment from striving, and temporary dissolution of structural thought.

However, the most widely used modification of TM is the relaxation response, developed by Herbert Benson, Professor of Medicine at Harvard University and Director of the Hypertensive Section at Boston's Beth Israel Hospital, who with Keith Wallace, Principal of the Maharishi International University in the USA, pioneered much of the empirical research into TM, and subsequently stripped it of all philosophical and political features (see Chapter 9) and applied it in health care settings.

Biofeedback

For the past 5,000 years, the self-regulation experts of India have taught their students to consciously self-regulate their psychological and psychophysiological processes. Many other people around the world have used various aspects of self-regulation in their rituals, particularly in healing rituals, for centuries.[87]

Yet it is only in the past 30 years that Western research has established that bodily functions, previously thought of as involuntary or autonomic, can be influenced by yoga, zen and other forms of meditation. Even so, until Swami Rama demonstrated his ability to stop his heart pumping by putting it into atrial flutter and to control vascular behaviour in his hand, and Jack Schwarz demonstrated control of pain and bleeding at the Menninger Foundation, it was questioned whether individuals could control these functions at will.

Studies by Pavlov in the early years of the twentieth century showed that dogs could learn to salivate on cue and change their body temperature to the extent of controlling blood flow to one leg at a time. Subsequent studies went further, demonstrating that by rewarding desired performance, rats could salivate, accelerate or slow heart rate, alter blood pressure, control circulation in the stomach wall, and direct heat to one or other ear. One celebrated rat learned to fire an individual nerve cell.[88]

In subsequent research on human subjects it became clear that if an individual could become aware of a function of which they were normally unaware they could learn to control it, and that such awareness could be achieved by providing some feedback of information about that function. The concept of biofeedback thus came into being, although the principle has been used for many thousands of years in that most basic feedback device, the mirror. Bathroom scales are also a biofeedback instrument, providing information about body weight. Like all such instruments they are merely an aid to achieving self-control and do not in themselves produce effects. They cannot cure over or under-weight, or maintain weight at a certain level; they can only indicate the success or otherwise of one's attempts to do so. They highlight an important principle of biofeedback, which is that to be effective it requires more than a simple reading of an instrument; it requires a response.

Biofeedback may be provided by electromyography which, when muscles contract or relax, records and displays, usually as a pen tracing, information transmitted through electrodes on the skin. More subtle biofeedback is provided by the electrical skin resistance meter or ESRM, a simple device, which when attached to the palm of the hand indicates the degree of an individual's arousal or relaxation by measuring changes in the polarisation of sweat gland membranes resulting from change in the rate of blood flow, which varies with body tone. The ESRM therefore indicates the activity of the autonomic nervous system and can be used as an aid in modifying tension.

During the 1960s the electroencephalograph, which measures the electrical activity of the brain, was first used as a biofeedback device.[89,90] It revealed that every physiological state is accompanied by an apparent change in emotional and mental state, conscious or unconscious, and conversely that every conscious or unconscious emotional or mental state is accompanied by apparent change in physiology. By producing a pleasant sound which increases when alpha waves fall below a certain level, it was found that most subjects could learn to produce or suppress alpha waves at will, and that alpha seemed to be associated with feelings of well-being. Gradually it emerged that any neurophysiological or other biological function that can be monitored or amplified and fed back can be regulated. It was established that over a period of weeks subjects could acquire control of their heartbeat;[91] overcome rhythmic disabilities of atrial fibrillation and premature ventricular contraction;[92] control high blood pressure without the use of drugs;[93] vary the temperature of the hands;[94] regulate stomach acidity;[95] and alter blood platelet formation.[96] Research into these functions was greatly assisted by the development of the polygraph, an instrument for simultaneous electrical or mechanical recording of several involuntary physiological activities including blood pressure, pulse rate, respiration and perspiration. Using this equipment it became possible for a subject to see the volatility of heart rates and appreciate that physical changes in breathing and posture can have profound effects on the heart. Simply sitting upright slows heart rate, whereas slouching or shallow breathing increases it. Such an awareness enables individuals to recognise links in their behaviour and makes regulation possible. So while only a few years earlier it was considered 'paranormal' to claim self-regulation feats, such as control over blood pressure, by the early 1970s it was possible for a subject in a psychological experiment to lean some measure of blood pressure control in half an hour.

Therapeutic applications of biofeedback

Biofeedback has been used successfully in the treatment of migraine and tension headache (where it has been demonstrated to be more effective than diazepam),[97] ulcerative colitis, spastic colon, and in regaining control after periods of dysporesis.[98] It has been used to teach individuals to recognise bronchial tube diameter, which has implications for the control of asthma and other respiratory diseases;[99] to assist in the regulation of chronic diarrhoea and constipation;[100] and to retrain patients with faecal incontinence resulting from organic impairment.[101] Encouraging results have also been reported in treating hemiphlegic patients paralysed for over a year,[102] and partial paralysis resulting from stroke; in cases of Bell's palsy, and other muscular problems.[103] Severed facial nerves have successfully been retrained by biofeedback,[104] and various cardiovascular disorders also respond well.[105] Improved immune function has been reported following biofeedback-assisted relaxation.[106] Biofeedback has also been used successfully and routinely in the treatment of tension and migraine headache, angina pectoris, painful menstruation, sacroiliac pain, neurodermatitis, rheumatoid arthritis, asthma, tachycardia, gastric and duodenal ulcer, cardiospasm, pylorospasm, nausea and vomiting, regional enteritis, and frequency of micturation. Disorders of the circulatory system, including Raynaud's disease, Burger's disease, intermittent claudication, other peripheral vascular disorders and circulatory complications accompanying diabetes and other illnesses, can be controlled and eliminated with self-regulation. Anxiety disorders, including panic disorders and phobias, can also be effectively treated with biofeedback.[106]

However, while many effects have been demonstrated in the laboratory or clinic these are not necessarily or readily achieved outside these situations. Schwartz[108] was only able to demonstrate reduction of blood pressure within a clinical setting. This is a major drawback of biofeedback which is essentially laboratory based, involving as it can do a good deal of bulky and expensive equipment capable of monitoring precisely subtle biological changes. For biofeedback to be of lasting benefit, the individual has to be able to transfer what is learned in the clinic to the outside world. Hence therapists are increasingly supplementing or substituting biofeedback with meditation and other forms of relaxation. A further drawback, indicated by Benson,[109] is that usually no more than one physiological function can be fed back upon and changed at any one time. This is disputed, as individuals have been taught to regulate several functions simultaneously.[110] It was found that when they reduced both heart rate and blood pressure together these subjects spontaneously and consistently reported feelings of relaxation and calmness. Advocates of biofeedback insist it has clear advantages over meditation and other forms of relaxation in which stress reduction is achieved through an overall response.

This is certainly beneficial, but there is no evidence to indicate that an overall relaxation response has any effect upon the particular organ system in which the individual expresses his stress. There is a general tendency for all neuro-physiological functions to move towards a state of deep relaxation during the meditation periods. However, the particular area of affliction, such as the high blood pressure of the hypertensive patient, may not necessarily drop during this overall relaxation period; therefore one major advantage of biofeedback is that the specific physiological function which needs to be corrected can be monitored, feeding information back to the patient to help him assess his progress in alleviating that dysfunction. This instantaneous feedback is a major asset in stress reduction therapy.[110]

The disadvantage is that self-regulation of a particular function such as heart rate does not necessarily mean that the person can generalise this. Pelletier[112] argues that as individuals differ in patterns of response to stress and these manifest in a different organic system for each individual, a comprehensive approach to clinical intervention is needed which can be applied for relaxation in specific situations, and monitoring of the specific systems in which the person is manifesting the stress in order to help the individual self-regulate that system as unequivocally as possible.

Psychological applications of biofeedback

It has been demonstrated that just as people can learn to control physiological functions for medical purposes, they can also do so in order to achieve altered states of consciousness. Hence biofeedback can be used as an aid to the development of meditational skills and self-development: it 'offers a bridge that can lead people from the ordinary waking state to the development of higher states of consciousness'.[113] A problem with biofeedback is, however, that the production of alpha waves in a laboratory does not necessarily help a subject in any way: 'The alpha wave can only be related to a new understanding if there is something new to understand'.[114] Training a person to produce alpha by means of biofeedback will not produce new insights, whereas if a person is taught how to gain insight he may show high levels of alpha. The process is not reversible.

C. Maxwell Cade and Geoffrey Blundell[115] produced a special type of EEG which enabled a clearer understanding of what occurs in the brain during meditation. This device, known as the 'Mind Mirror', differs from standard hospital encephalographs which show only pathological responses of the brain and not responses to mood, thought and so on. For medical purposes the latter are considered a nuisance since they interfere with readings for psychological purposes. However, for psychological purposes such knowledge is an essential guide to the subject's development on the path of self-regulation. The Mind Mirror measures rhythms from both hemispheres of the brain simultaneously and displays them in the form of a frequency analysis which allows the relationship between them to be seen as a pattern. Using this measure, it has been found that meditation produces a combination of theta and alpha waves in both hemispheres, whereas normally a person produces primarily beta in one or other hemisphere. Thus meditation integrates the two hemispheres, effecting a balance or psychosynthesis between rational and intuitive functions; and a utilisation of the full mind. Cade calls this state 'the awakened mind'. Using the Mind Mirror, it has been demonstrated that yogis and swamis produce the awakened mind pattern of brain waves throughout their everyday lives, thus supporting the claim that the effects of meditation generalise into all aspects of daily living.

8

Hypnosis, Auto-Suggestion and Autogenic Training

Misconceptions about hypnosis

Most people think of hypnosis as a trance-like state in which the subject, at least partially, loses awareness of reality, and under the control of the hypnotist becomes able to perform a variety of feats that would be impossible in the normal state. This view is reinforced by popular writers, the media, stage performers and professional hypnotists anxious to maintain the mystique of their methods, and by dictionaries, which typically define hypnosis as a special state of mind resembling sleep, characterised by extreme suggestibility. Such a view is highly misleading. There is abundant evidence that so-called hypnotic behaviour is not so remarkable as is commonly supposed, the feats performed under hypnosis being achievable under normal conditions,[1] and the notion of a special state unnecessary since well-established psychological processes can account for the effects very adequately. Nevertheless, the widespread belief in hypnosis as an altered state of consciousness 'by which the hypnotist can induce distortions in the areas of volition, memory and sensory perception'[2] persists in spite of contrary evidence and argument. Accordingly hypnosis is still regarded by a large section of the general public more with fear than scepticism. Their fears are of being unconscious while under hypnosis and unaware afterwards of what occurred during the session; being hypnotised against their will, or without being aware of it; having the mind dominated by another person; losing verbal control and revealing secrets when hypnotised, and not returning to normal afterwards.[3]

The reality is that consciousness is not lost during hypnosis. The traditional view of hypnosis as a trance-like state, that is, as a condition of unawareness of external things in which visions and hallucinations are experienced and acts performed unconsciously, has been undermined over the past thirty years in numerous experimental studies.[4-11] Hypnosis is not a trance in which awareness is even partially lost, nor is it sleep. On a scale of human awareness hypnosis is the very opposite from coma, with ordinary consciousness in the middle.[12] During hypnosis a person is fully aware of what is happening, and if anything, his or her awareness is enhanced. Moreover, despite the claim that hypnosis is a fourth organismic state distinct from waking, sleeping and dreaming,[13] there appears to be nothing particularly unique about hypnosis which justifies it being termed a state. There is no difference in the EEG readings of subjects when normally awake or hypnotised;[14] no difference in cortical potential, pulse rate, skin resistance or palmar electrical potentials, peripheral blood flow, or blood clotting.[15,16] There is a slight rise in body temperature brought about by vasodilation of blood vessels, and small changes in the voltage of the life field, but these are very subtle and can be recorded in response to normal emotional reactions,[17] and are a characteristic feature of relaxation.[18] In fact, the only way to tell if a person is hypnotised is if he or she responds to test suggestions, or declares afterwards that he or she has been hypnotised. Hypnosis appears to be merely an extension and more systematic use of the spontaneously occurring everyday phenomenon of deep absorption, which most people have experienced when 'carried away' by a task or situation. It has been established[19] that when given a choice – an alternative scheme for classifying their experience – most subjects prefer to describe themselves as 'absorbed' rather than hypnotised. However, because the hypnotic condition does not involve the wonderful aspects the uninitiated tend to expect, it is not uncommon for people to express doubts as to whether or not they actually have been hypnotised. 'Subjects such as these have to learn to apply the label "hypnotised" to a set of experiences different from the ones expected'.[20] Furthermore, those who when hypnotised find it to be nothing exceptional often conclude incorrectly that they have not been hypnotised successfully and that it cannot be effective. Thus a person's declaration as to whether or not they have been hypnotised is not a very satisfactory criterion.

In this sense it is possible to be hypnotised without knowing it. Similarly, it can be argued that if a person does not know he or she is hypnotised because the experience has not been explicitly defined as such, it is possible to be hypnotised against one's will. Even so, this would not affect the subject's awareness of what is going on. Therefore it is generally accepted by hypnotists of all theoretical persuasions that a person cannot be hypnotised against his will, and that hypnosis is a condition of consent.

As to the mind being dominated by another person, it is clear that the effects attributed to hypnosis are produced and determined by the person 'hypnotised'. Subjects employ a number of strategies to achieve these effects.[21] Certainly the picture of the hypnotised person as being in a zombie-like state of complete subjection and unawareness is wide of the mark, and hypnotic subjects cannot be conceptualised simply as passive recipients of hypnotic suggestions. The experimental evidence is very clearly in opposition to the long-cherished notions that the hypnotised person is in the hypnotist's power and cannot resist his or her suggestions. Claims, such as those made in Australia by two women that they had been sexually assaulted by a hypnotist and, although aware of what was happening, were unable to offer any resistance because hypnotised,[22] have to be treated with caution. So too does the counter-claim made in this instance by the hypnotist, that since hypnotic coercion is impossible because a hypnotised person would immediately resist suggestions of an unwanted nature. Neither explanation is adequate and other factors need to be taken into consideration. For example, the women's belief in their inability to resist hypnotic suggestion might have been sufficient to create a self-fulfilling hypothesis. Alternatively, their behaviour might be seen as constituting motivated helplessness in which their subsequent testimony was a retrospective rationalisation. 'Like alcohol, it is possible that hypnosis might be used by some people as a way of disowning responsibility for their own behaviour, which is otherwise perceived by them as being taboo'.[23] Certainly this might be a factor in the often uncharacteristic behaviours of those volunteering as subjects for stage hypnosis. However, the question of whether hypnotised persons can be made to perform acts against their will remains controversial. Although it is argued that people cannot be made to do anything they don't want to, it remains a possibility that within the hypnotic situation what a person 'really wants' might be changed. Accordingly, if the hypnotist seems to the client to be in control, even if this control is illusory, it is wise for a person to choose a trustworthy hypnotist.[24]

Given that there are no indications that the hypnotised person is ever in a special state, it follows that the fear of not returning to normal after hypnosis is unfounded. Similarly, the evidence suggests that the fear of post-hypnotic phenomena is unjustified. Subjects trained to scratch their ears post-hypnotically to a cue word did so, but failed to respond to a staged conversation in which the word occurred several times.[25] This suggests that post-hypnotic suggestion works only because subjects do what they think is expected of them.

Fears that hypnosis may precipitate psychiatric illness are also unsupported by the evidence. Controlled experimental studies have found that subjects undergoing hypnosis are less likely to experience disturbance in everyday life than those in control groups, and that they report more relaxation, less anxiety, more pleasure and feelings of enhanced well-being after hypnosis.[26] The idea that hypnotisability may be a sign of mental weakness is also confounded by the understanding that hypnosis is actually concentration or absorption and is fostered as such by scientists and artists.[27]

Nevertheless, the ability of subjects to endure severe pain when under hypnosis is often taken as evidence for the existence of a special hypnotic trance state. However the issue is not quite so straightforward. Pain is not a simple sensation but a complex psychophysiological response which involves expectation, interpretation and suffering.[28] If any of these variables is modified, so too are the perception and sensation of pain. Task-motivated instructions are as effective as hypnosis in reducing subjective and physiological responses to painful stimuli,[29] hence there is no need to invoke the concept of a special state to explain pain control. However, stereotypical and misleading views about hypnosis are still evident, even within the scientific community, and these have seriously impeded research and teaching on the subject.[30] Negative attitudes have led to instruction on hypnosis being opposed in principle, with the result that as recently as 1985 only 4 out of 50 university and polytechnic departments of psychology in Britain introduced their students to theories and methods of hypnosis. Such attitudes are part of a legacy of mistrust and scepticism which originates in the discrediting of Franz Anton Mesmer (1734–1815), the modern pioneer of hypnotism.

Mesmerism

Mesmer did not discover the phenomenon which came to be named after him. The priest-doctors and shamans of primitive societies brought about similar trance-like states to those Mesmer induced in others. There are indications that a similar practice was used by healers in ancient Egypt, Greece and Rome,[31] and subsequently others such as Paracelsus[32] and the seventeenth century healer Valentine Greatraks.[33] Mesmer was distinguished from them by his formulation of scientifically testable propositions which linked the phenomena with the manifestations of 'a universally distributed and continuous fluid... of an incomparably rarefied nature', with 'properties similar to those of a magnet'.[34]

In fact there was nothing new or original in Mesmer's formulation. The sixth century physician Galen, whose views were still influential in eighteenth century Europe, had claimed that an invisible essential fluid filled the universe, planets and all living creatures, and that health consisted of a balance of the fluid essences of mind, body, soul and the environment. Accordingly the universe was a living organism of balancing forces, and health lay in each part adjusting to every other part so that it reserved to the fullest, the capacity to direct, control and sustain the life of the whole. Such a view was, and still is, fundamental to Western traditions of magic, and has recently been revived within Western scientific thinking.[35]

Also current in Mesmer's time was the notion disseminated by Paracelsus that magnets possessed special healing properties and with their powers of polar attraction and repulsion could be used to influence this ethereal fluid. Healing by stroking and touch was common during this period.

Mesmer simply combined these three principles, viewing the body as a magnet and illness as faulty distribution of magnetic fluid, which he attempted to redistribute by passing his hands over the body in much the same way that a metal is magnetised. He believed that in this way he could realign the magnetic field associated with a sick person and effect a cure. As he was able to demonstrate striking cures, his concepts of animal magnetism and magnetic treatment, which became known as Mesmerism, became very popular, especially among the poor who could not afford orthodox medical treatment. In France, where Mesmer was practising, this led to an investigation of Mesmerism by a Royal Commission, led by the US Commissioner to France, Benjamin Franklin.

Mesmer's claims for magnetic effects were systematically tested using magnetometers, which failed to detect any magnetism. The French Commission reported in 1785 that there was no substance to Mesmer's claims and that all the effects attributed to magnetism were the result of the patient's imagination. By dismissing animal magnetism in this way the commissioners implied that Mesmeric procedures had no validity. What they failed to do was to distinguish between the procedures, which clearly did have therapeutic value, and Mesmer's explanation of how they worked. They also failed to recognise that their conclusions as to how the procedures achieved their effects raised important questions about the therapeutic possibilities of the imagination. However the Franklin Report dismissed imagination along with Mesmerism. It was some 200 years later before the importance and implications of the commissions' conclusions were recognised and given serious consideration.

The Franklin Report discredited Mesmer, who retired into obscurity, but interest in Mesmerism and its practice continued. Dugald Stewart (1753–1828), professor of moral philosophy at Edinburgh University, was the first to recognise its scientific potential. He claimed the phenomena produced by Mesmer as 'inestimable data for extending our knowledge of the laws which regulate the connection between the human mind and our bodily organisation'.[36] Following a demonstration of Mesmerism by Charles Lafontaine in 1841, a Scottish physician, James Braid (1795–1860), commenced a series of experiments which led him to reject Mesmer's theories and to develop new concepts and methods. In *Neurypnology,* published in 1843, he proposed that the combined state of physical relaxation and altered awareness entered into by persons who were mesmerised should be called hypnosis, from the Greek *hypnos* meaning sleep.

Hypnosis

By this time the rapprochement between medicine and psychology had been furthered by the Edinburgh physician John Abercrombie. In 1830 he noted that in madness, fever and other abnormal states the mind betrays capacities and extensive systems of knowledge of which it is at other times wholly unconscious. He claimed this as evidence of the existence of an unconscious region of the mind. However it was by way of hypnosis that the influence of unconscious factors on behaviour became clearly demonstrated. As a result the doctrine of the unconscious mind ceased merely to be a philosophical abstraction.

Hypnosis proved to be of great interest to both physicians and psychologists. Before the introduction of ether and chloroform, which were easier to administer and less time-consuming, it was used as the sole anaesthetic in a great number of painless operations by a number of surgeons in Britain and elsewhere. In continental Europe Liebault (1835–1904) effected many remarkable cures with hypnosis. J. M. Charcot (1835–1893), a neurologist at the Salpetrière mental hospital in France, demonstrated that paralysis and anaesthesia could be produced and abolished by hypnosis. The psychiatrist Paul Janet (1859–1947) used hypnosis in the exploration of multiple personality. In so doing he anticipated by several years the importance of unconscious processes in mental illness, and the means of accessing them in psychotherapy, which subsequently were the focus of Freud's theorising and practice. It was Freud, however, who finally and irrevocably pulled medicine and psychology together:

> the striking manifestations of hypnosis brought to public attention by Mesmer towards the end of the eighteenth century and studied intensively during the early half of the nineteenth, together made it hard to deny that mind also had an influence on the functions of the body. It seemed increasingly clear that mind and body were part of a single system. Later, in the 1920s and 1930s the term psychosomatic was introduced to express this unity.[37]

A report by the British Medical Association in 1893 stated that 'as a therapeutic agent hypnosis is frequently effective in relieving pain, procuring sleep and alleviating many functional ailments', and a wealth of research worldwide has since supported these claims. The literature on the uses of hypnosis in psychotherapy and psychosomatic medicine is vast. Some idea of its scope can be gleaned from the papers presented at the 38th Annual Workshops and Scientific Program of the Society for Clinical and Experimental Hypnosis, held in Los Angeles in 1987. These report on the application of hypnosis to problems including anxiety, depression, neurological disease, trauma, obstetrics, gynaecology, smoking, drug dependence, psychoticism, asthma, malignant disease, bulimia and other eating disorders, sexual deviance, impotence, phobias, aphasia, hypertension, memory loss, child abuse and multiple personality.

The most widely reported effects of hypnosis are anaesthesia and analgesia. James Esdaile (1808–1859) carried out hundreds of painless operations during the nineteenth century using hypnosis as the sole anaesthetic, and hypnosis has since been used in obstetrics and operations such as appendectomy, caesarian section, breast surgery, skin grafting, heart surgery, cataract removal, prostrate resection, haemorroidectomy, nerve restoration and the ligation and stripping of veins.[38] It is claimed that 90 per cent of all minor fractures in casualty departments could be treated without anaesthesia if hypnosis were employed.[39] Less time consuming methods of achieving anaesthesia are now used, although many dental operations are still performed under hypnosis, and several studies have found that it is a valuable method for inducing conscious sedation in operations using local anaesthesia which might otherwise be difficult to achieve, such as plastic surgery;[40] and as an alternative to cerebral sedatives in high-risk and fearful patients.[41]

Hypnosis has proved to be a potent analgesic, of value in terminal illness,[42] and childbirth,[43] although its pain-killing effect is not yet fully understood. Certainly relaxation reduces anxiety, which by increasing muscle tension, increases pain. Relaxation may therefore be effective in reducing pain, with suggestions of warmth and comfort also playing an important role in augmenting relief. Another possibility is that hypnosis may work by getting the brain to ignore painful influences,[44] or to dissociate from them. [45]

Hypnosis has been found to be better than acupuncture, valium, aspirin and placebos in the relief of experimentally induced pain, and its effects more or less equivalent with those of morphine.[46] This is suggested by the fact that naloxone, which blocks the effect of opiate-like substances including endorphin, has been found to reverse analgesia artificially induced by hypnosis,[47] although this result has yet to be replicated, and other studies have suggested that hypnosis does not release endorphins.[48] Understanding of the role of endorphins has developed in recent years and it is now clear that while not all endorphins are involved in pain control, some have a role in pain modulation as part of the body's general response to stress. The effects of hypnosis may therefore be due to chemical factors.

Hypnosis has been used to control pain, anxiety and insomnia associated with cancer.[49-52] It has been found to help restore the sense of self-control that is often lost during the course of invasive cancer treatment;[53] overcome anticipatory emesis and nausea associated with cancer chemotherapy, which is commonly resistant to anti-emetic drugs;[54] improve immune function by increasing the number of lymphocytes;[55] and help coping with advanced cancer.[56] It has proved effective in reducing the anxiety associated with surgery and to significantly reduce consumption of analgesics post-operatively.[57] It has also been found to profoundly improve patients' quality of life and to reduce absenteeism from work, in addition to significantly relieving symptoms in patients with irritable bowel syndrome.[58] However, although hypnosis has a wide range of clinical applications, it is considered more effective when the aetiology of pain is known and the pain is chronic in nature.

Hypnosis also has a wide variety of application in psychotherapy. Freud recognised its value and promoted it as a means of accessing repressed unconscious material. However, he observed that much of the material produced under hypnosis was fanciful, fantasy or confabulation, and eventually abandoned its use. Nevertheless it has proved effective in the treatment of anxiety and phobic reactions; psychosomatic disorders such as asthma, migraine, headache, psoriasis, eczema, warts, high blood pressure, peptic ulcer, bedwetting, backache and insomnia; and in the treatment of repetitive and engrossing behaviours and addictions, such as smoking, overeating; obsessive compulsive reactions;[59] and depression.[60]

Nevertheless, despite incontrovertible evidence of its therapeutic effects, a good deal of suspicion about hypnosis remains in both psychology and medicine. Many doctors and psychologists regard it as unscientific and mysterious. This is largely because research has failed to find a single explanation for its effects. It may be that the various phenomena require different explanations,[61] with a range of processes interacting to give rise to effects which may vary from situation to situation and person to person. Also the explanation offered by the Franklin Commission (that imagination is solely responsible for observed effects) is generally regarded as insufficient to account for phenomena that are widely and erroneously regarded as highly unusual and otherwise impossible to achieve.

Feats performed under hypnosis are achievable under normal conditions.[62] Nevertheless the supposed discrepancy between 'normal' and hypnotic behaviour has led to a number of theorists to explain the latter in terms of unusual psychological and physiological mechanisms.[63-67] This view is challenged by other theorists who consider that well-established psychological and social processes can account for the effects very adequately.[68-74] Two processes considered to be of central importance in understanding hypnosis are compliance and belief. The power of the former was highlighted in controversial research[75] which demonstrated very clearly that having committed themselves to an experiment, the majority of subjects complied with instructions even to the point of being prepared to administer lethal electric shocks to subjects. These findings supported that of earlier research[76] which found that experimental subjects enact roles they are given to an alarming degree. Hypnotic suggestion has been likened to this phenomenon. It is argued[77] that motivation to comply with the hypnotist's suggestions might come partly from a desire to 'have a go', which results in a social commitment. From this perspective, hypnosis is a form of role play. Support for this view comes from a study[78] which demonstrates that reports of post-hypnotic amnesia could be eliminated by providing instructions that allowed subjects to admit role playing rather than being in a hypnotic state or trance. The most important finding of the study was that amnesia was removed when compliance was eliminated, which may be seen as suggesting that compliance could play a significant role in the hypnotic response.

Nevertheless some subjects genuinely believe themselves to be hypnotised. According to the traditional view of hypnosis this is because they have fallen into a unique 'state'. However there is evidence to show that in the face of ambiguous information subjects tend to rely on external factors to label their experience,[79,80] and that ambiguous inner states can be manipulated by giving people cues to their situation.[81,82] A number of features of the hypnotic situation may evoke ambiguous sensations in subjects that they then interpret as evidence for their being hypnotised. These may include feelings of giddiness, changes in temperature, floating and detachment, sleepiness and reduced attention to external stimuli, all of which are readily experienced by individuals who have been trained to relax. However, although relaxation may form a major source of the sensations that the subject labels as hypnosis, the two are not to be equated because 'even when relaxation is not present, then as long as a situation is defined as hypnosis subjects may continue to show a high level of responsiveness to suggestions'.[83] This supports the contention that subjects will report their experience as evidence for hypnosis if it accords with their beliefs about it. Thus, although it seems that compliance and belief may interact in the hypnotic situation, there are grounds to suggest that the latter explanation would be more acceptable to most subjects.

Although compliance may be a major motivating force in hypnotic responding, it has obvious disadvantages to its perpetrator; the compliant subject may feel deceitful, the self-image may be threatened, and even intense personal disappointment may be experienced. If given the choice, therefore, between *believing* something has happened and experiencing the *pretence* that something has happened there will be strong internal pressures to accept the former. It can be argued that the motivation to believe something has happened or is happening will be particularly strong in the clinical context where 'pretence' would offer little relief from medical problems. There is evidence from social-psychological studies of cognitive dissonance theory, indicating that people can be strongly motivated to reduce discrepancies between private attitudes or beliefs. There is no obvious reason why such a mechanism should not operate in the hypnotic situation. In this way hypnosis subjects would be motivated to make hypnotic suggestions 'work' within the limitations of the hypnotic context. If possible the subject will attempt to carry out suggestions so that the resulting responses are both publicly and privately acceptable. The interaction between compliance and belief may therefore be seen as a three-stage process by which, when confronted by a suggestion or set of suggestions, subjects (1) decide what the hypnotist 'really' wants; (2) attempt to employ cognitive strategies to produce congruent actions and experiences; (3) if (2) fails, resort to behavioural compliance.[84]

If this analysis is correct, then hypnotic behaviour is first and foremost social behaviour.

Like other complex social enactments, hypnotic responding is strategic rather than automatic. Hypnotic subjects retain rather than lose conscious control over their behaviour. These subjects guide their enactments in terms of their understanding concerning the requirements of the test situation and the social impressions they wish their enactments to convey. From this perspective individual differences in hypnotic susceptibility reflect individual differences in attitudes, motivations, and interpretations concerning hypnosis and the hypnotic situation, and individual differences in imaginal abilities required to experience these effects.[85]

Nevertheless, irrespective of these factors, it is the person who 'hypnotises' him or herself and brings about the various effects. Thus hypnosis can be more properly thought of as guided self-hypnosis.[86]

Auto-suggestion

Alexandre Bertrand[87] took the view that hypnosis and its effects were brought about by the person's imagination acting upon himself. Liebault concurred with this view, claiming that hypnosis is entirely due to auto-suggestion: self-administered suggestions meant to bring about either psychological or physical change without subsequent effort or involvement. Subsequently Emile Coué (1857–1926) observed that if this was the case then it should be possible to devise a method which dispensed with the hypnotist. As a chemist he was interested in whether auto-suggestion could bring about the same effects as drugs. He experimented with auto-suggestion and found that it could, so he developed a form of self-healing or psychotherapy, which became known as Couéism, and for which he claimed a 97 per cent success rate in overcoming his patients' presenting problems.

Initially each person was given a series of hypnotic suggestibility tests to ensure that they were amenable to suggestion. Then Coué proceeded to give a series of suggestions intended to promote psychological and physical well-being. He insisted that the patient repeat these 15 to 20 times daily until improvement in the presenting problem was achieved. This method of treatment became extremely popular prior to World War I, when an estimated 40,000 people were treated annually by Coué.[88] It greatly influenced Mary Baker Eddy, the founder of Christian Science, who is often associated with Coué's formula 'every day and in every way, I'm getting better and better'. However, the very simplicity of Couéism, comprising as it did the mental rehearsal of a series of suggestions, led to its falling into disrepute. Practitioners of Couéism simply repeated the relevant formulae and ignored the preparatory stages of the process, such as relaxation, the resolution of unconscious conflicts, and subsequent vivid imagining of the desired outcome. Indeed Couésim came to be seen as the mobilisation of will-power, despite Coué's claims that it is not the will but the imagination which is of crucial importance in bringing about physiological effects. Clearly, Couéism did not dispense with the therapist and was in most respects indistinguishable from hypnosis, so in no sense did it serve to demystify hypnosis and the power of the hypnotist. It did, however, highlight the power of suggestion.

Autogenic training

The principle of auto-suggestion was taken further in autogenic training, 'a physiologic form of psychotherapy which the patient carries out himself by using passive concentration upon certain combinations of psychophysiologiocally adapted stimuli'.[89] In contrast to most forms of psychotherapy, autogenic training is directed to mental and bodily functions simultaneously. It was developed in the 1930s by the German neurologist and psychiatrist, Johannes Schultz. He described it as 'a method of rational physiological exercises designed to produce a general psychobiologic reorganisation in the subject which enables him to manifest all the phenomena otherwise obtainable through hypnosis'.[90]

Schultz based his system on the work of the distinguished brain physiologist Oskar Vogt who, in his research into sleep and hypnosis between 1890 and 1900, found that some people are able to put themselves into a state resembling sleep for predetermined periods. He observed that those persons who achieved what he termed 'autohypnosis' had a substantial reduction of fatigue and tension, and a decrease in the incidence and severity of psychosomatic disorders, such as headache. Drawing on these observations, Schultz combined the concept of auto-hypnosis with a number of exercises designed to improve and integrate mental and physical functioning and eliminate maladjusted behaviour and its manifestations in neurotic and psychosomatic symptoms.

He noted that hypnotised subjects generally reported two characteristic sensations, a pleasurable feeling of warmth in the limbs and torso, and heaviness. Both are in fact psychological correlates of relaxation, the subjective sensation of warmth being the psychological perception of vasodilation in the peripheral arteries, and the sensation of heaviness being the perception of muscular relaxation. Schultz concluded that if he could design exercises which would enable subjects to induce these sensations in themselves he might be able to teach them to achieve the 'passive concentration' characteristic of hypnosis. He thought that once they were able to achieve this easily and rapidly it might be possible for them to progress to subtle psychological effects and to achieve a degree of autonomy over bodily functions. Passive concentration is described[91] as a casual attitude toward the intended outcome of concentrated activity, thereby distinguishing it from active concentration which is characterised by concern, interest, attention and goal-directed efforts regarding its outcome and functional result. During passive concentration subjects 'learn to abandon themselves to an ongoing organismic process rather than exercising conscious will',[92] and in so doing achieve a state of mind and body similar to the low arousal state of meditation which allows the body to self-regulate to a more harmonious state.

Indeed in Schultz's system, as in meditation, it is necessary to minimise external stimulation and turn attention inwards. To this end there must be monotonous input to various sensory receptors and concentrated attention towards somatic processes. This is achieved primarily by mental repetition of psychophysiologically adapted suggestions, while focusing attention on the parts of the body referred to in these formulae. As such it is similar to mantra yoga and meditation which have an affinity with Couéism in that they deal with positive affirmations.[93] Furthermore Schultz claimed that given these conditions dissolution of ego boundaries occurs, as it does in yoga, producing a dream-like state of consciousness and plasticity of imagery. Like yoga it commences with physiologically oriented exercises, progressing to exercises which focus primarily on mental imagery, and finally to special exercises developed for normalisation of certain functional and organic disorders. With regular practice these lead ultimately to the self-regulation of numerous mental and physical functions. There is thus a step-wise progression through physical relaxation and mental imagery, to self-healing.

Most of the advanced stages of autogenic training aim at increasing the person's ability to experience inner psychological phenomena visually[94] and involve the exploration of the effects of visual images on consciousness.[95] This process commences with the rotation of the eyeballs upward and inward so that they look towards the centre of the forehead. This procedure is often recommended in other mystical and meditative practices and in hypnosis, and has been shown to induce an increase in the production of alpha rhythms of the brain,[96] or to deepen a hypnotic trance-like state of consciousness. Both the therapist and patient may derive significant insights into the patient's unconscious from the images generated while in this state, which can be valuable in resolving both psychological and physiological states of disorder and psychosomatic stress.[97] Schultz recommended use of the advanced exercises of autogenic training in psychotherapy, and in clinically hopeless cases or desperate situations.

Schultz used his system to treat psychological and physical conditions, including peptic ulcers, indigestion, circulatory problems, angina, heart arhythmia, obsessive behaviours, phobias, sexual problems, diabetes, asthma, migraine and allergies; and claimed a considerable degree of success. He reported that after training, subjects could modify pain thresholds in different parts of the body, block the pain of dental drilling, warm their feet by raising foot temperature by as much as three degrees Fahrenheit, and that hypertensive patients could achieve decreases in blood pressure of 10–20 per cent.

Autogenic training has been subjected to considerable research and the impressive claims made for it by Schultz have found much support. It would appear that in the autogenic state, subjects are capable of regulating a wide range of physiological functions by way of auto-suggestion. Numerous studies[98] have reported significant physiological effects, including reductions by as much as 10 per cent in respiratory rate, blood pressure and heart rate; and significant decreases of muscle potentials, and patella response. Changes in peripheral circulation during passive concentration have been verified by a number of independent researchers.[99,100] Studies[101-103] have confirmed earlier findings of a rise in skin temperature, more pronounced in distal extremities than in more proximal areas, and an increase in weight in both arms during passive concentration. Changes in blood sugar during concentration on warmth in the liver area have also been demonstrated,[104,105] as have changes in heart rate during autogenic training.[106] Changes in the shape of the eyeballs and improved distance vision have been found in near-sighted people.[107] Autogenic training has also eliminated stomach contractions resulting from great hunger,[108] and anaesthetised against third degree burns.[109]

Autogenic training is used as a standard pre-operative procedure in Germany and is widely used throughout Europe, where it is integrated into the medical training programmes of many universities. It is also now used in Canada, the USA and Japan. Until recently it has been little known or practiced in Britain. However, the situation is changing as a result of research. One study[110] found that 82 per cent of all patients referred for autogenic training with a wide range of problems found it generally helpful, 74 per cent found that it also helped specific symptoms, and most reported feeling more relaxed and confident. Another study[111] of 100 healthy persons aged between 25–60, half of whom were allocated to physical exercise and half to autogenic training following physical and physiological tests designed to select stress variables and heart risk factors, found after two months that both groups had experienced considerable reductions in anxiety and depression, improved their scores on general health questionnaires, reported an enhanced sense of well-being, improved sleep, reduced physical tension, and showed significant reduction in resting pulse rate, blood pressure and blood fatty acids. In every respect, autogenic training proved to be as useful as exercise, which is an important finding given the finding[112] that only 14 of 215 patients having suffered heart attack were prepared to continue exercise therapy. Almost half the patients reported finding exercise inconvenient; 30 per cent found it boring; 25 per cent disliked exercise without medical supervision; and a further 35 per cent gave medical reasons for discontinuing the exercise programme. The advantage of autogenic training over exercise is that, being essentially sedentary, it can be practised by anyone, whether confined to bed or a wheelchair, and it can be successfully used in work or leisure contexts. Moreover, once mastered, it is the fastest method of achieving passive concentration. Unlike yoga, it doesn't take much time. Another advantage[113] is that the body is not expected to react in a stereotyped way. Apart from increasing speed of reaction to suggestions, subtle changes constantly take place as the intensity of practice grows and the suggestions can be changed to suit current needs as well as distant aims.

Certainly contemporary research supports the conclusion that 'both clinical results and experimental data indicate that autogenic training operates in a highly differentiated field of bodily self-regulation and that with the help of autogenic principles it is possible to use one's brain to influence bodily and mental functions effectively'.[114] A review of controlled outcome research involving 76 studies[115] reported positive effects of autogenic training on migraine, insomnia, test anxiety, angina pectoris, asthma, childbirth, eczema, hypertension, infertility, Raynaud's disease and recovery from heart attacks. It has been recommended as a first line of treatment for patients with excessive circadian blood pressure, a condition which, even in the absence of elevated blood pressure, is associated with a large increased risk of developing ischaemic stroke or nephropathy, following the finding that significant reductions of systolic blood pressure can be achieved with autogenic training.[116] Huge improvements in childhood migraine have been reported following autogenic training;[117] also improved stamina, concentration, intellectual performance, physical coordination, diminished arousibility and reduced symptoms in most diseases;[118] improved management of stress and emotions in HIV-infected individuals;[119] and success in treating psychiatric patients suffering severe anxiety disorders.[120]

Nevertheless autogenic training is often viewed with suspicion because it relies on auto-suggestion. Practitioners insist that there is a critical distinction between autogenic training and auto-suggestion in that in the former people are trained over a long period of time to achieve a meditative state. Autosuggestion is only used initially as a means of training them to achieve a low arousal state.

9

Relaxation

The quieting of the sympathetic nervous system, as manifested in altered skin resistance, brain wave and breathing patterns, and reduction in other measures of physiological arousal such as muscle activity, heart and pulse rate, blood pressure and blood hormone levels, is striking and similar in yoga, meditation, biofeedback, hypnosis, and autogenic training. Indeed none of these self-control strategies is unique in eliciting these effects, which are now recognised as being consistent with a physiological state of deep relaxation. However, the tendency to attribute these effects to altered states of consciousness, which has become fashionable since the 1960s, is not altogether unjustified since relaxation is an *altered* state in that it is not commonly experienced and does not occur spontaneously but must be consciously and purposefully evoked. Relaxation is not merely a shift in physiological functions but is an integrated combination of these which is not achieved simply by lounging in front of the television or chatting with friends. This was not fully appreciated until advances in technology facilitated precise recording of subtle physiological processes.

The physician Edmund Jacobsen first investigated relaxation systematically during the 1920s. Yet relaxation or rest has long been recognised as the opposite of nervous hypertension, which is a feature of many conditions and occurs in the guise of symptoms, causes or effects throughout almost the entire range of medical practice, surgery and specialities.[1] Rest has been seen as an antidote which increases general resistance to infection and other noxious agents, decreases blood pressure and strain on the heart, diminishes energy output and movement of body parts, thereby averting strain or injury. Accordingly it has been prescribed in the treatment of numerous conditions including acute infections, ulcers, gastro-intestinal disorders, cardiac and renal disease, high blood pressure, arthritis, systemic disease, neurosis, after surgery and frequently in preparation for it. Traditionally various means have been used to promote rest including tepid baths, massage and warm drinks, but the agents now most frequently used by physicians are sedative drugs. Nevertheless, patients often fail to derive the full benefits of rest, especially in hospitals where ward routines are typically put before the patients' need for peace and quiet.[2]

Directing a person to 'rest' or 'relax' is in itself quite futile as many people simply don't know how to, and their restlessness may be increased by distress and vice versa. Normally people are unaware that their muscles are tense and they cannot judge accurately whether or not relaxation has been achieved. Therefore what is customarily called rest or relaxation is in many instances inadequate, which accounts for the failure of many rest cures. A person may lie apparently quietly for hours but remain sleepless and restless. She may show signs of mental activity, organic excitement, anxiety or other emotional disturbance, breathe irregularly, fidget, move her eyes or fingers, or start in response to sudden noise. Following such 'rest' the person often does not feel refreshed and retains symptoms of fatigue and other ills. Moreover, even when the person feels fairly relaxed there are often clinical signs of residual tension and 'restlessness' such as irregular respiration, increased pulse rate, voluntary or local reflexes indicated in wrinkling of the forehead, frowning, movements of the eyeballs, tightness around the eyes, frequent or rapid blinking, shifting of the head and limbs, swallowing and startle responses. In true relaxation, residual tension is absent, respiration loses its irregularity, pulse rate drops, there is no tightness in the jaw and throat, the knee jerk and other reflexes are absent. The person lies quietly with flaccid limbs and no visible traces of stiffness, no reflex swallowing, and motionless, toneless eyelids. Residual tension disappears only gradually and so relaxation is achieved slowly and progressively rather than suddenly and immediately. Recognising this, Edmund Jacobsen attempted to devise a method whereby extreme neuromuscular relaxation could be achieved by progressive elimination of muscle tension.

Progressive relaxation

Jacobsen took the view that it is only when a person knows what tension is that he can begin to relax. His system of progressive relaxation involved the individual learning to identify tension in muscle groups by contracting them. It is the cultivation of 'muscle sense',[3] and can be thought of as a method of nervous re-education which helps the individual to become increasingly observant of muscle contractions in various parts of the body, and to recognise that subjectively relaxation is not a positive 'something' different from contraction, but simply a negative, non-doing. The aim is to show those who insist that they cannot relax that if they can progressively tense muscles they can cease the same contraction, and that it is not necessary for them to move body parts or 'do' anything to achieve it. In principle it can be taught to anyone in much the same way as any physical skill, providing that they are willing, motivated to learn and practice, and able to follow instructions. Nevertheless some people are not successful in cultivating muscle sense and fail to gain fine control.

Progressive relaxation has many forms depending on the condition to be treated, whether acute or chronic, and the ability of the person to follow directions. It may be brief and occasional, with only 2–3 training periods, or longer, extending over months. Periods of instruction may also vary from 30 minutes to an hour, and may be daily or 3–4 times weekly. However, as repetition is the keynote of the method, daily practice by the individual is required.

In a quiet room the person either lies on his back with arms by the sides and legs uncrossed, or sits in a chair. He is then taught to recognise the presence of muscle contraction, however slight, and to relax it in all the noteworthy muscle groups of the body in a certain order. Jacobsen adopted the sequence of left arm and hand, right arm and hand, left foot and leg, right foot and leg, abdomen, respiratory muscles, back, shoulders, chest, face and mouth.

The degree of relaxation is assessed in a number of ways: by palpation of muscle groups and passive motion of body parts by the therapist; visual observation of the flaccidity of muscle groups; the absence of movement or contraction; the presence of involuntary start or jerk of a local part (as sometimes occurs before sleep); increasingly slow responses to interruption or failure to respond; and sleepy-eyed or vacuous, expressionless appearance. Relaxation of mental activities is then achieved through the introduction of imagery. Visual, auditory and other sensory images are presented to enable the subject to recognise the subtle tensions of the small muscles or the sense organs which accompany imagery. This is a delicate matter that requires practice but Jacobsen claimed[4] that when this is done mental imagery dwindles and ceases with the approach of general relaxation, and that without faint attention the image fails to appear. Motor or kinesthetic imagery may likewise be relaxed away. Thus inner speech ceases with progressive relaxation of the muscles of the lips, tongue, larynx and throat. Furthermore, attention, recollection, thought processes and emotion gradually diminish, and Jacobsen claimed that this is registered in a totally expressionless face.

> The thesis that progressive relaxation brings with it absence of thinking, is apparent, literally on the face of it. This thesis also harmonizes with the experience of all the subjects and patients who considered that it was impossible to be relaxed extremely and to have images at the same time. With the advent of one condition, the other invariably ceases.[5]

Clearly Jacobsen is suggesting that the end state of perfect or complete relaxation, achieved in a clinical manner without recourse to esotericism of any kind, is a state of inner silence, emptiness, or void which is the aim of meditation. Moreover, as in meditation, this state is an ideal, which according to Jacobsen is not as a rule achieved, and then only for brief periods of time.

Regular and extensive practice is required to master progressive relaxation, but the method can be simplified or shortened in a number of ways, for example by restricting the training to a few muscle groups. When the person recognises that relaxation can be effected as quickly as muscle contraction, he can be taught to scan the body for tension and to concentrate on relaxing only those muscles. It is possible to use everyday events such as traffic signals, hourly radio bulletins or workshift bells as signals of when to scan and relax muscles. A person may also achieve differential relaxation by learning to identify and relax the muscles not required in the execution of a task while achieving a minimum of tension in those that are.

Jacobsen claimed that progressive relaxation is effective in the treatment of hypertension, insomnia, anxiety neuroses, cardiac conditions, compulsive neuroses, tics, hypochondria and stuttering, and that following relaxation drugs and dietary restrictions could be abolished in many cases. In addition to these conditions, he recommended it as particularly suitable for cases of nervousness or emotional disturbance; functional neuroses such as phobias; habit spasm, fatigue, exhaustion and debility; pre-operative and post-operative conditions; toxic goitre; sleep disturbances; alimentary spasm; peptic ulcer; chronic pulmonary tuberculosis; organic and functional heart disorders, and vascular hypertension.

Wolpe's relaxation method

Wolpe[6] subsequently developed a system of relaxation based on that of Jacobsen which he used with systematic desensitization in the treatment of phobias and anxiety states. His method is quite brief, comprising six periods of instruction with twice daily 15-minute practice periods. Like Jacobsen he commenced the training by focusing on the muscle groups of the arms, largely because they are easy for demonstration purposes and easily checked upon by the therapist, progressing to the head, where relaxation produces the most marked anxiety inhibiting effects. Initially the subject grips the arm of a chair to see if he can distinguish any qualitative difference between sensations in the forearm and hand. He is directed to take particular note of the quality of sensation in the forearm, caused by muscle tension in contrast to sensations in the hand which are caused by touch and pressure. The subject is encouraged to note the exact location of forearm tensions. The therapist then grips the subject's wrist and asks him to tense his arm against this resistance, thus making him aware of the tension in his biceps. Then, by instructing him to straighten his bent elbow he calls attention to the extensor muscles of the arm. The therapist shows the subject how to achieve deep relaxation by asking him to resist the pull at the wrist by tightening the biceps and noting the sensations in that muscle, then instructing them to let go gradually as the force exerted against them is diminished. The subject is instructed to notice that the letting go is a non-activity – an uncontracting of muscle – and told to continue relaxing the muscle when the arm is resting on the chair. This is repeated until the subject understands what is required of him, when he is asked to place both hands on the lap for a few minutes, relaxing all muscles and reporting any sensations experienced – usually warmth and heaviness. Initially, only limited success is likely, hence the need for regular practice.

In the second session training focuses on the facial muscles. Sensations are demonstrated through contraction of the muscles of the forehead. Focus in the third session is upon tensing the muscles of the temple, jaw and neck by clenching the teeth, while the fourth session is concerned with the neck and shoulder muscles, which when contracted keep the head erect. The fifth session concentrates on the muscles of the back, abdomen and chest, through arching the body, and the feet; and finally, in the sixth session, all the previously trained muscle groups are worked on. Wolpe found this method effective in bringing about desired emotional changes and it has since been widely adopted in the treatment of phobias and anxiety conditions.

Farmer and Blows' method of relaxation

Most of the methods of relaxation currently used in psychological and medical therapy are modifications of those of Jacobsen or Wolpe. Ron Farmer, a South African psychologist, has developed an even shorter method than that of Wolpe which incorporates principles of yoga practice, psychological learning theory and auto-suggestion. This has been extended by Blows,[7] who, influenced by TM, introduced passive observation or 'letting go' of cycles of thinking. This method entails lying in a supine position similar to the *sarasana* or corpse posture of yoga, awareness of breathing movements, passive observation of thought, and letting go of internally triggered cycles of mental activity. Blows observes that in the methods of Jacobsen and Wolpe the state of relaxation is continually disrupted by the action of tensing the muscles, and for this reason progressive relaxation does not always yield the same neurophysiological indices as meditation. Farmer addressed this problem by using the principle of stimulus generalisation derived from learning theory. Instead of tensing a series of muscles in the whole body, the subject does the preliminary training with the dominant hand, tensing only that part of the body and allowing the experience of letting go to generalise to other parts in turn with no further tensing actions. Blows claims that once commenced the relaxed state is not disrupted but enhanced.

The exercise begins with the subject focusing on her breathing and saying the word 'relax' softly on each breath. Relaxation is introduced in two simple steps so that without actually being told to do so the person concentrates on her breathing and prepares for the word 'relax' to become an affective signal on the brain, enabling her to relax quickly in everyday situations. Blows suggests that saying the word 'relax' aloud helps to establish the habit. It also allows the therapist to monitor the coordination of breathing and relaxation. Tensing and release of the dominant hand is introduced coarsely at first in one cycle of breathing, then extended to gradual releasing over a number of breaths, becoming progressively finer. In the last stages of this preliminary procedure the subject, while mentally rehearsing the word 'relax', is asked to imagine that after his hand feels fully relaxed a little more tension flows away each time he breathes out. Blows claims that gradual refinement of the contraction and release of the hand, commencing with coarse tensing which can be felt easily, prepares for generalised release of tension in other areas of the body which is enhanced by imagining further release of tension.

The instructions include the statement that effort is not required, only letting go, and a suggestion of heaviness of the limbs is also added. Each section of the body is then covered using common sense rather than strictly anatomical sections, consistent with ordinary people's body images. Normally two training sessions are required before the subject can reproduce the experience reasonably well at home, where it is recommended that practice takes place twice daily.

Blows has included an additional phase of pleasant imagery of the subject's own choice, and claims that with modification the original Farmer method can be extended to produce a state similar to that attained during Transcendental Meditation. Thus it is not restricted to muscular relaxation but can also achieve mental calmness. Blows maintains that given a range of relaxation methods most people prefer the Farmer and Blows method, but as it has not yet been submitted to physiological tests or evaluative studies its efficacy has yet to be verified. Nevertheless it does have advantages over other relaxation methods in as much as that it avoids not only interruption of the relaxation process by muscle tensing but also a good deal of verbal instruction which is widely held to stimulate mental activity and logical thought.

Attempts to avoid interruption of the relaxation process by muscle tensing has led to the development of progressive relaxation methods which use muscle stretching exercises as an alternative to tension-release methods. **Stretch-based relaxation training** has been found to be effective in decreasing subjective measures of muscle tension and activation and to show potential for stress management.[8] Such methods are not new. The Ancient Egyptians used a system of stretching and deep breathing, known as **sesh**, meaning expansion or freedom, as a means of releasing the self from the bondage imposed by its physical limitations. It was designed to 'stretch' the individual in every possible way and to extend personal abilities. It develops both mental and physical fitness, achieves a healthier balance between mind and body, and helps people to feel good about themselves. In fitness terms sesh is unique because it uses four forms of flexibility in each move or posture. Sports scientists now recognise that certain kinds of stretching can improve fitness. These include ballistic or movement stretches, static stretches, such as those used in yoga, isometric or flex and relax stretches, and passive stretches where a joint is held in a certain position and pressure is applied to it. Each of these kinds of stretching are used in sesh movements, and this traditional form of fitness training is now being taught in Britain.

In order to avoid the distractions of verbal instruction, non-verbal quieting methods based on gentle touch and sound have also been developed.[9] Music has been combined most effectively with relaxation procedures and has been found to alleviate pain in a number of studies.[10]

Relaxation tapes

There is an increasing tendency to use music as an aid to relaxation and numerous audio-cassette tapes have been produced commercially. However, although a very popular means of promoting relaxation, audio-cassettes, whether verbal or musical, lead to reliance on external devices and the failure of the person to develop his or her own internal cues to relaxation. As such they are antithetical to the principal aim of all forms of relaxation, which is to train the individual in self-reliance and self-awareness. Furthermore they tend to give the false impression that muscle control can be acquired instantly. This frequently leads those who fail to do so to believe that they cannot relax. Certainly the promise of a speedy means of achieving relaxation is very attractive, especially when compared with those lengthy and time-consuming methods which achieve relaxation by sequential contraction of muscle groups and focus on breathing. Hence the popularity of the relaxation methods devised by Herbert Benson, professor of Medicine at Harvard University Medical School, and Director of the Hyper-tensive Section of Boston's Beth Israel Hospital.

The relaxation response

Benson insists that the ability to relax is not a learned phenomenon or skill but an innate and universal human capacity, which he terms the relaxation response, and requires no special educational attainment or aptitude, nor any lengthy period of training. 'It is not necessary to meditate or to be wired up to a machine to achieve it, nor is there any necessity to engage in any rites or esoteric practices to bring it forth and to reclaim its benefits'.[11]

Benson developed a simple technique for eliciting the relaxation response derived from traditional forms of meditation. This involves the person adopting a comfortable posture in a quiet environment and a passive attitude, achieved by redirection of attention to a silently repeated sound, word or phrase, and to breathing. Once seated comfortably the person is directed to close the eyes, or focus with open eyes on a fixed point or object, and to become aware of breathing by inhaling through the nose and exhaling through the mouth. He is directed to say 'one' silently as he breathes out, thereby establishing a pattern which is rehearsed for 10–20 minutes. He is encouraged not to worry about success in achieving a deep level of relaxation but merely to maintain a passive attitude and permit relaxation to occur at its own pace. He is also told not to dwell on distracting thoughts which may occur, but simply to turn attention back to breathing and repeating the word 'one'.

Benson indicates that subjective feelings accompanying the relaxation response vary among individuals. The majority experience a sense of calmness, while some experience ecstatic feelings, and others describe pleasurable sensations. In this respect their experiences are consistent with the response patterns to meditation, which include sensations of dizziness and foggy consciousness, calmness and tranquillity, pleasant bodily sensations, vibrations and waves, feelings of the body being suspended or light, lucid consciousness with detachment from thoughts and feelings, and extensive loss of bodily sensation.[12] However, regardless of the subjective feelings experienced, the physiological changes associated with the relaxation response are similar to those of TM.[13]

Therapeutic effects of relaxation

Benson[14] reported the effectiveness of the relaxation response in treating hypertension, headache and a wide range of other conditions. The therapeutic benefits of relaxation are now widely recognised. It has been used successfully in the control of asthma;[15,16] in cancer treatment;[17] and reducing the side effects of cancer chemotherapy;[18,19] in improving immune response;[20] reducing diabetics' need for insulin;[21] in reducing anxiety, reactivity to anxiety,[22] and coping without anxiolytic drugs.[23] Compared with hypnosis, relaxation has been found to produce greater reduction in physical arousal and subjective distress.[24] Relaxation is also effective in the control of chronic pain.[25–27]

Relaxation and pain control

The role of relaxation in pain control is increasingly recognised. It may alleviate pain associated with involuntary muscle tone, which may be confined to an area immediately around the primary pain, more generalised, or even at a site far distant from its source.[28] Hence clenching of the jaw may accompany abdominal pain and low back pain often involves an increase in tension of back, buttock and leg muscles, whereas some chest and abdominal pain results in increased muscle tone all over the body. While the primitive function of the increased muscle tone might be to protect the primary pain site and prevent damaging movement, it is not useful in pain which is not associated with acute inflammation or injury. Indeed in non-acute pain the increased muscle tension often causes secondary pain which exacerbates the original problem. Moreover, increased pain interferes with relaxation and sleep and leads to an increasing spiral of tension and pain.

Severe pain is also accompanied by subjective feelings of distress and physiological arousal which can be brought under control by successful relaxation training. Attention to breathing can inhibit these effects in the short term. Relaxation may also have long-term effects. Eighty-six per cent of patients with a variety of conditions who continued relaxation with biofeedback, when followed up after five years, were found to show improvements compared with only 5 per cent of those patients who discontinued relaxation.[29]

Pioneers of relaxation in the treatment of cancer[30] recognised that it serves a variety of functions. For some patients it appears to be a way of recharging batteries, whereas for others it helps to break the cycle of fear and tension that often builds up and overwhelms people suffering from serious illness. With fear reduced it is easier for people to develop a more positive expectancy, which may further reduce their fear and may be a significant feature in cancer regression.

Notwithstanding its many therapeutic applications, it is as an antidote to stress that relaxation is now gaining most recognition.

Stress, illness and immunity

There is nothing new in the idea that stress is linked with serious illness. This connection was established in ancient times. In 1759 the surgeon Richard Guy highlighted the possible role of adverse life events in the development of cancer, and loss has since been cited as an antecedent condition in the development of cancer by numerous commentators.[31-36] Studies have demonstrated a link between stressful events and cancer;[37-41] and in the recurrence of cancer,[42] with the result that such a view is now widely accepted and promoted.[43-45] However, the most compelling evidence for the link between stress and illness comes from the newly emergent interdisciplinary field of psychoneuroimmunology or PNI.

Psychoneuroimmunology

Psychoneuroimmunology attempts to explain the mechanisms by which the mind works upon the body to influence illness, health and healing. Its central focus is to advance understanding of immunity. The functions of the immune system can broadly be classified into cellular and humoral immunity. The former refers to the responses of cells that combat viral infection and bacteria and are involved in reactions against transplanted tissue and tumours. T-lymphocytes, white blood cells involved in the cellular immune response, are subdivided into several classes on the basis of their function. They include T-helper/inducer and T/suppressor/cytoxic lymphocytes. The former stimulate the production of antibody from B-lymphocytes and also several important substances called lymphokines which enhance immune response and promote the replication of T-helper cells, the functions of which are critical for the immune response and deficiency of which can result in immunodeficiency.

T-suppressor lymphocytes down-regulate the immune response and inhibit antibody production through their influence on T-helper cells. The helper to suppressor cell ratio is sometimes used as a global index of immune function, hence low helper to suppressor cell ratios are often found in AIDS patients and other populations of immune-suppressed individuals. The relative percentages of T-helper and T-suppressor lymphocytes are measured using specific monoclonal antibodies.

In contrast to cellular immunity, humoral immunity refers to the production of antibodies by B-lymphocytes. Antibody molecules are synthesised against, and bind to, foreign proteins or antigens, foreign substances which may trigger the immune response.

During the 1920s, Pavlov established that guinea-pigs could be conditioned to produce specific antibodies in response to being handled by research workers in the laboratory. Some 50 years later a similar discovery was made during a Pavlovian learning experiment on conditioned aversion. It was found that the immune system of rats can be conditioned by experience, and that they can learn to enhance or suppress immune functions. The finding that cells in the immune system of rats could be trained in the same manner as Pavlov's dogs initially attracted a good deal of scepticism, but has now been conclusively demonstrated in numerous studies. Research findings from hundreds of studies relating to the influence of the mind on immunity have now been published. All of them point to the conclusion that the immune system is controlled by the brain, whose structures, particularly those involved in emotion, such as the hypothalamus and pituitary gland, can be artificially stimulated to increase or decrease immune functioning.

The connection between the autonomic nervous system and emotional states was first indicated by W.B. Cannon in 1929. By the 1950s it had been established that a close affinity exists between some neurotransmitters and some endocrines, and between the pituitary, or master gland, and one of the chief regulating systems of the brain, the hypothalamus. It has thus become clear that hormones are a more important regulator of behaviour than had previously been suspected by most psychologists. This new awareness gave rise to a new field of investigation, that of psychoneuroendocrinology, which was the precursor of psychoneuroimmunology.

The endocrine system was thought to be the sole mediator between the brain and the immune system. Then in the 1980s, neural projections were identified in both rats and mice from the spinal cord and medulla to the thymus gland, (which stimulates the production of the immune system's T-cells). This suggested a role for these structures in the regulation of thymic functions, and established the role of the so-called lower brain areas with regard to immunity, but not of the mind, which is usually synonymous with the higher areas or cortex of the brain. However, the hypothalamus, which has an important regulatory role in immune function, is intimately connected to the limbic system, part of the brain involved in emotion. The limbic system, in turn, forms a connecting network with the frontal lobes, which are the most evolved part of the cortex. The existence of connections between the brain and immune system raised the question of whether actual behaviour or events known to be modulated by various brain areas can be associated with changes in immune functions, and whether the findings of animal studies can be generalised to man.

The effects of stress on immunity

PNI research has shown how psychological distress can lead to adverse immunological changes providing one physiological pathway through which major and minor life changes might result in an increased incidence of infectious and malignant disease.[46] It is now widely accepted that both the neuroendocrine and immune systems can be influenced by external stress once it has been perceived by the central nervous system. Stress is characterised by activation of both the autonomic nervous system and the hypothalamo-pituitary-adrenal axis (HPA). The resulting neurochemical changes have been demonstrated to affect immune function both directly and indirectly. Direct effects are possible because lymphocytes bear receptors on their surfaces for many neurohormones and transmitters, and lymphocytes are exposed to neurochemicals in lymphoid organs and in peripheral blood. More indirect mechanisms for neural-immune interactions may involve changes in lymphocyte trafficking resulting from changes in sympathetic vascular tone.[47]

Elucidation of the pathways of communication between the central nervous system and the immune system has advanced largely from animal studies but there is also a wealth of evidence from human studies. There is a growing body of literature showing that acute stress, whether physical or emotional, can produce transient manifestations of immunosuppression in humans and animals. Moreover, chronic stress may cause significant dysfunction of the immune response leading to increased susceptibility to disease.[48] In response to stressors the adrenal cortex produces glucocorticoids through the HPA. Individuals with an adreno-cortical insufficiency such as Addison's disease have physiological difficulty handling stress. An over-abundance of glucocorticoids during stress can also have major physiological consequences. Research on the relationships between the CNS, immune system and endocrine systems provides evidence of physiological pathways, including the glucocorticoids, and other 'stress hormones' such as the catecholamines, prolactin, and growth hormone, through which distress may modulate immune function.[49] Knowledge about the mechanisms of action is still limited, but there is a growing literature describing such relationships, and their health-related consequences.

Stress and autoimmune disease

> With the recent realization of the interrelationships and networks existing between the nervous, endocrine and immune systems, the catalytic effect of stress on individuals with a predisposition for autoimmune disease can now be explained.[50]

For over a century the association between the central nervous system and the immune system, as it relates to the development of autoimmune disease, has been recognised.[51] In 1881 Charcot reported an association between multiple sclerosis (MS) and affective disturbances. Since that time there have been many reports which support the claim that stress and psychosocial factors contribute to the appearance or exacerbation of human autoimmune disease. A large body of evidence suggests that the onset of rheumatoid arthritis usually follows one of two patterns: occurring after a single abrupt life event such as bereavement following the death of a spouse or relative, separation from a loved one due to illness or divorce, loss of employment, or abrupt financial loss; or after a long-standing series of unpleasant experiences, which may include long-term family discord, work stress, or pressures associated with other responsibilities. The onset of autoimmune thyroid diseases and insulin-dependent diabetes mellitus also show a link with stressful life events;[52] and patients with multiple sclerosis report a higher level of distress or stressful life events occurring just prior to the onset of MS symptoms. Other studies have revealed an association between MS and affective disorders. There is a greater incidence of overt depressive disorders in MS populations, and a large proportion of MS patients exhibit depressive characteristics.[53]

Affective factors and illness

Research in the field of psychoneuroimmunology has shed light on the mechanisms by which stress and affective states can have such a profound effect on immunity only recently. Yet the role of psychological factors in the development of disease has long been recognised. Galen observed that cancer more commonly occurs in women of melancholic disposition than in those of more sanguine personality type, and this view has found support among physicians throughout history. It has also been supported by modern research.[54-61] Other psychological factors have been identified in cancer patients, including repression and denial of emotions, inability to express hostile feelings, poor outlet for emotional discharge, a tendency towards self-sacrifice and blame, rigidity, impaired self-awareness and a predisposition to hopelessness and despair. Cancer has also been described as a disease following emotional resignation and loss of hope,[62] which is found in those who in trying to gain approval from others, suppress anger and other negative emotions.[63] Research evidence strongly suggests that cancer patients characteristically suppress emotion and seem to ignore negative feelings such as hostility, depression and guilt. A link between breast cancer in women and inability to 'get something off the chest' has been identified. Differences have been found[64] between benign and malignant breast cancer patients in their expression of anger. Long-term survivors of breast cancers express much higher levels of hostility, anxiety, alienation and other negative emotions than short-term survivors.[65] Patients with malignant tumours have also been found to be more repressed in the expression of anxiety,[66] and to be more passive and appeasing. Patients who express emotion freely and show active determination to fight their disease live longer than those who are meek, passive, compliant or defeatist.[67] Cancer patients have also been identified as characterised by a greater tendency to hold resentment and not forgive, self-pity, poor ability to develop and maintain meaningful long-term relationships, and poor self-image. The belief systems of those patients who eventually succumb to cancer are characteristically negative, whereas those patients whose cancers show spontaneous remission tend to be positive.[68] Cancer patients also report more subjectively experienced stress than controls.[69] Indeed the link between cancer and stress is well-established in the psychological literature.[70-76]

Recognition of the psychological characteristics of cancer patients has led to the notion of a cancer-prone or Type C personality.[77] There is some evidence to support such a proposition,[78-80] but it is far from conclusive.[81] It has also been argued[82,83] that cancer patients are no different from patients who develop other serious diseases, and that there is a common group of causes for cancer, heart attack, stroke and related thrombotic diseases, which includes chronic stress, a predisposed personality type and chronic hyperactivation of neural, endocrine, immune, blood clotting and fibrinolytic systems. A number of studies have suggested a common pattern of psychological helplessness and hopelessness in various diseases. Women with rheumatoid arthritis have been found to be tense, moody, depressed, concerned with rejection they perceived from their mothers and the strictness of their fathers; to show denial and inhibition of the expression of anger; and to reflect these traits, compliance, subservience, conservatism, shyness, introversion and the need for security, on standard tests of personality.[84-86] Affective factors have also been linked with respiratory and infectious diseases.[87-90]

Nevertheless there are numerous difficulties in studying possible psychological causes of any illness, especially cancer. Although spoken of as one illness, cancer takes many forms which may have quite different causes, and factors which may be responsible for the initial onset of the disease may be different from those involved in its subsequent development. Onset of cancer may occur many years before any signs of the disease are evident, and factors that are cited as antecedent conditions may in fact have occurred after the cancer became established. Retrospective studies of cancer thus have several pitfalls, including the possibility that the presence of cancer, whether recognised by the patient or not, may influence her psychological state by its physical effects on the brain and body chemistry. The problems involved in designing research studies that will produce valid information about psychological precursors of cancer or other disease are formidable. Currently there is no generally accepted means of exactly defining and measuring many of the psychological variables investigated, with the result that the findings of different studies vary with the different methods used, and are not comparable. Nevertheless there is abundant evidence supporting the influence of psychological factors on endocrine and immune functions.[91-100]

Psychological modifiers of stress

It is becoming increasingly evident that factors such as coping style are instrumental in determining the impact of stress on the autonomic nervous system, immune system, and susceptibility to disease. Repression as a coping style has attracted considerable attention, particularly the association between a repressive coping style and the onset and progression of cancer. One hypothesis is that because people with a repressive coping style display inattention to internal cues of distress, they may also fail to detect significant bodily feedback. Some support for this theory comes from the finding that repressive cancer patients report fewer and less severe side effects of treatment,[101] yet are no different from other patients in terms of disease and treatment status. However, this theory does not account for the association between repression and increased cancer risk.

Another possible link between repression and disease is that the repressor's immune system is adversely affected by evoking stressors, which is implied by high levels of autonomic response.[102] Repressors typically deny the experience of stress, yet react to stressful stimuli with high autonomic arousal.[103] Repressors who report low anxiety and high defensiveness actually show physiological responses to anxiety-provoking stimuli that equalled or surpassed those subjects who reported high anxiety.[104] Repressors also report significantly lower levels of affective pain than non-repressors, and it has been suggested that since they fail to experience the emotional discomfort associated with anxiety and pain, they may lack the motivation to gain control over a stressful stimulus or event. This is significant because animal studies have shown that variations in perceived control of a stressor affect arousal level and lymphocyte responses. Hence the controllability of stress factors appears to be critical in modulating immune function.

Expectation is also known to influence blood levels of the hormones cortisol and prolactin which are important in activating the immune system.[105] Positive and negative expectations have opposite effects, respectively enhancing or depressing the immune response. The importance of expectancy or belief is well recognised in orthodox medicine, to the extent that doctors frequently prescribe a placebo, or imitation medicine, in cases where reassurance for the patient is more useful than conventional medication. Placebos have been demonstrated to be as or more effective than real medicine in the treatment of pain and a wide variety of diseases ranging from hay fever to rheumatoid arthritis[106] which implicate the automonic, endocrine and immune systems. However it is only relatively recently that the placebo has been investigated seriously. Although it is not yet understood exactly how, it is now recognised that the placebo can have more profound effects on organic illness – including 'incurable' malignancies – than conventional drugs. The placebo is not so much a pill as a process, which begins with the patient's confidence in the doctor and then extends through to the full functioning of his own immunological and healing system.[107] The placebo effect offers proof that there is no separation between mind and body, and that illness and health are always an interaction between both. In the light of new evidence about the way the human mind/body system functions 'attempts to treat most mental diseases as though they were completely free of physical causes and attempts to treat most bodily diseases as though the mind were in no way involved must be considered archaic'.[108]

The placebo will not work in all circumstances. The chances of success appear to be directly proportional to the quality of the patient's relationship with the healer. The healer's attitude to the patient, his or her ability to convince the patient that he or she is not being taken lightly, and his or her success in gaining the patient's full confidence, are all vital factors, not only in maximising the usefulness of the placebo, but in the treatment of disease in general. However it is doubtful whether the placebo or any other treatment would prove effective without the patient's will to live; that is, without a positive attitude to life. The importance of a person's psychological attitude in health and illness is currently the focus of much attention.

Healthy attitudes

This is nowhere more evident than in relation to stress. There is now little doubt that stress contributes to a great deal of illness, both psychological and physical, and it has become fashionable to think of stress itself as the major disease of the twentieth century. Increasing concern about the stress of modern life led to various attempts during the 1960s and subsequently to score the stress impact of life events and produce 'stress' tables as a guide to the amount of stress a person can withstand. Typically events were rated on a scale between 0 and 100, with an event such as the death of a spouse being assigned the maximum stress rating. Consequently the view of stress most widely promoted in recent years is that stress is caused by external factors beyond personal control and so must be avoided. Stress has therefore become a negative concept and stress avoidance the goal of many people pursuing health and happiness. However, it is now recognised that the interaction between life events and the individual is considerably more complex than was first recognised. An unhappy marriage or poor working conditions, while not events *per se*, may nevertheless be highly stressful. Moreover, not only life events but also ordinary mundane occurrences and irritations need to be taken into account because major life events are frequently accompanied by minor concerns, and in the short term these are better predictors of both psychosomatic and physical symptoms than are major life events.[109-111]

While awareness of these factors would appear to justify growing concern with stress, the stress impact of an event, whether major or minor, may be very different when viewed objectively from the way it is experienced subjectively. Furthermore the impact of the same event may vary, often dramatically, from person to person. Assigning a fixed numerical stress rating to an event can therefore be very misleading. Recent stress scales[112] are more sensitive and score individual events on a ten-point scale and include items such as buying and selling a house, increasing a mortgage, having a child commence school, and pet-related problems. Nevertheless the emphasis on stressful events implies that stress is beyond the control of individuals and obscures their role in determining stress. However, 'people construct circumstances for themselves which they then react to with stress; that is, they are not being stressed by external events beyond their control, but are stressing themselves'.[113] Hence stress is an option rather than an inevitability, which arises mainly from the individual's attitude towards and interpretation of events.

The stress associated with an event depends to a great extent on whether the person appraises it as a threat or a challenge; as positive or negative. Those who view an event positively tend to see it as an opportunity to learn, grow and develop, whereas those who view it negatively tend to experience it aversively, as stressful, and try to avoid it. The former not only cope with a series of stressful events without becoming ill, but may actually thrive as a result.[114]

Differences in appraisal can result in enormous differences in how people respond to potentially stressful events and the amount of stress they experience.[115] 'Hardy' executives who remained healthy in circumstances where their less hardy colleagues became ill, were found to have totally different attitudes than their fellow workers, despite being similar in terms of other psychosocial variables. Characteristically they had a strong sense of commitment to themselves, their work and families; a sense of control over their lives; and an ability to see change in their lives as a challenge rather than a threat. They accepted change as an opportunity for growth and self-development and sought novelty, tolerated ambiguity, and showed mental flexibility in dealing with life's problems. They also availed themselves of social support when they needed it. By contrast, the less hardy executives experienced a sense of powerlessness, were threatened by change, anxious in the face of uncertainty and lacked social support. The characteristics of psychological hardiness identified in this study have since been confirmed in studies of managers, other professional groups and patients. However, a significant factor emerged in relation to army officers. While a sense of commitment and control appeared to protect officers from stress, those who were oriented towards challenge were in fact more prone to illness. This suggests that when a person's need for stimulation is not matched by opportunities for it, more illness can result. The tendency to accentuate the negative outcomes of stress obscures the important stimulus value of change, challenge, and novelty in spurring people on to achievements and satisfactions. If avoided entirely inertness and boredom would result, which ultimately might prove more stressful and hazardous because studies of sensory deprivation show that under-stimulation can cause the central nervous system to go awry and produce both mental and physical disorders. Hence 'the bored brain may be as damaging as the blitzed one'.[116] Accordingly, the concept of stress has been modified over recent years so as to distinguish between stress, that is, the subjectively experienced effects of an event, and stressors, the events per se; and takes into account not only the nature of the stressor – its frequency, duration and intensity – and the individual's resources for dealing with it, but also other psychological variables such as the person's need for stimulation and excitement, and attitude toward, and interpretation of, events.

Studies of cancer patients[117] have suggested that their attitude is vitally important in determining the outcome of the illness. Those with spontaneous remission of cancer are found to be positive in attitude. A clear correlation is also found between mental attitude and length of survival.[118] Cancer patients who outlive predicted life expectancies have been found to refuse to give up in the face of stress, to be more non-conformist, with greater psychological insight and flexibility.[119] Flexibility, or the willingness to make changes, seems to be a particularly crucial factor in recovery. Those who respond poorly to treatment are usually characterised by rigidity and holding on to self-image and the familiar.

Relaxation as an antidote to stress

The importance of relaxation as an antidote to stress, in the prevention and treatment of illness, and the maintenance of health, rests not only on relaxation of the body and bodily tensions, and concomitant physiological changes, but also on a number of other factors. By promoting muscle sense it increases bodily self-awareness and attention to bodily cues, and may reveal pain and other symptoms of illness ordinarily masked by high levels of tension.[120] This is particularly important in persons with a tendency to repress painful and distressing experiences. Relaxation also promotes relaxation of mental attitudes, beliefs, negative emotions and expectancies. Indeed, relaxation can only be fully effective when this is achieved, because physical tensions are the inevitable consequence of mental tensions and conflicts. Relaxation is most effective when positive expectancy is instilled.[121] Positive attitudes, emotions and beliefs can thus be considered life-enhancing, even life-giving experiences.[122] Therefore creating attitude change – sometimes referred to as attitudinal healing – focuses on trying to shift a person in a more positive direction. It works on the principle that if a person can change his outlook he can change the world around him and himself. Rigidity is viewed as a response to threat or fear, so the person is encouraged to let go of the fear and transform it into a positive emotion and acceptance.[123,124] This idea forms the basis of various widely popularised self-healing approaches. The requirements for such attitude change are the ability to accept criticism, recognising it as the other person's problem, and often as an expression of jealousy; acceptance of the self, and affirming self-worth; seeing the positive in all circumstances, and problems as situations from which one can learn; looking forward with joy rather than backwards in sorrow; focusing on what one has rather than what one lacks; learning from mistakes and converting them into successes; letting go of what is no longer needed and making the most of what one attracts.[125] In essence, attitudinal healing can be viewed as cultivating a relaxed approach to life.

Humour and laughter

Humour and laughter can play an important role in relaxed living. A sense of humour enables people to see the funny side of situations that might otherwise be stressful and also to take themselves less seriously. Not only can it help overcome negative attitudes and emotions but it may also assist in overcoming illness.[126] Sigmund Freud observed that humour is liberating because it enables us not to be distressed by the provocations of life, or compelled to suffer its traumas.[127] An essential element of humour is that it shows that life's traumas can also be opportunities for pleasure. It puts a new perspective on stressors and alters attitudes and responses to them. Hence James Thurber's observation that 'humour is the only solvent of terror and tension'.[128] In the East humour has always been regarded as healthy or wholesome, in the sense that a person responds as a whole to it. The observable reaction to humour, laughter, is regarded as medicine in its own right. In the West the idea that mirth is 'sufficient cure in itself' is not new. Mirth was recommended as medicine in the Bible, by the early Greek philosophers and healers who prescribed comedy as treatment, and by philosophers such as Hobbes, Kant, and the famous physician Sir William Osler. Its most enthusiastic proponent in modern times was Norman Cousins who attributed his recovery from an apparently incurable condition to the healing power of laughter.[129] Yet it is almost certainly true that in the West, we don't take humour seriously enough. While it is widely accepted that laughter might help a person feel better it is only relatively recently that its physical effects have been investigated. Psychologically laughter is inconsistent with anger, which is widely considered to be a factor in the onset of many cancers and other illnesses associated with suppression of the nervous system.[130] Claims regarding the beneficial effects of laughter focus on neurotransmitters. The preliminary results of studies suggest that laughter reduces levels of neurotransmitters such as cortisol and adrenaline, whose levels increase in response to stress and bring about immunosuppression. Laughter also seems to stimulate the secretion of catecholamines, which in turn release endorphins, neurotransmitters that stimulate the pleasure centre in the brain,[131] and promote feelings of well-being and relaxation. In this way laughter may counteract the negative effects of stress and negative emotions which can trigger suppression of the immune system.

Recognition of the therapeutic value of humour has led to the formation of the Nurses for Laughter Group at Oregon Health Sciences University, which has introduced laughter-producing paraphernalia on hospital wards; and to clowns helping children to cope psychologically with illness in the Big Apple Circus/Clown Care Unit at New York Babies' Hospital. A 'humour room' has also been opened at St. Joseph's Stehlin Foundation for Cancer Research, Houston and St. John's Hospital and Health Center in Santa Monica, California, offers patients a humour channel on closed-circuit television. In France specially trained clowns are being used on children's wards, and in Britain laughter therapy workshops are being promoted as part of health care and stress management programmes by some regional health authorities.

The ability to see the lighter side of life is now being widely claimed to be advantageous in the cure of illness, in the control of pain, and in increasing chances of survival and improving the quality of life of those who are seriously ill. These claims find support in a number of studies.[132] It has been established that showing elderly patients humorous movies has a significant effect in relieving pain and improving mood, and that listening to humorous audiotapes reduces stress levels.[133] Laughter does have measurable physical effects on bodily processes. A 'good' laugh exercises the muscles of the face, shoulders, diaphragm and abdomen, and more robust laughter involves the arm and leg muscles. It has been claimed that laughing 100–200 times a day is equal to about ten minutes of rowing. 'Hearty' laughter speeds up heart rate, raises blood pressure, accelerates breathing and oxygen consumption. It produces 'huffing and puffing' similar to that resulting from exercise, and so has been described as 'internal jogging'.[134] As laughter subsides, it is followed by a brief period of relaxation during which respiration and heart rate slow down, often to below normal levels, blood pressure drops and muscles relax. 'Mirthful laughter' can also have a significant effect on immune functioning. It has been found to produce significant reductions in the plasma levels of cortisol, 3, 4-dihydrophenylacetic acid, epinephrine, and growth hormone.[135] 'If stress is found to be associated with an increased susceptibility to immunologically mediated disease through mechanisms that are associated with activation of the sympathetic nervous system, this study suggests the possibility that psychologic relevant activities which relieve stress may have a beneficial effect on health'.[136] While the findings of research do appear to confirm the biblical claim that 'a merry heart works like a doctor', it is as yet unclear whether the brief immunological changes associated with laughter can exert lasting health benefits. It my be that possessing an enduring sense of humour is more important.

The suggestion that teaching cancer patients a variety of self-help methods which encourage attitudinal change could increase their chances of survival[137] has found support in various studies.[138-141] Patients using psychological methods have been found to survive 2–3 times longer than would have been predicted on the basis of national norms. After five years, 51 per cent of those who did so were living compared with only 16 per cent of patients who had not received the same treatment.[142] However, medical opinion on the issue remains divided. On the one hand doctors agree that patients' attitude is vitally important to their survival and that it is important to do everything possible to support those with serous illness. Yet on the other hand they tend not to agree on whether or not it is appropriate to offer specific psychological approaches and imply that they may cure or influence the course of disease.[143] Accordingly the medical establishment has been slow in implementing psychological approaches, or carrying out controlled trials of their effectiveness. Attempts to establish a scientific basis for psychological approaches have been hampered because accounting for psychological factors complicates medical investigation with multiple variables that exceed the capacity of current research paradigms.[144] Findings concerning psychological interventions are thus still limited, and both controlled clinical trials and carefully documented case studies are still needed. In practice, doctors often ignore psychological factors totally, and programme patients with negative rather than positive expectancies. Conventional medical approaches are therefore likely to increase the likelihood of stress rather than reduce it, and to prompt patients to seek other approaches which offer hope, and the prospect of recovery.

10

Visualisation

Research in psychoneuroimmunology offers clear proof that what passes through the mind can produce alterations in the chemistry of the body and affect physiological functioning, health and illness. Although understanding of the processes involved is still rudimentary, awareness of this mind–body connection is not new. It is at the very core of shamanic belief and practice, and has informed most traditional healing practices throughout the world. Some 400 years before PNI emerged the French essayist Montaigne anticipated modern understanding by indicating that a 'powerful imagination begets the thing itself', and supported this claim with numerous observations. He considered it 'likely that miracles, visions, enchantments and the like extraordinary phenomena derive their credit chiefly from the power of the imagination', but indicated that ordinarily the imagination is quite powerful: 'We sweat, we tremble, we turn pale and blush through the shock of our imagination, and lying back in our feather-bed we feel our body agitated by its power, sometimes to the point of expiring... I do not wonder that imagination brings on fevers and death in those who give it a free hand and encourage it'.[1] He was in no doubt as to the potentially deadly consequences of a person's worst imaginings, relating the incident of a woman, who being told in jest that she had eaten a cat pasty, 'was taken with a looseness of the bowels, accompanied by fever, and it was found impossible to save her'.[2] He also related the case of a man about to be hanged, who died as his eyes were being unbandaged to have his pardon read to him, 'killed by the mere stroke of his imagination'. He considered that imagination killed passion as effectively as people, citing numerous incidences of male impotence which he attributed to this cause. Nevertheless, he recognised the imagination's power to cure as well as kill, and detailed ways in which it could be successfully used to remedy this and other conditions.

Montaigne also realised that physicians routinely employed powerful imagery when dealing with patients. He gave the example of a man normally prescribed several enemas who responded as effectively when the usual procedures were followed without the enema. Montaigne therefore anticipated the role of the imagination in health, illness and healing, by several centuries.

A dramatic contemporary example of the role of the imagination in healing relates to the cardiologist Bernard Lown, who while on his rounds with his students, pointed out a patient who had what he called 'a wholesome, very good third-sound gallop' to his heart. In medical terminology a gallop rhythm means that the heart is badly damaged and dilated. The patient was critically ill and, as nothing further could be done for him, had little hope of recovery. Yet he made a full return to health. He explained later that as soon as he heard Dr Lown describe his heart as having a 'wholesome gallop', which he took as meaning that it had a strong kick to it, like a horse, he became optimistic about his condition and knew that he would recover.[3]

A contemporary American doctor[4] has described one of his colleagues 'pitting his medicine against that of an adversary' by conducting a 'de-hexing' ceremony, and thereby successfully curing a patient who was dying in response to a shaman's spell. The specific aim of shamanic ritual and spells is to capture the imagination of individuals and direct it to certain ends, healing or otherwise. Throughout history medical practitioners have quite deliberately exploited the power of the imagination in their use of placebos.

The placebo effect

The placebo is a medicine or procedure with no intrinsic therapeutic value which is applied more to please and placate the patient than for any organic purpose. It originates in the Latin *placebo* meaning 'I shall please'. It is highly probable that until relatively recently most medicines were placebos. In ancient Egypt patients were treated with lizard's blood, crocodile dung, swine's teeth, asses' hooves, putrid meat and such like, yet there is little doubt that patients considered these treatments effective, paid highly for them, and revered their physicians.[5]

Placebos have been demonstrated to be as or more effective than real medicines in the treatment of pain and a wide variety of diseases[6,7] which implicate the autonomic, endocrine and immune systems. However, within Western medicine the placebo or 'doctor who resides within'[8] is widely regarded as a nuisance factor that contaminates the effects of 'real' treatments. For this reason placebos are used in control studies to determine the efficacy of medicinal drugs. When a drug is tested, a group of subjects are given placebos – fake substances – in order to find out exactly how much of the drug's effectiveness is really the patient's imagination. It is only relatively recently that these effects have been investigated seriously. Traditionally within Western medicine 'placebo' is a pejorative term, with connotations of quackery and pseudomedicine. Nevertheless within medicine it is also widely acknowledged that the prescription paper, rather than what is written on it, is often the vital ingredient in recovery. However, the doctor is the most powerful placebo of all, in that the chances of successful treatment seem to be directly proportional to the quality of the doctor–patient relationship, that is, the extent to which the patient imagines that the doctor's interventions can and will be effective.

It may well be that any effective treatment may simply be a ritual that culminates in some patients believing that it will work. It has been suggested that hypnosis may be a placebo, which for some patients, in some circumstances, is highly effective.[9] Such a view is consistent with the observation that 'human suffering responds to the spoken word rendered by compassionate persons cast in the role of healer',[10] and with the recently acknowledged negative placebo or *nocebo* effect[11] whereby treatment known to be effective does not work because the patient doesn't expect it to.[12] This phenomena is well illustrated by the case of Mr Wright who achieved a remarkable remission in his cancer in response to the newly introduced and much acclaimed 'wonder drug' Krebiozen, only to succumb quickly to the disease when the drug was derided as ineffective.[13]

Some degree of placebo reaction is probably involved in the administration of every medication and therapeutic procedure. Studies suggest a 55 per cent placebo response in many, if not all, healing procedures.[14] This response is likely to vary according to the circumstances and physiological make-up of the individual.[15] However, to claim that the effectiveness of these approaches is no more than a placebo effect is highly controversial. Nevertheless, the use of placebos in drug trials is an implicit acknowledgement of the power of the imagination.

The Franklin Commission which reported in 1785 concluded that the effects attributed to Mesmerism were due solely to the imagination. By so doing they 'threw out the baby with the bath water', effectively dismissing imagination along with Mesmerism as a subject for scientific investigation. Almost 200 years later scientists attributed the effects of hypnosis to the vividness of the imagery created by the subject in response to suggestion.[16] Indeed the effects of meditation, hypnosis, auto-hypnosis, auto-suggestion, autogenic training and biofeedback have all been attributed largely to the individual's ability for visualisation.

Imaginative medicine

The imagination has always played a key role in medicine. Folk medicine throughout the world is based on vivid imagery, and the oldest and most widely used system of healing in the world, shamanism, has been described as the 'medicine of the imagination'.[17] Shamanic healing works on the body by creating powerful imagery in the patient. So too, it is claimed,[18] do shrines such as Lourdes, miracle cures, unproven remedies and placebos. Common to each of these events is that they all serve to alter the *images* or the expectancy that the persons hold regarding their state of health; and this, it seems, brings about physiological effects.

Although the imagination has been used throughout the history of medicine, whether explicitly as a means to manipulate cure, or implicitly in every interaction between the medical practitioner and the patient, its role in health and illness has been ignored or overlooked in orthodox Western medicine. It is only relatively recently that the physiological effects of intense imagery have been determined.

Physiological effects of imagery

During the 1920s it was found that the Russian mnemonist Shereshevskii could increase his heart rate by imagining himself running, and alter the size of his pupils and his cochlear reflex by imagining sights and sounds.[19] However, Jacobsen[20] was the first investigator to establish that subtle tensions of small muscles or sense organs accompany imagery and that appropriate motor neurons are activated when particular body movements are imagined. It was subsequently demonstrated[21] and more recently confirmed,[22] that muscle tension increases in subjects who imagine lifting progressively heavy weights.

Later studies indicated that salivation could be induced by imagining sucking a lemon[23] and that imagery can also elicit changes in blood sugar levels, gastrointestinal activity and blister formation.[24] It was established that intense sexual and phobic imagery is accompanied by dramatic physiological changes;[25-31] that changes in heart rate, galvanic skin response, respiration and eye movement are associated with negative images; and that images of sadness, happiness, anger and fear can be differentiated by cardiovascular changes.[32,33] Research[34] also suggested that aspects of immune functioning could be influenced by imagery.

More recently the effects of imagery on various physiological functions, notably heart rate, blood pressure, blood flow, electrodermal activity and immune response, have been confirmed. Many studies have reported an increase in heart rate in responses to images of emotional and physical arousal[35-44] and decreased heart rate in response to relaxing imagery.[45-49]

Increases in electrodermal activity have also been demonstrated in response to images of emotional and physical arousal.[50-59] Experimental studies have confirmed that the diastolic blood pressure of normal subjects is raised in response to images of anger; and systolic blood pressure elevated by images of both anger and fear.[60,61]

Experimental studies have also demonstrated changes in blood flow in association with imagery,[62-65] while clinical studies have shown that vivid images can be used to either increase internal blood flow or decrease external bleeding.[66-68]

Within the past decade experimental and clinical studies have confirmed earlier suggestions that immune functioning may be influenced by imagery. The response of white blood cells and the efficiency of hormone responses to standard tests of physiological stress can be enhanced by appropriate imagery,[69] increasing the number of white blood cells in circulation, and the levels of thymosin-alpha 1, a hormone especially important to the T-helper cells. Other indices of improved immune function have also been reported in response to imagery;[70-73] and it has been suggested[74] that patients recovering from AIDS owe much to the effects of imagery on immune function. These findings prompted an awareness that it might be possible to control physiological functions formerly thought to be auto-nomomic or involuntary by imagery, and to harness this ability more systematically in the treatment of illness.

Studies have demonstrated that heart rate can be controlled, blood pressure lowered and homeostatic balance achieved by way of imagery.[75-81] In applied research relaxing imagery has been used successfully to reduce systolic blood pressure in patients receiving chemotherapy.[82] Long-lasting reductions in systolic blood pressure of hypertensive patients have been induced[83,84] using relaxing images. Imagery has also been shown to increase the likelihood of cancer regression;[85-93] to relieve pain, nausea and anxiety in cancer patients;[94,95] and reduce the side effects of cancer chemotherapy.[96,97]

Visualisation

How the imagination achieves physiological effects remains unclear, but in recent years a clearer understanding of the processes of the imagination has emerged. Individuals vary in the range of images they produce and as to whether they are predominantly 'visile, audile or motile',[98] but for most people visual images tend to predominate. The ability to produce visual images – to 'see in the mind's eye' – something not at the moment visible or capable of being viewed, is termed visualisation or fantasy (from the Greek *phantazein*: to make visible). With the exception of a small minority of individuals suffering certain kinds of brain damage, everyone is capable of visualisation, although not everyone is aware of the extent to which they do so in everyday life. While the externalistic standpoint of the West typically may train an impoverished imagination relative to the 'visionary mode' of the East, it is simply not the case, as has been claimed,[99] that people in the West do not use visualisation to any great extent in their daily lives. For most people, visualisation is a normal feature of their cognitive functioning, used in the planning, coordination and execution of everyday activities, decision making, problem solving and creative thinking. It is true, however, that the emphasis within psychology has been upon the study of language and verbal memory, and that scientific investigation of imaginal processes has only very recently begun. Moreover, it has been concerned almost exclusively with visual imagery and has largely neglected auditory, kinaesthetic and olfactory imagery.

Research into visual imagery

Since the 1970s, studies of visual imagery[100-104] have suggested that subjects perform very similar mental processes when perceiving and imagining objects, and that these processes operate on properties of the relevant objects, even when those objects are not physically present. The finding that a purely mental image that is internally generated and transformed is virtually as effective as an external comparison stimulus is perhaps the most direct evidence available for a functional equivalence between imagery and perception.

These studies have only considered static images, yet scientists' self-reports suggest that performing dynamic operations with images, such as rotating them in space, is what confers most of their creative power.[105] Certainly the notion of 'turning something over in one's mind' is commonplace. It would seem that 'equipped with the awareness of the physical form of an object, we can clearly imagine all the perspective images which we may expect upon viewing from this or that side'.[106] Studies confirm that this is the case,[107-110] and that mental transformation is the internal analogue of the corresponding physical transformation of the external object. This analogue process can be particularly effective for dealing with complex structures and operations of such structures. By imagining various objects and their transformations in space many possibilities can be explored without taking the time, making the effort or running the risk of carrying out those operations in reality.

Neuropsychological bases of visual imagery

The equivalence of visual imagery and perception as indicated by this research has given rise to the belief that they activate similar physiological mechanisms. That is, visual images generate similar, albeit not necessarily identical, internal response states to those generated by the actual stimuli themselves. The main source of supporting evidence comes from studies of brain-damaged patients with selective visual disorders and, more recently, from brain-imaging techniques, some of which investigate regional brain activity during mental activity. Studies of brain-damaged patients provide further evidence in support of the premise that non-sensory visual structures that normally subserve object recognition are also involved in object imagery.[111-113] A number of studies using brain imaging techniques with normal subjects have revealed activation during mental imagery in sensory regions of the visual system. Studies using electrophysiological techniques have also provided evidence that mental imagery evokes visual sensory activity in normal subjects.[114] Conversely, stimulation of the sympathetic nervous system leads to an increase in visual imagery. This, it is suggested,[115] results from release of the memories in the right temporal lobe, mediated through the amygdala and limbic system as part of the stress response. When this excessive sympathetic state occurs, the visual imagery can be very vivid.

Neurological bases of visual imagery

However, little progress has been made in understanding the neurological basis of visual imagery. Research initially appeared to suggest that the two cerebral hemispheres are specialised for different cognitive functions: the left hemisphere being primarily concerned with language and language-related functions, and the right hemisphere with a variety of non-linguistic visual/spatial functions,[116,117] mental imaging[118] and emotion.[119,120]

Achterberg drew on the well-established assumption that the right hemisphere is primarily implicated in imagery and emotion, and activated during stress, in proposing a neuroanatomic model of image function in the mediation of brain and bodily processes. However, as she indicates 'other areas of the brain besides the cortical hemispheres are obviously necessary to move consciousness downward to contact and alter physiology'.[121] She argues that if the right hemisphere is primarily implicated in emotion it must have a direct relationship with the autonomic nervous system. She supports this supposition by pointing to the vast network of neural connections between the right hemisphere and the limbic system, which she identifies as a processing area for the emotions, the activities of which involve the autonomic nervous system. She also points to structural and functional relations between the limbic system, and the hypothalamus (which regulates body rhythms, heart rate, respiration, blood chemistry, glandular activity and immune functions) and between the hypothalamus and the pituitary gland (which regulates the hormonal systems of the body, affecting every organ, tissue and cell of the body). Achterberg claims that there is sufficient evidence about the specific functions of the right hemisphere, and its connections with other brain and body components, to support the premise that images 'can and do carry information from the conscious fore to the far reaches of the cells'.[122] In this way they mediate between mental and bodily processes: 'The evidence for the neuroanatomic bridge between image and cells, mind and body, exists. It is solid, and can be viewed when brain tissue is placed under a microscope'.[123]

Achterberg suggests that because the verbal functions of the left hemisphere are one step removed from the autonomic processes, both in evolution and function, messages have to undergo transformation by the right hemisphere into non-verbal or imagerial terminology before they can be understood by the involuntary or autonomic nervous system. Similarly, before the imagery characteristic of right hemisphere functions can be processed into meaningful logical thought it must be translated by the left hemisphere. The images intimately connected with physiology, health and disease are, she argues, preverbal, without a language base, except what is available through connections with the left hemisphere. If these connections were to be severed and the left hemisphere thereby rendered inaccessible, untranslated messages would continue to affect emotions and alter physiology, but without intellectual interpretation. She points to the disorder alexithymia (literally, without words for feelings) as suggesting that this does occur. In this, as yet little understood, condition emotions and images which remain untranslated are thought to be expressed physically in various body systems, and the resulting damage eventually diagnosed as rheumatoid arthritis, ulcerative colitis, asthma, hives, migraine and other psychosomatic disorders.

By virtue of linguistic communication with others the left hemisphere may be conceptualised as an interface with the external world. Accordingly, Achterberg proposes that imagery of the right hemisphere is the medium of communication between consciousness and the inner world of the body, serving as the means whereby 'unconscious' non-verbal physiological processes become conscious or verbalisable. The limbic system is the area in which this 'translation' occurs. Moreover, as is the case with any bridge or 'border' area (from the Latin *limbus* meaning border) it can, in principle at least, be used in two directions, and therefore translate verbal messages into non-verbal imagerial terminology. Imagery is therefore construed as a bridge not only between left and right hemispheric processes but also between different levels of the self: between psyche and soma. As such, Achterberg claims a role in psychology for imagination similar to that conceived by Aristotle, in whose cognitive psychology it was the bridge between sensation and thought: 'imagination is impossible without sensation, and conceptual thought is impossible without imagination'.[124]

In the context of imaginative medicine the notion of images as transformers or translators of different kinds of 'message' or information in the brain is in itself quite persuasive. It accounts quite adequately for both the physiological effects of imagery and its diagnostic reliability. Furthermore, PNI research suggests that the limbic system is a probable location for such processes. However, the neuropsychological links between imagery, emotion and immune functioning are not as clear cut as Achterberg suggests. Indeed, the complexity of the problem is evident in the diversity of views concerning cerebral localisation of imagery.[125] Although the most common and long-standing view, supported by considerable evidence[126] is that imagery is predominantly a right hemisphere function, it now seems clear that neither hemisphere can be excluded. The assumption made by numerous authors that imagery is a right hemisphere function is not supported by all the available evidence. Other well-established notions about cerebral laterality, such as the links between the right hemisphere and emotion have also been challenged.[127] This research suggests that the left hemisphere is involved in processing positive emotions and stimulating the immune system, while the right hemisphere is involved in processing negative emotions and suppressing the immune system, either directly or by mediating and/or inhibiting the activity of the left. This finds some support in observations[128] that left-handed people are more susceptible to auto-immune disorders. Other research[129] have suggested that patients who exercise the right hemisphere during imagery exercises may 'distract' it from suppressing the immune system. It has been claimed that 'comprehending these neurophysiological mechanisms of cognitive activation and control will be critical to understanding immunological competence'.[130]

Despite research findings linking specific functions to each hemisphere, it may be that such differences relate more to the 'style' of information processing than the information processed.

> In other words, it is not so much the case that each hemisphere is uniquely specialized to work with different things (e.g. the left hemisphere with phonemes and the right hemisphere with musical tones) rather, it is that each hemisphere is organized structurally to provide a different cognitive style. Each style is more or less well adapted to processing different types of information.[131]

It has also been argued[132] that the left hemisphere is best suited for 'detailed' processing that can be most aptly considered as 'high resolution' or 'high-frequency' information, and the right hemisphere better suited to processing larger non-detailed 'low-frequency' information.

One conclusion to be drawn from the available evidence, is that all the suggestions emerging from the research are partly correct. 'Neural structures in both hemispheres must have the representational information and processing capacities associated with imagery phenomena, but they participate differentially in different functions of imagery'.[133] In this view, imagery is multifaceted and not localised in any specific brain area; different regions in both cerebral hemispheres, and possibly subcortical regions, being responsible for different imagery functions.

Psychological functions of visual imagery

While the precise neurophysiological and neuropsychological mechanisms underlying imagery remain unclear, it seems that the key to understanding its psychological function lies in its role as a transformer or transducer of information in the brain. It facilitates the translation of both verbal and non-verbal outputs, and 'communication' between relevant processes. Contemporary research supports the ages-old wisdom that images effect a link between cognition and sensation (mind and body) and thus between essentially conscious processes amenable to language and those that are not. They may therefore provide an insight into the archaic mind of man.

As an alternative, albeit complementary, cognitive representational mode to the verbal, imagery provides quite literally a new perspective on, or way of looking at, issues. It is particularly suited to the representation of issues which in themselves are non-verbal. For example, physiological and emotional processes that are relevant to both physical and psychological health. By so doing it increases the range and flexibility of mental functioning, providing a tool which greatly benefits problem solving, decision making and creative thinking. As imagery and perception are neurologically similar processes, experience in the imagination can be viewed as psychologically equivalent to actual experience. Thus as a means of reality testing and problem solving it is often superior to 'rational' strategies. Moreover, because imagery is isomorphic with perception it has a greater capacity for descriptive accuracy than verbal logic which is linear rather than a simultaneous representation. This 'patterning of ideas and images gathered up in a simultaneous constellation'[134] means that thinking in images is very much quicker than verbal thinking. It is instantaneous and global rather than sequential, and, in the manner of visual perception, conveys complex information more immediately than verbal language. A picture *is* worth more than a thousand words, it seems.

The simultaneous representation of images results in a time sense or perception of time quite unrelated to serial clock time. This effectively relieves pressure and tensions associated with time-related stress. Together with the absorbing quality of imagery, it promotes relaxation, thereby increasing the flexibility of functioning (both mental and physical) and awareness, two key characteristics of healthy functioning and survival.

Images relate to physiological states in ways suggesting both a causative and reactive role,[135] therefore the physiological effects produced by imagery can be induced consciously and deliberately or unconsciously. Imagery can also provide important clues to physiological functioning. It therefore provides a tool for accessing and utilising mental and physiological processes of which people are generally unaware or unconscious, and as such is an important tool for self-discovery and creative change. It has been suggested that imagery may be a more direct expression of the unconscious than linguistic expression; it is less likely to be filtered through the conscious critical apparatus, because generally words and phrases must be consciously understood before they can be spoken.[136]

In the light of contemporary understanding of the functions of visual imagery

it seems reasonable to believe that images hold enormous potential for healing, and it is not surprising that extensive claims about the promise of imagery for therapeutic benefits have been made. A large body of recent scientific research on imagery indicates that these claims are justified.[137]

Hence it is unsurprising that visualisation has been a key feature of healing throughout the history of medicine.

Visualisation in the history of Western medicine

The promise of imagery for yielding therapeutic benefits has been recognised since the earliest times and is evident in the practices of shamans throughout the world. Shamans invoke powerful images in themselves and others as a means of discovering unconscious clues to the onset of illness; emotional and mental factors that might have contributed to its development, and in order to influence the course of illness directly or indirectly. As such shamans use imagery in both diagnosis and treatment.

Dream imagery was used diagnostically and in treatment by the ancient Egyptians and Greeks. Diagnosis and treatment also took place during the state of consciousness just prior to sleep, when what are now known as hypnogogic images would occur, bringing insight and healing. Many cures were ascribed to this procedure.[138]

In the Hippocratic system of medicine, imagery, notably that of dreams, was thought to reveal clinically important diagnostic information and to foster the development of malignancy once established. Galen anticipated modern research findings by indicating that images of sadness, terror, or fright produce discrete physiological effects.

During the Middle Ages medicine was largely practised by witches or wise women whose 'flights on broomsticks' may more properly be regarded as 'flights of fantasy' within the unconscious for the purpose of divining information relevant to the treatment of illness. There is little doubt that they were powerful and effective healers, and their understanding of the healing process is reflected in Paracelsus' assertion that 'man is his own doctor... the physician is in ourselves and in our own nature are all the things we need'. Nevertheless in the eyes of the Church their cures were the work of the devil and had to be purged.

However, with the decline of physical medicine, imaginative medicine flourished. 'The treatments of choice specified by the early Church were medicine of the imagination in every sense; shrine cures, processions and pilgrimages to holy places, relics of the saints and martyrs'.[139] Healing was no longer attributed to Asclepios and his family but to saints, notably Cosmas and Damian, who became the patron saints of the healing profession throughout Western civilisation. Churches dedicated to them used the method of incubatio, or incubation sleep, modelled on the divine sleep cures of the Greeks. In these the sick received diagnostic information and cures from revered healers, images of whom appeared during the twilight state between sleep and wakefulness. This practice continues within the Christian church, as does its reputation for effecting exceptional cures. Hence, 'the methods of the shamans and the wise women – healing in non-ordinary reality and invoking visions of spirit guides – has been a part of Christianity since its inception. Only the names have been changed'.[140]

Imaginative medicine continued to flourish even when the heretics and witches did not. By the sixteenth century (the era of Paracelsus and Montaigne), the imagination was generally considered to be a powerful factor in health and illness, capable of producing illnesses and curing them. Paracelsus considered it a most important tool in medicine, describing it as man's 'invisible workshop'.[141] However, by the seventeenth century philosophical rationalism and science had created a split between mind and body, and the role of the imagination in healing was ignored as emerging 'medical science' focused its attention solely on the body. In the eighteenth century the role of the imagination in healing was tacitly acknowledged by the Franklin Commission but nevertheless dismissed from further consideration.

Visualisation in Eastern medicine

As in the West, Eastern medicine has relied heavily on imagery since the earliest times. In Eastern cultures health is viewed as a harmonious balance between constituent qualities and energies of man and the universe. Its fundamental premise is that man must be regarded as a whole, with no separation of body, mind or soul. Imagery has been used for many thousands of years in these cultures to achieve this state of health or wholeness.

Visualisation in Indian traditions

Mantra yoga combines the use of sound with imagery. A mantra may be repeated as a person imagines healing light,[142] or imagined as a mandala, a complex circular pattern which represents symbolically the intricacies of the Ultimate Reality. Kundalini yoga also achieves its aims of mastery of the senses and generation of intense body heat primarily by way of meditation and imagery. Imaginative methods are also commonly used in tantric yoga.

Imagery in Tibetan traditions

Imaginative exercises which derive from ancient Tantric texts are also a feature of Buddhism, notably that of Tibet.[143] Typically these direct the person to imagine being 'eternally in the shape of a deity', the precise details of which are vividly and meticulously specified as in the manner of guided fantasy, or involve mandalas. Exercises in self-control may involve attention to and focus on images.

In traditional Tibetan medicine, healing practices are complex and often elaborate, and diverse imaginative methods are used. A widely used visualisation exercise involves the mandala of the medicine Buddha. A variation of this is to visualise oneself as the medicine Buddha. Visualisation of light plays a large part in Tibetan medicine. Brilliant white or coloured light is imagined radiating from a deity and purifying both mentally and physically as it flows through the person. The light can be directed by the person to a diseased area of his or her body, or outwards into the universe if healing others. Another healing meditation involves imagining the deity of purification sitting on the top of one's head. The light streaming from him descends into and illuminates the body, and all mental anguishes and physical ailments dissipate and exit the body in the form of blood, pus, smoke and insects.

Visualisation in Chinese and Japanese medicine

Traditional Chinese medicine also uses visualisation in the promotion of health. Individuals are encouraged to enhance, redirect and normalise chi by imagining it in various ways. As chi is commonly conceived as the vital energy or breath which animates the cosmos, considerable emphasis is placed on energising the individual through correct breathing, and visualisation is used to assist this process. In Chinese martial arts traditions a common breathing exercise is to imagine the breath being drawn in through the nose as light and travelling down the spine to a point approximately two inches below the navel referred to as T'ian T'ien or the Golden Stone, before being drawn up through the chest and out of the mouth. The image of fog or nothingness filling up the body from bottom to top may also accompany deep breathing. T'ai Chi Chuan, a system of exercises designed to promote the flow of chi through the body-mind, also incorporates specific images of chi. A feature of perhaps the best known technique of Chinese medicine, acupuncture, is that the practitioner imagines blending his or her chi with that of the patient during treatment.

Reiki and other forms of Japanese healing aim at channelling, directing and balancing the universal life energy within oneself and from person to person through the hands by way of visual images and symbols.

Common to all Eastern traditions is an emphasis on the importance of meditation for achieving wholeness or health and it is central to most healing practices. The basis of much meditational practice is visualisation of symbols, objects, deities or abstract qualities. The physiological effects achievable by meditation, like those attained through biofeedback, have focused attention on the role of imagery in the control of bodily processes, or self-regulation.

Visualisation and self-regulation
Biofeedback

We have long known that the muscles of the heart, stomach and intestines have responded to images and emotions; thinking of something frightful leads to fear, which leads to vascular and intestinal responses. Biofeedback is showing us that these same 'involuntary' muscles also respond to volition and visualisation. Biofeedback is making the most of this knowledge and these abilities accessible to everyone, and biofeedback is making our potential for conscious control of the unconscious scientific, measurable, and verifiable.[144]

Pavlov found that not all subjects can be successfully conditioned, and attributed unsuccessful conditioning to innate physiological inhibition in subjects. However, studies have linked the variability of conditioning in human subjects to differences in visual imaging. Poor visualisers who are unable to fantasise and who seldom remember dreams have most difficulty in achieving the biofeedback response.[145] The strength of appetitive galvanic skin response conditioning is positively correlated with the vividness of subjects' tactile imagery.[146] Heart rate deceleration conditioning has also been found to be stronger in a group of vivid visualisers than in a group of poor imagers.[147] On this basis it has been claimed that Pavlovian conditioning of autonomic responses is mediated by mental imagery.[148]

Individual differences in the effectiveness of biofeedback have been attributed to differences in imaging ability. Subjects who produce more vivid imagery have been found to produce greater heart rate increases,[149] greater electrodermal activity,[150] and greater electrodermal control.[151] The effectiveness of biofeedback has also been linked not only with the ability to visualise but also to the use of imagery during biofeedback. Subjects who successfully altered skin temperature were found to be those who spontaneously imagined such temperature alteration.[152] Similarly subjects who successfully lowered and raised blood pressure and heart rate were those who spontaneously imagined tranquillity in association with the former and emotional agitation with the latter.[153–156] Other studies[157,158] have shown that during biofeedback for relaxation, subjects who successfully attenuated their electromyographic responses were those who spontaneously imagined tranquillity.

Research has explicitly compared the effectiveness of biofeedback alone, biofeedback with imaging instructions, and imaging without feedback. In research on vasomotor control[159,160] it has been found that biofeedback with instructions to imagine warmth, produces greater skin temperature increases than biofeedback alone. In research on relaxation, biofeedback augmented by visual imagery has been found to produce greater electromyographic decrements than biofeedback alone.[161] However, for some subjects biofeedback interferes with imagery.[162] In a study of heart rate control[163] smaller heart rate changes were produced by biofeedback than by emotional imaging without biofeedback and by hypnotic suggestion without biofeedback.

Collectively the above studies suggest that many successful effects of biofeedback can be reduced to autonomic effects of visualisation. Moreover the last study raises the possibility that many autonomic effects of hypnotic suggestion can also be the effects of visual imaging.[164]

Visualisation and hypnosis

Although it remains a controversial area in both theory and practice, what is not contested is the importance of mental imagery in hypnosis.

> Hypnotic suggestions do not ask subjects explicitly to enact overt behaviour, rather they inform subjects that a specific behavioural event will occur, while inviting them to engage in imaginings that are consistent with the occurrence of that behaviour... For instance, imagine a force attracting your hands toward each other... As you think of this force pulling your hands together, they will move together.[165]

These suggestions may be augmented by visual imagery. Thus, for example, arm levitation, where a subject is instructed that one arm will rise higher and higher (which is a common index of a subject's hypnotisability) may be accompanied by appropriate imagery, such as balloons or strings attached to the subject's hands, tugging upwards and drawing the fingers up with them. Hence the effects of hypnosis have been attributed to the vividness of the imagery created by the subject in response to suggestion.[166] Certainly many nineteenth century commentators considered, as did the Franklin Commission in the eighteenth century, that hypnosis and its effects were brought about by the subject's imagination. Liebault concurred with this view, claiming that hypnosis was brought about by auto-suggestion, the physiological effects of which Coué claimed, were the result of the imagination.

Visualisation in autogenic training

Visualisation is a key element in autogenic training, most of the advanced stages of which involve 'the summoning and holding of certain images in the mind for examination and exploration of their effects on consciousness'.[167] The images are intended to produce an intensification of psychic experience by increasing a person's ability to experience inner psychological processes visually.[168] Visualisation exercises include holding a static uniform colour in the mind's eye, then imagining various colour formations such as clouds, shadows or movements, then multicoloured patterns or forms, and eventually objects, such as faces, masks, statuettes and the like. Abstract concepts such as freedom and justice are then transformed into images and elaborated upon. Over a period of weeks the training progresses to the generation of complex, dynamic images in which archetypal and religious themes often emerge.

> At this point the individual may become an active participant in the material which comes to him and experience himself as an actor in the tableau which his mind presents... The quality of the state the trainee achieves is very like that of dreaming and is at least equally vivid and real. He begins to experience the collective dimensions or the transpersonal dimensions of consciousness. When

the mind calls up scenes in which the individual begins to see himself as an active participant, the exercises are called 'film strips'. Later, when there are prolonged periods of self-participation, the visualisation is called 'multi-chromatic cinerama'. In this last, most elaborate phase, where fantasy and reality alternate in the subject matter of what is 'seen', both therapist and patient may derive significant insights into the patient's unconscious. Such insights can be of great use in resolving both psychological and physiological states of disorder and psychosomatic stress.[169]

Finally the individual progresses to imaging other persons, the aim being to provide insight into and modification of affective relationships.

It is highly probable that the effects achieved in all these healing approaches and relaxation methods owe their effects largely to visual imagery.

Visualisation in psychological medicine

Apart from any physiological processes they might affect, the processes of the imagination are widely acknowledged as potent therapeutic agents. The clinical efficacy of images have been ascribed to a variety of processes, both cognitive and emotional.[170] These include the individual's clear discrimination of his or her ongoing fantasy processes; the clues regarding alternative approaches to various situations afforded by images; awareness of usually avoided situations; the opportunity images provide for covert rehearsal of alternative approaches; consequent decrease in fear of overtly approaching avoided situations,[171] the feeling of control and enhanced coping skills gained from monitoring and rehearsing various images.[172,173] Images are also a source of detail about past experiences[174] providing access to significant memories of early childhood before language became predominant,[175] and other features of which a person is largely unconscious. They afford a richer experience of a range of emotions,[176] are effective in by-passing defences and resistance;[177-179] and frequently open up new avenues for exploration when therapy reaches an impasse.[180] For these reasons visual imagery is widely used in psychological medicine.

Schultz recommended that the advanced stages of autogenic training which involve visualisation could be used effectively in psychotherapy. These 'waking dreams' are fully consistent with a long-standing tradition of using imagery within psychological medicine. Freud and Jung focused attention on the importance of imagery in providing insights into the unconscious mind.

Guided imagery

The influence of Freud and Jung can be seen in the work of Carl Happich who developed his approach to psychotherapy in the 1930s and 1940s.[181-183] Rather than work with images produced spontaneously by a person in dreams or fantasy,

Happich chose to present certain symbols which his patients were invited to explore in the context of an imaginary journey, guided by him, until their meaning had been discerned.

Unlike Jung, Happich was to remain a fairly minor figure in the history of imaginative medicine. His importance lies in having introduced into therapy the method of guided imagery. This can be likened to a waking dream, or a 'movie in the mind' which the person is guided through by another.

Directed daydreaming

Robert Desoille also advocated the therapeutic use of the 'waking dream' or 'directed daydream'.[184,185] In this approach the person journeys in the imagination, relating psychic experiences and reactions to the therapist, who does not suggest the whole fantasy but directs and controls it by offering symbols which can serve as crystallisation for the fantasy.

Using methods he called 'deep relaxation and symbolism', Walter Frederking[186] also encouraged his patients to engage in fantasy during progressive physical relaxation and to describe their experiences and discoveries as they progressed from unclear visions to increasingly clear productions of a kind of 'symbolic stripthought'.[187] This symbolic thought, which Frederking considered to have significance similar to dreamlife, was allowed to flow by with the patient as both playwright and actors. In this way, Frederking believed the person could directly confront the contents of his or her personal unconscious and relate them directly and dramatically to psychic problems.

Freidrich Mauz[188] used a related method with psychotic patients. By way of monologue, he depicted the patient in representative scenes from childhood, with the aim of unlocking suppressed emotions so that a meaningful dialogue could later emerge. He also led patients on imaginary journeys which he believed would awaken positive feelings and meanings in the person, and enable them to contact their feelings and the world around them.

Hanscarl Leuner[189-192] developed Guided Affective Imagery along similar lines. His patients were invited to enter and explore a series of ten predetermined scenes representing major conflict areas in life and to provide the therapist with a commentary on the experience. It was used originally without music but music was added by Leuner and others in the belief that it enhanced the efficacy of the method. Extended visual fantasies with a narrative commentary are also a feature of Oneirodrama,[193] which is initiated by certain standard symbolic scenes and preceded by relaxation procedures. The Italian psychiatrist Roberto Assagioli used guided imagery, day dreams or symbols as a means of allowing his patients to mediate between conscious and unconscious material themselves. He conceived of symbols as 'containers' of meaning, and therefore as transformers and conductors, or channels of psychic energies. For Assagioli, as for Jung, wholeness or health requires the integration of imagination, intuition and inspiration with rational, conscious processes. It is a psychosynthesis, a bringing together of different modes of consciousness. The goal of his therapy was not only to explicate these various levels of awareness but by thorough exploration of them to reconstruct the total personality, shifting it to a new centre through examination of its fundamental core, and thus enhancing personal and spiritual potential. Assagioli viewed every element of images as representing, at one level or another, a personality trait, albeit distorted, misplaced or projected. He encouraged identification with all aspects of the images as a means of assimilating repressed or otherwise dissociated material into a new construction of the self.

All of these dream or waking dream therapies, collectively termed oneirotherapy (from the Greek *oneiros* meaning sleep), rest on the belief that the symbolism inherent in visual imagery constitutes an affective language that expresses unconscious motives without fully imposing them on conscious recognition. Therefore, it is assumed that the participant will show less resistance to the expression of underlying motives. In general, these methods have been reported to be effective in uncovering the structural details of the client's personality, in discovering the nature of affective trauma, and in quickly ameliorating symptoms.[194] These methods also have the advantage of being suitable for use with relatively unsophisticated persons and those prone to rationalisation.[195]

Guided imagery is often used where a person's representation of issues is too limited to enable coping in a given area, or where a therapist wishes to challenge existing representations. Indeed the effectiveness of this method has been attributed to two major functions: the opportunity it provides to present a person with an experience which is the basis for representation of issues in his or her cognitive model where previously there has been little or none; and to challenge the person's previously impoverished model.[196] Although it is preferable to work with a person's spontaneous imagery where possible, recognition of the effectiveness of guided imagery in introducing greater flexibility of cognitive functioning has led to its proliferation within psychotherapy and counselling.

Visualisations used include the 'inside the body' journey, where a person imagines journeying through his or her body in order to gain insight into physical problems and attitudes; taking an imaginary inventory of the body, engaging in imaginary dialogue with internal parts of oneself, creating and interacting with an imaginary inner guide, dying in one's imagination, visualising communication between the two hemispheres of the brain, exorcising the parents from various parts of the body, and regressing into the previous life; and much more. Exercises in guided imagery (also referred to as 'creative visualisation'), directed towards personal growth, psychological transformation and positive mental health commonly used in psychotherapy, have been compiled and published for a general audience.[197-209]

Behaviour therapy

The publications in English by Assagioli[210-214] helped to draw attention to the techniques of imaginative medicine. These had been widely disseminated throughout Europe in the early twentieth century by clinicians influenced by Freud and Jung, but because of the influence of behaviourism, they were virtually ignored within the field of psychological medicine in Britain and North America until the 1970s.

Even so, imaginal methods were not entirely obliterated, and many behavioural approaches serve to demonstrate that images are powerful stimuli which elicit emotional responses. Procedures such as systematic desensitisation and emotional flooding[215,216] use imagery in conjunction with relaxation in the modification of phobic behaviour, and in attempts to change or reduce inappropriate or exaggerated responses to stress. Indeed, a prerequisite for effective application of desensitisation is the ability to conjure up reasonably vivid images.[217]

Systematic desensitisation

Systematic desensitisation, sometimes referred to as the method of reciprocal inhibition, is the most widely used of all behaviour modification techniques for the amelioration of emotional problems. It has been applied extensively in the treatment of irrational fears or phobias and expanded to deal with a great variety of other symptomatic patterns associated with neurotic disturbance.

Initially it involves careful analysis of the nature of the phobia and the range of situations in which the phobic individual experiences anxiety. A hierarchy or sequence of different images relating to the feared event or object is then constructed, ranging from the least to the most frightening. The person is then encouraged to engage in progressive relaxation and while relaxed is confronted progressively with items in the hierarchy. In theory, as each image is presented to a deeply relaxed person it loses a certain increment of its associated anxiety.

In a variation of this procedure the relaxed person is encouraged not only to produce the frightening images but to replace them with pleasant images. The entire method critically depends on the private imagery of the individual. In effect the therapist merely establishes conditions of relaxation and a systematic way for the person to engage in the imagery. Essentially the images or the responses that will be desensitised are developed by the individual and are completely under his or her control.

Since the key feature of the treatment is the patient's ability to produce imagery and to carry out, in the presence of the therapist, the day dream about various events in his life, the effect of the treatment is in part a testimonial to the great human capacity for producing fantasy material with the power to modify behaviour. So in a curious way, we come full circle. The behaviourists, who have been most critical of the emphasis by psychoanalysts and humanists on private experience and internal events in the personality, have ended up developing a treatment method that is particularly effective because it relies extensively on the imaging capacities of the patient.[218]

Aversion therapy

An approach employed by behaviour therapists in the treatment of alcohol and drug abuse, sexual deviation and anti-social behaviours has been to provide the patient with an extremely unpleasant or negative experience when he or she actively participates in the undesired behaviour. Electric shock and nausea-producing drugs have been used widely in the 'treatment' of homosexuality, alcohol and drug abuse and sexual festishes. However, as administration of these is often hazardous and complex, a number of behaviour modification therapists have now moved towards using the patient's own imaging capacities rather than external agents to provide a repellant experience for those who are trying to control unwanted behaviour. The covert desensitisation method[219,220] is based on this approach, and similar principles have been used in other procedures.[221,222]

A highly controversial 'implosive therapy' has also been developed[223] in which, rather than the patient forming suggested images in a state of calm relaxation, the therapist uses images to create a situation of intense anxiety, hoping thereby to 'implode' away symptom formation. The therapist therefore presents the patient with his or her worst imaginings surrounding an event or situation, the assumption being that if the patient imagines the worst and nothing happens, the tendency to associate fear with this image in subsequent confrontations will be reduced.

Humanistic psychotherapy

Humanistic psychologists during the 1960s and subsequently once again focused attention on imagination, dreams, and fantasy. Influenced by the practices of imaginative medicine in Europe and the East, many of them developed novel imaginative methods.

One of the most influential was Frederick (Fritz) Perls. Through his Gestalt therapy he demonstrated that imagery is a rich source of information about the self and that there is no limit to the kinds of imagery that can be created and used effectively in therapy. He highlighted a diversity of methods by which these images may be accessed and explored. These included guided fantasy, the famous 'empty chair technique' (see Chapter 4, p.105), dreamwork and psychodrama.

Psychodrama is a psychotherapeutic approach developed by a contemporary of Freud, the Viennese psychiatrist Jacob Moreno. In developing psychodrama, Moreno was seeking an alternative to the predominantly verbal approach of orthodox psychoanalysis that facilitated psychological healing through powerful emotional release or catharsis. In psychodrama a principal actor or protagonist dramatises his or her problems and conflicts in the company of several auxiliaries under the direction of a therapist who assumes overall responsibility for the ensuing drama, and uses a number of imaginative techniques in facilitating the dramatic process. These methods include imagination, role playing, and play acting, and were subsequently widely adopted by many therapists, including Perls who recognised their value in the exploration of fantasy.

> We can make use in therapy of fantasizing and all its increasing states of intensity towards actuality – a verbalized fantasy, or one which is written down, or one which is acted out as psychodrama.[224]

Acting has been described[225] as the 'physicalisation of the imagination'. Perls, like Jung, appreciated this, and saw the importance of exploring everyday fantasy, in addition to dreams. Instead of inviting other people to play the different roles in the fantasy, as in psychodrama, he asked the client to play all the roles. Perls termed this form of dramatisation, **'monotherapy'**. He claimed that by requiring a person to create and enact his or her own stage, characters, props and dialogue and to direct and orchestrate every performance 'monotherapy thus avoids the contamination of the precepts of others, which are usually present in ordinary psychodrama'.[226] Perls also required his clients to 'shuttle' or alternate between the manifest content of a fantasy or dream and its associations, so as to understand its symbolic significance and sharpen their awareness by providing them with a clearer sense of the relationships in their behaviour.

Perls' ideas and methods have been assimilated directly and indirectly into other psychotherapeutic approaches.

Arts therapies

Dramatic methods are among other image-based 'healing' arts widely used in psychotherapy. These include all forms of artwork, painting, sculpting, modelling, mask making, puppetry, dance, poetry, the creation of mandalas, and much else. Art therapy *per se* was not used in Britain until the 1940s, and until the 1980s there were no criteria for the professional training of art therapists. There is still no generally agreed consensus about its scope and applicability. Commonly it is viewed as a way of dealing with mental illness, because it has been developed and most widely used in the field of mental health, but it can be used by anyone who wishes to use art as a medium for exploring and expressing themselves.[227] Some proponents of art therapy view it purely as a diagnostic tool. Certainly it has been applied effectively in this way in the field of physical medicine.[228-231] Freud viewed art diagnostically, as evidence of a patient's pathology, while Jung viewed the images of artwork therapeutically, in the same way as those of dreams, as a key to the artist's unconscious life, and a means to healthy self-expression and transformation. These differing views are still evident within art therapy. Some art therapists pay little attention to the production of art. They consider that the therapy lies in discussion of the completed work, while others feel that the process of making art is intrinsically therapeutic and is the most important aspect in promoting change in a person.

> The healer has used art – painting, sculpture, dance, music, poetry, storytelling, all art forms – in patient care for many reasons. Art therapy and expressive arts have concentrated on releasing inner stories in a psychotherapeutic way to free emotions and heal the psyche. Healing art programs have concentrated more on the power of the creative process to heal directly, without analysis. Their belief is that just making art heals by freeing images from the inner world and putting patients in a place where they are in a creative state. This state is similar in physiology to other healing states and to prayer. Thus, making art is similar to meditation, relaxation or guided imagery in that it changes physiology by having the person concentrate on images that produce the autonomic nervous system shift and the adrenal, immune system changes that tend to produce healing states.[232]

However, for both the healer and artist, art heals in the same way. Images held in the brain stimulate the hypothalamus and the autonomic nervous system and change the autonomic parasympathetic nervous system, brain waves, immune state, and the neurotransmitters. They also affect others, transpersonally and affect the person's spiritual state. For healers art is a complementary therapy similar to guided imagery, but with the advantage of not appearing as threatening to some patients and directors of health care.[233]

> Art heals in several ways. Broadly, it heals as a process, where the patient makes art, or as an experience, where the patient meditates on or views art. First, as the patient makes art, images from the inner world are freed and they resonate spirit, mind and body.
>
> ... images surface that are transformative in nature. They are the images of deep space, relaxation, ascension, change and birth. They are the images of pain and darkness brought to light and changed into images of love and control. Second, art is used as a device to access and hold mental images. When patients concentrate on an image, hold it in their minds, a mental shift occurs. These images are made by artists to heal the viewer, and meditation on them produces a state similar to that of the artists when the images were made.[234]

A leading exponent of the use of the arts in therapy, Shaun McNiff, insists that

> virtually everyone who uses art in psychotherapy believes in the ability of the
> image to explore and communicate and offer insight outside the scope of the
> reasoning mind. However, there are sharp distinctions in how we treat pictures
> once they appear. These attitudes range from approaching them as graphic
> designs for evaluating the mental conditions of artists, to greeting them as angels
> who come to offer assistance.[235]

Nevertheless they all recognise that everything that a person makes or creates has
an autobiographical aspect in that these products are expressions of imaginal
experience and therefore a self-portrait of psychic life. This is certainly the view of
Violet Oaklander,[236] an exponent of using Gestalt therapy in the treatment of
children. She observes that a child's fantasy process is usually the same as the life
process so it is possible to look into the child's inner realms through fantasy. In
this way it is possible to expose what's hidden or avoided and find out what is
going on in the child's life from the child's perspective. She observes that fantasy
is often a means of expressing those things a child has trouble admitting to in
reality, and that many art techniques, including string painting, inkblot painting,
finger painting, and drawing the family as symbols or animals, lend themselves to
fantasy. Her declared goal in using these techniques is to help the child to become
aware of him or herself and his existence in the world.

McNiff considers that the use of the arts in therapy represents a return to the
shamanic origins of art as medicine. 'Images and the artistic process are the
shamans and familiar spirits who come to help people regain the lost soul.' Thus
the creative art therapies are 'contemporary manifestations of ancient shamanic
continuities'.[237] He takes the view that loss of soul is a metaphor for detachment
from feelings and the essential self. As he points out, it cannot be lost in a literal
sense because it is ever-present, but contact with or sight of it can be lost, and he
believes that this estrangement from our nature results in mental and physical
illness. He insists that it is the nature of soul to be lost to that aspect of mind that
strives to control it. In other words, people lose a sense of themselves and contact
with their feelings because of the influence of the rational, logical, intellectual
mind that always strives for self-control. This aspect of mind has to be relaxed in
order for them to experience their essential selves. He maintains that salvation of
the soul comes about when people engage in their environment and restore their
relationship. He uses a quotation from Ferrini's play *Shadow Talking*[238] to convey
this idea: 'If you could forget who you think you are you might catch up with what
you really are and can't see'.

Clearly theatre is one way in which this occurs. Engaging in the dramatic
process, whether by acting or watching, brings about these kinds of insights and
transformations when the fantasy is entered into wholly. It then becomes a reality,
but can only do so because there is a suspension of disbelief, of rational thinking.

This state can be regarded as being on automatic pilot, because the normal control mechanism, the reality factor, the thinking or conscious mind, is relaxed. McNiff considers that automatism – painting from this dreamlike state – is central to art therapy. The dramatic element comes about through the process of establishing dialogue with images. This focuses attention on what is present in the phenomena that have been created by the mind. In art therapy this is initially based on observation of the structural properties of images, their shape, colours and so on. Psychological significance comes about by relating these visual features to the intimate details of the interpreter's life – the interpreter always being the person who produced the image and never the therapist.

The visual arts and music

The connection between the visual arts and music has a long history. Specific paintings have often inspired composers. And music has always evoked visual images.'[239] One way of enhancing appreciation of music is through creative visualisation, 'seeing' images, colours and scenes that the music suggests, or creating 'stories' to accompany music. Musical performance can also be enhanced by dramatic means such as role playing: 'becoming' a successful performer; 'becoming' the music by imagining being the performance, or imagining being a musical instrument.[240] Absorption in and involvement with music in this way may also be therapeutic. Indeed music therapy is based on this premise, and it is widely acknowledged that music has healing properties which can be applied in the treatment of various conditions.

For centuries people have believed there is a profound link between music and health. Modern research has established that music can influence blood pressure, circulation, metabolism, respiration and muscular energy in both animals and humans[241] and as a result music is increasingly used in treatment. Vibro-acoustic therapy where patients are placed in a music bath whilst played specially chosen music is known to improve the condition of children with cerebral palsy, to relieve back pain, arthritis, circulatory problems and benefit other conditions.[242] It reduces heart rate and other indices of anxiety in patients prior to surgery.[243] These effects are due partly to the relaxing effects of music, and also because it is now known to stimulate the release of serotonin and norepinephrine, which alleviate depression and create a sense of well-being, and endorphins which block pain. However, music therapists consider that the therapeutic benefits of music extend far beyond its physical effects. ' "Creative music therapy" provides a means of communicating, interpreting and understanding the body and mind beyond language, and beyond its common use as a simple pleasurable activity'.[244]

This awareness is evident in healing practices since the earliest times. Shamanic practices traditionally incorporate sound as an integral part of healing rituals. This may be produced by chanting and drumming but in many cultures other instruments are used.[245]

> The shaman is the musician, i.e. he or she makes the music and induces trance. The repetitive rhythmic patterns of instrument or voices serve to induce trance states in which the shaman 'sees' the cause of illness as disharmony in the sick person's world (Samuels and Samuels 1975).[246] Often the shaman employs acceleration or deceleration of tempo and an increase and decrease (crescendo and decrescendo, respectively) in volume. Sometimes she or he uses both accelerando and crescendo together, further increasing an excitatory state that enhances trance.[247]

Although many therapists use verbal suggestions or guided imagery to induce imagery, and some use drumming,[248] sounding a gong[249] or chanting,[250] it is perhaps the case, as Skaggs has suggested, that introducing drumming or chanting into clinical practice would be unacceptable to most traditionally-orientated therapists and their clients. Nevertheless, Skaggs argues that it is not necessary to abandon the musical aspects of shamanism. She claims that the **Bonny Method of Guided Imagery and Music** (GIM), 'which integrates ancient and contemporary beliefs and practices in a dynamic, transformational therapy in service of physical, psychological and emotional healing' (Skaggs 1990, *op. cit.* p. 19), features many similarities to shamanic practices, and may be the link between the past and the present.

GIM was developed in the late 1960s by Helen Bonny as 'a process of evoking imagery through music-listening'.[251] It focuses on inducing an altered state of consciousness in the client by playing specially chosen music on cassette tape as an accompaniment to visualisation exercises centred around the 'standard situations' of Leuner's Guided Affective Imagery. It is claimed that focusing on the music serves to deepen the altered state of consciousness. 'At the same time, through its form and structure, music provides a container for the process as it serves to dissolve barriers to deeper levels of consciousness'.[252]

From the perspective offered by McNiff, all arts therapies, and all those which rely upon visualisation, afford access to and exploration of what Aboriginals refer to as the 'eternal dreamtime', the unconscious areas of the mind beyond rational thought, which is the traditional 'hunting ground' of the shaman. Implicitly, therefore, they represent a return to the shamanic tradition of healing.

The return of the shaman

There has been an upsurgeance of interest in shamanism in recent years, prompted partly by recognition that its practices are relevant to contemporary health issues and partly by the realisation that, unless preserved, this ancient source of knowledge, already obscured by generations of rational 'scientists', will be obliterated. Symbolic imagery from a wide variety of occult, mystical, magical and shamanistic sources has been incorporated into various forms of psychotherapy. [253–255] Imaginary 'power animals' typically invoked by shamans in healing rituals, have re-emerged as allies of the therapist. [256–259] Native American wisdom has become *de rigueur* as traditional totemic symbolism has been absorbed into therapeutic approaches, and the vision quest has become an accepted psychotherapeutic procedure. Within this climate numerous self-appointed and controversial shamans[260–262] have emerged or been identified[263–265] and have drawn popular attention to shamanism. Michael Harner, Associate Professor of the New York School of Social Research has helped to make the experience of shamanic reality more accessible to Westerners and taught them how to access and apply the healing powers of the shaman in workshops throughout the USA and Europe. Courses and workshops on contemporary shamanism are increasingly commonplace in the USA, Britain and Europe. The shamanic world view is also increasingly evident in the field of psychological medicine. Articles in psychiatry journals frequently liken the work of psychiatrists to that of the shaman, and 'shamanic' approaches to health and healing are being advocated within the health care professions in Britain,[266–268] and practised in America.[269] Given the growing recognition of their usefulness it is becoming increasingly difficult to find areas of psychological medicine where imaginative methods are not used.

Visualisation in contemporary Western health care

Nevertheless, it is quite probable that imaginative methods would have remained within the confines of psychotherapy had it not been for Carl Simonton, an oncologist, and his wife, Stephanie Matthews-Simonton, a psychotherapist. Combining the insights derived from many different fields of research, they argued[270] that as emotional and mental factors, including stress, play a significant role both in susceptibility to and recovery from all disease, including cancer, the first step in getting well is to understand how these factors have contributed to illness, and to find ways of influencing them in support of treatment. They also recognised that a cancer diagnosis in itself creates stress and other negative psychological responses such as fear, hopelessness and despair, which further depresses the immune system of the cancer patient, leading in many cases to a poor prognosis.

They believed that visualisation might help such patients in a number of ways: firstly enabling the person to relax, so decreasing tension and counteracting the effects of stress. This, they suggested, would improve immune function. They considered that visualisation might also help cancer patients confront their fears of hopelessness and helplessness, enabling them to gain a sense of control and change in attitude. The visual images produced might also provide a means of accessing and exploring unhealthy beliefs hidden in the patient's unconscious mind and so yield valuable insights into their condition. Carl Simonton taught his patients a simple form of relaxation and encouraged them to hold in their mind the image of a pleasant place. They were then asked to visualise their illness in any way it appeared to them, and the form of treatment they were receiving. Having done so, they were to imagine the cancer shrinking or otherwise responding in a positive way to treatment. Patients were also encouraged to imagine pain in the same way rather than trying to suppress it, and they were encouraged to draw their cancer and their pain and to use these drawings as a basis for exploring these issues with those treating them.

Of 159 patients with a diagnosis of a medically incurable malignancy treated over a four-year period, none of whom were expected to live more than a year, 22.2 per cent were reported to have made a full recovery. The disease regressed in a further 17 per cent of patients and stabilised in 27 per cent. Further tumour growth was reported in 31 per cent of patients but average survival time increased by a factor of 1.5–2. Those who eventually succumbed to malignancy maintained higher than usual levels of activity, and achieved a significant improvement in their quality of life.[271]

Abundant anecdotal evidence, including accounts by children[272] has since supported the Simontons' claim that relaxation and visualisation have an important role to play in the treatment of cancer as adjuncts to orthodox medical treatment. Improved cancer outcome related to the use of imagery has been reported,[273] and support has also been forthcoming from a number of studies,[274,275] which confirm that visualisation has numerous effects, including cancer regression. Guided imagery and visualisation have been found to provide cancer patients with considerable relief from pain, nausea, vomiting, anticipatory emesis, and anxiety,[276–278] and to be effective in reducing the negative effects of cancer chemotherapy.[279]

Increasingly, contemporary practitioners are using imagery in diagnosis and treatment, and to relieve the pain and anxiety associated with medical conditions. The pioneers of these imaginative methods in modern medical practice have been described[280] as trying to bridge the gulf between the different worlds of magic and medical science, mind and body, and termed 'shaman/scientists'. Arguably, however, such a term is misleading, because to a large extent modern practitioners ignore the spirit, which shamans traditionally consider the most important factor in disease, health and healing.

Imagery techniques have been applied and studied in a variety of health care settings for many years 'in the belief that the shamanic techniques that served the world so well in medicine since the beginning of recorded history should not be discarded but improved on'.[281] The techniques have been validated on patients suffering from chronic pain, severe orthopaedic trauma, rheumatoid arthritis, cancer, diabetes, burn injury, alcoholism, stress disorders and childbirth. Moreover, a significant increase in natural killer cell (NK) activity, together with a decrease in antibodies to the herpes simplex virus suggestive of better control of the virus by the immune system, has been demonstrated in a controlled study of patients taught guided imagery techniques.[282] More recently randomised clinical trials of breast cancer patients practising relaxation and visualisation during chemotherapy found higher levels of lymphokine activity. Relaxation frequency and self-rated imagery quality were positively correlated with NK activity, suggesting that relaxation and guided imagery produce immunological change, and that they can modify host defences.[283] Relaxation and imagery were also found to improve mood in women receiving treatment for locally advanced breast cancer,[284,285] although the researchers indicate that it is not clear whether the relaxation or the visualisation is responsible for the results. However, an investigation into pain management in patients with rheumatoid arthritis suggests that visualisation, rather than relaxation, is responsible for pain reduction and improved emotional states.[286]

Evidence for immunoenhancement has also been demonstrated in response to essentially image-based stimuli such as humour,[287] humorous films and audiotapes[288] and compassionate films.[289] In the latter study subjects exposed to a film about Mother Theresa's work caring for the sick and poor showed increased immunoglobulin (IGA) levels regardless of whether they outwardly approved of her work or not. These results suggest that information and suggestions can be acquired by subjects unconsciously and may enhance immune function whether or not the subjects are aware of an effect or emotional reaction. Positive and immune enhancing imagery techniques have also been shown to have specific immunological consequences. Hypnotised subjects, who were encouraged to imagine their white blood cells as sharks attacking the germs in their bodies, showed an actual increase in the number of lymphocytes.[290] Taken together, these studies suggest the possibility of increasing the ability to enhance and control the immune system through conscious or unconscious suggestion, or by exposure to positively enhancing stimuli. Accordingly, interventions with imagery might prevent, or at least delay, the progress of AIDS in seropositive males.[291] Anecdotal support for the role of imaginative interventions in the treatment of AIDS has also been provided;[292] and one of the most significant studies in the area[293] has demonstrated voluntary regulation of a specific immune function through imagery by a subject. Such findings are consistent with the earlier research on biofeedback[294] which provided the first unequivocal evidence that adept meditators could voluntarily control pain, bleeding and infection from self-induced puncture wounds.

Conversely, there are indications that difficulty in visualisation may have adverse consequences. Just as immunological benefits may be achieved by visualisation, the opposite may also be true. Attention was first drawn to the possible relationship between rigidity of imagery and rigid mental attitudes in the 1960s.[295] Mental rigidity is known to be a feature of a number of conditions such as cancer, rheumatoid arthritis, heart attack, and other stress-related conditions. Type A persons, for example, successful as they may appear on superficial scrutiny, are nevertheless handicapped in their ability to indulge in 'introversive experiences of creative thought',[296] a defect which might increase their dependence on achievement in the external mundane world and work. (Arguably, however, their drive to achieve could have decreased their dependence on the satisfactions to be derived from introversive experience.)

Although there is still need for further carefully controlled studies, imaginative methods have been widely adopted in the USA and Europe where they have been enthusiastically promoted by some physicians.[297-299] Certainly over the past 20 years or so research has produced a considerable body of research which has shown that images are a powerful force, with both physiological and psychological effects. It has been claimed[300] that the effects associated with imagery are as potent and real as those produced by any drug and that accordingly, visualisation should be regarded as medicine in the truest sense of the word.

Timely Interventions
as Methods of Energy Conservation

Although in recent years there has been a grudging acceptance, in some quarters at least, that 'timely interventions' such as hypnosis, autogenic training, biofeedback, meditation, relaxation and visualisation may be effective and have a place in modern medicine, they are generally insufficiently understood for their full ramifications to be appreciated. They 'work' by relaxing the predominantly 'left-brain' mode of logical, linear, rational, verbal thought, and crucially, the sense of time as linear, proceeding inexorably from the past, through the present, to the future. This promotes relaxation by relieving time-related stress, and by suspending ordinary thought which generates much of the tension experienced by individuals. Considerable energy is expended in maintaining muscle tension. This energy becomes available when muscle tension is relaxed. Hence relaxation is energising.

Relaxation makes energy available in other ways. Relaxation of verbal thinking enables access to ordinarily inaccessible regions of the self which, because they are beyond normal awareness, may be considered unconscious. These regions constitute non-ordinary reality and awareness of them is a substantially altered state of consciousness in which the person establishes contact with living energies conveying information and ideas.

These energies have been differentiated in various ways. Freud described an unconscious mind underneath ordinary consciousness in which primal energies reside. Jung conceived of the collective unconscious as a realm beneath the individual unconscious – a domain of archetypal energies which may be differentiated and represented symbolically in various forms. Roberto Assagioli considered both these concepts unjustifiably limiting. He argued for the existence of a higher consciousness, which he termed the 'higher' or transpersonal self, in addition to the 'underworld' of the unconscious. One way of conceiving this distinction might be to consider the former as above consciousness and the latter as below it, in a manner analogous to the heavens and the underworld of the shaman. Whereas the energies of the underworld can be differentiated and represented symbolically as gods or guides in various forms, the heavens occupy an undifferentiated frequency domain that can only be experienced directly. A similar distinction between the world of spirits and the world of Spirit is frequently encountered in religious and mystical traditions, notably those of the

East, and in traditions of healing, which strive towards union with and direct experience of the ultimate reality or universal mind. These traditions emphasise that true seeing or direct perception of reality involves 'pure' consciousness, a nothingness or emptiness variously termed Brahman, Atman, the universal Tao, and described as 'the clear light of the void' in Buddhism, or undifferentiated uncoloured light. Irrespective of how it is described, this reality is encountered by looking inwards to the centre of one's being. This realm of consciousness is beyond all forms and appearances, albeit that from which all such forms, appearances and images derive. Meditation or concentration on images and symbols is therefore a means to this end, which ultimately must be transcended. By differentiating the primitive, archaic contents of the collective consciousness and the 'superconscious', as attempted by Assagioli, it is possible to make subtle distinctions between the various kinds of psychic experience in a manner fully consistent with ancient and oriental traditions.

These distinctions are particularly relevant to healing, as will be examined in the following chapters. Those timely therapies already examined not only allow access to normally unconscious domains but also enable a person to *intervene* so as to influence health at these energy levels. Provoking powerful imagery is the means by which this is normally achieved. Other interventions, although manifestly different from those identified here as 'timely', and from each other, also influence health energetically, and can therefore be considered energetic treatments or 'energy medicine'. These approaches to treatment are considered in the following chapters.

Part III

ENERGY MEDICINE

11

Energetic Treatments

Asked to explain the apparent convergence of ideas in modern physics and ancient mysticism, Maria von Franz[1] asserted that Western physicists, extroverts looking outwards towards the cosmos, and introverted mystics looking inwards into their own unconscious minds, had discovered the same truth: that the universe is one great unity; that the process of this whole is an energy dance; and that everything is an energy phenomenon. Both conceive this energy not as some underlying substance or 'stuff' but as dynamic patterns of activity, movement or change (hence the Greek *energeia*: activity) to be understood in terms of vibrations, pulsation, flow, rhythm, synchrony, resonance, and as relative to time.

The understanding that time and energy are relative and reciprocal, interdependent aspects of one and the same phenomenon, found expression throughout the ancient world in mythologies where various gods representing movement were personifications of both time and world-creating energy. In the Hindu tradition the god Krishna reveals his divine role as creator and destroyer of the world with the words, 'Know that I am Time which causes the world to perish when the time is right for it', and the god Shiva bears the title *Maha Kala* (great time) or *Kala Rudra* (all consuming time), and is depicted as the cosmic dancer, who symbolises the energy of the universe.

The gods of ancient Iranian, Greek, Roman and Mayan civilisations were also equated with time:

The archetypal image of god in his world-creating energy is behind most personifications of time. Psychologically speaking this god personifies psychic energy in its multivalent instinctual image-generating spiritual creative power which embraces all psychic processes.[2]

In these cultures time is energy, or change in nature.

Within contemporary physics the same 'truth' is encountered, expressed in the symbols of mathematics rather than those of myth. The modern statement of this relationship is Einstein's celebrated formula $E=mc^2$, where energy is equivalent with matter (or nature as we know it), changing over time. This transformation is also upheld in the psychological domain where the concept of time

> seems to express a relationship of (1) its (time's) content, i.e: what happens in it (travelled space, achieved work etc.), with (2) the speed of its flow in the form of speed – motion being either a speed frequency or a power (force)[3]

and the psychological experience of time[4] is determined largely by the amount of energy – physical or mental – expended in a given activity. It follows, therefore, that modification of one feature will result in change in the other. This is demonstrable in time therapies. Following meditation, biofeedback, hypnosis, autogenic training and relaxation people typically report feeling more energised. The interrelationship between time and energy is also evident in everyday behaviour. Invariably those people who claim never to 'have time' do not use their energies effectively, while those who claim to have no energy rarely use their time effectively. Most stress conditions or 'time sicknesses' are manifestations of energy extravagance in as much that 'tense people spend too much energy',[5] and hence excessive adenosine triphosphate or cyclic ATP, the basic chemical utilised in nerve and muscle cells. However, this relationship is consistently overlooked in orthodox Western medical practice, despite 'lack of energy' being one of the most common presenting problems. Yet it is fundamental to all effective healing practices, which are essentially energetic treatments concerned with the conservation and regulation of vital energy processes.

Energy medicine

Traditional approaches to healing throughout the world since antiquity share a belief in the existence of subtle energies in and around the person. Mobilisation and balancing of these energies are seen as fundamental to health, and illness as the result of their stagnation or disruption. 'In ancient hippocratic medicine the patient was called "asthenis" meaning a person who lacked strength or vital energy; the doctor was "iatros", which means the healer who re-established the "sthenos" or vital energy in the person … medicine has moved away from this model toward the pathology of life omitting the source of health which is the vital energy'.[6] In the West most concepts of energy, such as Mesmer's magnetic energy, Bergson's Élan Vital, Reich's orgone or bio-energy, von Reichenbach's odic force and the Theosophists's ether, were developed when Western science was formulated in exclusively objective, mechanistic terms. Accordingly life energy is frequently conceived as some kind of substance which flows through the organism. This notion is reflected in Freud's use of the term 'libido', which derived from the Latin *libare*: to pour.

In the East concepts of energy, variously referred to as chi, ki, prana, Kundalini, or Shakti, are markedly different, and akin to those of pre-scientific Western civilisations, notably ancient Greece and Egypt. Energy is conceived not as 'anything' but as continuous movement or change. It is relative, and rests on an inner polarity, or regulative function of opposites which flow into one another. This view was revived in more recent times by the German embryologist Dreisch, who adopted Aristotle's concept of *entelehkia* or *entelechy* – the vital force which directs the life of the individual – to describe the impetus which urges the organism to self-fulfilment: a concept similar to the vital force described by the founder of homeopathy, Samuel Hahnemann, and to the self-actualising tendency of psychologists Abraham Maslow and Carl Rogers, and the psychotherapist Fritz Perls.

However, the most striking similarities with ancient and Eastern concepts of energy are found in the ideas of Carl Jung. He claimed that psychic and physical energy are two aspects of one and the same reality, the world of matter appearing as a mirror image of the world of the psyche, and vice versa. He designated energy as physical when it is physically measurable, and as psychic when it becomes psychically or introspectively perceptible. Accordingly, 'the psyche should be capable of appearing in the form of mass in motion, and insofar as psychological interaction takes place, matter should possess a latent psychic aspect'.[7]

The fundamental concept common to these views is that all matter, including the human body, the psyche and all phenomena, comprise energy in a particular state of vibration, and have both physical and psychic aspects. Such a view is fully consistent with modern physics. Accordingly wave motion, light, heat, colour and sound are merely different forms of vibration, as are thoughts, images, and emotions. Healing approaches based on this view use the various states of vibration to restore energy imbalances within the mind and body. Energy medicine therefore involves a number of techniques which are believed to influence the organism at a more fundamental level than the physical or psychological symptoms of illness.

> When we realise that in the final analysis our bodies are in fact made up of nothing but energy in constant transformation it is easier to understand how subtle non-physical energetic influences such as emotions and thoughts can have a direct influence on our physical functioning, just as our physical functioning can have a direct influence on our emotional and mental experiences.[8]

Unfortunately not enough people do realise this. Even within the scientific community many find it hard to accept the principles of contemporary science, much less accept that these have been mapped out with striking similarity throughout the world since antiquity. Yet this is clearly the case.

The Chakra system

The Hopi Indians, who believe themselves to be the oldest inhabitants of the earth, view the human body and that of the earth as isomorphic. Both have an axis (in man, the spine) along which, they maintain, there are several vibrating centres or vortices which distribute energy through the body. The first centre at the top of the head receives life energy at birth and is the seat of communication with the creator. The second centre is situated at the brain, the third at the throat, the fourth at the heart, and the fifth at the solar plexus. Similar beliefs are common among Native American Indians and the Inuit. They are also a feature of early Egyptian, Tibetan and Indian thought, hence the similarity between Hindu symbols and those of Native American totem poles.[9] However, in addition to the centres described by the Hopi, the Hindu system includes a centre situated below the navel and another located over the sacral bone. These are described as three-dimensional pulsating wheels, known in Sanskrit as *chakras*, which rotate rhythmically from the centre, rather like Catherine wheels, in a way which appears to seers and clairvoyants as like a cone, trumpet or convolvulus flower. According to the direction of spin, they either draw energy in or direct it out of the body, thereby energising or enervating it.

Most of what is written about these centres is in Sanskrit or Indian Vernaculars, the minor Upanishads and Puranas, and Tantric works. They were first described in English early this century[10,11] but became more widely known through the writings of Theosophists, members of the Theosophical Society founded in 1875, whose system of beliefs was derived from the sacred writings of India. Nevertheless, evidence that early European mystics were familiar with them comes from the *Theosophica Practica*, issued in 1696 by Gichtel, who was probably a Rosicrucian, from Egyptian monuments, and the ancient rituals of freemasonry.

Leadbetter described the location and Sanskrit name of each chakra as (1) Base of the spine, *Muladhara;* (2) gonads, *Svaddhistana;* (3) solar plexus, *Manipura;* (4) heart, *Anahata;* (5) throat, *Vishuddhi;* (6) between eyebrows *Ajna;* (7) top of the head, *Sahasrara.* In the Hindu system these were traditionally stimulated or 'awakened' by Raja, Karma, Jnana, Hatha, Laya, Bhakti and mantra yoga respectively.

The position of the chakras was described somewhat differently by the Theosophists, who located the second centre at the spleen rather than in the area of the sexual organs. 'From our point of view the arousing of such a centre would be regarded as a misfortune, as there are serious dangers connected with it'.[12] This was not merely a Victorian prudery, for as Leadbetter pointed out, Hindu scriptures warn that 'it gives liberation to yogis and bondage to fools', and the ancient Egyptians had taken elaborate precautions to prevent such an awakening. In addition to these major chakras, a number of minor chakras are variously described in different traditions.

According to ancient wisdom, organisms draw vital energies from the atmosphere and earth by way of a finer, immaterial body on whose surface they are situated. This is variously known as the *vital body* in certain Rosicrucian schools, the *astral, etheric body* or *double* in other Western occult traditions, the *ka* in ancient Egypt, the *doppelgänger* in medieval Europe, *linga sharirah* in the East, and *perispirit* in French spiritism.[13] It is generally regarded as synonymous with the spirit and as surviving physical death. In the Theosophical tradition man was viewed as a soul who possesses a body – several bodies in fact – rather than vice versa. In addition to the visible vehicle by which he conducts his business in the physical world, he has other bodies invisible to normal sight by means of which he deals with emotional and mental worlds. This is also the centuries-old claim of many seers and philosophers, and St. Paul, who stated that 'there is a natural body and there is a physical body'.[14]

The ancient view is that energy in the form of light is drawn into the body's immaterial counterpart, which acts like a prism, breaking it down into seven streams corresponding with the frequency bands of the colour spectrum. Each of these is drawn through resonance to a chakra whose vibrations are of the same frequency. These vibrations become progressively more dense, heavy and lower in frequency along the vertical axis of the body. At its base they merge and arise with earth energies, represented in Indian thought as the coiled serpent Kundalini and in Chinese thought by a dragon. The upward spiral motion of these energies around the central axis of the spine is also represented in the caduceus, the traditional symbol of the healing arts since ancient times in the West.

The chakras, which may be thought of as transmitters or transformers of energy, are believed to vibrate at a characteristic frequency as they distribute energy throughout the body. The energy patterns around each chakra, although always changing, are mostly of a certain colour whose vibrations correspond with its basic frequency. The prevailing colour of a chakra indicates how well its energies are being transformed and transmitted at a given time and therefore reflect current experience.

In ancient traditions each chakra is also associated with a musical note, a symbolic form and certain elements of the same characteristic vibrational frequency. These vary according to tradition. In the seventeenth century Gichtel assigned planets to the chakras, suggesting that they are sensitive to planetary influence, thereby providing a physical basis for astrology. More recently the chakras have also been associated with the location and functioning of the major nerve plexuses of the body, each of which is connected to one of the glands of the endocrine system. The slightest imbalance of energy in any of the chakras is believed to influence the corresponding gland, giving rise to fluctuations in hormones which are secreted directly into the bloodstream, producing immediate changes in mood, appearance, tension, respiration, digestion, intuition and intelligence.

The various traditions hold that by understanding its character, function, associated colour, sound and symbolic form, each chakra can be cleansed, opened and balanced. The correct and balanced action of these chakras is expressed as absolute and perfect health on all levels. These beliefs form the basis of most ancient forms of healing, including the colour and sound therapies of ancient Egypt and Greece, the various practices of yoga, and the use of 'power' objects such as crystals and stones by shamans and witch doctors.

The principal features of the human chakra system common to many traditions are as follows:

The first, root or base chakra, Muladhara, located at a position corresponding with the base of the spine, is the first manifestation of the life force in the physical body. It determines the person's level of physical energy and the will to live in physical reality. It is concerned with basic survival and physical health; and being intimately connected with the prostate and testes in men and the uterus in women, it influences sexual activity and regulates creativity. This energy primarily affects the legs, the hip joints and the base of the spine, overlapping into the pelvic area, providing the strength to support the physical body and influencing safety and security. The coccyx functions on the etheric level as a pump, directing the flow of energy up the spine and connecting each chakra with the life force.

Psychologically, the first chakra is associated with feelings of being securely grounded, 'well rooted', and belonging. It is thought to be mostly red, influenced by Saturn, associated with the element earth, the symbolic form of the square, the metal lead (base metal), the sense of smell and the sound vibration LA. (The symbols and sounds given here are from the Tantric tradition.)

The second or sacral chakra, Svadhisthana, located in the pelvic region midway between the pubis and navel, is considered in traditional systems to be the centre of sexual activity. Because sexuality is an expression of the life force, this chakra is closely related to the base chakra, and influences physical and sexual vitality. It is situated in the region referred to as the gut or belly, which the Japanese term the *hara,* and is associated with the liver, pancreas, spleen, kidneys and bladder and therefore with metabolism, digestion, detoxification, immunity to disease and the balance of fluids and sugars within the body. It is also thought to have glandular connections with the testes and ovaries, and to influence the production of the hormones testosterone and oestrogen.

On the psychological level it relates to passions or 'gut feelings' and emotions, and to issues people care deeply about – power, sex and material wealth. It is associated with the colour orange, the influence of Jupiter, water, tin, the sense of taste, the symbolic form of a pyramid with its capstone removed, and the sound BA.

The third or solar plexus chakra, Manipura, positioned slightly above the navel, is thought of as the centre of personal power or the power to act, and therefore with the sense of vision. It is associated with the adrenal glands, which through the production of adrenaline profoundly affect the sympathetic nervous system, and thereby muscular energy, heartbeat, digestion, circulation and mood.

Traditionally it is related to mental functioning – the intellect or rational mind, intentionality and will – but it is also directly related to the second chakra and so to emotional life. Thought to be primarily yellow, it is associated with Mars, fire, iron, sight, the symbolic form of the circle, and the sound RA.

The fourth or heart chakra, Anahata, found in the centre of the chest over the breast bone, is believed to relate to the thymus gland situated behind the sternum, the main function of which in adults is to create immunity to disease. Traditionally it is associated with love and compassion, feeling, sensitivity, touch, the skin and the hands and with the colour green. Interestingly it is known that many of the body's immune cells are located in the skin and can be stimulated by touch. It is thought to be influenced by Venus, associated with air, copper, the symbol of the equilateral cross, and the two-syllable sound Ya Mn.

The fifth or throat chakra, Visuddhi, located at the front of the throat, is thought to influence the thyroid gland, which affects the metabolism, musculature and heat control of the body. Traditionally it relates to communication and self-expression, to hearing and taking responsibility for one's personal needs. It is associated with sky blue, the planet Mercury, ether, hearing, the symbolic form of the chalice and the sound HA.

The sixth or brow chakra, Ajna, found just above and between the eyebrows in the centre of the forehead, is traditionally known as the 'third eye' and is identified with visual imagery, insight, intuitive understanding, clairvoyance, psychic abilities and ecstasy. It is associated with the pineal gland, which according to contemporary research has a significant role in processing mental imagery and unconscious processes, and is also responsible for the production of the hormones serotonin and melotonin. Its colour is midnight blue or indigo, and its symbols are the moon, gold and silver, the six-pointed star, and the sound AH.

The seventh or crown chakra, Sahasrara, is positioned in the centre of the upper skull. Traditionally regarded as the seat of the soul, it is identified with pure or enlightened being, spirituality and integration of the whole being. It is associated with the pituitary, the master endocrine gland, which regulates the functioning of the other glands, and is closely associated with the pineal gland. Its colour is purple or violet, its symbol the thousand-petalled lotus and its sound the sacred OM (oh a um), which is considered to be the total amalgam of all sound and of all creation.

According to the chakra system, the nature of man is sevenfold. The first and second chakras are mostly concerned with receiving and distributing physical energies, and combine to give a person potency, vitality and the will to live. The third, fourth and fifth chakras are concerned with psychological energies and so with personality and intelligence rather than physical traits; and the sixth and seventh chakras with spiritual energies which express the individual's relationship to the spirit or soul.

The chakras function as an integrated system, rather than in isolation. If one begins to malfunction, so will others, as they attempt to compensate for reduced energy transmission in one centre by working overtime. So the chakra system provides the impetus for the regulated, balanced flow of energy throughout the whole person which is necessary for health.

The aura

Traditionally the flow of energy is not confined within the physical body as this is ordinarily conceived. In the ancient view, the body emits a radiant energy which relates specifically to the location and intensity of energy within it, and reveals how it is functioning. This three-dimensional emanation, which surrounds the body in all directions and extends for some distance beyond its surface, is widely referred to as the aura, and represents the sum total of the energy emitted by the chakras.

Normally invisible but discernible by seers and clairvoyants – who since the earliest times have described it as a large shimmering oval, comprising a mass of fine bright fibres or rays arranged in seven bands, each corresponding with the functioning of a chakra – the aura reveals the physical, psychological and spiritual well-being of the person it envelops.

When the chakras are functioning normally, each will 'open' by spinning clockwise and drawing energy from the universal energy field to distribute throughout the body. When the transmission of energy has occurred, the colour originating from each should be very pale and translucent.

However, when the chakra spins anti-clockwise it remains closed to incoming energies, which consequently are not distributed within the body and show themselves as darker, more dense patches or blotches of colour in the aura. The space between the body and the first colour emanation of the aura is referred to as the ovum. It is not 'empty' as such, being the most dense and therefore most easily visible part of the energy field, but it is colourless or a dull white/gold, so appears to be blank.

The first layer of the aura, the health band, emanates from the base chakra and reflects the overall vitality of the physical body. It is traditionally described in metaphysical literature as red. *The second layer of the aura, known as the emotional or astral band,* emanates from the second chakra. It reflects physical and sexual activity, and 'gut feelings', and is orange in colour. *The third layer of the aura, the mental band,* comes from the solar plexus chakra and reflects mental functions based on the intellect and personal power. It is yellow, and shiny or brilliant in a mentally alive person. *The fourth layer of the aura, or heart band,* emanates from the heart chakra. It is green and reflects inspiration in all forms. *The fifth layer of the aura, or causal band,* comes from the throat chakra and is blue, reflecting self-expression and the karma of the soul – its progress through successive incarnations. *The dark blue sixth layer, or spiritual band,* emanates from the sixth chakra, reflecting the person's spiritual development and intuitive awareness; and *the seventh layer or cosmic band,* reflects the soul principle or cosmic consciousness of the individual. It is purple in colour.

Each band radiates different colours of varying intensity that reveal to those who can discern them the state of a person's health, character, emotional disposition and tendencies, abilities, attitudes, past problems and spiritual development. The aura can therefore be used for diagnosis, and throughout history seers (or sensitives) have reported using it as the basis for healing.

In North America and Canada there has been extensive investigation of clairvoyants such as Jack Schwarz and Rosaline Bruyere, and medical intuitives such as Carolyn Myss, who perceive chakra and aura energies and use them in diagnosis and treatment. This research appears to confirm the observations of the ancients. A study of orthodox Western physicians[15] has also revealed that many diagnose illness through the energy field they perceive around their patients, or through the energy vortices connected with the endocrine system. One doctor who uses auric diagnosis, John Pierrakos, has conducted extensive investigations into the phenomenon,[16] as has physicist and clairvoyant healer Barbara Ann Brennan. She believes that auric diagnosis is especially helpful because 'the aura is really the 'missing link' between biology and physical medicine and psychotherapy. It is the 'place' where all emotions, thoughts, memories and behaviour patterns are located.[17]

Diagnosis of disorder through the aura/chakra system

Traditionally those who understood the principles of the aura/chakra system were seers or clairvoyants, mystics who could perceive the subtle energies of the human energy field directly. Contemporary clairvoyants believe that others can also learn to perceive these energies because this sensitivity is latent in everyone. Those who cannot 'see' the human energy field directly can become attuned to its vibrations. Certainly energy terms are commonly used to describe others as brilliant, sparkling, dim, dull, blue, in black moods, in the pink, or as giving off good or bad 'vibes'.

It has been established that blind and blindfolded subjects can distinguish colours by 'feel'.[18-20] People can also detect various physical sensations in their hands and fingertips when they pass their hands through the energy field of another person some two or three inches above the surface of the body. Heat and cold, tingling, pins and needles, pulsation, pressure or electric shock can provide reliable information about pain and other symptoms of disease, as has been recognised through masseurs and healers throughout history.

The art of dowsing

An ages-old technique for detecting subtle energies is dowsing. This is an ancient art which has been used to locate water, minerals and lines of force deep within the earth, and more recently to sex newly-born chicks and detect submarines.[21] Although depicted on Mayan and Egyptian reliefs and practised throughout medieval Europe, the earliest references to dowsing in English were by Robert Fludd in 1638. The term 'radiesthesia' was applied to the practice at the turn of the century by the Abbé Alexis Bouley in the belief that the phenomena observed in the act of dowsing result from some kind of radiation.[22] Medical radiesthesia became popular in England during the 1930s. It is used in detecting hidden causes of disease which do not lend themselves to identification by means of standard clinical tests, and to find treatments which will eliminate the disease. Psionic medicine developed by Dr George Lawrence represents a modern development in the application of radiesthesia to health.[23]

Although ostensibly a physical method, dowsing or radiesthesia ultimately depends on the sensitivity of the practitioner to subtle radiations of varying vibrational frequencies. The dowsing instrument, whether a rod, stick, pendulum or a more complex device, merely serves to indicate what the human 'instrument' initially detects. Hence while a person may be unconscious of subtle energies they are nevertheless processed by the nervous system and expressed through unconscious pathways of neurological and motor activity. Tiny muscle movements register these influences and produce movement in the dowsing instrument.

According to this ancient art, the amount and direction of the energy flowing through a chakra can be detected using a pendulum. After a few seconds the pendulum will usually begin to move, and the direction and radius of the movement show the amount and direction of the energy flowing through the chakra. The wider the radius the greater the energy flow. The speed of movement indicates the rate of energy flow through the chakra. Clockwise movement of the pendulum indicates an open chakra that is functioning effectively. The feelings and processes governed by it are therefore balanced and healthy. Counter-clockwise movement indicates that the chakra is closed or blocked so that energy cannot flow through it. The result is that feelings and functions governed by it are not balanced and are probably experienced negatively by the person. Between these two extremes various other movements may be described by the pendulum, all of which have diagnostic validity.[24]

Applied kinesiology

Another form of diagnosis based on similar principles is applied kinesiology, developed during the 1960s by American chiropractor George Goodheart. It uses manual muscle testing to provide muscular biofeedback on responses to given stimulation, to evaluate body function through the muscle–meridian connection and indicate appropriate treatment. A kinesiology muscle test involves the practitioner placing a person's limb in a certain position in order to isolate and contract the muscle being tested. Light pressure is applied in the direction which would extend the muscle. On the practitioner's instruction to 'hold' the person tries to match the practitioner's pressure. The muscle will either lock in place or give way. This is not a test of muscle strength but of neurological function, which, it is argued, can be used to test the individual's response to any stimulus, whether a remedy, food, or emotional word or phrase, and to locate dysfunction in the body, assess imbalances in the energy field and those that may undermine future health. The explanation given for this is that if a given stimulus produces stress, the resulting neurological responses can be detected by way of imperceptible muscle movements. Applied kinesiology is widely used diagnostically by practitioners of complementary therapies, although the reproducibility and reliability of muscle testing remains the subject of considerable debate.

Scientific measurement of the chakra-aura system

> Energy fields are invisible structures around the body. They are invisible in the same way that television and radio waves are invisible. Their existence is made manifest by the presence of a receiver (the body), much in the same way that we need a TV or radio to detect television and radio waves. Unfortunately energy fields around the body are nothing like as simple as radio and TV waves.[25]

While the subtle energy fields around the body are evident to many healers, they have eluded scientific measurement until recently. This may be because these energies can only react with and be detected by living organisms. Hence a detectable reaction only occurs when they find their counterpart in a living being. This, it is claimed,[26] is the basis for healing diagnoses, dowsing and water divining. However, because these forces are not easily detected by physical instruments in the orthodox scientific world, they are deemed to have no physical reality.

It is clear from the history of Western research into subtle energies during the twentieth century that science is blinkered by the limitations of its own tools. In 1911 Dr Walter Kilner of St. Thomas' Hospital, London, published a dissertation on the human aura, *The Human Atmosphere* (republished in 1984 as *The Aura* by S. Weiser), in which he claimed that a force field exists around the human body which can be charted and analysed. He subsequently developed a special kind of glass, the Kilner screen, which, he claimed, allowed the aura to be seen objectively. This – and his prediction that it would in future be possible to photograph the aura and use it for more accurate diagnosis of all kinds of illness – was dismissed as fanciful. The views of Dr F.S.C. Northrup of Yale University, who proposed the existence of dynamic life fields around living organisms was similarly rejected, as was the discovery of an energy body possessed by all human beings claimed by Yale professor of anatomy H.S. Burr.

In the late nineteenth century a Russian researcher, Yakub Yodko-Narkevitch experimented with electrography or corona-discharge photography which does not require the use of a camera. Instead, a film is exposed directly through the agency of a high voltage, high-frequency electric discharge which passes between the object to be photographed, through the film, to a conducting plate on the other side. In the course of this he discovered that a picture from a healthy person differed to one from a sick person, and that tired, excited, sleeping or awake individuals could be discriminated by the same means. His publications and research tools were lost in the Russian revolution.

Electrography was rediscovered only by accident during the 1930s by Semyon Kirlian. He developed high voltage photography which revealed streams of apparent energy flowing from the fingertips in a manner suggested by traditional aura theory. Subsequently other devices, such as the verograph, were developed that produced images similar to those obtained by Kirlian photography, and during the 1960s another Russian researcher, Leonidov, developed a lightless microphoto which provided further objective evidence for the aura by capturing the fading life of a dying plant.

Over the course of many years of research, Kirlian and his wife and co-researcher, Valentina, became convinced that these energy streams reflected the well-being or otherwise of an organism, and this view subsequently gained support from research on plants and humans. Working with a surgeon, Ruben Stepanov, they found that electrography could be used to diagnose illnesses in human beings. They found that tissue from cancer patients produced many tiny white and grey spots on photographs, whereas non-cancerous tissue produced large well-defined spots.[27]

The Kirlians' research was further developed by Professor Vladimir Inyushin.[28] He described the energy field around living forms as a biological plasma body, claiming – as Burr had done previously – that this is a whole unified organism emitting its own electromagnetic fields, which are the basis of all biological fields. He considered bioplasma, as he termed it, to be a fourth state of matter which could take on highly organised patterns and influence the Kirlian images. As such it may be equivalent to the etheric or astral body described by the ancients.[29]

Using Kirlian photography, Professor Viktor Adamenko subsequently claimed to have found concentrations of 'bioplasma' at hundreds of points on the human body corresponding to the acupuncture points of traditional Chinese medicine, and that these varied with different illnesses. However, Adamenko points out that there is as yet no proof that the plasma state can exist naturally in living beings. What is clear, he suggests, is that the Kirlian image is strongly influenced by electrical processes within the organism which are much more organised than is generally recognised. He therefore prefers to describe the phenomenon not as bioplasma or the aura but as a corona, which he defines as the cold emission of electrons from the live object into the atmosphere.

Adamenko also found that Kirlian photography revealed changes in the corona of a famous Russian healer during a healing session, and could be used to discriminate genuine healers from charlatans, and to discover the ability to heal in people who never suspected it in themselves.[30] (This work has been continued at Milan University by Professor Arnaldo Zanatta.)

Research with electrography convinced the Kirlians that their method provided evidence not only of a person's physiological state but also of mental states. Adamenko has found that stress can be detected in mentally healthy people using Kirlian photography, which can also be used as a tool in diagnosis of psychological illness.[31] Comparisons of Kirlian images from several hundred schizophrenics with controls has provided not only convincing evidence that Kirlian photography can be used in psychiatric diagnosis but also that it can be used to predict a worsening of clinical symptoms.[32]

Kirlian photography did not become known in the West until the mid-1960s, and initially it was met with scepticism. The suggestion that the observed phenomenon is simply the result of physiological variations at the surface of the skin, was rebutted by Professor Thelma Moss of the Neuropsychiatric Institute of the University of California School of Medicine, who was the first serious researcher of the phenomenon in the USA. She demonstrated that while there is no correlation between the observed corona and variations in skin temperature, peripheral states or perspiration, there are apparent correlations with psychological states. Relaxation produced by meditation, hypnosis, and acupuncture is characterised by more brilliant coronas, while states of tension and emotional excitement result in a contracted corona with red blotches at the fingertips: a finding which appears to reflect the relationship between these 'time' therapies and energy.

Further evidence that the phenomenon is not a physical variation of the photographed surface comes from the discovery that when a leaf has pieces removed or human fingers are amputated the corona discharge in each case shows as a whole, albeit poorer quality, image.[33] William Tiller of Stanford University has suggested that the energy apparently emitted from the fingertips is present prior to the formation of solid matter. This, he claims, may be another level of substance producing a hologram; a coherent energy pattern organises matter so that it produces a physical network in the manner of a hologram. Thus if one part of the network is cut away the forming hologram still remains. Adamenko observes that while a complete image can be reproduced from any part of a hologram, the smaller the piece of hologram, the worse will be the quality of the image. Since electrons can be considered waves as well as particles, he suggests that there is no reason why they could not form a holographic image just as well as light.

> Indeed electron-wave holography has already been achieved in 1975 by physicists in the USA. Just as with light holography, though, it is necessary that the waves are in a highly-ordered, or coherent state, such as is produced by a laser. Could a living organism really be so perfectly organised to emit coherent electrons in the intense electric field? If the answer is yes, then we shall see great developments of what is at present an embryo science: *quantum biophysics*. Kirlian photography will then be making a substantial contribution to the science of life.[34]

The German professor of Biophysics Fritz-Albert Popp argues that organisms are organised in precisely such a coherent way. Research since the 1930s has shown that virtually all living organisms give off exceedingly small amounts of light. Although many scientists dismiss this phenomenon, known as ultraweak biological light, as a waste product of metabolism, systematic investigations using highly sensitive instruments have revealed that these 'biophotons' have remarkable properties that cannot be explained in terms of random metabolic errors. Popp proposes that the light is released from a coherent electromagnetic field which can account for biological organisation and biocommunication. Many significant correlations between features of the weak biological light and a number of fundamental biological processes such as cell division, death and major shifts in metabolism, exist. These correlations may indicate that the light is a sensitive global expression of biological regulatory processes. Furthermore, there are strong grounds for believing that rapid communication takes place by way of electromagnetic fields. Studies of light emission have provided evidence for long-range communication between cells, and have shown such communication to be defective in cancer cells.[35] Hence, 'there is a fundamental sense in which all organisms are "beings of light" '.[36]

> An organism may be likened to a candle flame. The structure of the flame is only maintained by the dissipation of energy in the process of burning. It is a very simple example of what Prigogine calls a 'dissipative structure'. Likewise an

organism only maintains its structure by the constant dissipation of metabolic energy. The instant this is cut off it starts to fall apart. The organism should therefore be thought of as a process or a 'happening' rather than as an object.[37]

Over the past few decades the new science of bioelectromagnetics, which studies the interaction of electromagnetic or EM fields and life, has emerged. It 'has already opened the door towards another way of seeing life, from the viewpoint of a nonlinear dynamic system that collectively interacts within a sea of EM fields'.[38] From this perspective 'life turns out to be electromagnetic through and through'.[39] There are a growing number of electromagnetic applications in medicine, whereby a large variety of externally applied electric, magnetic and EM fields of low intensities are used to diagnose and/or treat disease.[40]

> Energy fields offer a tantalizing opportunity for early diagnosis and the selection of appropriate treatment in a way that some of us have not even begun to grasp. We are slowly groping our way to a more objective way of looking at these fields and thereby experimenting with them. In my view this must be a most exciting area of potential development for biology in general and medicine in particular.
>
> Already the measurement and healing of energy fields has generated the fast growing field of energy medicine, sometimes called vibrational or non-local medicine. This has enabled enormous progress to be made with a whole range of chronic diseases which so far have been untreatable. We are clearly on the brink of several breakthroughs in this area of medicine which will herald an era of highly focussed causally directed medicine.[41]

As a possible means of detecting EM fields, there is growing interest in Kirlian photography in the West, where it has been used successfully to identify patients with cancer.[42,43] However, although there have been some successes in a number of applied fields, many scientists simply do not take it seriously. Nevertheless, attitudes are changing, and the full potential of this method is being explored in high-quality research.[44]

The chakras have also been the subject of considerable scientific research, most notably by Japanese professor, Hiroshi Motoyama, who has developed various physiological devices for measuring subtle energies in and around the body. Over a 15-year period he devised AMI (Apparatus for Measuring the Functional Condition of Meridians and their Corresponding Internal Organs) which measures the flow of energy within each of the acupuncture meridians. This instrument measures the initial skin current and steady state current in response to DC voltage externally applied at the terminal points of meridians, the *sei* or 'well' points. 'Experiments on some 2000 subjects strongly suggest that the relative magnitudes of such skin currents reflect the functional conditions of Ki energy in the meridians'.[45] He also developed the Chakra Instrument to detect minute changes in energy emitted by the body. It measures the electromagnetic fields around the body, and can show subtle changes in these when chakras are naturally active or activated by some other means.[46,47] On the basis of experimental studies using these devices, Motoyama has concluded that the energy systems underpinning traditional Chinese and Indian medicine are fundamentally the same, despite differences in terminology, and consistent with the ages-old observations of clairvoyants and mystics.

Taken together, the chakra and aura systems provide a comprehensive and consistent account of the distribution and functioning of the human energy field, and a framework for energy medicine such as is traditionally practised in India, Tibet, China, Japan, among Native American Indians, Aboriginals, and the Kahunas of Hawaii. These include ages-old practices such as acupuncture, acupressure or Shiatsu; and more recent practices such as reflexology, and homeopathy.

Acupuncture

Traditional Chinese medicine (TCM), the system of Eastern medicine that includes acupuncture, has few similarities with Western biomedicine.

> Stimulation of acupuncture points treats distal regions of the body; the meridian pathways do not correspond to familiar organ systems and are not easily comprehensible to the West. Furthermore, many more interconnections – 12 major meridians, 8 auxiliary tracts as well as other channels and up to 1000 acupuncture points – are part of TCM. Western medicine has focused on bodily fragments rather than interconnections, elucidating anatomy and physiology, from the level of organ systems, organs, tissues and cells, down to the chemistry of biomolecules and genes. The present dominant scientific paradigm in biology and medicine is mechanical reductionism... it is doubtful whether central features of acupuncture such as the flow of *qi* (subtle life energy) and the meridian map could ever be comprehensible from such a viewpoint.[48]

Nevertheless, attempts have been made to explain acupuncture within the framework of the dominant paradigm of biomedicine. Biomechanical theories, which have hypothesised that meridians are mechanical pipelines along which chi flows, and that acupuncture points are anatomically distinct from surrounding tissues, have largely proved unsatisfactory in explaining how acupuncture works. These theories offer no explanation of what chi or acupuncture points are. Nor do they explain how applying needles to one point on the body can treat a remote region of the body or even the whole body.[49]

Biochemical theories have also been advanced to account for acupuncture. These have focused on biochemical mechanisms of action, and specifically on the mechanisms of acupuncture analgesia. Acupuncture is 70–80 per cent effective in treating pain. Although there is controversy as to how much of the pain relief is placebo effect, and more placebo-controlled trials are needed, there is little doubt that it is a particularly effective remedy for conditions involving pain. Pain relief is to some extent the result of the deep relaxation induced when certain points are needled. However, research has shown that it activates small myelinated nerve fibres in the muscle that send impulses to the spinal cord from where three centres are activated to cause analgesia: the spinal cord, midbrain and pituitary-hypothalamus.[50] It is now widely believed that the release of endorphins – natural morphine-like substances in the body that act as opiate receptor sites and inhibit pain transmission – and other neuroactive substances such as neuropeptides, is responsible for causing acupuncture analgesia. A considerable body of research evidence supports the hypothesis that endorphins mediate acupuncture analgesia. Naloxone, an opiate receptor antagonist, blocks acupuncture analgesia, as do other opiate receptor antagonists; genetically altered mice resistant to morphine show no acupuncture analgesia; endorphin levels rise in blood and cerebral spinal fluid and fall in specific brain regions during acupuncture analgesia; and acupuncture analgesia is enhanced by protecting endorphins from enzymatic degradation.[51]

While endorphin release may explain short-term pain-killing effects of acupuncture, it does not explain the long-term cumulative effects such as the treatment of chronic pain over months. Nor does the biochemical approach explain the non-local and holographic features of acupuncture. Moreover, it proposes only an explanation for the mechanism of acupuncture analgesia and doesn't consider the other physiological effects of acupuncture, or how neurotransmitters other than endorphin and neuroendocrines substances in the body might be involved in these effects.

In traditional Chinese medicine acupuncture is a broad-based therapy for conditions ranging from hypertension to paralysis. It is extensively used in the treatment of neurological conditions and stroke.[52] Nevertheless the volume of acupuncture research is modest. Many studies are flawed methodologically and results tend to be inconclusive.[53] However, animal and human studies demonstrate a vast array of effects on immune function, autonomic function, hormonal activity, gastric acid secretion, intestinal motility, and release of a variety of opioid peptoids;[54] and that it enhances immunity in patients with malignant tumours.[55]

Anaesthesia is another of the effects traditionally claimed for acupuncture. Its contemporary protagonists argue that it is cheaper and causes fewer side effects such as vomiting and headache than conventional anaesthetics. Support for this claim comes from a study,[56] which compared acupuncture and epidural anaesthesia in caesarian births and found that acupuncture gave rise to on average 112 ml. less blood loss than epidurals and faster post-operative recovery with fewer complications. Of the mothers who received acupuncture, only 5.2 per cent needed the pain-killer pethidine, compared with 29.9 per cent of those who received epidurals. However, these effects tend to be overlooked in Western medical journals, where its pain-related role has been emphasised to the exclusion of its other applications.[57]

Bioelectrical theories

Bioelectrical theories appear to hold greater promise for a comprehensive understanding of acupuncture. The determination of the existence of acupuncture points by way of electrical means began in the 1950s. Acupuncture points were first measured by Dr Reinhold Voll in the 1950s using a standard circuit to measure resistance. Dozens of studies since published confirm that there is a significant difference between the electrical activity of true and non points, and have concluded that acupuncture points represent at least an area of high conductivity (electrical permeability) relative to nearby tissues.

Research also suggests that meridians can be identified with measurements of electrical impedance and conductance. 'In fact the objective existence of the meridian system is argued most strongly by the electrical specificity of acupuncture points'.[58] Various studies have found that by applying a direct current over the body surface points on the skin of higher electrical conductance could be identified and these corresponded with the meridians.[59] In general, the research appears to acknowledge the bioelectrical identity of both acupuncture points and channels as specified in traditional acupuncture. This has led to a bioelectric theory of action. This postulates that acupuncture points and channels are electromagnetic in nature; that acupuncture treatments induce alterations in the electromagnetic properties of channels and local tissues; and that electromagnetic fields significantly influence biological matter and physiological functions. The available evidence indicates that acupuncture points and their connecting channels are definable electrically. Relevant research has focused on electromyogram readings which correlate with subjective reporting of propagated sensations along the channels in both healthy subjects and patients with neuromuscular disorders.

A theory of acupuncture action has been developed based on the concepts of the organismic energy field.[60] This Zhang-Popp hypothesis – otherwise known as the 'standing wave superposition hypothesis' – infers that acupuncture has the capacity to induce changes in the standing wave pattern of the patient, and that shifts in EM fields created by such interference can produce changes in biological response that may promote healing. The theory is attractive because it accommodates many of the features of acupuncture, including its holographic nature – that is, the way in which the entire body is represented in parts such as the ears, feet, or hands. It also explains the anomalous skin resistance properties of acupuncture points and their interconnectedness.

Twenty years ago acupuncture was unacceptable to Western medicine but it is now becoming integrated into orthodox health care. In Britain it is available in most district general hospitals. There are increasing numbers of medical acupuncturists and provision of training programmes for doctors and orthodox health care professionals. It is also increasingly used by physiotherapists worldwide as a modality of treatment.[61]

More widespread use of acupuncture has led to various technological developments in its application. Sonoacupuncture, which applies high frequency sound to acupuncture points, has been developed. In Russia Adamenko has substituted the traditional needles with a tobioscope, an instrument containing photoelectric cells which records the skin resistance over acupuncture points and meridians, registering any imbalances, which are then treated by various means including lasers. Electroacupuncture, which involves the application of electricity to acupuncture needles, has been successfully used in relieving pain in obstetrics, in the management of addictions, epilepsy, rheumatoid arthritis and fibromyalgia.[62] However, traditionalists insist that diagnosis and treatment by electronic instruments are insufficiently sensitive to the whole process, which involves the practitioner's ability to blend his chi energy with that of the patient.

Acupressure and Shiatsu

Many conditions are claimed to be amenable to acupressure and Shiatsu, including headache, migraine and other pain conditions, respiratory illnesses, sinusitis, circulatory problems, digestive and bowel disorders, urogenital difficulties, tension, anxiety, depression, loss of libido and insomnia. Many of these conditions are stress related and the effects claimed are in part due to the relaxation induced by these treatments, which are becoming increasingly widespread and popular. However there is as yet little research on their efficacy. Nevertheless simple acupressure bands have been found to significantly reduce post-operative nausea and vomiting and the use of anti-emetic drugs,[63] and acupressure has also proved effective in the treatment of early morning sickness.[64]

Reflexology

Reflexology is a treatment which applies varying degrees of pressure to different parts of the body, usually the hands and feet, in order to effect change, not only in specific organs of the body but also in the relationships between them, and other systems and processes, thereby achieving balance. It is based on the assumption that every part of the body is connected by energy channels or pathways, known as reflex zones, that terminate on the soles of the feet, palms of the hands, ears, tongue and head. These pathways relate to all areas of the body, through ten zones which divide the body longitudinally on either side of the medial line. These divisions are conceptual rather than actual, as the energy is considered to flow in a continuum. Tension or imbalance in any part of the reflex zone will affect the entire zone and give rise to malfunction in organs of the body affected by it. Whenever an organ is dysfunctional the corresponding reflex in the feet or hands will be very tender on pressure. The fundamental principle of treatment is that tension can be released by applying pressure to the reflexes on the feet or hands. This stimulates subtle energy flow along the zone and vitalises it. Working on all reflex points in the feet returns the body to a relatively stable equilibrium of interdependent elements.

The origins of reflexology are obscure. Foot massage is depicted on a wall painting in the Egyptian tomb of Ankhmahor at Saqqara dated circa 2300 BC. Foot and hand pressure are known to have been used therapeutically over 5000 years ago in China and India, and by Native American Indians. It appears to be based on energy principles similar to oriental medicine, and its 'zones' are equivalent with the 'meridians' of acupuncture. However, modern reflexology is attributed to an American ear, nose and throat specialist, William Fitzgerald, who found that gentle pressure applied to specific areas of the hands and feet produced partial local anaesthesia in areas of the ears, nose and throat, and claimed to have used this method of anaesthesia in minor operations. He mapped the zones of the hands and feet, and with Dr Edwin Bowers in 1917, published a treatise on 'reflex zone therapy'. This method was further developed as Zone Therapy by Dr Joseph Riley in the 1920s and subsequently by his research assistant Eunice Ingham, and Doreen Bayley. Various different schools of reflexology have since emerged: the original Ingham method or traditional reflexology;[65-67] Metamorphic Technique;[68] multidimensional reflexology;[69] Morrell reflexology;[70] Reflex Zone Therapy;[71] Vacuflex reflexology;[72] and the Rwo Shr method;[73] which differ in the precise location of some reflexes and in methods of treatment.

Reflexology is used to treat a variety of conditions, especially pain, gastro-intestinal tract disturbances, skin and menstrual problems, asthma, anxiety and stress-related problems. There is much anecdotal evidence to support its effectiveness, mostly reported by nurses, midwives and health visitors in health care journals.[74-79] It has been described as relieving symptoms of cystic fibrosis,[80] and of multiple sclerosis,[81,82] and improving the well-being of cancer patients.[83] Beneficial effects of reflexology are also claimed in midwifery.[84-86] It is probable that many of these effects are a result of relaxation. Relatively little scientific research has been conducted on reflexology. The few research reports available appear to be positive. They suggest that reflexology may be effective in relieving headache,[87] reducing symptoms of premenstrual sydrome;[88,89] post-operative analgesia;[90] chest pain;[91] back pain;[92,93] blood sugar levels; and anxiety.[94] However, there is a need for more carefully controlled research. Many of the studies conducted have been criticised as methodologically flawed, or too small-scale to be of value[95] in determining the effectiveness of reflexology. Nevertheless, the research does suggest that in the treatment of some conditions, reflexology may be as effective as conventional treatments with drugs.

Homeopathy

Although generally not recognised as such, homeopathy has a similar conceptual basis to acupuncture and its variants. It was developed in the nineteenth century by the physician Samuel Hahnemann (1755–1843). He considered there to be certain basic vibrational patterns of disease or miasms, which originate in the aura, setting up patterns in the individual's life and body which spread their subtle influence through all the energies of the person. These miasms may be inherited genetically, or acquired by resonance, the principle whereby energies vibrating with a certain frequency and amplitude reverberate with similar energies in the environment. The former, in the genetic code, and the latter in the form of bacterial or viral attack, toxic pollution in food or the environment, can lie dormant for years, flaring up at times of weakness. Then the organism reacts to this disease or imbalance of its energies by attempting to restore balance, and in so doing produces the symptoms and signs the patient feels and the doctor observes. The homeopath, unlike the orthodox physician, does not consider these to be the illness *per se*, but rather the body's reactions to the original state of imbalance. They are an indicator of the extent of the imbalance, and of how profoundly the organism is affected by it, and can be used to determine appropriate treatment for restoring balance.

Homeopathic treatments restore the balance of subtle energy fields of the body by matching various natural remedies of different vibrational characters with the disharmonies of the body, thereby restoring harmony and inducing health. They utilise the principle of resonance, applying remedies which subject the organism to a periodic disturbance of the same frequency of the body, at which frequency the body displays an enhanced oscillation or vibration. The principle of treating 'like with like' (often rendered in Latin as *Similia similibus curentur*) is also used in orthodox medicine, notably in vaccines, but also in many cytotoxic drugs and radiation used in the treatment of cancer, which are in themselves carcinogenic. The same principle also underpins the layman's 'hair of the dog' remedy in the treatment of hangover. However, within homeopathy it is recognised that the therapeutic relationship between the person to be healed and the healer is crucial. It has been suggested[96] that this is the crucial resonance and that the remedies are merely a crutch. Arguably the therapeutic relationship and the remedies in homeopathy are mutually reinforcing.

The effects of homeopathy, where acknowledged at all, have often been dismissed as placebo effect because the doses of remedies used are considered too minute to have any pharmacological potency. In many homeopathic remedies the 'active' ingredient is generally thought to be so diluted that it is unlikely to contain a single molecule of the original substance. The counter-argument is that the vibrational character of that substance is retained and 'potentised' through succussion or vigorous shaking. The active component of the homeopathic remedy is thus physical rather than chemical; and operates on similar principles to dissipative structures in as much as that by shaking up existing patterns of energies within the body it enables the system to reorganise.

Attempts to explain the action of homeopathic remedies have led to the concept of 'information medicine'. In a fundamental sense energy *is* information, and it is hypothesised that this information can be transferred to water or other solvents, stored and passed to a biological system if it is in a sensitised state. An appropriate model for its action is the computer disk.

> If you had a homeopathic 'ultra-molecular' dilution chemically analysed, it would be found to contain nothing but water, ethanol (the dilution medium) and lactose (from the tablets onto which the dilutions are absorbed). However, if you had the same chemist analyse a computer disk, it would be found to consist only of vinyl and ferric oxide, yet for all the chemist knew, it might contain the collected works of Shakespeare! The point is that the information is stored in physical, not chemical form. This model also emphasises the importance of pre-sensitisation – you could only read the information on the disk if you had the right kind of computer with the right operating system and software.[96]

Although the concept of information medicine hypothesis is relatively new and tentative, it does find support in physics.[97] Nevertheless, the effectiveness of homeopathic remedies still remains at issue. From the outset homeopaths have conducted 'provings' of remedies on volunteers in order to determine their effects. Orthodox physicians often dismiss this proof, claiming that their efficacy has not been demonstrated in clinical trials. These are complicated in homeopathy by the highly individualised nature of the treatment. However, there is growing evidence from appropriately controlled studies reported in leading medical journals that homeopathy may be effective in the treatment of various conditions. A review of 107 clinical trials of homeopathy[98] found that 77 per cent gave positive results, albeit insufficient evidence to draw definite conclusions. Similarly cautious but positive conclusions have been drawn from other studies on homeopathic treatment of premenstrual symptoms[99] menopause,[100] alcohol-related problems;[101] and in the management of pregnancy and labour.[102] Well-controlled studies have found that homeopathy performs better than placebo in the treatment of allergic asthma, a result supported by a meta-analysis of research in this field. These results have been interpreted as either proof of the efficacy of homeopathy, or a demonstration that clinical trials may produce false-positive results. However, it has been pointed out that given the strength of the evidence, it is difficult to accept the latter hypothesis, which 'is possibly a tongue-in-cheek dig at the intransigence of certain of the medical profession to accept the positive research evidence'.[103] Support for the effectiveness of homeopathic remedies also comes from a growing number of studies in veterinary medicine, where placebo effect is controlled for in the very nature of the animal subjects. Clearly, however, there is a need for further rigorous research on human subjects.

In stimulating energy levels towards more harmonious arrangement homeopathic treatments may operate to bring about transformation in the manner of dissipative structures. Similar transformations are effected by a number of psychological therapies, whose 'shake-up' of existing energy forms is more clearly perceptible but nonetheless subtle.

12

Psychosomatic Treatments

The psychological treatments which more obviously fit within the framework of 'energy medicine' are those which derive from the work of Wilhelm Reich (see Chapter 5) who devised a number of devices for concentrating energy, and techniques for removing obstacles to its natural flow, which have become known as bioenergetics.

Bioenergetic therapies

Reichian therapy

The aim of Reich's therapy was to unblock body tensions and free breathing patterns in order to increase the flow of bio-energy through the body. He described[1] seven rings of tension caused by muscle armouring. These lie at right angles to the main axis of the body and divide it into horizontal segments. The limbs can also be divided into segments and parallels are drawn between the feet, hands and head; between wrists, ankles and neck; forearm, lower leg and heart, and so on. There are two segments on the head: *ocular*, which includes the forehead and scalp muscles; and *oral*, which includes the muscles of the lips, chin, jaw and cheek but not the tongue. The third segment, the *cervical*, covers the neck muscles, including those of the tongue, throat and larynx. The fourth *thoracic* segment contains the heart, ribcage, lungs and arms. The fifth *diaphragmatic* segment covers the stomach, pancreas, liver, kidneys and solar plexus. The sixth *abdominal* segment covers the intestines and lower back; and the seventh, *pelvic segment*, the pelvis, genitals and legs.

Tension or muscle armouring may lead to symptoms as follows:

- *ocular*: various, ranging from dizziness to schizophrenia
- *oral*: tight or constricted facial expression, and voice tone
- *cervical*: sadness, fear
- *thoracic*: blocked feelings of love, anger, pain
- *diaphragmatic*: stomach ulcer, liver conditions, diabetes

- *abdominal:* sexual problems
- *pelvic:* fear.

Reich found that people with similar childhood experiences and relationships with their parents had similar bodies, and people with similar bodies had similar psychological dynamics. On this basis he identified five major types of 'character structure': *schizoid, oral, psychopathic, masochistic* and *rigid;* and their psycho-physiological features.

Reich's concept of bio-energy and the system he built upon it bears a striking similarity to the chakra system. Indeed, an alternative way of construing the principal character structures of Reichian theory is to regard them as primary functional disturbances of the chakras.

Reich's students, Drs Alexander Lowen and John Pierrakos, mapped out the major physical and psychological features of the character structures, and on this basis co-founded Bioenergetic Therapy. Pierrakos subsequently added spiritual features to the character structures and related them to chakra functioning. He went on to develop a system of diagnosis and treatment of psychological and physical disorders based on visual observation of the human energy field and dowsing. Before he was able to perceive auras directly, Pierrakos experimented with and modified instruments devised by Reich and the screens developed by Kilner, to study the human energy field. He has combined the information derived in these ways with the methods developed in bioenergetics to develop a system of diagnosis and treatment which he terms **Core Energetics.**[2] Its primary aim is dissolving energy blocks in the human energy field. This work has been developed further in conjunction with Barbara Brennan to include general auric patterns of each character structure and energetic defence mechanisms.[3,4]

Bioenergetic analysis

Alexander Lowen developed bioenergetic analysis as a systematic methodology for dealing with the relationship between somatic functioning and psychological trauma.[5,6] He established the Institute of Bioenergetic Analysis in the USA in 1956 and it has since been developed throughout the Western world. According to Lowen, defensive blocks in the body resulting from emotional trauma in early life are revealed in patterns of breathing which have established chronic muscle tensions. The aim of bioenergetic analysis is the healthy integration of the body and mind through breathing, the relaxation of character structures and grounding: a method which teaches a particular stance whereby the person can make positive contact with the ground enabling bodily energies to move in a harmonious flow and the individual to make contact with reality, literally and metaphorically, and discover a sense of identity. Breathing is developed by placing the body under stress, typically through use of a breathing stool over which the person's body is positioned.

Biosynthesis

Reich's work was also developed by David Boadella, who termed his approach biosynthesis.[7] Its fundamental concept is that there are three major energetic currents or lifestreams in the body which are expressed as a flow of movement through muscular pathways; and a flow of emotional life in the core of the body through the deep organs of the trunk. Stress before birth, during infancy and later life is seen as breaking up the integration of these three streams giving rise to dysfunctional character structure. Biosynthesis aims to reintegrate them through breath release and emotional centring, retoning of muscles and postural grounding, and with the facing and shaping of experience through eye contact and voice communicaton.

Boadella relates character patterns to dysfunction of the chakras as follows:

The primary function of *the root chakra* is *grounding* in the sense of commitment to the body and the will to survive. Where well developed there is a sense of independence and personal power. Where dysfunctional there are tendencies to over-groundedness and fear of dependence, or under-groundedness and fear of independence. It expresses a polarity between rigidity and helplessness; control and collapse.

The primary function of the *hara or second chakra* is *charge*. It is closely related physically to the navel and the sense of contact (via the umbilical cord). In infancy it is the centre of well-being and later is the sex centre. Dysfunction shows as over or under-charge: the former as hypersexuality, casual contact and difficulty in achieving satisfactory relationships; the latter as hyposexuality, impotence, frigidity and sexual anaesthesia through inability to make satisfactory contact.

The *solar plexus chakra* relates to power and mastery, so is related to boundaries, anger and anxiety. In anger there is a tendency to invade others and in anxiety to be invaded. Basic conflicts are expressed in identification with power and domination, or submission, rather than blending and compassion. As the core function of the heart chakra is compassion, deep love and the formation of strong relationships, it is the centre of *bonding*. Dysfunctions can be distinguished as over-bonding, addictive and stifling patterns in relationships, or under-bonding, expressed as superficial or transitory relationships, perhaps with a degree of indifference; or as total withdrawal from relationships.

The *throat chakra* relates to communication or *sounding* and how well the heart is expressed through the voice. Expressiveness is a sign of health but dysfunctions show as distortions in language, introjection or swallowing the views of others whole, without discrimination or reference to one's own feelings; and projection

– believing others to have attributes one is unwilling to ascribe to oneself. Guilt and blame are strongly implicated when the centre is blocked.

The *brow chakra* or 'third eye' is concerned with vision and contemplation, looking out and seeing in, and the ability to see oneself and others clearly. It is related to imagination and insight. Dysfunctions show in obsession, narrowing of vision to a single fixed beam, loss of imagination and insight; feelings of possession, being invaded by others and too telepathically open.

The *crown chakra* is concerned with openness to something greater than self, and with contact between inner and outer space. Disorders relate to 'spacing out' and fear of extinction in a void. Hence dysfunction may lead to messianic delusions and feelings of omnipotence; or, on the other hand, the sense of ultimate meaninglessness, nihilism, despair, existential depression, and fear of death.

These dysfunctions are treated by working directly on the body to stimulate the flow of energy through the chakras. However, biosynthesis recognises that an inner ground underlies the outer ground of the body, and action, feeling and thought. This expresses the essence or spirit of the person which is integrated using visualisation.

Biodynamic therapy

Gerda Boyeson, a Norwegian clinical psychologist, physiologist and Reichian analyst, derived biodynamic therapy from Reichian notions of bio-energy and armouring. Like Reich she considered Freud's libido theory limited and postulated that it must be an actual force moving in the body rather than solely psychological. She conceived of it in material form as a fluid which accumulates if blocked. She reframed Freud's theory of child development in terms of the physiological circulation of this energy within the body, and in so doing elaborated a biological theory of psychology. This postulates that psychological events are also an organic or neurological reality, and that mind and body are thus interfunctioning aspects of one biodynamic development. Every emotion, shock or frustration has a direct physiological consequence in a person as well as a psychological one. When emotions are repeatedly unexpressed and conflicts unresolved the consequences become chronic. Stress builds up layer on layer until neurotic symptoms develop somatic or behavioural manifestations. Hence a person literally embodies his or her neurosis. In Boyeson's theory, the primary personality is seen as becoming submerged during development in a secondary personality which corresponds with Reich's concept of the armouring by which people protect themselves from the onslaughts of the environment and their own socially unacceptable emotions. Thus a child punished for expressing an emotion may suppress it through muscular effort, which over time becomes part of his or her muscular armouring and body structure, and no longer feels that emotion.

However, Boyeson takes Reich's concept of muscle armouring further in terms of her concepts of visceral tissue armour, central to which is the principle of the emotional cycle. This is both a physical and psychological process in the sense that emotional events cause physiological changes which cease when the emotional event has passed. This can only occur in conditions of relaxation when the organism is no longer tensed for action, because under stress the self-regulating process is inhibited. The body then loses its capacity to clear itself with the result that the effects of trauma are retained. This loss of homeostatic response constitutes visceral armouring. When it prevents bio-energy flowing freely in the body, every cell is impaired and this results in tissue armouring. Boyeson's theory is similar to traditional ideas that when ill or stressed the energy field or aura of the body shrinks and loses its ability to absorb vitality and energise the body.

Biodynamic therapy derived from this theory aims to restore the body's capacity for self-healing and to reach the alive core of a person, encouraging it to expand (a similar concept to Pierrakos' core energetics). It varies for each client but often involves special massage techniques to disperse the body armouring. It is claimed as an effective treatment in all conditions where stress is an important component, low back pain, angina, migraine, multiple sclerosis, Parkinson's disease and rheumatoid arthritis.[8] In some persons this process achieves results only at the organic level while in others it is accompanied by profound psychological change.

Structural integration

This therapy, also known as **rolfing** after its originator Ida Rolf, was developed during the 1930s in America, and is strongly influenced by the work of Reich. It is a method of deep – some would claim, brutal – massage in which the therapist manipulates the client's body in order to return it to its desired postural and structural position, and in so doing releases imbalances resulting from the armouring process and discharges emotional and psychic blockages. Energies locked up in physical armour and defence mechanisms are released, promoting insight into the fears and inhibitions that initially provoked these responses. It is therefore not simply physical massage but a technique for freeing the body, mind and emotions from their conditioning. Its goal is to produce a more resilient, higher energy system through achieving balance in the energies of the body tissue from front to back, side to side and top and bottom of the body; and also balance between the deeper layers of tissue nearer the bone and those nearer the skin.

Rolfing involves loosening and lengthening of specific muscles and fascia of the body, repositioning of muscle fibres and returning them to their natural position. A course of therapy usually entails ten one-hour sessions. The first seven sessions attempt to remove ingrained stress patterns, postures and habitual responses. The initial session typically focuses on freeing the muscles of the chest area and ribcage to improve breathing, while the second focuses on the feet and ankles, which are seen as having an important bearing on the individual's standing in the world and the way in which the individual maintains contact with reality. The focus of subsequent sessions is on the integration of newly loosened muscles into new patterns of movement by manipulation of the fascia in appropriate directions. Releasing the physical component of chronic physical tension allows release of the system as a whole. This can manifest in the resurfacing of a buried memory or specific images, or it may show in insights into habitual behaviour patterns. As the therapy progresses, deeper and deeper tensions and resistances become apparent, and the increasing self-awareness of the client assists the therapist's hands in their dissolution. So, although Rolfing is not a psychotherapy *per se*, psychological changes do occur during the process and Rolfers are required to have a background in psychology before training.

Rolfing is fundamentally an 'energy' therapy.

[T]he body operates on energy, with energy, by energy; creating its own energy and taking in outside energy. A body is an individual energy machine. As you add together the parts of the machine... inappropriately you get... subtraction from the energy of the machine as a whole.[9]

Rolfing is a way of reversing this process.

In a study of the effects of rolfing on the body and psyche at UCLA[10] recordings were taken of low millivoltage signals from the body while the clairvoyant healer Rosalind Bruyere observed the auras of both the rolfer and the client. Her observations were recorded simultaneously with the electronic data.[11] When the wave patterns recorded by Fourier analysis and a sonogram frequency analysis were subsequently mathematically analysed, a correlation was found between the consistent wave forms and frequencies and the colours reported by Bruyere in any specific location. The experiment was repeated with seven other clairvoyants. They too saw auric colours that correlated with the same frequency/wave patterns. The researchers claimed their findings as the first objective electronic evidence of frequency, amplitude and time, which validates the subjective observations of colour discharge from the aura by sensitives throughout history. Moreover the colours observed in relation to the chakras were frequently those stated in the metaphysical literature.

Hellerwork

Hellerwork, a bodywork approach developed in the USA by Joseph Heller, is similar to rolfing. Indeed it is directly based on rolfing. Heller underwent rolfing and claimed that it had changed his life. He was trained by Ida Rolf, practised rolfing for several years and was president of the Rolf Institute for three years. Hellerwork follows the same pattern as rolfing. During eleven 90-minute sessions of deep tissue massage and movement awareness, the therapist releases habitual patterns of tension and reorders the entire body. With the release of tension, flexibility is restored and the body can be structurally realigned for optimum performance. In general the body lengthens; the two sides of the body are realigned and the pelvis relaxes towards the horizontal, allowing the weight of the trunk to fall directly over it. However, Hellerwork differs from rolfing in that it goes beyond changing the physical structure of the body and incorporates movement education. Heller believes that movement is a sensitive biofeedback device which constantly measures inner tensions, state of mind and habitual attitudes. Therefore, without physical re-education regular realignment will be needed as the formerly dysfunctional patterns will otherwise be re-established. When the body is misaligned and tense, enormous amounts of energy are expended in ordinary activities, such as sitting on a chair, so in Hellerwork sitting, walking and other movements are retrained.

Psychomuscular relief therapy

Psychomuscular relief therapy or PMRT, developed in Britain by Peter Blythe, and known in Scandinavia as **Release Therapy,** is based on the premise that most chronic and persistent psychoneurotic conditions such as anxiety states, depression, and phobias are the result of people being unable to relax certain muscles which are permanently in spasm, having tightened initially against intense emotional responses to specific incidents and situations. These spasms can be viewed as a natural way of coping with life but through continued usage the muscle tension becomes permanent. It then ceases to be an adaptive response, habitually transmitting strong signals via the afferent branch of the central nervous system which the brain interprets as anxiety. PMRT aims to release the feelings locked behind muscle tension which continually threaten to break through. It clearly owes a debt to Reich in both theory and practice.

Shen therapy

Shen therapy, developed by Richard Pavek, also focuses on treating psycho-somatic disorders by releasing hidden, hurtful emotions from deep within the body. It is based on the concept of a normal pattern of movement in what is referred to as the 'biofield' which becomes disrupted around sites of physical and emotional pain. Emotions are conceived as vibrating regions deep within the biofield, inside the physical body. The physical body relaxes when it feels a pleasurable emotion but contracts when it feels a painful one. These unconscious contractions prevent the organs in that region from functioning properly and trap the painful emotion inside. The energy flows from the Shen practitioner's hands are used to break these contractions and restore normal energy flow to the biofield. During the process, it is claimed[12] the painful, bodily held emotions are often released; the deeper, healthy emotions are accessed; and real healing begins.

The Alexander technique

A technique developed by and named after F. Matthias Alexander (1896–1955) for the improvement of postural and muscular activity is related to bioenergetic therapies, sharing with them the holistic assumption that there is no separation between body and mind. It adds the observation (supported by empirical research)[13] that every activity, mental, physical or spiritual, is translated into muscular tension, which may become habitual and distort thought, emotion and action. The technique is not a set of exercises as such, but the development of an individual's self-awareness as to how certain activities are performed. It is concerned not with what is done, but how it is accomplished, and as such, demands the same kind of awareness as zen and other oriental 'bodywork' disciplines such as yoga, aikido and T'ai Chi. It presumes that by increased personal awareness of physical attitudes the individual will perceive choices in the way he or she acts and will choose more natural and spontaneous expression. Thus, although not promoted as such, the principles of the Alexander technique ae fully consistent with those of humanistic psychotherapies, and its effects are considered similar in that it produces profound psychological and emotional changes, and feelings of well-being.[14]

The Feldenkrais method

Moshe Feldenkrais[15] has developed a technique for developing full efficiency and functioning of the body which incorporates elements of the Alexander technique and martial arts disciplines. It focuses on the gradual training of bodily awareness and sensitivity, but differs from the Alexander technique in its emphasis on body motion rather than posture. In this sense it can be regarded as a Western form of T'ai Chi.

Anthroposophical medicine

The Feldenkrais method is in many respects similar to **curative eurythmy,** the system of exercises and movements developed for the treatment of energy imbalance by Rudolph Steiner (1861–1925), the originator of anthroposophical medicine, which is an holistic system based on occult science,[16] and as such fully consistent with traditional energy medicine.

Although popular in Europe, particularly in Germany and Switzerland, anthroposophical medicine remains little known in Britain. It was initially welcomed by the theosophists because Steiner incorporated Hindu ideas about life energy, but they later developed along separate paths.

The influence of Eastern traditions is clearly evident in anthroposophical medicine. Steiner put forward a 'fourfold picture of man'. He considered there to be three energy 'bodies' or levels of existence and consciousness beyond the physical: the etheric, astral and spiritual. Etheric forces are the formative energies that underlie and shape all animate matter. Astral bodies underlie the etheric bodies in all living forms, while spiritual bodies underlie the astral only in humans. Disease results when a person's four bodies malfunction in some way. As these four levels of being interrelate, psychosomatic processes work both ways; the mind can produce malfunctions in the body and the body can produce mental disturbances. For this reason Steiner believed that any physical treatment should always be supported by treatment for the mind in the form of eurythmy or art therapy, which may properly be regarded as physical psychotherapy. However, in Steiner's system the root cause of all disease, whether physical or mental, is spiritual. The anthroposophical physician (only medically qualified doctors are allowed to train and practise anthroposophical medicine) works to discover what underlies an illness and requires a spiritual awareness not demanded of orthodox medical practitioners. They also administer remedies, mainly natural substances whose energies can be utilised to rectify energetic imbalance in the different energy bodies of man, notably homeopathic remedies, which were recognised by Steiner as working on the spiritual level.

Polarity therapy

Bioenergetic 'bodywork' is distinguished from the Alexander technique and the methods of Feldenkrais and Steiner in that touch – in some cases of a particularly vigorous and forceful nature – is used by a trained specialist to break up or otherwise shake up energy blockages as they manifest in dysfunctional patterns in the body. They generally require in the therapist, and promote in the patient, awareness of and sensitivity to, subtle energies. A specific awareness forms the basis of polarity therapy which was developed during the 1940s and 1950s by Dr Randolph Stone, who for many years studied Hindu healing techniques. Stone identified energy as the core focus of understanding health and he developed many techniques for relieving energy congestion using touch. In developing his approach Stone integrated knowledge of **osteopathy** and **chiropractic** (systems of treating bodily disorders by manipulation of the spine and other parts of the musculo-skeletal system); **naturopathy** (a method of treating disorders by natural means such as herbs, organic foods, sunlight and fresh air); and the understanding of energy in the Ayurvedic tradition.

Underpinning his therapy is the belief that the body is a magnified cell with a natural polarity, an expansion of the life force, which has its seat in the brain and the cerebro-spinal fluid. Accordingly its axis is neutral, the right hand side positive, holding positive electrical potential and radiating positive energy, and the left hand side negative. Stone claimed that with this knowledge it is possible to balance energies and so relieve pain and discomfort, because pain is the result of obstructions of the flow of vital energy at molecular, electromagnetic and even more subtle levels. Stone regarded thoughts and emotions as energy forms and negative thoughts and feelings as energy blocks which manifest ultimately in degenerative conditions. He claimed that these blockages could be relieved by hand movements and stroking which have energising effects. In polarity therapy light touch is used to free constricted fascia and so relieve energy congestion and facilitate energy flow. Inflammation or pain caused by excessive energy is relieved by placing the cooling (negative) energies of the left hand over it, while spasm, congestion or stagnation are vitalised by application of the positive energies of the right hand. All polarity treatments take place from side to side, front to back, above and below.

Polarity therapy also used reflexes – points on the body which have a connection with and effect upon different parts of the body. If these are sore to the touch, it indicates congested energy. While reflexology primarily makes use of reflexes on the feet and hands, polarity therapy recognises and makes use of reflex points all over the body, and specifies hand positions to be applied to each of them. Polarity therapy also involves use of the elements, different qualities of energy, air, water, earth and fire, in healing.

The electrical potentials of the body have been charted and it is claimed[17] that in the healing techniques used by Dr Stone there is a direct correspondence between the electrical polarities of the hands and the parts of the body where they are placed, and that this form of natural healing is used spontaneously and to good effect by most people. A mother, for example, might soothe a child by placing the front of her left hand or the back of the right hand (both negative in energy) on the child's forehead (also negative). Similarly, she may instinctively apply her right hand palm to the back of its head. In so doing, it is suggested, she is using the natural polarity of her body to balance the energies of her child. It is claimed that this natural polarity forms the basis of all treatments involving touch.[18]

Certainly practices can be found in ancient traditions where energies of the bodies are balanced by placing the palms of the hands at the crown of the head and the base of the spine, and in present-day healing practices such as cranial osteopathy and craniosacral therapy.

Cranial osteopathy

Cranial osteopathy originates in **osteopathy** which was developed during the American civil war by Andrew Still Taylor, an army doctor, who sought an alternative to the brutal surgery and indiscriminate drugging of medicine at that time. He developed osteopathy, which involves manipulation of the spine and other body parts, describing it as 'a scientific knowledge of anatomy and physiology in the hands of a person of intelligence who can apply that knowledge to the use of people who are sick or wounded by strains, shocks, falls or mechanical derangement'.[19] He considered the cerebro-spinal fluid 'a great river of life', and the highest known element in the human body.

William Garner Sutherland subsequently showed, contrary to current belief, that motion is possible and does occur in the sutures of the skull, and that there is a persistent involuntary movement of the tissues such as the brain, spinal cord, sacrum, trunk and limbs independent of breathing. He termed this process the primary respiratory mechanism or PRM, and its rate of movement the cranial rhythm impulse or CRI. The principles of CRI and the palpable movement of the body and the cerebro-spinal fluid were presented in the first textbook for practitioners,[20] and became important in the osteopathic approach.

It is recognised that the bones of the head and face must work in harmony, and that tension membranes lining the sutures where the bones vault together must also be in synchrony. If this is not so, cranial nerves, which are primarily parasympathetic autonomic controllers of all the senses, the movements of vital organs and the secretions of endocrine and exocrine glands, may be affected grossly or subtly, affecting all aspects of functioning. **Cranial osteopathy** is a process of assisting the respiratory system in moving the membranes of the cranial vault into a harmonious relationship through gentle touch.[21]

Craniosacral therapy

It is now recognised that pulsation occurs along the cranio-sacral axis. (In the chakra tradition the sacrum is regarded as an energy pump on the etheric level.) This rhythmic cranio-sacral pulsation, with a normal frequency of 6–12 cycles per minute, is palpable around the head and body. It is unrelated to breathing or heart rate and is not to be confused with brain waves, some of which pulse at 3–30 cycles per second. The rate of the cranio-sacral pulse may be slower or faster but is rarely more than 60 beats per minute. In craniosacral therapy, the therapist corrects abnormalities in the rhythm through light pressure on the patient's head and/or sacrum. Craniosacral manipulation is claimed as effective in alleviating a wide range of problems, especially post-traumatic symptoms of head injury, meningitis and encephalitis, migraine, behavioural, developmental and learning disorders in children, and sacral injuries – problems for which orthodox allopathic medicine often has little to offer – and to be successful in treating common childhood conditions such as colic, regurgitation, poor feeding, glue ear, ear infections and inconsolable screaming.[22] Research-based texts have been produced,[23] and there have been similar developments in chiropractic.[24]

The functions of the cranio-sacral rhythm are still being explored. Modifications of it are known to exert profound effects on systemic functions, reducing blood pressure, changing respiratory and cardiac rhythms, gastro-intestinal and neuroendocrine functions.[25] Research has also shown that cranio-sacral therapy to some extent parallels the effects of yoga and biofeedback.[26]

Therapeutic Touch

Dolores Krieger, a Professor of Nursing at New York University, spent many years developing Therapeutic Touch and pioneering it as a nursing modality. It is now widely taught and practised in the USA and Canada, where it is regarded as a natural extension of professional nursing skills.

Therapeutic Touch is based on the principle that healing is the rebalancing of energies within the body, which can be achieved through the direction of a healer's own energy, or their redirection of the energies within the body and energy field of a patient. It rests on belief that human beings are open energy systems, and transfer of energies between them occurs naturally and continually; and that illness is imbalance in an individual's energy field, and can be sensed as fine energetic cues, such as changes in the pattern of the energy field a few centimetres from the body.

Therapeutic Touch is performed using either direct physical contact (TT), or by holding the hands 2–6 inches from the subject's body (non-contact Therapeutic Touch, or NCTT). It has five stages. The first is that the healer must learn to centre herself psychologically and physically, that is to relax and focus attention inwards so that a meditative state is maintained during healing. Hence Therapeutic Touch may properly be regarded as a healing meditation. Indeed, healers' brain wave patterns during Therapeutic Touch resemble those of meditators.[27]

Having achieved this meditative state, the healer then makes an assessment of the patient's energy balance by passing her hands through the energy field surrounding the body, some 2–3 inches above its surface. Difference in energy flow resulting from energy imbalance and disease are detected through sensations in the healer's hands such as variations in temperature, 'pins and needles', tingling, pulsing, pressure or electric shock. The healer then 'unruffles the field', relieving congestion and freeing bound energy by stroking or sweeping gestures away from the affected part. This is often sufficient to relieve symptoms and mobilise the patient's own healing resources. After this the healer washes her hands or shakes them to remove the charge picked up from the patient. The healer then places both hands on either side or over the affected area of the patient and imagines directing energy to it. It is not considered sufficient merely to channel energy to the patient, because it is claimed that in an ill person whose energies are depleted this may do more harm than good. The energy must be modulated through use of colour imagery. The healer mentally pictures sending blue energy to cool or sedate, red to warm or stimulate, and yellow to energise; and continues doing so until such time 'when there are no longer any cues; that is, relative to the body's symmetry there are now no perceivable differences bilaterally, between one side of the field and the other as one scans the healer's field'.[28] In other words, until the patient's body 'feels all the same' to the healer.

Therapeutic Touch is distinguished from most other bioenergetic therapies in having been subjected to extensive empirical investigation, and has been demonstrated to be effective. Results suggest that it can be used to accelerate the regeneration of salamander forelimbs;[29] elevate serum haemoglobin in humans;[30] decrease overall muscle tension as indicated by multi-site electromyogram analysis;[31] decrease state anxiety;[32] and subjective measures of tension headache pain;[33] accelerate human dermal wound repair;[34,35] alleviate the effects of stress;[36] and acute pain in post-operative patients.[37] In a study to test the hypothesis that movements or passes could be hypnotic and so produce their effect, reduction in post-test anxiety was found to be far greater in subjects receiving actual Therapeutic Touch than in those who received imitation procedures.[38,39] An intriguing study[40] found that healing by NCTT was ineffective when the healer was unwell, and that similar physiological symptoms were also exhibited by 81 per cent of the treatment group during treatment sessions. Since the healer was physically separated from the healing subjects by a one-way mirrored door it is unlikely that the response can be attributed to viral or bacterial transmission from healer to subject. This is claimed as the first double-blind experiment to demonstrate that an inhibitory response can occur independent of any physiological or psychological interaction between healer and subject.

Therapeutic Touch has been successfully employed in a number of settings including prisons, and in the operating theatre, where it is found to greatly assist the induction of general anaesthesia. It has also been found to be of benefit to dying patients as an adjunct to pain relief and emotional support; in the reduction of clinical symptoms of fever and intestinal inflammation; and in assisting bone healing in children.[41] Its effectiveness in a wide range of physical and emotional health problems has led to it being used increasingly by health visitors and nurses,[42] and it is now being used widely in conjunction with physiotherapy and osteopathy. Since its introduction in the 1970s Therapeutic Touch has been introduced in 67 countries, and US universities now offer masters and doctoral theses in Therapeutic Touch.

Krieger's achievements have been considerable. Not only has she pioneered and effectively promoted Therapeutic Touch within orthodox Western medicine, but in so doing she has also revived the ages-old natural healing tradition of laying-on-hands which is the basis of her approach, and established a means by which it can be systematically trained. However this has led to controversy in

Britain, where interest in Therapeutic Touch began only in 1989 with the Didsbury Trust, a registered charity dedicated to developing it in the UK. The increasing interest has led to its acceptance within nurse education, and a diploma level course in TT has been established at the University of Manchester. In 1994 the British Association of Therapeutic Touch was also established to promote its practice, research and education. However, progress has been slow because its principles

> are not generally understood among all levels of nursing, including nurse lecturers. There seems to be growing awareness of its existence, but awareness does not always mean acceptance. A great deal of mysticism still causes furrowed brows on many listener's faces... Integrating something new into the nursing curriculum is not an easy task, especially when the topic area challenges the present belief system.[43]

There is uneasiness among British nurses about introducing a form of healing into nursing associated with spirituality,[44] which some nurses associate with religions, and in some cases reject because it is based on belief systems other than their own.[45]

Laying-on-hands, or contact healing

Contact healing by laying-on-hands, most commonly referred to simply as 'healing', is almost certainly the most widespread therapy in the world, the most ancient, and possibly the most misunderstood. It is one of the complementary therapies least accepted by modern medicine, yet there is more supporting evidence for its efficacy than for most of the other complementary therapies combined.[46,47] There is documentary and pictorial evidence for its use in Western civilisations since those of ancient Egypt and Greece, but nowhere is it more evident than in the scriptures of the early Christian Church.

Christ appeared to teach of a spiritual realm in which healing energies work more powerfully than man ever dreamed, (a view consistent with those of ancient traditions of both the East and West), and he directed his disciples to heal with this knowledge. There can be no doubt that Christ's original mission was to establish a healing ministry.[48] The healing of the body therefore played an enormous role in the early Christian period, as the Gospels and Acts of the Apostles reveal. Numerous acts of healing by Christ are documented, as are those of his followers, Peter, John, Ananais and Paul.[49] Laying-on-hands therefore became a recognised religious practice. Indeed, as a result of its purges on witches and other 'lay' healers whose practices were condemned as 'the work of the devil', the Church held a monopoly on healing from the Middle Ages onwards. In Britain until 1951 lay healers were under threat of the Witchcraft Act which carried a death penalty, and in the USA were subject to a legal prohibition on anyone without a recognised qualification manipulating another's body. The practice of healing in both countries has therefore tended to be confined within churches, outside which it has flourished only since relaxation of these laws.

Healers in Britain have been able to treat patients in hospitals since 1959, but only in 1977 did the General Medical Council change its policy and allow doctors to suggest or agree to patients seeing healers. Negative attitudes towards healing no doubt owe much to the legacy of the Church and its opposition to witchcraft, but a good deal results from widespread misunderstanding of what it involves. Largely owing to its religious connotations, laying-on-hands is widely thought to be synonymous with faith healing, and its effects the results of suggestion.

Belief and suggestion have an undisputed role in all healing, including orthodox medical treatment and cure, as is amply demonstrated by the placebo effect, and they unquestionably play a similar role in complementary treatments, but they do not account adequately for the effects of laying-on-hands. Faith, belief or suggestion are merely an auxiliary to actual healing,[50] and if this were not so, the healing of children, the mentally ill, those with learning difficulties, animals and those unaware of receiving this form of healing could not occur. Yet it does. 'There is solid experimental work and enough careful evaluation of reported claims to make this clear.'[51]

One of the most intensive investigations of the phenomenon[52] demonstrated that the effects of healing are not attributable to the patient's beliefs. This possibility was eliminated by using plants and animals as experimental subjects. In a series of double-blind experiments, it was demonstrated that injured mice healed much faster than controls when a noted healer, Oskar Estebany, held his hands over them.[53] His ability to prevent the development of thyroid goitres in mice was also demonstrated, and that plants and fungi can be significantly affected by healing.[54]

Further experiments[55,56] revealed that Estebany was able to increase enzyme reactions over time, and that the longer he held a test-tube of enzymes the more rapid the reaction. Similar effects have been noted in response to high intensity electromagnetic fields. Indeed it was found that Estebany's hands, although not emanating any measurable 'energy', affected the digestive enzyme Trypsin in a way comparable to the effects of an electromagnetic field measuring 8–13,000 gauss (normally human beings live in an electromagnetic field of 0.5 gauss). Irrespective of the type of enzyme investigated the change noted after exposure to the healer's hands was always in a direction of greater health of the cells and greater energy balance. Other noted healers, such as Olga and Ambrose Worrall, could cause damaged enzymes to reintegrate and return to normal structure and function, and enhance plant growth. The latter effect was subsequently confirmed in other experiments.[57] Other studies of Olga Worrall[58] used a cloud chamber – an electron detection device developed by nuclear physicists to make the path of high energy particles visible. The experimental procedure involved the healer placing her hands around the apparatus in an attempt to determine whether they might exert an influence on its uniform vapour pattern. They were found to produce a wave pattern in the vapour which seemed to move vertically from her palms, and altered course when she changed the position of her hands: an effect not found in non-healer control subjects. Furthermore she could affect the cloud chamber from a distance of 600 miles, when it was found that the aftermath of the energy turbulence in the chamber took about eight minutes to subside.

Studies of healers have shown that they can affect living tissue *in situ.* Following treatment by Estebany the haemoglobin levels of patients exceeded pre-treatment levels,[59] and other healers could also accelerate repair in living organisms.[60] Furthermore, after receiving training from Estebany, nurses could also produce statistically significant effects.[61]

Matthew Manning, Britain's most extensively investigated healer, was found in various studies to be able to prolong by up to four times the life of red blood cells in a weak salt solution in which they normally burst (the probability of this occurring by chance is 100,000:1); and to influence cancer cells in sealed containers. Indeed, 140 controlled trials of healing on enzymes, cells *in vitro,* yeasts, bacteria, plants, animals and humans, 61 per cent demonstrate highly significant effects and another 16 per cent marginally significant effects.[62]

Manning's brain wave patterns during healing have been found to show a large increase in low theta and delta range frequencies, a pattern which has been termed a 'ramp function' because of its appearance on EEG records. This pattern, suggestive of very deep sleep, has been found to originate in the limbic system of his brain, and Canadian studies have shown that it is transferred to people receiving healing from him. Moreover, when held by him, the hands of those receiving healing show a highly unusual Kirlian image with a brilliant white corona. Other healers have also been found to produce greater corona emanations during healing.[63,64]

The EEG patterns of healers while healing are similar to those of clairvoyants and yogis,[65] and the brain wave patterns of those receiving healing alter simultaneously with those of the healer. 'The diverse range of experimental data on the biological effects of healing is supportive of the hypothesis that a real energetic influence is exerted by healers on sick organisms'.[66] Furthermore this would appear to be exerted while healers are in a highly relaxed state.

Most healers believe they are originators or transmitters of energy and that they obtain their best results when calm, relaxed and under as little pressure from outside events as possible.[67] Nevertheless, there is no personal healing technique.[68] Healers do not consider that they heal and are not technically responsible for the result. They believe they are merely an instrument, a channel for energy, which is variously attributed to God, other deities or entities, or spirits, and frequently invoked by prayer, chanting and other rituals. Some healers experience this energy physically as a pattern of activity within their hands and body, and heal by trying to transmit it to another person. The feeling has been described as a 'pulsing vibration that is not just mental, but is an actual physical sensation which may be felt pouring over the entire body. The portion of the anatomy which is more acutely conscious of the feeling... is the hands, and it is through the hands that the actual transmission takes place'.[69] Therefore healers usually place their hands on patients.

The attempt to heal by 'doing' something to or for a person has been distinguished as quite different from, and less important than, healing where the healer does not attempt to do anything but simply experiences a feeling of being 'at one' with the person to be healed.[70] However this is a false distinction because there are universal features common to all healing of this kind.[71] Irrespective of idiosyncratic rituals, all healers do one thing similarly, which is to shift consciousness and become one with the person to be healed, albeit momentarily. This is not achieved by concentration but, on the contrary, by mental abandonment or relaxation. The resulting state of being united or in harmony with another is reminiscent of Roger's concept of empathy in which the therapist, rather than doing anything, reaches out with his being to another, attending to him or her fully and without barriers. Accordingly, 'true healing is a partnership between healer and patient. The removal of the personality barrier results in a condition known as contact and rapport'.[72] It is this communication or relationship between them which sets up an interplay of energy that is frequently experienced physically by one, other or both parties and accelerates the patient's self-healing. In physical terms this may be thought of as a state of attunement or harmony in which the healer 'gets on the same wavelength' as the other person, enabling healing to occur through the principle of resonance. This psychological harmony between healer and patient is the essential 'contact', and it is only after this is established that hands are laid on the body. However, it is difficult for many novice healers to accept that healing is so simple, and that no effort is required. Misunderstanding of the process often leads them to engage in various rituals which are unnecessary, and may be an impediment. The passes have no healing value, as no physical movement can produce the healing result.[73]

It follows that laying-on-hands is not necessary either, other than in reinforcing the psychic contact already established between the healer and patient, and that healing can be achieved without any physical intervention of any kind. That this is in fact the case is suggested by the phenomenon of absent or distant healing in which the healer makes psychic contact with a person at a distance, without even being in their presence. Hence, despite appearance to the contrary, all healing by laying-on-hands achieves its effects psychologically, and can properly be decribed as psychic or psychoenergetic.

13

Psychoenergetic Treatments

Lawrence LeShan has claimed that despite numerous references to 'forces' and 'energies', the concept of energy is not especially helpful in attempting to understand healing. In a seminal study[1] he found that in the state of consciousness associated with healing, the healer does not 'act' as one does in the ordinary world of sensory reality, but simply and literally perceives him or herself and the healee as one entity (each with their uniqueness maintained), within a metaphysical system which he termed 'the clairvoyant reality'. Within this frame of reference, (which LeShan claims is common to mystics, mediums and physicists), reality is clearly perceived as a timeless and unified whole, in which there are no boundaries and nothing is separated from anything else. All things flow into each other and are part of a larger whole where neither time nor space can prevent exchange of information and energy. LeShan suggests that when healers alter their consciousness to this clairvoyant mode with the person to be healed as its focus, they are able to mobilise the self-repair system of that person, even at a distance, simply by bringing them to mind. In this mode the healer does not attempt to 'do' anything to the person but simply 'is' at one with them.

> When the healer – for a moment – absolutely knows this to be true, that he and the healee are one, the healee sometimes responds with a mobilization of his self-repair and recuperative abilities.[2]

LeShan proposes that when the healer attends with love, this is in some way transmitted to the healee so that he or she knows it also. The healee is in a different existential position: part of a unity or whole, and more complete. This, LeShan observes, constitutes healing, and under these conditions positive biological changes may occur. Accordingly it is the interaction between the healer and healee which is healthy, in the sense that it is integrative. Nevertheless, LeShan considers that the changes which occur in the healee's body as a result of this union are confined to the kinds of results the body can achieve on its own naturally under optimal conditions, and that the healer cannot influence these energies in any way. The healer is therefore constrained to 'be' rather than to 'do'.

LeShan considers that everyone has the ability to heal in this way, and that it can be trained. In 1970 he established a five-day training programme and found that of some 400 people who took this course over a ten-year period, 80–90 per cent learned to alter consciousness to the clairvoyant mode and achieve positive biological changes in others. Nevertheless, although having trained himself and others to heal in this way, LeShan admitted having 'not the faintest idea as to why it gets results or what is happening'.

LeShan's observations support the claims of the renowned healer Harry Edwards who observed that, despite appearances to the contrary, any ritual or 'doing' is unnecessary in healing, and may be an impediment, because ultimately healing is a state of mind or quality of being. As such it is a psychic rather than a physical phenomenon. This is reflected in LeShan's use of the term 'psychic healing' to describe what is more generally known as 'laying-on-hands'. He clearly distinguishes this phenomenon from what he terms 'transpsychic healing', in which he considers the concept of energy to be of central importance.

Transpsychic healing

LeShan distinguishes transpsychic healing as that in which the healer, rather than merely arousing and strengthening the patient's own healing resources through a partnership of harmony and cooperation, mentally attempts to use this knowledge of unity to direct the immense resources of the cosmos on behalf of the healee. Here there is a conscious attempt to influence the greater 'one', of which the healer is part, to move to the aid of another part. LeShan observes that this 'one' may be conceptualised as God, and the healer's influence exerted through prayer; but other constructs can be used just as effectively for attaining and using this state of consciousness. He acknowledges that for many individuals, including himself, the concept of energy is then particularly useful:

> Knowing for the moment that you are part of the total One of the cosmos, and that there are vast energies which maintain the universe on its course (so to speak, the cosmic 'homeostatic forces'), you attempt by total concentration and 'will' to bend these energies to increase the harmony of the healee, another part of the cosmos. Knowing yourself a part of an all-encompassing energy system, you will the total system to direct additional energies to the repair and harmonization of a part that needs it.[3]

However, as he indicates, wilful determination is not necessary to direct these energies. It is sufficient for the healer to become so attuned to these forces that he becomes a channel for them.

> If I can perfectly align myself with the harmonies of the universe then their energies can flow through me to the healee whom I hold in consciousness.[4]

This requires a complete surrender of will other than the desire for what is best for the healee, and a complete identification with the 'All'. LeShan describes it as reaching towards a state 'where you wear the universe like a glove, and it wears you'. This state where the healer reaches out beyond mind to Unity – which LeShan refers to as the transpsychic reality – is superconscious or transcendent rather than conscious or psychic. He claims that the results of this mental action can be remarkable, even miraculous, producing physical change beyond the body's ability for self-repair. He suggests that it may account for the perception of the flow of energies by some healers and their patients, which appears to be captured by Kirlian photography; dramatic effects of famous healers, such as Harry Edwards and George Chapman; and the so-called 'psychic surgeons', whose controversial miracle cures are well documented.[5–11]

Psychic surgery

> The phenomena which occur are at times incredible, sometimes amusing, but always remarkable. For instance, tissue anywhere on the body is parted using only the bare hands of the healer; tissue or strange objects may be removed from the opening – egg shells, broken glass, old plastic bags, pieces of seaweed, a live shrimp. Cotton wool, dipped in oil, may be dematerialized into the chest of the patient and a few minutes later rematerialized in one ear and later removed from another.
>
> A healer may point his own forefinger or that of a bystander from a distance of about eight inches at the spot on the body where he wishes to make an incision, whereupon a clean cut, oozing a few drops of blood appears almost instantaneously. Some healers have been seen to remove an eyeball, remove connective tissue from the rear and then replace it. A healer may also use a knife, sharp or blunt, which he wipes on his sleeve before manipulating around the eye of a patient whilst he removes a small growth without causing any pain or damage.[12]

These phenomena are not necessary for actual healing, but they frequently satisfy the 'seeing is believing' principle.[13] Whether believed or not, extraordinary numbers of people are treated by these healers, throughout the world. It is claimed[14] that psychic surgery achieves its remarkable results by way of the etheric body. Working with this energy body the psychic surgeons alter its blueprint, whereupon changes take place in the physical body, often with startling suddenness. The process may be likened to 'charging' the battery of the body by joining it to the main supply, a far greater power source than merely another battery. This being the case, it could be argued that the healer, through applying vibration (from the Latin *vibrare*: to shake or move) is creating a perturbation in the system which enables it to escape to a higher order of organisation; and thus creating new forms through dramatic 'shake-up' of the old.

Nevertheless, an external agency may not be necessary to effect healing of this kind. This is suggested by the Indonesian practice of *Subud*, the central feature of which is *latihan*, a collective exercise in which people submit themselves to 'an energy which activates the inner nature, and through its purifying process tends to move and vibrate even those parts of us that we cannot see, which are 'out of mind'.[15] This force is received through complete non-doing and may be 'sufficient to disrupt and to traumatise the patterns of the psyche and the nervous system'.[16] During the exercise healings often occur as a result of individuals being brought into new harmony. Nevertheless, the exercise also carries with it the danger of spiritual crisis, and a 'Subud syndrome' or 'psychosis' similar to, but differing from, schizophrenia has been identified in a number of medical journals. This phenomenon serves as a reminder of Prigogine's observation that reintegration or disintegration may follow shake-up of energies. Therefore the intensification of energy through healing is not necessarily curative, and this important distinction between healing and curing cannot be over-stressed.

LeShan believes that transpsychic healing can also be trained, but only in those with a serious background in meditation and contemplation. Although admitting to not knowing how it 'works', he believes it to be 'the mobilisation and focusing of some as yet undefined type of energy'.[17] His own enquiries into its nature led him 'against all [my] expectations and preferences into fields hitherto left to religion',[18] and to conclusions similar to those reached by Reich and Jung before him, and various Eastern and Western traditions.

> The recurring theme 'God is love' appears to mean exactly what it says; that there is a force, an energy, that binds the cosmos together, and moves always in the direction of its harmonious action and the fruition of the separate connected parts. In man, this force emerges and expresses itself as love, and this is the 'spark of the divine' in each of us. When this force is acknowledged and reinforced by the culture it is possible for human beings to relate harmoniously to themselves, to others, to the rest of the cosmos, and to move toward the most unique and awesome self-fulfilment.[19]

LeShan suggests that when this force is ignored or discouraged, the energy becomes blocked and distorted, and in all human history has been expressed in self-hatred, a hunger for power, materialistic greed and ultimately the real possibility of man's so disrupting the expression of this energy as to end his part of the cosmic design.

> It seems to me that the challenge to science, to man, to the human experiment, is finally and irrevocably, whether or not man can accept that he is a part of the energy of the universe and can only function harmoniously within it through his capacity to love – infinitely.[20]

Thus, although not explicitly stated as such, LeShan's transpsychic healing may be regarded as spiritual in nature.

Spiritual healing

The term 'spiritual' lends itself to much confusion and misunderstanding, especially in materialistic cultures which are markedly 'aspiritual'. It may be taken as referring to the spirit or soul, and interpreted as relating to churches and religions. Accordingly spiritual healing tends to be attributed to God or gods, and is typically invoked by prayer and other rituals. Healing flourishes in all religions and movements including the Christian Church, and in less orthodox movements such as Christian Science, which was developed in the last century with the aim of reinstating the healing ministry of early Christianity. Many healers deplore the tendency of some Christian communions to regard healing as only possible for those who are members of a particular branch of the Christian faith.

> Spirit healing is not the prerogative of any religion or race; it is a common heritage for the whole of the human family. It is extensively practised in the lamaserys of Tibet, and every Mohammedan priest invokes the healing aid for his supplicants. The gift of healing is no more a perquisite of Christianity than any other religion.[21]

Moreover,

> There is not a set of healing laws for the Spiritualist and another for the Methodist or Christian Science practitioner. There are general laws that govern healing, as there are laws that govern every other effect produced in the universe.[22]

Church membership and theological terminology may be unacceptable to the vast numbers of people who have a deep belief in the power of God as the ruling force of the universe, but do not subscribe to any particular religious beliefs, and to the very great number who are members of faiths other than the Christian. The term 'primal healing' has been proposed[23] to refer to a form of healing that arises from complete attunement of the human mind and body with the first cause of the universe, whether described as God, Spirit, Universal Force, or otherwise.

Nevertheless the term 'spiritual healing' persists, and is often further confused by the common belief that it pertains to 'spirits', discarnate beings surviving in another realm and communicating with those on earth through mediums. This widespread belief is fostered in the emphasis on healing within the Spiritualist Church.

In Britain The National Spiritualists' Association recognises several different ways by which healing is effected: by spiritual influences working through a medium and infusing curative, stimulating and vitalising energies into the diseased body of another; by the spiritual forces illuminating the brain of the healing medium thereby intensifying perception of the cause of the disease and its remedy; and through absent treatments where spiritual energies blending with those of the medium are directed to a person distant from them. It therefore covers all aspects of spiritual healing, including psychic or intuitive diagnosis and absent treatment.

Confusion undoubtedly arises as a result of a failure to distinguish between 'spirits' and 'Spirit'. The former may be regarded as non-physical entities which function to transmit information or energies through the medium of one person's body or mind to that of another; and the latter as the source of these energies: a great cosmic power which pervades the entire universe. The latter concept, which forms the basis of Spiritualist philosophy, owes much to the influence of ancient and Eastern traditions, and to Theosophy, where 'poor spirits' – mental or physical – are thought to arise from a person's inability to attune themselves mentally to the great forces of nature which are essential for life.

Irrespective of what they choose to call it, most spiritual healers believe in this spiritual reality and are concerned to channel this Absolute Energy. A minority subscribe to belief in 'spirits' and claim to channel these energies. Therefore spiritual healing has, for the most part, little to do with spirits. Nevertheless, all spiritual healers are mediums in the sense that they mediate between an energy source and its eventual recipient.

Mediumship

Spiritual healing depends largely on an understanding of universal energies and the means of attunement with them. Central to this is the principle that the physical body can be acted on and influenced from higher spheres or planes of activity through or by means of the vital or etheric body which acts as a vehicle through which cosmic energy flows. The problem for the healer is to connect the etheric body with the physical body, on the one hand, and with the great reservoir of spiritual energy on the other.[24] It may well be that these are two different processes. What has been described as psychic healing involves the creation of 'a mind bridge'[25] between healer and healee which establishes the channel or wave band over which the cosmic or primal force then travels directly into the mind or body of the patient, whether they are in contact with or distant from the healer.

This mental connection is considered possible because both parties are immersed in a common etheric field through which energy and information can be transmitted. Accordingly the patient need not be present for the purposes of diagnosis and treatment. Such a view is consistent with holographic theory, according to which information about the whole is available at once in each of its parts. It is therefore sufficient to 'bring to mind' the patient in order to affect, and be affected by them.

Intuitive diagnosis

Like any bridge, the mind bridge can work in two directions. Hence by 'tuning' in to the energies of another person information can be obtained about them, even when they are not physically present. Intuitive diagnosis, whereby a person obtains reliable information about a person's state of health, and uses this as the basis for treatment is probably as old as medicine itself. It certainly goes back to Hippocrates, the intuitive physician widely regarded as the founder of Western medicine.[26] Celebrated intuitives such as Edgar Cayce, Jack Schwarz, Rosalind Bruyere and Carolyn Myss, have all been subjected to scientific investigation, although formal studies of intuitive diagnosis are relatively recent.

US neurosurgeon Norman Shealy has conducted research on several intuitives and claims to have found a 'significant rate of accuracy as determined by computer validation'. He concludes that intuitive diagnosis is not only possible but also highly successful.[27] One of the most outstanding intuitives of those he studied was the internist Dr Robert Leichtman, who was found by Shealy to be 96 per cent accurate in his evaluation of 'patients', as compared with about 80 per cent accuracy among physicians generally. Many doctors acknowledge that there is a strong element of intuition in all medical diagnoses, and so might be more persuaded by the claims made in respect of Dr Leichtman than those made by intuitives with no medical training. However, Leichtman demonstrated his accuracy using only photographs, the patients' names and birth dates.

Carolyn Myss has no medical training. She has developed her capacity to perceive a person's energy field or life force to such a degree that she can intuit the nature and precise location of physical disease within a person's body. This intuitive diagnosis, which forms the basis of a book co-authored by Shealy,[28] has been found to be 93 per cent accurate. Shealy provides insufficient detail to enable independent evaluation of his findings. However, the most compelling evidence for the accuracy of Myss' diagnosis is that he has successfully conducted surgery based upon it, and has sufficient confidence in it to do so. Nevertheless, other studies of intuitive diagnosis[29] are inconclusive, and there is a need for more rigorous investigations.

The therapeutics prescribed by many medical intuitives have been found to be appropriate and effective, despite their lack of medical knowledge.[30] Edgar Cayce, probably the best known and most widely researched intuitive diagnostician of all time, made some 15,000 diagnoses and therapeutic recommendations. The latter included conventional and unconventional medications. Many of the more unorthodox remedies, which are not recognised or understood by conventional medicine, have been found to be effective.[31] However, perhaps the most influential medical intuitive is the physician Dr Edward Bach, whose intuitively derived flower remedies are widely and increasingly used and researched.

It has been suggested[32] that healers (and medical intuitives) establish this mind bridge or channel by means akin to radio waves, albeit of a very much higher vibration, and that the healing forces operated by healers are also conceived as states of vibration. Hence when a healing takes place the healer applies a set of correcting vibratory forces to a given condition so as to bring about the change necessary to restore true balance and harmony. This 'may be the ABC of spirit healing'.[33] It is claimed[34] that these vibrations can be directed and timed to a split second by the healer, and that those to whom they are attuned actually receive an influx of energy. This claim finds support in studies[35] which have demonstrated that the EEG patterns of the recipients of healing alter simultaneously with those of the healer, even during absent healing; and the discovery that Olga Worrall could influence patterns in a cloud chamber when giving absent healing from 600 miles distant.[36] The same principle is the basis for radionics, which diagnoses and treats illness from an energetic frequency perspective.

Radionics

Radionics 'is a method of healing at a distance through the medium of an instrument using the ESP faculty'.[37] It provides a comprehensive system of health analysis and treatment.

Basic to radionics theory and practice is the concept that man and all life forms share a common ground in that they are submerged in the electromagnetic energy field of the earth; and further, that each life form has its own electromagnetic field which, if sufficiently distorted, will ultimately result in disease of the organism. By sensing the energy field, radionics practitioners can discover the cause of disease within any living system, be it a human being, animal, plant or the soil itself; and suitable therapeutic energies can then be made available to it to help restore optimal health.

Radionics originated in the work of Dr Albert Abrams (1863–1923), a neurologist and author of several textbooks, teacher of pathology and later Director of Studies at Stanford University Medical School. Finding that he obtained a hollow sound in the same place as disease when examining the abdomen of patients, he pioneered within orthodox medicine diagnosis by percussion, or tapping various parts of the body to produce resonating sounds. His investigations led him to conclude that some kind of energy was involved, and he developed a box containing resistors to measure disease reactions in ohms. This met with hostility among the medical orthodoxy, despite the fact that the practice of percussion has a very long history in traditional medicine and is demonstrably effective as a diagnostic technique. Abrams wrote many papers on his new diagnostic system, claiming that in this way disease could be detected before it was clinically identifiable in any orthodox way. He also began to experiment with reversing the energy flow in order to restore the patient's health, and developed an 'oscilloclast' to treat the patient by means of vibrations.

Doctors from all over the world went to California to learn about Abram's system and in 1924, the year of his death, it was investigated by the Royal Society for Medicine in London. It was concluded that Dr Abram's fundamental proposition 'had been proved to a high degree of probability'.[38] Nevertheless, as doctors of that era did not understand the relationship between energy and matter, it was decided that the system could not be taught in medical schools. Although some doctors continued to use the system, most practitioners of radionics today are not medically qualified.

The basis of radionics theory and practice as set out by Abrams[39] was subsequently developed and refined by a number of pioneers, most notably Dr Ruth Drown and George De La Warr[40,41] and more recently by David Tanstey,[42] Malcolm Rae and Aubrey Westlake.[43]

Radionics sees organs, disease and remedies as having their own characteristic frequency or vibration which can be expressed in numerical values known as 'rates' and calculated on radionics instruments. Using instruments she had developed for the purpose, and which are still in use today, Dr Ruth Drown, a chiropractor, identified a series of rates which in effect constitutes the vibrational pattern of known diseases. She was the first radionics practitioner to use distant treatment.

The radionics practitioner, in making an analysis, uses the principle of dowsing, detecting disease in much the same way that the dowser detects the location of water, oil or mineral deposits. The particular form of ESP used in radionics is often referred to as 'the radiesthetic faculty' through which the practitioner, by means of a series of mentally posed questions, obtains information about the health of his patient to which the conscious thinking mind has no direct access.[44]

Radionics systems which indicate this sensitivity more accurately than dowsing devices such as rods, pendulums or sticks, have been developed and tested in the USA and Europe for several decades. These have been termed 'psychotronic technologies'[45] because of the central role of the operator's consciousness in obtaining information from the device. The operator achieves a psychoenergetic link with various subtle energies through a process of attunement.

> This psychic process of tuning in… occurs at the level of our higher frequency vehicles of expression. In most individuals this energy linkup takes place at an unconscious level. The unconscious mind acts as a passageway through which higher frequency levels of consciousness may interact with the physical body. Higher psychic impressions are translated into various forms of the body's neurological circuitry. If the psychic information reaches conscious awareness, it

does so through the expressive mechanism of the cerebral cortex. Unconscious intuitive information may filter through the right cerebral hemisphere and then be transferred to the left hemisphere where it is analyzed and expressed verbally. While psychic information may not always reach conscious awareness, it is still processed by the nervous system and expressed through unconscious pathways of neurological and motor activity.[46]

The medium of expression is the dowsing instrument or radionics device.

The mechanical output of the pendulum, like the radionics device, is dependent upon the unconscious nervous output induced by psychic perceptual functioning. In the instance of the radionics device, the unconscious output is conveyed through the autonomic nervous system. In the case of the pendulum, the medium of expression is tiny unconscious skeletal muscle movements. Both systems capitalize on electrical changes in the nervous system of the physical body as a means of translating unconscious psychic data into conscious diagnostic energetic information.[47]

At its most simple, the radionics procedure involves a biological specimen – usually a drop of blood or a lock of hair – referred to as the 'witness'. This is placed in the well of the radionics instrument, a device consisting of a black box with a number of tuneable dials on the front, each numerically calibrated, and usually attached to variable resistors or potentiometers inside the box. These are also connected by wires to the circular metallic well and to a rubber pad which forms the interface between the operator and the device. While mentally tuning in to the patient, the radionics operator then lightly strokes a finger across the rubber pad. While doing so he or she slowly turns one of the dials.

The operator will register a positive response when he/she feels a sticking sensation in the finger as he/she strokes the pad. This might be viewed as a type of sympathetic resonance reaction. The resonance occurs between the energetic frequency of the patient and the subtle energy system of the radionics operator's nervous system. The dial is left tuned to the setting which induced a resonance response. The operator then moves on to a second dial, repeating the same procedure with the finger stroking until he/she has tuned all the dials to their appropriate settings. Each dial represents a digit in sequence which, when combined produces a multidigit number referred to as a 'rate'. The rate reflects the energetic frequency characteristics of the patient being remotely tested by the radionics device.

Based on a comparison of the patient's rate with a type of 'rate reference table', the radionics practitioner is able to make a presumptive diagnosis of the patient's pathological condition. Comparison of patients' rates with the standard rate reference tables allows matching of the patient's frequency with known vibrational frequencies associated with particular illnesses.[48]

This frequency matching procedure is similar to that in homeopathy, except that radionics directly measures the patient's primary energetic frequency disturbance rather than depending upon empirical frequency matching of remedy to symptom complex. To most orthodox physicians this process may appear nonsensical, although it conforms with the principles of biological resonance and holography. According to the latter, the witness reflects the total energetic structure of the entire organism and continues to do so because of resonance with the person from which it came, remaining in energetic equilibrium with its source regardless of distance. Readings are taken of the main physical systems and structures, the state of mental and emotional bodies, the chakra system and meridians.

Having divined the energetic frequency imbalances within the patient, radionics devices allow the practitioner to transmit vibrational energy of the needed frequency back to the patient by way of the chakras and meridians. The radionic rates of homeopathic, herbal, flower, gem and many other remedies can also be established in order to determine the most helpful treatments for any condition.

George de la Warr developed the radionics instruments so as to incorporate sound waves. Based on his work practitioners have been able to transmit simulations of homeopathic remedies, which are related to each other and to other forms of spiritual healing in that they involve the application of corrective vibratory forces. These forms of healing are claimed by their exponents to exert their influence at the etheric level by attempting to restore energy imbalances in the etheric body which controls the physical body. They are considered to achieve their effect by attunement to and amplification of the higher vibrations of man, which results in the stimulation of the body's self-healing processes. Such healing can be likened to applying 'jump leads' to a car battery, the depleted energies of which are 'boosted' by those of another, after which it is able to 'charge' itself. In all these apparently different methods of healing it is the psyche which mediates between spiritual, or higher mental energy and physical energy. Mind is thus the medium whereby energy is transmitted and transformed.

Mind as the medium of energy transformation

The notion of the mind as an energy transformer is misleading, however, suggesting as it does different energy factors. Yet, as Jung and others have observed, the striking similarity between the concept of energy in present-day physics and that underlying numerous psycho-spiritual traditions, both ancient and modern, suggests that 'they may well designate one and the same factor viewed from two complementary angles'.[49] Accordingly mind might more appropriately be thought of as a refractor which imposes a different 'angle' on this energy, transforming only in the sense of directing it. The healer's belief that they are mentally 'channelling' energy seems consistent with this notion, but how this is achieved remains open to question. Efforts to represent a comprehensible picture of what is known about energy – which, since it is conserved might be viewed as the modern successor of substance – require a conception of 'form'. This is no less true of relativity and quantum theories, in the former energy being pictured as the curvature of space-time, and in the latter as a periodicity of waves.

Energy transforms
Number and rhythm

Amorphous energy probably does not exist, in as much as that when it manifests in either psychic or physical dimensions it is always 'numerically' structured, as 'waves' for example, or as (psychic) rhythm.[50] Jung observed the tendency of all emotional and energy laden psychic processes to become rhythmical; 'Any kind of excitement... displays a tendency to rhythmical expression, perseveration, and repetition'.[51] This may explain the basis of various rhythmic and ritual activities performed by primitive peoples, and the dependence of work-achievement on music, dancing, singing, drumming and rhythm, in general; 'Through them, psychic energy and the ideas and activities bound up with it are imprinted and firmly organised in consciousness'. Hence, the application of rhythm to psychic energy 'was probably the first step towards its cultural formation, and hence its spiritualization'.[52]

According to Jung,[53] the Chinese concept of number is based on association with this type of rhythmic activity in man. From the earliest times the Chinese used number to assess feeling-intensities of all things that had a psychic effect on man. Number remains the common ordering factor of both physical and psychic manifestations of energy, and is consequently the element that draws mind and matter together.

> Natural numbers appear to represent the typical, universally recurring, common motion patterns of both psychic *and physical energy*. Because of these motion patterns (numbers are identical for both forms of energy), the human mind can, on the whole, grasp the phenomena of the outer world. This means that the motion patterns engender 'thought and structure' models in man's psyche, which can be applied to physical phenomena and achieve relative congruence. The existence of such numerical constants in the outer world, on the one hand, and in the preconscious psyche, on the other... is probably what finally makes all conscious knowledge of nature possible.[54]

Number can therefore be regarded as a mediator between psychic or 'inner' situations and physical or 'outer' ones. Thus when trying to understand these latter patterns consciously one makes use of the abstractions of higher mathematics for the observation of quantitative manifestations of energy.

Accordingly, mathematics is the language of physics, and through its use physicists attempt to provide accurate descriptions of physical reality.

Symbolism

However, there is no branch of mathematics for the observation and description of qualitative manifestations of energy.[55] To make them comprehensible one must first develop a qualitative view of number, such as has been attempted in relation to rhythm.[56] Arguably, however, 'comprehensive pictures' of the qualitative aspects of energy are provided, quite literally, by the symbols of visual imagery, which is why imagery is traditionally the language of the mystic, the medium and the poet, and why, in recent times, striking parallels have been noted between their descriptions of reality and the mathematical descriptions of the physicist.

Symbols are the supreme mediators between different worlds of experience, and thus transformers of energy.[57] That they are used as such by healers can be gleaned from the accounts of contemporary healers;[58-62] and from traditional healing traditions such as Japanese Reiki or Tibetan healing. Common to all of these is an emphasis on the use of imagery combined with relaxation.

Olga Worrall described[63] imagining energy in the form of light flowing from her hands into the patient during healing. LeShan also describes his use of symbols in training himself and others to attain the clairvoyant mode in which he believes healing is achieved:

> For example, I might use the symbol of two trees on opposite sides of a hill with the tops visible to each other. From one viewpoint they looked like two separate trees but inside the hill the two root masses met and were one. The two trees were really one and inseparable. Further, their roots affected the earth and the rocks until I could know that in the whole planet and cosmos there was nothing that was not affected by them and affecting them. This sort of symbolization, different in each case, as the healee and I are different in each healing encounter, would often be useful in helping reach the Clairvoyant Reality with the healee and myself centred in it.[64]

Symbols appear to function as a means of attunement to subtle energies of the self and other life forms. Some forms of healing rest on understanding of cosmic symbols which offer a precise technique for accessing universal transcendental energy. In this way they can be considered to build the 'mind bridge' between the cosmos and the healer, on the one hand, and the healer and the healee, on the other.

According to tradition, Usui, a Japanese academic searching for an explanation of how Buddha and Christ healed by laying on hands, had a vision following meditation in which he saw symbols which later enabled him to channel the energy of Reiki or Universal Life for himself and others. He evolved the precise use of these symbols in a series of attunement processes designed to activate life energy which could then be directed by laying on hands.

The principle of resonance, whereby vibrational forms tend to attract energy of a similar quality and vibration, has been used to explain the role of thought and imagery in mobilising energy:

> The idea is like a blueprint; it creates an image of the form, which then magnetises and guides the physical energy to flow into that form and eventually manifests on a physical plane.[65]

Externalisation of these images, as in artwork, may be even more potent in mobilising energy.

> Symbols are transformers of energy. They have expressive and impressive features. On the one hand they express the intrapsychic processes in images, but on the other, when they become 'incarnated' in pictorial material they make an impression: i.e.: their meaning content influences the intrapsychic process and furthers the flow of psychic energy.[66]

Sound

Visual images and thoughts are not the only psychic mediators of energy.

> Sound, when understood generally as matter in a state of vibration, obviously encompasses much more than we can ordinarily hear with our ears. We can readily acknowledge that sound, even in the ordinary sense, has effects beyond bringing pleasant or unpleasant associations to mind. It can directly affect our body, just as certain sounds can break glass. Theoretically it is thus obvious that all sound has some effect on us, even though we may not recognise what it is.[67]

This understanding forms the basis of the traditional use of sound in healing. Sound vibrates in waves at different frequencies and is transmitted to the brain via the auditory nerve. These auditory messages may also reach the autonomic nervous system which regulates organs and body functions, and influence physiological functions such as heart rate and breathing. Rhythmic auditory stimuli such as drumming, singing and chanting have been widely employed by shamans and magico-religious practitioners throughout history during rituals. These may generate changes in brain wave patterns, and encourage rich imagery.[68] Rhythms corresponding to theta frequency have been identified in response to Native American drumming[69] and in Eastern mantra chanting.[70] Buddhist chanting has also been found to increase alpha response.[71]

Buddhist monks and Tibetan yogis have a long tradition of chanting to induce altered mental and physical states. Variations in energy may be regarded as different qualities of vibration and associated with different levels of reality, which correspond with a hierarchy of sound. It is therefore possible to equate divine energy with divine vibration or sound. This 'mantra theory' dates far back in the history of religion.

> Sacred language may from one point of view be defined as a system of sounds based on knowledge which we, in present times, do not have. Thus speaking very abstractly, a sacred language is a reflection of the entire spectrum of creative energies in the universe. The use of music and chanting, the arrangement of words in a song or myth, probably have to be understood in this context. Theoretically we would have to recognise the distinction between that aspect of language which provokes certain images and ideas which in turn affect our organism, and another aspect of language which directly affects our organism by vibration in a carefully controlled way. Surely scripture, if it is 'sacred' does both. 'Secular' or ordinary language may be understood simply as language in which these elements are poorly recognised and uncontrolled.[72]

It is said that Sanskrit is such a language and that the Vedic hymns, which are the root of all Hindu culture, were composed and sung as reflections of the divine play of creative energy. Many mantras used in traditional forms of meditation are short phrases or words from the Vedas and even those from other sources are all Sanskrit. Even when Indian disciples spread to foreign lands the mantras used tended to remain in Sanskrit because of what is understood to be the cosmic and psychological properties of the language.

Although certain mantras such as *Om* are supposed to produce the same effect for anyone who intones them correctly, the practical use of mantras is also based on the idea that individuals vary in regard to which particular sounds are helpful to them. The dispensation of mantras is therefore regarded as demanding an extraordinary psychological knowledge, 'not only of men as they are, but of men as they can become',[73] because repetition of any sound or mantra over months or even years will produce certain effects. It is generally considered to require the understanding of great masters.

Among Native Americans religious words have a special potency integral to their special sounds.[74] What is named is understood as present in the name rather than merely symbolised by it. Moreover, just as words bear power, a statement of thought is also understood to have a potency of its own.

In the religious traditions of Central and South America each individual is considered to have a particular note and pitch, knowledge of which can be used to effect their purification and healing, or their death. Similarly, throughout Africa and the East the human voice is widely used in healing and in influencing emotional states. The *kiai* or fighting cry of the Japanese Samurai is said, when uttered in a minor key, to produce 'partial paralysis by a reaction that suddenly lowers the arterial blood pressure.[75] It is probable that the famous 'blood curdling' cry uttered to devastating effect by Laurence Olivier in his much-acclaimed performance as Coriolanus was achieved similarly, albeit unwittingly.

Modern science uses the same principles, harnessing very high frequency sound waves in the form of the ultrasonic scanner within medicine, and at the other extreme, very low frequency sound waves are being explored as military weapons.[76]

Other physical effects of sound are claimed in the legends of Mexico and Peru. According to these, ancient peoples had such 'sound knowledge' that by this means alone they could split massive stone slabs along precise harmonic lines and then move them into position by resonance. The temples of Uxmal and Macchu Pichu are thought to have been raised and patterned in symphonies of sound.[77]

Navajo Indian legend tells of shamans who could produce pictures in sand merely by speaking to it, and that this may be possible was demonstrated by the eighteenth century German physicist Ernst Chladni, who discovered a way of making vibration patterns visible.

Chladni observed the changing patterns of sand scattered on steel discs in response to violin notes. He noted that the disc resonates to the violin only in certain places, shifting sand only to those areas which are inert. The resulting patterns, known as Chladni figures, have been extensively used in physics to demonstrate wave function, but they can also be used to show that different frequencies produce patterns with different forms. Using powders of different densities and a wide range of frequencies, it is possible to induce patterns of almost any form. Commonly they adopt familiar organic forms:

> Concentric circles, such as the annual rings in a tree trunk; alternating lines, such as the stripes on a zebras back; hexagonal grids, such as the cells in a honeycomb; radiating wheel spokes such as the canals in a jellyfish; vanishing spirals, such as the turrets of shellfish.[78]

Cymatics

The study of the effects of waves or vibrations on matter was termed cymatics by Hans Jenny, who expanded and refined Chladni's research, and in so doing, produced further evidence that form is a function of frequency.[79,80] He demonstrated that raising the pitch of the sound causes a pattern to invert itself into a moving one; and by raising it again, a static but different pattern is produced once more, and so on. Thus the formalised expression of the ascending musical scale alternates between static and fluid. This, it has been suggested, is a visual expression of the yin/yang concept of duality.[81] There are always patterns on the disc, the one formed by sand and the background, which is free of sand.

> The runnels of sand which we see are simply where it has collected at the 'dead' areas of the disc, whereas the 'life' of the pattern is vibrating in the background behind, or between the runnels, where invisible energy is causing chaos to

coalesce into form. The paradox is that the *visible* expression of energy is the inverse of the actual vibrationary pattern, which is invisible...

After centuries of concentrating only on what it can see and touch, science is now beginning to look *between* these runnels, into the background of metaphysical order. We are reminded again of the Gnostics' assertions that the physical world is but a pale shadow – the mirror image or outermost shell of a supreme ordering energy which exists in another dimension.[82]

Jenny further developed his experiments, devising a 'tonoscope' which transforms sound uttered into a microphone into a three-dimensional visual representation on a screen. When correctly intoned into it, the sacred Sanskrit syllable *Om* can be seen to produce a perfect circle, which then filled with concentric squares and triangles, and finally a *yantra* – the formal geometric expression of sacred vibration which is found in many world religions. This would seem to suggest that 'liturgical language and music supplied not only a special vocabulary through which the ancient priest classes could speak of different realities, but a vocabulary which itself resonated to the vibrations it described'.[83]

Sound therapies

Sound therapies attempt to harness sound waves in the diagnosis and treatment of disease. Their exponents maintain that disease, which manifests in a change of fundamental frequency of the vibrational or energy output of the body, can be treated by application of vibrations of a similar frequency which restore disturbed inner rhythms to their natural harmony. Practitioners use a number of different approaches in treatment.

In **Cymatics,** a machine is placed over the body part to be treated and sound waves are transmitted through the skin in an attempt to cause body cells to vibrate at an optimum healthy resonance.

Physioacoustic Methodology, developed in Finland, uses computer-generated sound waves which are played through speakers in a specially designed chair to relax the occupant, and thus reduce muscle tension and lower blood pressure. This therapy, and its variants, are becoming increasingly popular throughout Europe in the treatment of stress-related disorders.

Chanting techniques are also widely used in healing. Participants are taught, usually in workshops, to use tones in the voice to create pure sounds, which are said to resonate through the body and induce mental and physical well-being.

The Tomatis Method, developed by French ear, nose and throat surgeon, Alfred Tomatis, aims to retrain individuals who experience difficulty in processing certain sound frequencies, such as those with autism or dyslexia, to hear and listen properly. It is based on the premise that music and vocal sounds rich in high frequencies have an energising effect which corresponds to the effect of the mother's voice on the developing foetus. The Tomatis Method uses specially filtered music tapes of particular frequencies, such as pieces by Mozart and Gregorian chants, and, if possible, the sound of the mother's voice, directed via headsets that are modified to deliver through bone conduction as well as air.

Auditory Integration Training (AIT) is a similar method, developed by French ear specialist Dr Guy Berard. These methods have been promoted as an effective treatment for learning disabilities, depression and immune disorders. However, while increased alpha response has been found in complex rhythmic music such as Mozart symphonies,[84] there is as yet no convincing evidence from clinical studies to support these claims.

Although orthodox physicians are generally sceptical about the claims made for sound therapies, and to the idea of 'tuning in' to a person's physical vibrations, it is well established that body tissue can absorb and reflect sound waves differently, hence the extensive use in conventional medicine of ultrasound scans, the electrocardiogram, which records the vibrations or electrical frequencies of the heart, and the electroencephalogram, which measures brain waves. However, sonic and ultrasonic treatments are less well developed, their experimental use being largely confined to osteoplasty.

The most widespread form of sound therapy is music therapy.

Music therapy

According to Ethiopian legends language developed from song. Early man could only sing but eventually he forgot the tune and had to rely on speaking the words. 'The vibrations of music, such a primary part of primitive expression, hints at a forgotten awareness of the rhythms and tones which actually keep us alive.'[85] The central place occupied by music in the education of the Greeks was 'due to the recognition that the harmonics of sound unlocked in the student an awareness of the interplay of invisible relationships'.[86]

Music has long been recognised and used as a mediator between physical and metaphysical realities, and as a means of achieving psychic reintegration. Accordingly music had a widely acknowledged therapeutic significance in the ancient world, and healing with music is a long-standing tradition in both Eastern and Western cultures.

Contemporarily in the West, there are two broad approaches to music therapy: 'active', which requires the person to play instruments or sing, and 'passive' where the person listens to music. Within these approaches, there are various schools, some based on the work of particular teachers and others on certain psychotherapeutic approaches. There is a vast literature on the subject and its applications, and many positive claims made for it, but a lack of valid clinical research from which substantive conclusions can be drawn.[87] Hence the clinical value of music therapy remains somewhat speculative.

The measurable physiological effects of music include reduction of blood pressure and heart rate, changes in respiratory rate, and reduced muscle activity, which are consistent with relaxation. Music therapy has been applied within psychiatry and psychotherapy, principally to assist relaxation and in alleviating anxiety states; in the treatment of schizophrenia and depression, and Alzheimer's disease. It is similarly used in coronary care units and in hospices, in the treatment of cancer and some neurological problems, and in working with individuals, notably children, with learning difficulties and autism; and in the care of the elderly. Music therapy appears to be most effective in the relief of pain. The benefits of music, including analgesia, can largely be attributed to its relaxing effects. As yet its influence on immunological parameters has not been established, although this remains a possibility which needs investigation.[88]

Chromatics

Cymatics has demonstrated that sound and form are a matter of vibrational frequency, and it is now recognised that this is also true of light and colour. Chromatics, the science of colour, is the study of this relationship.

Ancient man viewed light as sustaining life and all the functions and processes of living things. 'En-lightenment' was synonymous with health in its literal sense of wholeness or holiness of body, mind and spirit. Hence to the ancients light was a spiritual as well as a physical phenomenon. In many ancient cultures the sun was worshipped. The most important aim of life was to realise the light and thereby God. Ancient magic attempted to achieve this connection by 'bringing down' the light, transferring and reflecting its power. Magic and religion were thus inextricably linked with each other and with healing.

Light and colour

Light is a narrow band of visible energy in the middle of a spectrum that embraces energies from cosmic rays to radio waves. These energies are graded according to wavelength and measured in nanometers, each equivalent to one millionth of a millimetre. The spectrum of visible light falls within 380–760nm. Each variation in wavelength within this band of energy can be sensed by our eyes and perceived as a specific colour. Reds have the longest wavelength, lowest frequency and least energy, while violets have the shortest wavelength, highest frequencies and most energy. Beyond the red end of the visible spectrum there are longer wavelengths of infrared radiation, microwaves and radio waves; beyond the violet end there are shorter wavelengths of ultraviolet radiation, X-rays, gamma rays and cosmic rays. The energy of sunlight produces all the wavelengths of colour from ultraviolet through the visual spectrum to infrared in a roughly equal distribution. This is known as full-spectrum white light.

Ancient man considered each of the energies that make up sunlight to show a different aspect of the divine and to influence different qualities of life. Colour was therefore an important feature in the symbolism of ancient cultures throughout the world, and the origins of healing with colour in Western civilisation can be traced back to the mythology of ancient Egypt and Greece.

Interest in the physical nature of colour developed in Ancient Greece alongside the concept of the elements. Each element was associated with a certain colour and so colour was intrinsic to healing, which involved restoring the balance of these elements. Coloured garments, oils, plasters, oils, ointments and salves were used to treat disease. Pythagoras and Hippocrates included their use in several treatises on medicine.

An Arab physician and disciple of Aristotle, Avicenna (980–c. 1037) indicated the importance of colour in both diagnosis and treatment in his *Canon of Medicine*. He noted that colour was an observable symptom of disease, and developed a chart which related colour to temperament and the physical condition of the body. He also used colour in treatment, insisting that red moved the blood, blue or white cooled it, and yellow reduced pain and inflammation. He prescribed red flowers to cure blood disorders and yellow flowers and morning sunlight to cure disorders of the biliary system.

Avicenna wrote about the possible dangers of colour in treatment, observing that a person with a nose-bleed should not gaze on things of a brilliant red colour or be exposed to red light as this would stimulate the sanguinous humour, whereas blue would soothe it and reduce blood flow.

During the Middle Ages, Paracelsus used light and colour extensively in treatment, but with the advent of physical medicine in the seventeenth century, and its emphasis on surgery and antiseptics, interest in healing with colour declined. It did not resurface until the nineteenth century.

In 1876 Augustus Pleasonton[89] reported his findings on the effects of colour on plants, animals and humans. He claimed that the quality, yield and size of grapes could be significantly increased if they were grown in glasshouses with alternating blue and transparent panes. He also reported having cured various diseases, increased fertility and the rate of physical maturation in animals by exposing them to blue light. Pleasonton also maintained that blue light was effective in treating human diseases and pain. His work gained supporters, but was dismissed by the medical establishment as unscientific.

In 1877 a distinguished physician Dr Seth Pancoast also advocated the use of colour in healing,[90] to little effect, but a subsequent book by Edwin Babbitt[91] attracted worldwide attention. In this he advanced a comprehensive theory of healing with colour. He identified the colour red as a stimulant, notably of blood and to a lesser extent the nerves; yellow and orange as nerve stimulants; blue and violet as soothing to all systems, and with anti-inflammatory properties.

Accordingly he prescribed red for paralysis, consumption, physical exhaustion and chronic rheumatism; yellow as a laxative, emetic and purgative and for bronchial difficulties; blue for inflammatory conditions, sciatica, meningitis, nervous headache, irritability and sunstroke. He developed special devices, including a special cabinet called a Thermolume which used coloured glass and natural light to produce coloured light; and the Chromo Disk, a funnel-shaped device fitted with special colour filters that could localise light onto various parts of the body.

Babbitt established the correspondences between colours and minerals, which he used in addition to treatment with coloured light, and developed elixirs by irradiating water with sunlight filtered through coloured lenses. He claimed that this 'potentised' water retained the energy of the vital elements within the particular colour filter used, and that it had remarkable healing power. Solar tinctures of this kind are still made and used today by many colour therapists.

Chromopaths subsequently sprang up throughout the USA and Britain, and they developed extensive colour prescriptions for every conceivable ailment. By the end of the nineteenth century, red light was used to prevent scars forming in cases of smallpox, and startling cures were later reported among tuberculosis patients exposed to sunlight and ultraviolet rays. Nevertheless, the medical profession remained sceptical of any claims made for healing with colour.

Investigations into the therapeutic uses of colour were carried out in Europe during the early twentieth century, notably by Rudolph Steiner,[92] the originator of anthroposophical medicine, who related colour to form, shape and sound. He suggested that the vibrational quality of certain colours is amplified by some forms, and that certain combinations of colour and shape have either destructive or regenerative effects on living organisms. In the schools inspired by Steiner's work, classrooms are painted and textured to correspond to the 'mood' of children at various stages of their development.

Steiner's work was continued by Theo Gimbel.[93-95] Among the principles he has explored are the claims of Max Lüscher, a former professor of psychology at Basle University, who claimed that colour preferences demonstrate states of mind and/or glandular imbalance, and can be used as the basis for physical and psychological diagnosis. Lüscher's theory, which forms the basis of the Lüscher Colour test,[96] rests on the idea that the significance of colour for man originates in his early history, when his behaviour was governed by night and day. Lüscher believed that the colours associated with these two environments – yellow and dark blue – are connected with differences in metabolic rate and glandular secretions appropriate to the energy required for night-time sleep and day-time hunting. He also believed that autonomic responses are associated with other colours.

Support for Lüscher's theories was provided in the 1940s by the Russian scientist S.V. Krakov[97] who established that the colour red stimulates the sympathetic branch of the autonomic nervous system, while blue stimulates the parasympathetic branch. His findings were confirmed in 1958 by Robert Gerard of the USA.[98]

Gerard found that red was disturbing to anxious or tense subjects, while blue had a calming effect. Red produced feelings of arousal and blue produced feelings of calm, tranquillity and well-being. The discovery that blood pressure increases under red light and decreases under blue light led Gerard to suggest that psychophysiological activation increases with wavelength from blue to red.

Although cautious about his findings and insisting on the need for further research, Gerard highlighted the possible therapeutic benefits of the colour blue, and recommended it as a supplementary therapy in the treatment of various conditions. Among other suggestions, Gerard pointed to the possible uses of blue as a tranquilliser and relaxant in anxious individuals, and as a way of reducing blood pressure in the treatment of hypertension.

Dr Harry Wohlfarth[99] also showed that certain colours have measurable and predictable effects on the autonomic nervous system. In numerous studies he found that blood pressure and pulse and respiration rates increase most under yellow light, moderately under orange and minimally under red, while decreasing most under black, moderately under blue and minimally under green.

Subsequent research on plants and animals conducted by the pathologist Dr John Ott[100,101] also demonstrated the effects of colour on growth and development. Plants grown under red glass were found to shoot up four times more quickly than those grown in ordinary sunlight, and to grow much more slowly under green glass. However, although red light initially over-stimulated plants, their growth was subsequently stunted, whereas blue light produced slower growth initially, but taller, thicker plants later.

Rodents kept under blue plastic grew normally, but when kept under red or pink plastic their appetite and growth increased. If kept under blue light they grew denser coats.

During the 1950s studies suggested that neo-natal jaundice, a potentially fatal condition found in two-thirds of premature babies, could be successfully treated by exposure to sunlight.[102] It was subsequently established[103] that exposure to full-spectrum or blue light was also effective, and white light replaced high-risk blood transfusions in the treatment of this condition. Intense blue light is now the most common form of treatment for neo-natal jaundice, but full-spectrum white light is also used and is considered by some to be natural and safer.[104]

Bright white full-spectrum light is now also used in the treatment of cancers, seasonal affective disorder, anorexia and bulimia nervosa, insomnia, jet lag, shift-working, alcohol and drug dependency and to reduce overall levels of medication. The blue light used successfully in the treatment of neo-natal jaundice has also been shown to be effective in the treatment of rheumatoid arthritis.[105] Most subjects exposed to blue light for variable periods of up to 15 minutes experienced a significant degree of pain relief. Blue light is also used in healing injured tissue, in the treatment of cancers and non-malignant tumours, skin and lung conditions. In 1990 scientists reported to the Annual conference of the American Association of the Advancement of Science on the successful use of blue light in a wide variety of psychological problems, including addictions, impotence, eating disorders and depression.[106]

At the other end of the healing spectrum, red light has been shown to be effective in the treatment of migraine, headache and cancer.[107] Red and green light has also been used in the treatment of seasonal affective disorder.[108] As a result, colour is becoming widely accepted as a therapeutic tool with various medical applications.

A technique developed in the USA over the past two decades, and recently introduced to Britain, is photodynamic therapy or PDT. This is based on the discovery[109,110] that certain intravenously injected photosensitive chemicals not only accumulate in cancer cells but selectively identify these cells under ultraviolet light. These photosensitive chemicals then exclusively destroy the cancer cells when activated by red light, whose longer wavelength allows it to penetrate tissue more deeply than other colours. PDT can be used for both diagnosis and treatment. In a worldwide experiment more than 3000 people with a wide variety of malignant tumours have been successfully treated with this technique.[111]

Colour is also used therapeutically in a variety of non-medical settings, including gymnasia, prisons, and reformatories. Studies have shown that viewing red lights increases subjects' strength by 13.5 per cent and elicits 5.8 per cent more muscular activity in the arm muscles,[112] and this method is now used to improve the performance of athletes. Red light appears to help athletes who need short, quick bursts of energy, whereas blue light assists in performances requiring a steady energy output.[113]

Colour has also been shown to affect emotion. Pink has been found to have a tranquillising and calming effect within minutes of exposure.[114] It suppresses hostile, aggressive and anxious behaviour, and has been found to reduce muscle strength within 2.7 seconds of exposure.[115] It appears that when in pink surroundings people cannot be aggressive even if they want to because the colour saps their energy. Hence pink holding cells are now widely used to reduce violent and aggressive behaviour in prisons.

Other studies have confirmed the effects of colour on the emotions,[116] as suggested in phrases such as 'seeing red', 'feeling blue', 'being in the pink' and so on, attributing them to the effects of the electromagnetic energy of colour on the endocrine system, notably the pituitary and pineal glands, and the hypothalamus, which influence mood.

Studies have also suggested that there may be some substance to the notion that there may be some benefits from viewing life through rose-tinted spectacles. American psychologist Helen Irlen discovered that colour-tinted spectacles can be highly effective in the treatment of learning difficulties, notably dyslexia.[117] This was regarded sceptically until recent investigations by the British Medical Research Council confirmed Irlen's claims. In 1993 a new device called the Intuitive Colorimeter, was made available to British opticians so they could measure which tint – bright pink, yellow, green or blue – best helps people who normally see text as swirling, wobbling or with letters appearing in the wrong order.

It has been established that colour need not be visually perceived for it to have definite psychological and physical effects. It can be distinguished by blind, colour-blind and blind-folded subjects.[118] This phenomenon has been researched since the 1920s when it was found that hypnotised blind-folded persons could recognise colour and shape with their forehead (third eye), and that non-hypnotised subjects could precisely describe colours and shapes presented under glass. Research in Russia during the 1960s was stimulated by studies which found that a blind-folded subject could distinguish colour and shapes with her fingertips. Subsequent studies found that people could be trained to recognise colour with their fingertips in only 20–30 minutes training and that blind people developed this sensitivity even more quickly.[119]

Colour therapy

Scientific discoveries about the effects of colour lend support to observations of seers since ancient times about the subtle energies of the body. Hence, although colour is widely and increasingly used in orthodox medicine, colour therapy is generally a complementary therapy which relies on the aura and chakras in diagnosis and treatment. In colour therapy disease is viewed as a depletion of energies within the physical and etheric bodies, which can be supplemented by the application of appropriate colour vibrations to the relevant chakras. Treatment may be through direct contact with the patient or by absent healing methods. In the former the therapist works with the aura, sensing imbalances clairvoyantly, or by passing the hands over the body and noting changes in vibration associated with various parts of the body. Chakra function may also be assessed by dowsing or by applied kinesiology. In the latter the therapist holds a colour at the patient's eye level with the left arm while extending the right arm horizontally. As each colour is perceived, he or she applies gentle downward pressure to the extended right arm. Lack of resistance to this pressure suggests that the person needs the colour he or she is perceiving.

A more complex form of diagnosis[120] involves dowsing the spine with the fingers. This is based on similar principles to radionics, but a signature or photograph of the patient is used as a 'witness' rather than a blood or hair sample. This is placed under a chart depicting the spine. Using the middle finger of his or her dominant hand the therapist makes passes over the chart vertebra by vertebra noting any sensations. This form of diagnosis is based on the idea that the subtle energy along the spinal channel is organised in sections relating to each chakra, and is associated with different physical and psychological functions. Diagnosis is determined by which vertebra, and hence which colours, are active (producing sensation) or inactive (producing no sensations) in any section.

Treatment in colour therapy involves the projection of coloured light to relevant chakras using various devices such as lamps and filters. In many instances the light provided is defined by shapes believed to enhance the colour's energetic effects. Full-spectrum lamps fitted with special quartz filters that produce colours of all wavelengths and frequencies may be used. Elixirs, pigments, gemstones, crystals, coloured essential oils and flower essences may also be also be prescribed. Aura-soma therapy, an increasingly popular form of colour therapy, uses colour choice in diagnosis, and 'synchronised wavelengths' of herbs, essential oils and crystal energies in treatment.

In absent healing the healer meditates on 'sending' a particular colour ray to the individual being treated. Whether healing at a distance or not, visualisation is considered to improve the power of therapy.[121] Visualisation of light and colour has always played an important role in traditional systems of healing, especially those of Tibet and China. It is also a component of Therapeutic Touch. The principle underpinning colour visualisation is that imagining colour produces vibrations of certain frequencies which can be directed to the energy centres of the body to bring about various physiological and physical effects. Visualisation of and meditation on colour are also thought to strengthen its energies and increase its healing properties. Imagining vital energies as light and colour is encouraged in many traditions, ancient and modern[122] as a way of enhancing, redirecting and normalising them.

Flower therapies

In all parts of the world since the earliest times flowering trees, plants, shrubs and herbs have been used for healing purposes. All parts of plants have been used. Ginseng, a substance derived from the aromatic roots of *Panax schinseng* or *Panax quinquefolius*, has long been used medicinally in China and is now widely used in the West. Quinine derived from chinchona bark, is used as a tonic, to relieve fever and pain, and in malaria therapy. Aspirin, also widely used to relieve pain, fever and colds and to reduce inflammation, derives from the stems of Spiraea. The narcotic drug, cocaine, widely used medicinally as a topical anaesthetic, is derived from coca leaves. Two of the most potent pain-killing agents, morphine and codeine, are alkoloids extracted from the unripe seed capsules of the opium poppy *Papver somniferum*. The heart stimulant digitalis is prepared from the dried leaves of foxglove. Linseed from the flax plant and mustard seed have long been used as poultices, and oils derived from various parts of plants have a wide variety of medical uses. Pharmacy throughout the ages has been based on the recognition of the medicinal properties of plants, as has medical herbalism. However, throughout history, flowers have been considered to embody the essential nature of the plant and to have particular healing powers.

The white lotus was regarded as sacred by the ancient Egyptians, and also in India, China and Tibet, where it represents the state of perfect health or holiness. To the Tibetans, the lotus flower is not merely a symbol of perfection, but a means of realising it. They teach that there is a direct link between the essential nature of plants and man's essential nature or soul, and that at an unconscious level he can make contact with his own essence through that of plants and so restore harmony within himself. Flowers therefore have a vital healing function.

The idea underpinning this teaching is that the essence of any phenomenon is its vibrational character and that there is a fundamental resonance between it and aspects of human nature which can be used to restore harmony to the latter. As such, systems of healing with flowers utilise similar principles to homeopathy, and have a similar method of preparation.

Flower therapies use flower essences: 'liquid pattern-infused solutions made from individual plant flowers, each containing a specific imprint that responds in a balancing, repairing and rebuilding manner to humans on their physical, emotional, mental and spiritual or universal levels'.[123] This imprint is the vibrational character of the flower. It is claimed that the effects of flower essences are comparable with hearing a particular moving piece of music whose sound vibrations evoke emotions that indirectly affect physiological processes such as breathing, pulse rate and other physical states.[124] This claim has yet to be established empirically. While there is abundant evidence emerging from PNI that emotions trigger biochemical responses which in turn bring about changes in nerve function, digestion, respiration, circulation and the immune system,[125] it needs to be shown first that infusions of flowers carry vibrations that trigger changes in the energy of the human body, and then that this particular energy change is related to emotions.

Nevertheless, systems of healing with flower essences, many of them long-standing, are numerous and widespread throughout the world. The first modern therapeutic system was based on flower essence developed by the British physician Edward Bach (1886–1936). From his two brief accounts[126,127] of the development of flower essences as a system of treatment, it is clear Bach was greatly influenced by Hahnemann, the originator of homeopathy.

> Disease will never be cured or eradicated by present materialistic methods, for the simple reason that disease is in origin not material. What we know as disease is an ultimate result produced in the body, the end product of deep and long-acting forces, and even if material treatment alone is apparently successful this is nothing more than a temporary relief unless the real cause has been removed.[128]

For Bach the 'real' cause of disease is conflict between soul and mind, or personality which manifests in a distortion of the wavelength in the energy field of the body which slows down, exerting a negative effect on the whole psyche and resulting in 'soul states' such as worry, anxiety and impatience. These negative states so deplete the individual's vitality that the body loses its natural resistance and becomes vulnerable to infection and illness. Bach's research led him to conclude that positive healthy states of mind could be restored by the energies found in flowering plants.

Initially Bach discovered 12 flowers, each with a natural affinity to certain mental traits. These, he believed, showed the same vibrational character as the quality concerned, but without distortion and at the natural rhythm, and could thus be used to re-establish its harmonious vibration through the principle of resonance. Accordingly by operating at subtle energy levels, these flowers can act as a catalyst for reintegration and healing.

> The action of these Remedies is to raise our vibrations and open up our channels for the reception of our Spiritual Self; to flood our natures with the particular virtue we need, and wash out from us the fault which is causing harm. They are able, like beautiful music or any glorious thing that gives us inspiration to raise our very natures and bring us nearer to our souls, and by that very act bring us peace and relieve our sufferings. They cure not by attacking disease, but by flooding our bodies with the beautiful vibrations of our Higher Nature, in the presence of whom disease melts away as snow in sunshine.[129]

He went on to identify 38 flowers which he believed could be used to remedy all the known states of mind that afflict humankind. He considered his flower remedies to be a complete system of healing requiring 'no extension or alteration'. Like Hahnemann therefore, Bach believed that the patient should be treated rather than the disease, and the cause rather than its effects. In each case the mental outlook of the person is chosen as the guide to the necessary remedies, because Bach believed that the mind shows the onset and course of disease more definitely than the body.

Bach tested his remedies on himself, and his findings were subsequently verified by a medical colleague who used them in his own practice. Bach also treated many patients successfully with his remedies. After his death his work was continued in his name and his flower remedies are now known and used worldwide.

Although Bach believed his system to be complete, in recent years other systems have been developed that are considerably more extensive. The repertory of California Flower Essences[130] includes 72 well-described and understood essences, with a further 24 essences still at the research stage of development, and 200 yet to be investigated. The system described by Gurudas[131] lists 112 remedies. Other systems include Australian Bush Flower Essences, Perelandra Flower Essences, and Bailey Flower Essences. Although widely tested in a manner similar to the provings of homeopathy, these flower therapies have not been subjected to clinical trials and are not recognised within orthodox medicine.

Aromatherapy

The effects of plant odours on the emotions has been recognised for centuries. The ancient sacred scriptures of India, *The Upanishads*, describe the art of energising body, mind and soul through breathing, and aromatic plant oils have been used for this purpose in many traditional healing practices. The chemistry of plant oils is now more widely understood, and it is recognised that some are nerve stimulants or sedatives and can be used to treat depression or anxiety.

However, a more recent approach to aromatherapy is concerned with plant oils not as chemical mixtures but as 'liquid vibrations', each having a certain resonance which corresponds with a colour and sound and with different bodily organs. Essential oils traditionally classed as Base Notes in perfumery and reddish in colour have been identified as resonating with the base chakra.[132] Hence Myrhh may have an energising effect when base chakra energy is depleted, and Frankincense an uplifting effect when spiritual energies are low. Green oils, such as Bergamot and Inula, correspond with the heart chakra, while blue oils resonate with the throat chakra, and so on. By stimulating the chakras these oils can bring about physical, mental, emotional or spiritual effects, whether simply warming the body, stimulating circulation, and relaxing muscle tension, enhancing positive emotions and feelings of well-being, or 'raising the spirits' in a more transcendent sense. Odours can thus be used to treat disease on a level which corresponds to the subtle energies of the individual in ways fully consistent with the principles of 'energy medicine', and can be used in conjunction with colour, sound, flower remedies or any other form of energy.

Time, Energy and Healing

The relationship of time and energy

The premise developed in the foregoing chapters is that all forms of healing are ultimately psychological modifications of the inextricably linked factors, time and energy. What have been referred to as 'timely interventions' modify the individual's relationship to time and facilitate greater mobilisation and utilisation of energy through relaxation, a process which may be thought of as relaxing the time sense in that it reduces reliance on linear verbal thought processes. This is assisted by visualisation which enables a person to access and explore the undifferentiated energy domain of the unconscious non-verbal mind, the timeless regions of inner space, thereby integrating dissociated features of the self, producing a more unified and more forceful whole. Energetic treatments or energy therapies work directly with subtle energies in and around the body and influence indirectly the individual's sense of time and other psychological processes. Modification of either time or energy in these ways has an effect on matter, or physical being, as these are inextricably related. So, change in one of these features will necessarily bring about change in the other. In all cases the medium through which this is achieved is the human mind or psyche. In this sense all healing, whether of the self or others, is psychological, and possible given time and energy. As such, its principles are fully consistent with contemporary scientific thinking.

It is therefore ironic that the British Medical Association in its adjudication on complementary therapies dismissed them as relying on little more than 'time, touch and compassion'.[1] These factors are frequently not 'given' within orthodox medicine, either in practice or principle, because in so far as expounded here, time, energy and the relationship between them are not properly understood, not merely as they relate to healing, but more generally, even though they are implicit in contemporary scientific formulations about the nature of the universe.

> If one asked a physicist a few years ago what physics permits us to explain and which problems remain open, he would have answered that we obviously do not have an adequate understanding of elementary particles or cosmological evolution but that knowledge of things in between was pretty satisfactory. Today a growing minority, to which we belong, would not share this optimism: we have only begun to understand the level of nature on which we live.[2]

New paradigms in science

Indeed the scientific vision of nature is undergoing a radical change which is proceeding on all levels and resulting in an understanding of the world totally new in the West.

Such a radical reformulation of reality is profoundly unsettling to those attached to the old scientific paradigm. This term derived from the Greek *paradigma* meaning pattern, and was coined[3] to refer to the pattern of the universe perceived by scientists. It is a kind of super-theory about the nature of reality, of such wide scope that it accounts for all, or most, of the major known phenomena in its field. It is an implicit framework or perspective for most scientists.

Inevitably it also becomes a set of blinkers[4] in that it defines certain kinds of endeavours and issues as trivial, impossible or meaningless. However, when the impossible becomes possible, or the apparently trivial yields results inconsistent with the dominant paradigm, a state of crisis arises in the fields so affected. Then most problems can be likened to zen *koans*, which cannot be solved at the level on which they are being addressed but have to be reframed in a wider context.[5] This change of context represents a new paradigm, and so such crises are a precondition for the emergence of a new perspective, or 'paradigm shift'.[6] The history of science is characterised by such shifts, because it is only as a result of these changes in perspective that scientific understanding develops.

A paradigm shift commences with the blurring of the existing pattern, and consequent loosening of the rules for normal research. This is ushered in by a proliferation of competing views, a willingness to experiment, the expression of explicit discontent, and argument over fundamentals.[7] Nevertheless, although scientists begin to lose faith in the existing paradigm, they do not renounce it. This is partly because it is impossible to embrace a new paradigm until the old one has been relinquished. The perceptual shift is rather like the Gestalt switch – the 'now you see it now you don't' principle – which operates in the perception of visual illusions, and must occur all at once. Hence all important advances are sudden insights, or new ways of seeing.

The 'old order' is threatened in other senses also. Established scientists who are emotionally and habitually attached to the old paradigm are rarely able to make the switch, and tend to react towards proponents of the new paradigm with scorn, scepticism, derision and hostility. So, where paradigm clashes occur, so also does profound antagonism.

> Science did not win its now dominant cultural position easily, and the scientific establishment (henceforth called Science, to distinguish it from science in practice) had reason to guard against non-scientific ideas that were opposed to Science. Yet while it proved less vicious than the formerly dominant Church in suppressing competitive ideas, it has been equally self-righteous in professing the 'one true science' and equally thorough in expunging 'non-scientific' ideas and

practices within its ranks and in denigrating them throughout its own and other cultures – non-scientific ideas being defined as everything identified as inner knowledge, and all outer knowledge gained within world views, theories or tests other than those officially recognised by Science. Indigenous science, for example, is not recognized because it has not separated itself from sacred or inner knowledge.[8]

Nevertheless, among the greatest advances of the twentieth century is the understanding of science itself as an evolving endeavour within an historical context.

In particular, philosophers of science have shown us that scientific world views – views of so-called 'reality' – are historically changing constructs – that the prevailing scientific paradigm of one era can be invalid in the next; that scientific theories can be judged only by their usefulness, not by their truth; that science is the endeavour to create maps to reality and differs from religion by constructing these maps rationally and refining them through experimental tests rather than accepting without question maps acquired by revelation.[9]

Discoveries therefore do not dictate a single world view or approach to science. On the contrary, they suggest the possibility of alternative world views, theories and experimental tests all within the realm of science. Nevertheless these advances in scientific understanding have not been easily implemented in scientific practice because it remains difficult to accept the implied uncertainty of scientific knowledge after taking such stock in its certainty. Thus much scientific pronouncement and practice suggests that most scientists still hold science to be the ultimate arbiter of truth in the world. Resistance to accepting a new perspective ensures that at least 50 years elapse before any major scientific discovery penetrates public consciousness.[10]

The current crisis in health care

The implications of this time-lag are considerable because in the meantime adherence to the old order results in attempts to solve problems with outmoded concepts and methods, rather than those appropriate to the task, and escalation of the crisis.

Such a crisis in orthodox Western medicine is only too clear. One in three persons in the developed world is likely to develop some form of cancer; while one in five will fall victim to coronary heart disease. Chronic degenerative conditions are also increasing, as are what appear to be new diseases, such as ME, Total Allergy Syndrome and AIDS. The optimistic hope is that in time and with increased financial resources, a cure will be found for all these conditions. So over the past 50 years there has been a vast expansion of and investment in the biomedical model of medicine which places a very high value on the use of drugs and sophisticated surgery. This trend continues despite a number of research programmes which suggest that these approaches are not fruitful. This is particularly evident in relation to coronary heart disease, the major 'killer' in the Western world. Three major causes of coronary heart disease claimed by biomedical theorists have been disproved several times in recent years; investigations into the effects of drugs have found in many cases that they actually increase the risk of coronary heart disease, and may also worsen quality of life; and similar reservations exist in relation to coronary artery by-pass surgery, the most common type of heart operation.[11]

The expression of discontent is not confined to learned medical journals. It is evident in the growing disillusionment of health care workers and the general public. The proliferation of 'alternative' medical practices is also testimony to dissatisfaction with orthodox approaches. The willingness of the public to experiment with these approaches and growing demand for their provision has led to a broadening of research as some of these methods are subjected to empirical test. As a result, traditionally excluded practices such as acupuncture, osteopathy, chiropractic and homeopathy, are becoming acceptable with orthodox medicine, and other approaches are being given more serious consideration. Inevitably these developments, all of which are consistent with a paradigm shift, have led to argument about the fundamentals of medicine.

HRH The Prince of Wales summed up the views of many when in his address to the British Medical Association in 1982 he observed that for all its breathtaking successes, the imposing edifice of medicine is, like the celebrated Tower of Pisa, slightly off-balance. He claimed that one of the most unfortunate consequences of this unhealthy imbalance – which he attributed to a move away from traditional methods of psychological healing towards biomedical therapeutics – is that the patient's individuality and his or her emotional, mental and spiritual needs are lost sight of. Another undesirable consequence, he claimed, is that by placing control of health care and rehabilitation in the hands of doctors and surgeons, insufficient emphasis is given to the role of the patients 'who could learn much more about the possibility of preventing their own illnesses through a different attitude to existence'.

Like the Prince of Wales, Norman Cousins argued that in order to create a balanced perspective in medicine, it is necessary to recognise that a strong will to live, a sense of higher purpose, a capacity for festivity, and a reasonable degree of confidence, are not 'alternative' to competent medical treatment but are ways of enhancing it.

> The wise physician favours a spirit of responsible participation by the patients in a total strategy of medical care. It is a truism that compliance is strengthened in an atmosphere of patient understanding and involvement.

Most of all the wise physician understands that there is no contradiction between compassion and competence, between the arts of reassurance where reassurance is possible, and cautionary notes where required, between personal observation and technological data; in short, between respect for the intangibles of medical care and respect for scientific quantification.[12]

Towards a psychology of healing

Reviewing in this light the considerable research on the connection between psychological and physiological factors, Cousins pointed to the emerging picture of the specific ways in which emotions, experiences and attitudes can create physiological change, and how complex psychological factors govern the functioning of the immune system. While admitting that not all research in this area is faultless, he nevertheless concluded that 'there has been enough replication involving controlled studies to point to a presiding fact, namely, the physician has a prime resource at his disposal in the form of the patient's own apothecary'.[13] He also pointed to the growing body of research which highlights the importance of the therapeutic relationship. These findings, which are increasingly featured in respected medical journals, have led to a more widespread recognition of the need for a 'biopsychosocial' or holistic approach to health which incorporates full utilisation of both medical science and the human healing system, and combines the high technology and symptom-suppression techniques of bio-medicine with an understanding of psychological and social factors in health and illness.

There is, of course, nothing new in this model. It is precisely that established some 2000 years ago by Hippocrates, having originated in the traditional magico-religious practices of the ancients. What is new is that for the first time in Western scientific medicine there is acknowledgement of the need to examine, understand and restore to their proper place in health care, the principles and practices of the psychology of healing. Such an endeavour will involve, in every sense, both time and energy.

Endnotes

Chapter 1: The Case for Complementary Medicine

1. Shah, I. (1973) *The Exploits of the Incomparable Mulla Nasrudin.* London: Paladin, p.26.

2. Dossey, L. (1982) *Space, Time and Medicine.* Boulder and London: Shambhala, p.11.

3. Illich, I. (1975) *Medical Nemesis: The Expropriation of Health.* London: Marian Boyars.

4. LeShan, L. (1984) *Holistic Health: How to Understand and Use the Revolution in Medicine.* Wellingborough, Northants: Turnstone.

5. Ornstein, R.E. and Sobel, D. (1988) *The Healing Brain: A Radical New Approach to Health Care.* London: MacMillan, p.24.

6. Stanway, A. (1982) *Alternative Medicine: A Guide to Natural Therapies.* Harmondsworth: Penguin.

7. Weitz, M. (1980) *Health Shock: A Guide to Ineffective and Hazardous Medical Treatment.* Newton Abbott and London: David and Charles.

8. McTaggart, L. (1996) *What Doctors Don't Tell You: The Truth About the Dangers of Modern Medicine.* London: Thorsons.

9. Fitzsimmons, C. (1988) 'Addicts sue over "happy pill" misery.' *The Observer,* 14 February.

10. Fulder, S. (1987) *How To Survive Medical Treatment: An Holistic Approach to the Risks and Side Effects of Orthodox Medicine.* London: Hodder and Stoughton.

11. McTaggart, L. (1996) *op. cit.*

12. Duquesne, M. and Reeves, J. (1982) *A Handbook of Psychoactive Medicines.* London: Quartet.

13. McTaggart, L. (1996) *op. cit.*

14. Illich, I. (1975) *op. cit.*

15. Weitz, M. (1980) *op. cit.*

16. McTaggart, L. (1996) *op. cit.* pp.95–96.

17. McTaggart, L. (1996) *ibid.* pp.155–156.

18. Fulder, S. (1987) *op. cit.*

19. Wolfe, S.M. and Hope, R.E. (1993) *Worst Pills, Best Pills II.* Washington, DC: Public Citizens Health Research Group.

20. Fulder, S. (1987) *op. cit.*

21. Fulder, S. (1987) *ibid.*

22. Stanway, A. (1982) *op. cit.* p.19.

23. Illich, I. (1975) *op. cit.*

24. LeShan, L. (1984) *op.cit.*

25. Hodgkinson, N. (1988) 'Surge in "needless" births by caesarian.' *Sunday Times,* 9 October.

26. Editorial (anonymous) (1988) *The Lancet,* September.

27. Hodgkinson, N. (1988) *op. cit.*

28. Weitz, M. (1980) *op. cit.*

29. Tew, M. (1995) *Safer Childbirth?* London: Chapman and Hall.

30. Weitz, M. (1980) *op. cit.*

31. McTaggart, L. (1996) *op. cit.*

32. Chalmer, I., Enkin, M, and Kierse, M. (eds) (1989) *Effective Care in Pregnancy and Childbirth.* Oxford: Oxford University Press

33. Illich, I. (1975) *op. cit.*

34. McTaggart, L. (1996) *op. cit.*

35. McTaggart, L. (1996) *ibid.*

36. McTaggart, L. (1996) *ibid.*

37. Coleman, V. (1994) 'The Betrayal of Trust.' *European Medical Journal 4.*

38. McTaggart, L. (1996) *op. cit.* p.6.

39. Illich, I. (1975) *op. cit.*

40. LeShan, L. (1984) *op. cit.* p.1.

41. Stanway, A. (1982) *op. cit.*

42. Stanway, A. (1982) *ibid.* p.23.

43. LeShan, L. (1984) *op. cit.*

44. Gillie, O. (1989) 'Treatment of pain.' *Health Independent.,* 3 January.

45. Ornstein, R.E. and Sobel, D. (1988) *op. cit.* p.30.

46. Ornstein, R.E. and Sobel, D. (1988) *ibid.*

47. LeShan, L. (1984) *op. cit.* p.2.

48. Siegel, B.S. (1986) *Love, Medicine and Miracles.* London: Rider, p.17.

49. Cousins, N. (1981) *Anatomy of an Illness as Perceived by the Patient: Reflections on Healing and Regeneration.* London and New York: Bantam, p.29.

50. Cousins, N. (1981) *op. cit.*

51. British Broadcasting Corporation (1997) *News At Ten,* 18 November.

52. Ornstein, R.E. and Sobel, D. (1988) *op. cit.* p.25.

53. Illiffe, S. (1988) *Strong Medicine.* London: Lawrence and Wishart, p.5.

54. McTaggart, L. (1996) *op. cit.*

55. McTaggart, L. (1996) *ibid.* p.5.

56. Illiffe, S. (1988) *op. cit.*

57. Rankin-Box, D.F. (ed) (1988) *Complementary Health Therapies: A Guide for Nurses and the Caring Professions.* London: Croom Helm.

58. Lindop, E. (1987) 'Factors associated with student and pupil nurse wastage.' *Journal of Advanced Nursing,* 751–756.

59. Lindop, E. (1988) 'Stress intervention in nurses.' Talk given at the Centre for Occupational Studies, Keele University, 11 January.

60. Adler, R.H. (1995) 'Is there a scientific alternative to alternative medicine?' Reported in *Positive Health 13,* 1996, pp.47–8.

61. Vincent, C. and Furnham, A. (1996) 'Why do patients turn to complementary medicine: An empirical study.' *British Journal of Clinical Psychology 35, (Part 1),* 37–48.

62. Burg, M.A. (1996) 'Women's use of complementary medicine: combining mainstream medicine with alternative practices.' *J. Fla Med Assoc 83,* 7, 482–488, August/September. Reported in *Positive Health 18,* 1997, p.49.

63. MacLennan, A.H. *et al.* (1996) 'Prevalence of alternative medicine in Australia.' *The Lancet 347(9001),* 569–573.

64. Peer, O. *et al.* (1996) 'Satisfaction among patients of a homeopathic clinic.' *Harefuah 130,* 2, 86–89, 15 January. Reported in *Positive Health 18,* 1997, p.49.

65. Bernstein, J.H. *et al.* (1996) 'Consultations with practitioners of alternative medicine.' *Harefuah 130,* 2, 83–85, 15 January. Reported in *Positive Health 18,* 1997, p.49.

66. Borkan, J. *et al.* (1994) 'Referrals for alternative therapies.' *Journal of Family Practice 39,* 6, 545–550.

67. Verhoef, M.J. and Sutherland, L.R. (1995) 'General practitioners assessment of and interest in alternative medicine in Canada.' *Social Science and Medicine 41,* 4, 511–515.

68. Spigellblatt, L. (1994) 'The use of alternative medicine by children.' *Pediatrics 94,* 6 (Part 1) 811–814.

69. Risberg, T. *et al.* (1995) 'Use of non-proven therapies: Differences in attitudes between Norwegian patients with a non-malignant disease and patients suffering from cancer.' Reported in *Positive Health 11*, 1996, p.35.

70. Furnham, A. and Kirkcaldy, B. (1996) 'The health beliefs and behaviours of orthodox and complementary medicine clients.' *British Journal of Clinical Psychology, 35, (Part 1)*, 49–61.

71. Ernst, E. *et al.* (1995) 'Complementary medicine: what physicians think of it: a meta-analysis.' *Archives of International Medicine 155*, 22, 2405–2408.

72. Bernstein, J.H. *et al.* (1996) *op. cit.*

73. Sutherland, L.R. and Verhoef, M.J. (1994) 'Why do patients seek a second opinion?' *Journal of Clinical Gastroenterology. 19*, 3, 1941–1947.

74. Spencer, M.H. (1995) 'Physicians should keep an open mind on complementary health care, Congress says.' *Canadian Medical Association 153*, 12, 1796–1797.

75. Verhoef, M.J. and Sutherland, L.R. (1995) *op. cit.*

76. Fulder, S.J. and Munro, R. (1981) *The Study of Complementary Medicine in the United Kingdom.* London: Threshold Foundation.

77. Consumers' Association (1986) 'Magic or medicine?' *Which?* October, 443–447.

78. Thomas, R. (1989) 'Give us more alternatives on the NHS.' *Journal of Alternative and Complementary Medicine*, 11 December.

79. Fulder, S. (1988) *The Handbook of Complementary Medicine.* (Second edition). Sevenoaks: Coronet Books.

80. Sharma, U. (1992) *Complementary Medicine Today. Practitioners and Patients.* London: Tavistock/Routledge, p.15.

81. Copper, R.A. and Stoflert, S.J. (1996) 'Trends in the education and practice of alternative medicine clinicians.' *Health 15,* 3, 226–238.

82. Sharma, U. (1992) *op. cit.* p.26.

83. Perkin, M.R. *et al.* (1994) 'A comparison of the attitudes shown by general practitioners, hospital doctors and medical students to alternative medicine.' *Journal of Research in Social Medicine 87*, 523–525. Reported in *Positive Health 5*, 1995, pp.36–37.

84. Berman *et al.* 'Physicians' attitudes towards complementary or alternative medicine: a regional survey.' *Journal of the American Board of Family Practitioners 8*, 5, 361–366. Reported in *Positive Health 11*, 1996, p.35.

85. Illiffe, S. (1988) *op. cit.*

86. Report of the Board of Science and Education on Alternative Therapy, London (1986) pp.61–75. In M. Saks (ed) (1992) *Alternative Medicine in Britain.* Oxford: Clarendon Press, pp.211–231.

87. Mendelsohn, R.S. (1979) *Confessions of a Medical Heretic.* Chicago: Contemporary Books, pp.xiii-xiv.

88. McTaggart, L. (1996) *op. cit.* p.xix.

89. McTaggart, L. (1996) *ibid.* p.7.

90. McTaggart, L. (1996) *ibid.*

91. McTaggart, L. (1996) *ibid.*

92. Dossey, L. (1982) *op. cit.*

93. Dossey, L. (1982) *ibid.* p.xii.

94. HRH Prince of Wales, cited in R. Holden (1988) 'Modern cardiology: the biophysical approach to heart disease.' *Caduceus, 4,* 6–9, p.6.

Chapter 2: Ancient Perspectives on Healing

1. Roszack, T. (1980) *The Making of a Counter Culture: Reflections on the Counter Culture and its Youthful Opposition.* London: Faber and Faber.

2. Jaynes, J. (1993) *The Origin of Consciousness in the Breakdown of the Bicameral Mind.* Harmondsworth: Penguin.

3. Colegrave, S. (1979) *The Spirit of the Valley: Androgyny and Chinese Thought.* London: Virago.

4. Blavatsky, H. (1888) *The Secret Doctrine: The Synthesis of Science, Religion and Philosophy Vols 1–3.* London: The Theosophical Publishing Society.

5. Besant, A. (1899) *The Ancient Wisdom: An Outline of Theosophical Teachings.* Second edition. Theosophical Publishing Society. London: Aberdeen University Press.

6. Freedom Long, M. (1954) *The Secret Science Behind Miracles.* Vista, CA: Huna Research Publications.

7. Gurdjieff, G. (1978) *Meetings With Remarkable Men.* London: Pan.

8. Ashe, G. (1977) *The Ancient Wisdom.* London: MacMillan.

9. Drury, N. (1978) *Don Juan: Mescalito and Modern Magic: A Mythology of Inner Space.* London: Routledge and Kegan Paul.

10. Drury, N. (1987) *The Occult Experience.* London: Robert Hale.

11. Butler, W.E. (1982) *Magic: Its Ritual, Power and Purpose.* Wellingborough: The Aquarian Press.

12. Scott, E. (1983) *The People of the Secret.* London: Octagon Press.

13. Butler, W.E. (1982) *op. cit.* p.11.

14. Russell, B. (1959) *Mysticism and Logic and Other Essays.* London: Allen and Unwin.

15. Harner, M. (1988) 'Shamanic counselling.' In G. Doore (ed) *Shaman's Path: Healing, Personal Growth and Empowerment.* Boston: Shambhala, pp.7–15.

16. Eliade, M. (1989) *Shamanism: Archaic Techniques of Ecstasy.* (Translated from the French by W.R. Trask, Penguin, Harmondsworth. First published 1964), Pantheon Bollingen Foundation.

17. Harner, M. (1988) *op. cit.* p.9.

18. Eliade, M. (1989) *op. cit.* pp.508–509.

19. Epes-Brown, J. (1985) 'North American Indian Religions.' In J.R. Hinnells (ed) *A Handbook of Living Religions.* Harmondsworth: Penguin.

20. Freedom Long, M. (1954) *op.cit.*

21. King, S. (1983) *Kahuna Healing.* Wheaton: Theosophical Publishing House.

22. Eliade, M. (1989) *op. cit.*

23. Kakar, S. (1982) *Shamans, Mystics and Doctors: A Psychological Enquiry into India and its Healing.* London: Unwin.

24. Watson, L. (1976) *Gifts of Unknown Things.* London: Hodder and Stoughton.

25. Eliade, M. (1989) *op. cit.*

26. Bergman, R.L. (1973) 'A school for medicine men.' *American Journal of Psychiatry, 130,* 6th June pp.663–666.

27. Epes-Brown, J. (1985) *op. cit.*

28. Castaneda, C. (1973) *A Separate Reality.* Harmondsworth: Penguin.

29. Castaneda, C. (1975) *Journey to Ixtlan.* Harmondsworth: Penguin.

30. Castaneda, C. (1976) *Tales of Power.* Harmondsworth: Penguin.

31. Castaneda, C. (1978) *The Second Ring of Power.* Harmondsworth: Penguin.

32. Castaneda, C. (1982) *The Eagle's Gift.* Harmondsworth: Penguin.

33. Castaneda, C. (1984) *The Power Within.* London: Black Swan Books.

34. Castaneda, C. (1988) *The Power of Silence.* London: Black Swan Books.

35. Castaneda, C. (1993) *The Art of Dreaming.* London: Aquarian Press.

36. Taylor, A. (1987) *I Fly Out With Bright Feathers: The Quest of a Novice Healer.* London: Fontana/Collins.

37. Kalweit, H. (1988) *Dreamtime and Inner Space: The World of the Shaman.* Translated by W. Wunsche. Boston: Shambhala.

38. Reid, D. (1985) 'Japanese Religions.' In J.R. Hinnells (ed) *A Handbook of Living Religions.* Harmondsworth: Penguin.

39. Saso, M. (1985) 'Chinese Religions.' In J.R. Hinnells (ed) *A Handbook of Living Religions.* Harmondsworth: Penguin.

40. Eliade, M. (1989) *op. cit.*

41. Watson, L. (1976) *op. cit.*

42. Matthews, J. (1991) *Taleisin: Shamanism and the Bardic Mysteries in Britain and Ireland.* London: Aquarian Press.

43. Cowan, T. (1993) *Fire in the Head.* New York: Harper.

44. Lévy-Bruhl, L. (1928) *The 'Soul' of Primitive Man.* London: Allen and Unwin, p.16.

45. Eliade, M. (1989) *op. cit.* p.8.

46. Watson, L. (1973) *Supernature: The Natural History of the Supernatural.* London: Hodder and Stoughton.

47. Drury, N. (1987) *The Occult Experience.* London: Robert Hale, p.23.

48. Achterberg, J. (1985) *Imagery in Healing: Shamanism and Modern Medicine.* New Science Library. London: Routledge and Kegan Paul.

49. Hultkrantz, A. (1997) 'Some points of view on ecstatic shamanism with particular reference to American Indians.' *Shaman 5*, 1, 35–46.

50. Eliade, M. (1989) *op. cit.*

51. Peters, L.G. and Price Williams, D. (1980) 'Towards an experiential analysis of shamanism.' *American Ethologist 7*, 398–418.

52. Harner, M. (1990) *The Way of the Shaman: A Guide to Power and Healing.* New York: Harper and Row.

53. Achterberg, J. (1985) *op. cit.*

54. Leshan, L. (1982) *Clairvoyant Reality: Towards a General Theory of the Paranormal.* Wellingborough: Turnstone Press.

55. Drury, N. (1987) *op. cit.*

56. Achterberg, J. (1985) *op. cit.* p.34.

57. Jacq, C. (1985) *Egyptian Magic.* Warminster: Avis and Phillips Ltd.

58. Pullar, P. (1988) *Spiritual and Lay Healing.* Harmondsworth: Penguin.

59. Pullar, P. (1988) *ibid*

60. Capra, F. (1978) *The Tao of Physics* (Third reprint). London: Fontana/Collins.

61. Capra, F. (1978) *ibid.*

62. Koestler, A. (1984) *The Sleepwalkers: A History of Man's Changing Vision of the Universe.* Harmondsworth: Penguin, p.27.

63. Koestler, A. (1984) *ibid.* p.25.

64. Koestler, A. (1984) *ibid.* p.25.

65. Koestler, A. (1984) *ibid.* p.27.

66. Russell, B. (1948) *History of Western Philosophy and its Connection With Political and Social Circumstances from the Earliest Times to the Present Day.* London: Allen and Unwin.

67. Bohm, D. (1980) *Wholeness and the Implicate Order.* London: Routledge and Kegan Paul.

68. Toffler, A. (1985) 'Science and Change.' Foreword to I. Prigogine and I. Stengers *Order Out Of Chaos: Man's Dialogue With Nature.* London: Fontana, p.xi.

69. Capra, F. (1978) *op. cit.*

70. Russell, B. (1959) *op. cit.*

71. Fromm, E. (1951) *Psychoanalysis and Religion.* London: Gollancz.

72. Achterberg, J. (1985) *op. cit.*

73. Achterberg, J. (1985) *ibid.*

74. Webster, C. (1988) 'The nineteenth-century afterlife of Paracelsus. In R. Cooter (ed) *Studies in the History of Alternative Medicine.* London: MacMillan Press.

75. Cooter, R. 1988 'Alternative medicine: Alternative cosmology.' In R. Cooter (ed) *Studies in the History of Alternative Medicine.* London: MacMillan Press.

76. Achterberg, J. (1985) *op. cit.* p.64.

77. Millenson, J.R. (1995) *Mind Matters: Psychological Medicine in Holistic Practice.* Seattle: Eastland Press.

78. Webster, C. (1988) *op. cit.* p.85.
79. Capra, F. (1982) *The Turning Point: Science, Society and the Rising Culture.* London: Wildwood House, p.47.
80. Capra, F. (1978) *op. cit.* p.56.
81. Hawking, S.W. (1988) *A Brief History of Time: From the Big Bang to Black Holes.* London: Bantam, pp.140–141.
82. Siegel, B.S. (1986) *Love, Medicine and Miracles.* London: Rider, p.65.
83. Achterberg, J. (1985) *op. cit.* p.69.
84. Achterberg, J. (1985) *op. cit.* p.7.
85. Kaptchuk, T. and Croucher, M. (1986) *The Healing Arts: A Journey Through the Faces of Medicine.* London: BBC Publications.
86. Illich, I. (1975) *Medical Nemesis: The Expropriation of Health.* London: Marian Boyars, p.112.
87. Dossey, L. (1982) *Space, Time and Medicine.* Boulder and London: Shambhala, p.230.
88. Davies, P. (1984) *God and the New Physics.* Harmondsworth: Penguin, p.vii.

Chapter 3: Modern Perpectives on Healing

1. Rosnow, R.L. (1981) *Paradigms in Transition: The Methodology of Social Enquiry.* Oxford: Oxford University Press, p.7.
2. Capra, F. (1978) *The Tao of Physics.* Suffolk: Bungay Press, pp.62–63.
3. Capra, F. (1982) *The Turning Point: Science, Society and the Rising Culture.* London: Wildwood House, p.177.
4. Capra, F. (1982) *op. cit.* pp.80–81.
5. Watson, L. (1973) *Supernature: The Natural History of the Supernatural.* London: Hodder and Stoughton, p.297.
6. Capra, F. (1978) *op. cit.* p.234.
7. Capra, F. (1978) *ibid.* pp.83–85.
8. Davies, P. (1984) *God and the New Physics.* Harmondsworth: Penguin, p.103.
9. Capra, F. (1982) *op. cit.* p.7.
10. Capra, F. (1982) *ibid.* pp.71–72.
11. Hawking, S.W. (1988) *A Brief History of Time: From the Big Bang to Black Holes.* London: Bantam, p.55.
12. Pagels, H.R. (1983) *The Cosmic Code: Quantum Physics as the Language of Nature.* London: Michael Joseph, p.101.
13. Davies, P. (1984) *op. cit.* p.601.
14. Berry, M. (1987) 'Quantum physics on the edge of chaos.' *New Scientist 116*, 1587, 44–47.
15. Zukav, G. (1980) *The Dancing Wu-Li Masters: An Overview of the New Physics.* London: Fontana, p.30.
16. Bohm, D. (1980) *Wholeness and the Implicate Order.* London: Routledge and Kegan Paul, p.145.
17. Gibran, K. (1978) *The Prophet.* London: Book Club Associates, pp.108–109.
18. Pribram, K.H. (1976) *Consciousness and the Brain.* New York: Plenum.
19. de St. Exupéry, A. (1974) *The Little Prince.* London: Pan Books.
20. Bohm, D. (1980) *op. cit.* p.206.
21. Lilly, J.C. (1977) *The Centre of the Cyclone. An Autobiography of Inner Space.* Frogmore, St Albans: Granada Publishing.
22. Grof, S. (1979) *Realms of the Unconscious.* London: Souvenir Press.
23. Huxley, A. (1954) *The Doors of Perception.* London: Chatto and Windus.
24. Prigogine, I. (1980) *From Being to Becoming.* San Francisco: W.H. Freeman.
25. Ferguson, M. (1982) *The Aquarian Conspiracy: Personal and Social Transformation in the 1980s.* London: Paladin, p.178.

26. Harwood, R. (1984) *All the World's A Stage*. London: Secker and Warburg, pp.53–54.

27. Freud, S. (1960) *Jokes and their Relation to the Unconscious*. New York: W.H. Norton and Co.

28. Levine, J. (1977) 'Humor as a form of therapy.' In A.J. Chapman and H.C. Foot (eds) *It's a Funny Thing, Humour*. Oxford: Pergamon.

29. Cousins, N. (1981) *Anatomy of an Illness as Perceived by the Patient: Reflections on Healing and Regeneration*. New York: Bantam.

30. Dillon, K.M., Minchoff, B. and Baker, K.H. (1985) 'Positive emotional states and enhancement of the immune system.' *International Journal of Psychiatric Medicine 15*, 13–17.

31. Saper, B. (1988) 'Humor in psychiatric healing.' *Psychiatric Quarterly 59*, 4, 306–319.

32. Holden, R. (1992) 'Laughter: the best medicine?' Presentation to the Second Annual Conference for the Promotion of Mental Health, Keele University, 28 September.

33. Capra, F. (1978) *op. cit.*

34. Zukav, G. (1980) *op. cit.*

35. LeShan, L. (1982) *Clairvoyant Reality: Towards a General Theory of the Paranormal*. Wellingborough: Turnstone Press.

36. Graham, H. (1986) *The Human Face of Psychology: Humanistic Psychology in its Historical, Social and Cultural Contexts*. Milton Keynes: Open University Press.

37. Holbrook, B. (1981) *The Stone Monkey: An Alternative Chinese Scientific Reality*. New York: William Morrow and Co.

38. Jung, C.G. (1978) *Psychology and the East*. London: Routledge and Kegan Paul, pp.8–9.

39. Dossey, L. (1982) *Space, Time and Medicine*. Boulder, CO, and London: Shambhala, p.xii.

40. Dossey, L. (1982) *ibid.*

41. Dossey, L.(1982) *ibid.* p.111.

42. Dossey, L. (1989) 'The importance of modern physics for modern medicine.' In A.A. Sheikh and K.S. Sheikh (eds) *Eastern and Western Approaches to Healing: Ancient Wisdom and Modern Knowledge*. Chichester: Wiley, p.400.

43. Rose, S., Kamin, L.J. and Lewontin, R.C. (1984) *Not in Our Genes: Biology, Ideology and Human Nature*. Harmondsworth: Penguin, pp.273–274.

44. Rose, S. *et al.* (1984) *op. cit.* p.276.

45. Rose, S. *et al.* (1984) *ibid.* p.276.

46. Achterberg, J. (1985) *Imagery in Healing: Shamanism and Modern Medicine*. New Science Library. London: Routledge and Kegan Paul.

47. Dossey, L. (1982) *op. cit.* p.89.

48. Dossey, L. (1982) *ibid.* p.91.

49. Dossey, L. (1982) *ibid.* p.91.

50. Ferguson, M. (1982) *op. cit.* p.183.

51. Laing, R.D. (1959) *The Divided Self: An Existential Study of Sanity and Madness*. London: Tavistock.

52. Ferguson, M. (1982) *op. cit.*

53. Lazlo, E. cited L. Purvis, (1987) 'Sage of the inner limits.' *Weekend Guardian*, 1 July.

Chapter 4: Eastern Perspectives on Healing

1. Scott, E. (1983) *The People of the Secret*. London: The Octagon Press.

2. Jung, C.G. (1978) *Psychology and the East*. London: Routledge and Kegan Paul, p.12.

3. Scott, E. (1983) *op. cit.* p.19.

4. Needleman, J. (1972) *The New Religions*. London: Penguin, Allen Lane, p.25.

5. Stutley, M. (1985) *Hinduism: The Eternal Law: An Introduction to the Literature, Cosmology and Cults of the Hindu Religion*. Wellingborough: Aquarian Press.

6. Nikhilananda, S. (1968) *Hinduism: Its Meaning for the Liberation of the Spirit*. Myalore, Madras: Sri Ramakrishna Math, p.29.

7. Nikhilananda, S. (1968) *ibid.* p.42.

8. Krishna, G. (1971) *Kundalini: The Evolutionary Energy in Man*. Boulder, CO, and London: Shambhala.

9. Ramaswami, S. (1989) 'Yoga and healing.' In A.A. Sheikh and K.S. Sheikh (eds) *Eastern and Western Approaches to Healing: Ancient Wisdom and Modern Knowledge*. New York: Wiley.

10. Isherwood, C. (ed) (1972) *Vedanta For Modern Man*. New York: Signet Books.

11. Vivekenanda, S. (1974) *Practical Vedanta*. Calcutta: Advaita Ashrama.

12. Crawford, C. (1989) 'Ayurveda; the science of long life in contemporary perspective.' In A.A. Sheikh and K.S. Sheikh (eds) *Eastern and Western Approaches to Healing: Ancient Wisdom and Modern Knowledge*. New York: Wiley.

13. Chopra, D. (1992) *Perfect Health: A Complete Mindbody Guide*. New York: Bantam, p.47.

14. Sharma, C.H. (1985) *The International Manual of Homeopathy and Natural Medicine*. Second Edition. Wellingborough: Thorsons.

15. Fulder, S. (1987) *How To Survive Medical Treatment: An Holistic Approach to the Risks and Side Effects of Orthodox Medicine*. London: Hodder and Stoughton.

16. Jacobs, J.S. (1987) 'Yoga and Ayurveda.' In M. Gharote and M. Lockhart (eds) *The Art of Survival: A Guide to Yoga Therapy*. London: Unwin Hyman Ltd.

17. Sharma, C.H. (1979) 'Ayurvedic Medicine.' In A. Hill (ed) *Unconventional Medicine*. London: New English Library.

18. Fulder, S. (1987) *op. cit.*

19. Chopra, D. (1987) *Creating Health*. Boston: Houghton Mifflin.

20. Chopra, D. (1992) *op. cit.*

21. Day, H. (1951) *About Yoga*. London: Thorsons Publishing Ltd., p.34.

22. Jung, C.G. (1978) *op. cit.* p160.

23. Jung, C.G. (1978) *ibid.* p.80.

24. Krishna, G. (1971) *op. cit.*

25. Eliade, M. (1970) *Yoga, Immortality and Freedom*. Princeton, NJ: Princeton University Press.

26. Vollmar, K. (1987) *Journey Through the Chakras*. Bath: Gateway Books.

27. Santa Maria, J. (1978) *Anna Yoga: The Yoga of Food*. London: Rider and Co.

28. Krishna, G. (1988) 'The true aim of Yoga.' In J.E.White (ed) *What is Enlightenment?* Wellingborough: Aquarian Press.

29. Wilson Ross, N. (1973) *Hinduism, Buddhism, Zen*. London: Faber.

30. Wilson Ross, N. (1973) *ibid.*

31. Wilson Ross, N. (1973) *ibid.*

32. Rajneesh, Bhagwan Shree, cited in Wadud, Swami Deva (1992) *Osho. Meditation: The First and Last Freedom. A Practical Guide to Meditation*. Cologne: Rebel Publishing House, p.xii.

33. Chogyam, N. (1990) 'Laughing possible!' *Caduceus 9*, 14–16.

34. Humphreys, C. (1962) *Zen*. London: Hodder and Stoughton.

35. Wilson Ross, N. (1973) *op. cit.* p.84.

36. Anderson, N. (1982) *Open Secrets: A Western Guide to Tibetan Buddhism*. Harmondsworth: Penguin.

37. Donden, Y., cited in N. Anderson (1982) *ibid.* p.219.

38. Anderson, N. (1982) *ibid.* p.88.

39. Donden, Y. (1977) *The Ambrosia Heart Tantra, Vol. 1 The Secret Oral Teaching on the Eight Branches of the Science of Healing*. (Translated by J. Kelsang) Dharamsala, India: Library of Tibetan Works and Archives.

40. Donden, Y. (1986) *Health Through Balance: An Introduction to Tibetan Medicine*. (Edited and translated by J. Hopkins). Ithaca, NY: Snow Lion.

41. Epstein, M. and Rapgay, L. (1989) 'Mind, disease and health in Tibetan Medicine.' In A.A. Sheikh and K.S. Sheikh (eds) *Eastern and Western Approaches to Healing: Ancient Wisdom and Modern Knowledge*. New York: Wiley.

42. Clifford, T. (1984) *Tibetan Buddhist Medicine and Psychiatry: The Diamond Healing.* York Beach, ME: Samuel Weiser.

43. Wilson Ross, N. (1973) *op. cit.*

44. Humpreys, C. (1962) *op. cit.* p.81.

45. Colegrave, S. (1979) *The Spirit of the Valley: Androgyny and Chinese Thought.* London: Virago, p.8.

46. Watson, L. (1986) *Dreams of Dragons.* London: Hodder and Stoughton, p.101.

47. Colegrave, S. (1979) *op. cit.*

48. Blofield, J. (1979) *Taoism: The Quest for Immortality.* London: Allen and Unwin.

49. Waley, A. (1942) (first printed 1932) *The Way and Its Power: A Study of the Tao-te-Ching and its Place in Chinese Thought.* London: George, Allen and Unwin, p.110.

50. Watts, A. (1976) *Tao: The Watercourse Way.* London: Jonathan Cape, p.26.

51. Chuang-Yuan, C. (1975) *Creativity and Taoism.* London: Wildwood House, p.31.

52. Colegrave, S. (1979) *op. cit.*

53. Chuang Tsai, cited in S. Colegrave (1979) *op. cit.* p.60.

54. Motoyama, M. (1987) 'Yoga and acupuncture.' In D. Gharote and M. Lockhart (eds) *The Art of Survival: A Guide to Yoga Therapy.* London: Unwin Hyman Ltd.

55. Gulliver, N. (1988) 'Shiatsu.' In D.F. Rankin-Box (ed) *Complementary Health Therapies; A Guide for Nurses and the Caring Professions.* London: Croom Helm.

56. Motoyama, M. (1987) *op. cit.*

57. Motoyama, M. (1987) *ibid.*

58. Motoyama, M. (1987) *ibid.*

59. Watts, A. (1961) *Psychotherapy East and West.* New York: Pantheon, p.19.

60. Ornstein, R.E. (1973) 'The traditional esoteric psychologies.' In R.E. Ornstein (ed) *The Nature of Human Consciousness.* San Francisco: W.H. Freeman.

61. Ornstein, R.E. (1975) *The Psychology of Consciousness.* Harmondsworth: Penguin.

62. Tart, C.T. (1975) *Transpersonal Psychologies.* London: Routledge and Kegan Paul.

63. Prigogine, I. and Stengers, I. (1985) *Order Out of Chaos: Man's New Dialogue With Nature.* London: Fontana.

64. Watts, A. (1961) *op. cit.* p.19.

Chapter 5: Western Perspectives on Healing

1. Jung, C.G. (1946) *Psychology and Religion.* New Haven, London and Oxford: Yale University Press, p.10.

2. Jung, C.G. (1946) *ibid.*

3. Szasz, T. (1979) *The Myth of Psychotherapy: Mental Healing as Religion, Rhetoric and Repression.* Oxford: Oxford University Press.

4. Jung, C.G. (1966) *Modern Man in Search of A Soul.* London: Routledge and Kegan Paul, p.344.

5. Frankl, V.E. (1969) *The Doctor and The Soul.* London: Souvenir Press.

6. Jung, C.G. (1978) *Psychology and the East.* London: Routledge and Kegan Paul, p.77.

7. Jung, C.G. (1966) *op. cit.* p.34.

8. Fromm, E. (1980) *Greatness and Limitations of Freud's Thought.* London: Cape.

9. Jacobs, M. (1992) *Freud.* London: Sage.

10. Jung, C.G. (1972) *Memories, Dreams, Reflections.* London: Fontana/Collins, p.173.

11. Hearnshaw, L.S. (1989) *The Shaping of Modern Psychology: An Historical Introduction.* London: Routledge, p.157.

12. Jackson, R. (1992) 'Psychotherapy: beyond a phoney love.' *Leading Edge 6*, 14–15.

13. Jacobs, M. (1992) *op.cit.*

14. Jung, C.G. (1978) *op. cit.* p.84.

15. Kakar, S. (1982) *Shaman Mystics and Doctors: A Psychological Enquiry into India and its Healing.* London: Unwin.

16. Capra, F. (1982) *The Turning Point: Science, Society and the Rising Culture.* London: Wildwood House, p.186.

17. Capra, F. (1982) *ibid.* p.186.

18. Capra, F. (1982) *ibid.* p.187.

19. Jung, C.G. (1966) *op. cit.*

20. Jung, C.G. (1959) *Face to Face with C.G. Jung.* BBC. First broadcast October 1959, repeated BBC2 16 October 1988.

21. Hearnshaw, L.S. (1989) *op. cit.* p.166.

22. Jung, C.G. (1972) *op. cit.* p.173.

23. Jung, C.G. (1966) *op. cit.* p.140.

24. Jung, C.G. (1966) *op. cit.* p.77.

25. Jung, C.G. (1966) *op. cit.* p.264.

26. Jung, C.G. (1966) *op. cit.*

27. Jung, C.G. (1946) *op. cit.* p.11.

28. Jacobi, J. (1962) *The Psychology of Jung.* London: Routledge and Kegan Paul.

29. Butler, W.E. (1982) *Magic: Its Ritual, Power and Purpose.* Wellingborough: Aquarian Press, p.16.

30. Jung, C.G. (1967) *Symbols of Transformation. Collected Works Vol 2.* (Second edition). London: Routledge.

31. Blair, L. (1975) *Rhythms of Vision.* London: Croom Helm, p.106.

32. Jung, C.G. (1963) *The Integration of the Personality.* Ninth impression. Translated by S. Dell. London: Routledge and Kegan Paul, pp.3–4.

33. Jaynes, J. (1993) *The Origin of Consciousness in the Breakdown of the Bicameral Mind.* Harmondsworth: Penguin, p.72.

34. Jung, C.G. (1963) *op. cit.* pp.53–54.

35. Jung, C.G. (1960) *The Structure and Dynamics of the Unconscious. Collected Works Vol. 8.* Princeton, NJ: Princeton University Press, pp.325–326

36. Prigogine, I. and Stengers, L. (1985) *Order Out of Chaos: Man's New Dialogue With Nature.* London: Fontana.

37. Serrano, M. (1966) *C.G. Jung and Hermann Hesse.* London and Prescott: C. Tinling and Co.

38. Jung, C.G. (1976) *The Symbolic Life.* Princeton, NJ: Princeton University Press, p.172.

39. Jung, C.G. (1955) *Mysterium Coniunctionis, Vol. 14 Collected Works of C.G. Jung.* Princeton, New Jersey: Princeton University Press, Princeton, para. 616.

40. Jung, C.G. (1954) *The Archetypes and the Collective Unconscious. The Collected Works of C.G. Jung, Vol.9,* Princeton, NJ: Princeton University Press, para. 204.

41. Storr, A. (1990) *Churchill's Black Dog: and Other Phenomena of the Human Mind.* London: Fontana, p.201.

42. Storr, A. (1973) *Jung.* Glasgow: William Collins, p.88.

43. Jacobi, J. (1962) *op. cit.*

44. Hochheimer, W. (1969) *The Psychotherapy of C.G. Jung.* Translated by Hildegard Nagel, G.P. Putnam, New York for the C.G. Jung Foundation for Analytical Psychology.

45. Hillman, J. (1975) *Re-visioning Psychology.* New York: Harper Colophon.

46. Von Franz, M.L. (1975) *C.G. Jung. His Myth in Our Time.* London: Hodder and Stoughton, p.112.

47. Jung, C.G. (1972) *op. cit.* p.155.

48. Jung, C.G. (1966) *op. cit.* p.56.

49. Jung, C.G. (1972) *op. cit.* p.185.

50. Jung, C.G. (1972) *ibid.* p.185.

51. Von Franz, M.L. (1975) *op. cit.*

52. Vaughan-Lee, L. (1992) 'The light hidden in the darkness; alchemical symbolism in dreams.' *Caduceus. 19*, 4–7

53. Butler, W.E. (1982) *op. cit.*

54. Jung, C.G. (1972) *op. cit.*

55. Drury, N. (1979) *Inner Visions: Explorations in Magical Consciousness.* London and Henley: Routledge and Kegan Paul.

56. Von Franz, M.L. (1975) *op. cit.*

57. Progoff, I. (1963) *The Symbolic and the Real.* New York: Julian Press.

58. Progoff, I. (1970) 'Waking dream and living myth.' In J. Campbell (ed) *Myths, Dreams and Religion.* New York: Dutton.

59. Von Franz, M.L. (1975) *op. cit.*

60. Hillman, J. (1975) *op. cit.*

61. Lilly, J.C. (1977) *The Centre of the Cyclone: An Autobiography of Inner Space.* St Albans, Frogmore: Granada Publishing.

62. Grof, D. (1979) *Realms of the Unconscious.* London: Souvenir Press.

63. Grof, S. (1985) *Realms of the Brain: Birth, Death and Transcendence in Psychotherapy.* Albany: SUNY Press.

64. Jung, C.G. (1959) *op. cit.*

65. Jacobi, J. (1962) *op. cit.* p.xi.

66. Jung, C.G. (1972) *Syncronicity: An Acausal Connecting Principle.* Translated R.F.C. Hull. London: Routledge.

67. Watts, A. (1961) *Psychotherapy East and West.* New York: Pantheon, p.19.

68. Totton, N. and Edmondson, E. (1988) *Reichian Bodywork: Melting Blocks to Life and Love.* Bridport, Dorset: Prism Press, p.36.

69. Ollendorff Reich, L. (1969) *Wilhelm Reich: A Personal Biography.* London: Elek Books, p.36.

70. Totton, N. and Edmondson, E. (1988) *op. cit.* p.36.

71. Reich, W. (1942) *The Function of the Orgasm.* Second edition. Translated by Thodore P. Wolfe. Orgone Institute Press (1961) New York, Ferraro, Strauss, Giroux.

72. Rycroft, V. (1979) *Reich.* London: Fontana/Collins.

73. Koestler, A. (1975) *The Ghost in The Machine.* London: Pan Books.

74. Heather, N. (1976) *Radical Perspectives in Psychology.* London: Methuen.

75. Skinner, B.F. (1959) *Beyond Freedom and Dignity.* Harmondsworth: Penguin.

76. Jung, C.G. (1959) *op. cit.*

77. Maslow, A.H. (1968) *Towards a Psychology of Being.* New York: Van Nostrand.

78. Reibel, L. (1984) 'A homeopathic model of psychotherapy.' *Journal of Humanistic Psychology 24*, 1, 9–48.

79. Hamlyn, E. (1979) *The Healing Art of Homeopathy: The Organon of Samuel Hahnemann.* Beaconsfield, Bucks: Beaconsfield Publishers.

80. Vithoulkas, G. (1980) *The Science of Homeopathy.* New York: Grove, p.140.

81. Jourard, S.M. (1971) *The Transparent Self.* London: Van Nostrand and Co.

82. Perls, F.S. (1976) *The Gestalt Approach and Eye Witness to Therapy.* New York: Bantam, p.16.

83. Perls, F.S. (1976) *ibid.* p.44.

84. Perls, F.S. (1969) *Gestalt Therapy Verbatim.* New York: Bantam, p.46.

85. Perls, F.S. (1976) *op. cit.* p.44.

86. Jung, C.G. (1978) *op. cit.*

87. Graham, H. (1986) *The Human Face of Psychology.* Milton Keynes: Open University Press.

88. Jung, C.G. (1966) *op. cit.* p.48.

Perspectives: A Synthesis

1.   LeShan, L. (1982) *Clairvoyant Reality: Towards a General Theory of the Paranormal.* Wellingborough: Turnstone Press.

2.   Cousins, N. (1981) *Anatomy of an Illness as Perceived by the Patient: Reflections on Healing and Regeneration.* London, New York, Toronto: Bantam, p.119.

3.   LeShan, (1982) *op. cit.* p.129.

4.   Cousins, N. (1981) *op. cit.* p.119.

5.   Patel, M.S. (1987) 'Evaluation of holistic medicine.' *Social Science and Medicine 24,* 2, 174.

Chapter 6: Time and Illness

1.   Ferguson, M. (1983) *The Aquarian Conspiracy: Personal and Social Transformation in the 1980s.* London: Paladin, p.111.

2.   Cooper, J.C. (1981) *Yin and Yang: the Taoist Harmony of Opposites.* Northampton: Aquarian Press, p.22.

3.   Luce, G.G. (1973) *Body Time: The Natural Rhythms of the Body.* St Albans: Paladin, p.30.

4.   Wittgenstein, L. (1978) *Tractatus Logico-Philosophicus.* London: Routledge and Kegan Paul.

5.   Eliade, M. (1959) *The Sacred and the Profane: The Nature of Religion.* New York: Harcourt Brace and World Inc, p.113.

6.   Hawking, S.W. (1988) *A Brief History of Time: From the Big Bang to Black Holes.* London: Bantam.

7.   Luce, G.G. (1973) *op. cit.* p.29.

8.   Dossey, L. (1982) *Space, Time and Medicine.* Boulder, CO, and London: Shambhala, p.25.

9.   Gottlieb, C. (1959) pp.157–188. In H. Feifel (ed) *The Meaning of Death.* New York: McGraw Hill.

10. Dossey, L. (1982) *op. cit.* p.21.

11. Dossey, L. (1982) *ibid.* p.21.

12. Dossey, L. (1982) *ibid.*

13. Dossey, L. (1982) *ibid.* p.23.

14. Ornstein, R.E. (1969) *On the Experience of Time.* New York: Penguin.

15. Ornstein, R.E. (1969) *ibid.*

16. Piaget, J. (1969) *The Child's Conception of Time.* London: Routledge and Kegan Paul.

17. Ornstein, R.E. (1969) *op. cit.*

18. Friedman, M. and Rosenman, R.H. (1974) *Type A Behaviour and Your Heart.* New York: Alfred A. Knopf.

19. Pelletier, K.R. (1978) *Mind as Healer, Mind as Slayer.* London: George Allen.

20. Matthews, K.A. and Volkin, J. (1981) 'Effort to excel and the Type A behaviour pattern in children.' *Child Development 52,* 1283–1289.

21. Musante, L., MacDougall, J.M., Dembroski, T.M. and Vanttorn, A.E. (1983) 'Component analysis of the Type A coronary-prone behaviour pattern in male and female college students.' *Journal of Personality and Social Psychology 45,* 1104–1117.

22. Cox, T. (1981) *Stress.* London: MacMillan.

23. Cannon, W.B. (1914) 'The emergency function of the adrenal medulla in pain and the major emotions.' *American Journal of Physiology 33,* 356–372.

24. Selye, H. (1956) *The Stress of Life.* London: McGraw Hill.

25. Charlesworth, E.A. and Nathan, R.G. (1987) *Stress Management.* London: Transworld Publishers.

26. Benson, H.D. with Zlipper, M.Z. (1975) *The Relaxation Response.* London: Collins.

27. Cooper, C., Cooper, R. and Eaker, L. (1988) *Living With Stress.* Harmondsworth: Penguin.

28. Whitacre, C.C., Cummings, S.O. and Griffin, A.C. (1994) 'The effects of stress on autoimmune disease.' In R. Glaser and J. Kiecolt-Glaser (eds) *The Handbook of Human Stress and Immunity.* San Diego: Academic Press.

29. Blumberg, E.M., West, P.M., and Ellis, F.W. (1954) 'A possible relationship between psychological factors and human cancer.' *Psychosomatic Medicine 16*, Part 4, 277–286.

30. LeShan, L. (1966) 'An emotional life-history pattern associated with neoplastic disease.' *Annals of the New York Academy of Science 125*, 780–793.

31. Solomon, G.F. (1969) 'Emotions, stress, the CNS and immunity.' Second Conference on Psychophysiological Aspects of Cancer. *Annals of the New York Academy of Science 1*, 335–342.

32. Stoll, B.A. (1979) 'Restraint of growth and spontaneous regression of cancer.' In B.A. Stoll (ed) *Mind and Cancer Prognosis*. Chichester: Wiley.

33. Jacobs, T.J. and Charles, E. (1980) 'Life events and the occurrence of cancer in children.' *Psychosomatic Medicine 42*, 1–24.

34. Rosch, P.J. (1984) 'Stress and cancer.' In C.L. Cooper (ed) *Psychosocial Stress and Cancer*. Chichester: Wiley.

35. Greer, S. and Watson, M. (1985) 'Towards a psychological model of cancer: psychological considerations.' *Social Science and Medicine 20*, 8, 773–777.

36. Alvarez, A. (1989) 'Stressful life events and the recurrence of breast cancer in women.' Reported in *Medicine Now*, BBC Radio 4, 15 February.

37. Editorial (anonymous) (1987) 'Depression, stress and immunity.' *The Lancet 11*, 133–134.

38. Cooper, G. *et al.* (1988) *op. cit.*

39. Dossey, L. (1982) *op. cit.*

40. Dossey, L. (1982) *ibid.* p.52.

41. Cassem, N.H., Hackett, T.P., and Wishnie, A. (1968) 'The coronary care unit: an appraisal of psychological hazards.' *New England Journal of Medicine 279*, 1365.

42. Dossey, L. (1982) *op. cit.*

43. Dossey, L. (1982) *ibid.*

44. Siegel, B.S. (1986) *Love, Medicine and Miracles*. London: Rider, p.39.

45. Dossey, L. (1982) *op. cit.* pp.93–94.

46. McKee, V. (1988) 'A fight to the death.' *The Times*. 27 October, p.14.

47. Burroughs, W.S. (1977) *Junky*. Harmondsworth: Penguin.

48. Dossey, L. (1982) *op. cit.* p.47.

49. Dossey, L. (1982) *ibid.* p.88.

50. Colt, E.W.D., Wardlaw, W. and Frantz, A.G. (1981) 'The effect of running on plasma beta-endorphin.' *Life Science 28*, 1637.

51. Goldstein, A. (1980) 'Thrills in response to music and other stimuli.' *Physiological Psychology 4*, 8, 126–129.

52. Dossey, L. (1982) *op. cit.*

Chapter 7: Meditation and Biofeedback

1. Laurie, S.G. and Tucker, M.J. (1982) *Centring: The Power of Meditation*. Wellingborough: Excalibur.

2. Shapiro, D.H. (1982) 'Overview: Clinical and physiological comparison of meditation with other self-control strategies.' *American Journal of Psychiatry 139*, 267–274.

3. Genesis 24: 63.

4. Timothy 1: 4, 15.

5. Goleman, D. (1978) *The Varieties of Meditative Experience*. London: Rider.

6. Maupin, E.W. (1969) 'Individual differences in response to a Zen meditational exercise.' In C.T. Tart *Altered States of Consciousness*. London: John Wiley and Sons.

7. Harding, J. (1988) 'Hello, John, got a new mantra?' *Sunday Times Magazine* 11 December, p.101.

8. Goleman, D. (1978) *op. cit.* p.68.

9. Goleman, D. (1978) *ibid.*

10. Maharishi, M.Y. (1969) *Science of Creative Intelligence*. Los Angeles: Maharishi International Press.

11. Goleman, D. (1978) *op. cit.* p.70.

12. Suzuki, T. (1958) *Essays in Zen Buddhism.* Second series. London: Rider.

13. Pirsig, R.M. (1974) *Zen and the Art of Motorcycle Maintenance: An Inquiry into Values.* London: The Bodley Head.

14. Roszack, T. (1970) *The Making of a Counter Culture. Reflections on the Counter Culture and its Youthful Opposition.* London: Faber and Faber.

15. Humphreys, C. (1962) *Zen.* London: Hodder and Stoughton, p.138.

16. Humphreys, C. (1962) *op. cit.* p.106.

17. Editorial (1977) 'The Psychology of Mysticism.' *The Practitioner No. 1306* April, Vol. 218, p.477.

18. Laing, R.D., cited in Clay, J. (1997) *R.D. Laing: A Divided Self.* London: Hodder and Stoughton, p.102.

19. LeShan, L. (1978) *How To Meditate: A Guide To Self-Discovery.* London: Sphere Books, p.7.

20. Krishnamurti, J. (1966) *Conversations with Krishnamurti In Europe.* Ojai, California: Krishnamurti Foundation.

21. Maupin, E.W. (1969) *op. cit.* p.178.

22. Hirai, T. (1975) *Zen Meditation Therapy.* Tokyo: Japan Publications Inc.

23. Maharishi, M.Y (1969) *op. cit.* p.287.

24. Sugi, Y. and Akutsu, K. (1964) *Science of Zazen – Energy Metabolism.* Tokyo: Japan Publications Inc.

25. Anand, B.K., Chhina, G.S. and Singh, B. (1961) 'Studies on Shri Ramananada Yogi during his stay in an airtight box.' *Indian Journal of Medical Research 49*, 82–89.

26. Green, E.E. and Green, A.M. (1977) *Beyond Biofeedback.* New York: Delacorte Press.

27. Schwarz, J. (1978) *Voluntary Controls: Exercises in Creative Meditation for the Activation of the Potential of the Chakras.* New York: The Aletheia Foundation.

28. Karamutsu, A. and Hirai, T. (1966) 'Studies of EEGs of expert Zen meditators.' *Folia Psychiatrica Neurologica Japanica 28*, 315.

29. Karamutsu, A. and Hirai, T. (1969) 'An electroencephalographic study of Zen meditation (zazen).' In C. Tart (ed) *Altered States of Consciousness.* New York: Wiley, pp.489–502.

30. Benson, H.B. with Zlipper, M.Z. (1975) *The Relaxation Response.* London: Collins.

31. Hirai, T. (1975) *op. cit.*

32. Anand, B.K., Chhina, G.S. and Singh, B. (1961) 'Some aspects of electroenecephalographic studies in yogis.' *Electrocephalograph Clinical Neurophysiology 13*, 452–456.

33. Karamutsu, A. and Hirai, T. (1966) *op. cit.*

34. Hirai, T. (1975) *op. cit.*

35. Bagchi, B.K. and Wenger, M.A. (1959) 'Electrophysiological correlates of some Yoga exercises.' In L. van Bagaert and J. Radermecker (eds) *Electroencephalography Clinical Neurophysiology and Epilepsy.* Vol. 3 of First Congress of Neurological Sciences. London: Pergamon.

36. Wallace, R.K. (1970) 'Physiological effects of transcendental meditation.' *Science 167*, 171–174.

37. Bloomfield, H., Cain, M. and Jaffe, R. (1975) *TM: Discovering Inner Energy and Overcoming Stress.* New York: Delacorte Press.

38. Schwartz, G.E. and Goleman, D.J. (1976) 'Meditation as an alternative to drug use.' Unpublished paper, cited in Pelletier, K. (1978) *Mind as Healer, Mind as Slayer.* London: George Allen.

39. Ormé-Johnston, D.W. (1973) 'Autonomic ability and Transcendental Meditation.' *Psychosomatic Medicine 35*, 341–349.

40. Linden, W. (1973) 'Practising of meditation by school children and their levels of field dependence-independence, test anxiety and reading achievement.' *Journal of Consulting and Clinical Psychology, 41*, 139–43.

41. Niddich, S., Seeman, W. and Dreskin, T. (1993) 'Influence of transcendental meditation: a replication.' *Journal of Counselling Psychology, 20*, 255–256.

42. Schwartz, G.E. and Goleman, D.J. (1976) *op. cit.*

43. Kirschner, S. (1975) 'Zen meditators: a clinical study.' *Dissertation Abstracts International, 36*, 361B–3614B cited by Ramaswami, S. and Sheikh, A.A. 'Meditation East and West.' In A.A.

Sheikh and K.S. Sheikh (eds) *Ancient and Western Approaches to Healing: Ancient Wisdom and Modern Knowledge,* pp.429–469. New York: Wiley.

44. Ottens, A.J. (1974) 'The effect of transcendental meditation upon modifying the cigarette smoking habit.' Dissertation Abstracts International, 35, 7131A cited in Ramaswami, S. and Sheikh, A.A. 'Meditation East and West.' *ibid.*

45. Schwartz, G.E. (1973) 'Pros and Cons of Meditation: Anxiety, self control, drug abuse and creativity.' Paper delivered at the 81st Convention of The American Psychological Association, Montréal.

46. Honsberger, E. and Wilson, A.F. (1973) 'Transcendental Meditation in treating asthma: Respiration therapy.' *Journal of Inhalation Technology 3,* 79–81.

47. Wallace, R.K. and Benson, H.B. (1972) 'The physiology of meditation.' In *Altered States of Awareness: Readings From Scientific American.* San Francisco, California: W.H. Freeman, pp.125–131.

48. Benson, H.B. *et al.* (1974) 'Decreased blood pressure in pharmacologically hypertensive patients who regularly elicited the relaxation response.' *Lancet 23,* March, 289.

49. Cooper, M. and Aygen, M. (1978) 'Effect of meditation on blood cholesterol and blood pressure.' *Journal of Israel Medical Association 95,* 2.

50. Boudreau, L. (1972) 'Transcendental meditation and yoga as reciprocal inhibitors.' *Journal Behavioural Therapy and Experimental Psychiatry 3,* 97–98

51. Patel, C.H. (1973) 'Yoga and biofeedback in the management of hypertension.' *Lancet 10.* November.

52. Patel, C.H. and Datey, K.K. (1975) 'Yoga and biofeedback in the management of hypertension: two controlled studies.' Proceedings of the Biofeedback Research Society. Monterey, California.

53. Dostalek, C. (1987) 'The empirical and experimental foundations of yoga therapy.' In D.M. Gharote and M. Lockhart (eds) *The Art of Survival: A Guide to Yoga Therapy.* London: Unwin Hyman.

54. Monjo, de V.P. (1987) 'The conditions of yoga therapy.' In D.M. Gharote and M. Lockhart (eds) *The Art of Survival: A Guide to Yoga Therapy.* London: Unwin Hyman, pp.66–78.

55. Wallace, R.K and Benson, H.B. (1972) *op. cit.*

56. Benson, H. with Zlipper, M.Z. (1975) *op. cit.*

57. Pitts, F.N. Jr. and McClure, J.N. Jr. (1967) 'Lactate metabolism in anxiety neurosis.' *New England Journal of Medicine 277,* 1329–1336.

58. Wallace, R.K. and Benson, H.B. (1972) *op. cit.*

59. Shapiro, D. (1975) *op. cit.*

60. Kirschner, S. (1975) *op. cit.*

61. Marron, J.P. (1973) 'Transcendental meditation: A clinical evaluation.' Dissertation Abstracts International, 34, 4551B, cited in Ramaswami, S. and Sheikh., A.A. 'Meditation East and West.' In A.A. Sheikh and K.S. Sheikh (eds) *Ancient and Western Approaches to Healing: Ancient Wisdom and Modern Knowledge.* New York: Wiley.

62. Delmonte, M.M. (1986) 'Meditation as a clinical intervention strategy: A brief review.' *International Journal of Psychosomatics 33,* 3, 9–12.

63. Rios, R.J. (1979) 'The effect of hypnosis and meditation on state and trait anxiety and locus of control.' Dissertation Abstracts International, 40, 5209A–6210A, cited in Ramaswami, S. and Sheikh, A.A. *op. cit.*

64. Comer, J.F. Jr (1977) 'Meditation and progressive relaxation in the treatment of test anxiety.' Dissertation Abstracts International, 38, 6412B–6143B, cited in Ramaswami, S. and Sheikh, A.A. *op. cit.*

65. Diner, M.D. (1978) 'The differential effects of meditation and systematic desensitization of specific and general anxiety.' Dissertation Abstracts International, 39, 1950B, cited Ramaswamai, S. and Sheikh, A.A. *op. cit.*

66. Ormé-Johnston, D.W. (1973) *op. cit.*

67. Wallace, R.K. and Benson, H.B. (1972) *op. cit.*

68. Fenwick, P.B. (1983) 'Can we still recommend meditation?' *British Medical Journal 287*, 12 November, p.1401.

69. Stoyva, J. and Budzynski, M. (1973) 'Cultivated low arousal – an antistress response?' In I.V. DiCara (ed) *Recent Advances in Limbic and Autonomic Nervous System Research*. New York: Plenum.

70. Benson, H.B. (1972) *op. cit.*

71. West, M. (1979) 'Meditation.' *British Journal of Psychiatry 135*, 457–467.

72. West, M. (1980) 'Physiological effects of meditation. *Journal of Psychosomatic Research 24*, 265–273.

73. Throll, D.A. (1981) 'Transcendental Meditation and progressive relaxation: their psychological effects.' *Journal of Clinical Psychology 37*, 776–781.

74. Sgapirom, D.H. (1982) 'Overview: clinical and physiological comparison of meditation with other self-control strategies.' *American Journal of Psychiatry 139*, 267–274.

75. Berkowitz, A.H. (1977) 'The effect of transcendental meditation on trait anxiety and self-esteem.' Dissertation Abstracts International, 38, 2353B–2354B cited in Ramaswamai, S. and Sheikh, A.A. *op. cit.*.

76. Willis, R.J. (1979) 'Meditation to fit the person: psychology and the meditative way.' *Journal of Religion and Health 18*, 2, 93–119.

77. Blanz, L.T. (1973) 'Personality changes as a function of two different meditative techniques.' Dissertation Abstracts International, 34, 7035A–7036A cited in Ramaswami, S. and Sheikh, A.A. *ibid.*

78. Polowniak, W.A. (1973) 'The meditation-encounter growth group,' Cited in Ramaswami, S. and Sheikh, A.A. *ibid.*

79. Riddle, A.G. (1979) 'Effects of selected elements of meditation on self-actualization, locus of control, and trait anxiety.' Cited in Ramaswami, S. and Sheikh, A.A. *ibid.*

80. Dice, M.L. (1979) 'The effectiveness of meditation on selected measures of self-actualization'. Cited in Ramaswami, S. and Sheik, A.A. *ibid.*

81. Ferguson, P.C. (1980) 'An integrative meta-analysis of psychological studies investigating the treatment outcomes of meditation techniques.' Cited Ramaswami, S. and Sheik, A.A. (1989) *ibid.*

82. Otis, L.S. (1974) 'The facts of transcendental meditation: If well integrated but anxious, try TM.' *Psychology Today 7*, 45–46.

83. Rogers, C.A. and Livingstone, D.D. (1977) 'Accumulative effects of periodic relaxation.' *Perception and Motor Skills 44*, 690.

84. Williams, P.M., Francis, A. and Durham, R. (1976) 'Personality and meditation.' *Perception and Motor Skills 43*, 787.

85. Otis, L.S. (1974) *op. cit.*

86. Blows, M. (1987) 'Relaxation and meditation: borrowing and returning.' In D.M. Gharote and M. Lockhart (eds) *The Art of Survival: A Guide to Yoga Therapy*. London: Unwin Hyman.

87. Norris, P. (1989) 'Current trends in biofeedback and self-regulation.' In A.A. Sheikh and K.S. Sheikh (eds) *Eastern and Western Approaches to Healing: Ancient Wisdom and Modern Knowledge*. New York: Wiley, pp.264–295.

88. Miller, N. (1969) 'Learning of visceral and glandular responses.' *Science 163*, 434–435.

89. Kamiya, J. (1968) 'Conscious control of brain waves.' *Psychology Today 1*, 57–60.

90. Kamiya, J. (1969) 'Operant control of the EEG alpha rhythm and some of its reported effects on consciousness.' In C. Tart (ed) *Altered States of Consciousness*. New York: Wiley, pp.600–611.

91. Lang, P.T. (1967) 'Effects of feedback and instructional set.' *Journal of Experimental Psychology 75*, 425.

92. Engel, B.T. (1972) 'Operant conditioning of cardiac functioning.' *Psychophysiology 9*, 161.

93. Elder, S.T. (1977) 'Apparatus and procedure for training subjects to control blood pressure.' *Psychophysiology 14*, 68.

94. Green, E.E. (1969) 'Voluntary control of inner states.' *Psychophysiology 6*, 37.

95. Gorman, P. and Kamiya, J. (1972) 'Voluntary control of stomach pH.' Research note presented at Biofeedback Research Society Meeting, Boston, November.

96. Norris, P. (1989) *op. cit.*

97. Paiva, A. (1982) 'Effects of frontalis EMG biofeedback and diazepam in the treatment of tension headache.' *Headache 22*, 216–220.

98. Pelletier, K.R. (1978) *Mind as Healer, Mind as Slayer: An Holistic Approach to Preventing Stress Disorders.* London: G. Allen and Unwin.

99. Vachon, L. (1973) cited in Pelletier, K.R. (1978) *op. cit.*

100. Stroebel (1972) cited in Pelletier, K.R. (1978) *op. cit.*

101. Miller, N.E. (1974) 'Biofeedback: Evaluation of a new technique.' *New England Journal of Medicine 290*, 12, 686–685.

102. Johnson, H.E. and Garton, W.H. (1973) 'A practical method of muscle reeducation in hemiphlegia: electriographic facilitation.' Unpublished manuscript. Casa Colina Hospital for Rehabilitation Medicine, Paloma, California, cited in Pelletier, K.R. (1978) *op. cit.*

103. Marinacci, A.A. (1969) *Applied Electromyography.* Philadelphia: Lea and Febiger.

104. Booker, H.E., Rubow, R.T. and Coleman, P.J. (1969) 'Simplified feedback in neuromuscular training: an automated approach using electromyographic signals.' *Archives of Physical Medical Rehabilitation*, 615–621.

105. Brener, J. and Kleinman, R.A. (1970) 'Learned control of decreases in systolic blood pressure.' *Nature 26*, 1063.

106. Peavey, B.S. (1982) 'Biofeedback assisted regulation. Effects of phagocyte immune functions.' Unpublished Doctoral Thesis, Texas State University, Denton, cited in Achterberg, J. (1985) *Imagery in Healing.* Boulder, CO, and London: Shambhala.

107. Norris, P. (1989) *op. cit.*

108. Schwartz, G.E. (1973) *op. cit.*

109. Benson, H. with Zlipper, M.Z. (1975) *op. cit.*

110. Schwartz, G.E. (1973) *op. cit.*

111. Pelletier, K.R. (1978) *op. cit.* p.268.

112. Pelletier, K.R. (1978) *ibid.* p.268.

113. Cade, C.M and Coxhead, N. (1979) *The Awakened Mind: Biofeedback and the Development of Higher States of Awareness.* Dorset: Wildwood House.

114. Blundell, G. (1979) 'Biofeedback'. In A. Hill *A Visual Encyclopedia of Unconventional Medicine.* London: New English Library, p.191.

115. Blundell, B. (1979) *op. cit.*

Chapter 8: Hypnosis, Auto-Suggestion and Autogenc Training

1. Spanos, N.P. (1986) 'Hypnosis and the modification of hypnotic susceptibility. A social psychological perspective.' In P.L.N. Nash (ed) *What is Hypnosis? Current Theories and Research.* Milton Keynes: Open University Press, pp.85–120.

2. Chertok, L. (1981) *Sense and Nonsense in Psychotherapy: The Challenge of Hypnosis.* Oxford: Pergamon Press.

3. Blythe, P. (1979) 'Hypnosis.' In A. Hill (ed) *A Visual Encyclopedia of Unconventional Medicine.* London: New English Library, pp.188–189.

4. Barber, T.X. (1961) 'Psychological aspects of hypnosis.' *Psychological Bulletin 58*, 390–419.

5. Barber, T.X. (1969) *Hypnosis: A Scientific Approach.* New York: Van Nostrand.

6. Barber, T.X., Spanos, N.P. and Chaves, J.P. (1974) *Hypnosis, Imagination and Human Potentialities.* New York: Pergamon.

7. Spanos, N.P. (1982) 'A social psychological approach to hypnotic behaviour.' In G. Weary and M.L. Mirels (ed) *Integrations of Clinical and Social Psychology.* Milton Keynes: Open University Press, pp.227–231.

8. Spanos, N.P. (1986) *op. cit.*

9. Wagstaff, G.F. (1977) 'An experimental study of compliance and post-hypnotic amnesia.' *British Journal of Social and Clinical Psychology 4*, 16, 225–228.

10. Wagstaff, G.F. (1981) *Hypnosis: Compliance and Belief.* Brighton: Harvester Press.

11. Wagstaff, G.F. (1986) 'Hypnosis as compliance and belief: a socio-cognitive view.' In P.L.N. Naish (ed) *What is Hypnosis? Current Theories and Research.* Milton Keynes: Open University Press, pp.59–84.

12. Spiegel, J. cited in Hariman, J. (1981) *How To Use the Power of Self-Hypnosis.* Wellingborough: Thorsons.

13. Chertok, L. (1969) *The Evolution of Research into Hypotheses in Psychophysiological Mechanisms of Hypnosis.* New York: Springer Verlag.

14. Casilneck, H.B. and Hall, J.A. (1959) 'Physiological changes associated with hypnosis.' *Journal of Clinical and Experimental Hypnosis 7,* 9.

15. Langen, D. (1969) 'Peripheral changes in blood circulation during Autogenic Training hypnosis.' In *Psychophysiological Mechanisms of Hypnosis.* New York: Springer Verlag.

16. Edmonston, W.E. and Pessin, M. (1966) 'Hypnosis as related to learning and electrodermal measures.' *American Journal of Clinical Hypnosis 9*, 31.

17. Ravitz, L.J. (1958) 'How electricity measures hypnosis.' *Tomorrow 6*, 49.

18. Schultz, J.H. and Luthe, W. (1959) *Autogenic Training: A Psychophysiological Approach to Psychotherapy.* New York: Grune and Stratton.

19. Spanos, N.P. (1982) *op. cit.*

20. Naish, P.L.N. (ed) (1986) In P.L.N. Naish (ed) *What is Hypnosis? Current Theories and Research.* Milton Keynes: Open University Press, pp.59–84.

21. Sheehan, P.W. and McConkey, K.M. (1982) *Hypnosis and Experience: The Exploration of Phenomena and Process.* Hillsdale, NJ: Lawrence Erlbaum.

22. Perry, C. (1979) 'Hypnotic coercion and compliance to it: a review of evidence presented in a legal case.' *International Journal of Clinical and Experimental Hypnosis 27*, 187–218.

23. Fellows, B.J. (1986) 'The concept of trance.' In P.L.N. Naish (ed) *What is Hypnosis? Current Theories and Research.* Milton Keynes: Open University Press, pp.37–58, p.46.

24. Naish, P.L.N. (1986) *op. cit.*

25. Fisher, S. (1954) 'The role of expectancy in the performance of posthypnotic behaviour.' *Journal of Abnormal Social Psychology 49*, 503.

26. Coe, W.C. and Ryken, K. (1979) 'Hypnosis and risks to human subjects.' *American Psychologist 34*, 673–681.

27. Krippner, S. (1969) 'Psychedelic state, hyponotic trance and creativity.' In C.T. Tart (ed) *Altered States of Consciousness.* San Francisco: Harper and Row, pp.271–290.

28. Melzack, R. (1973) *The Puzzle of Pain.* London: Penguin.

29. Barber, T.X. (1978) 'Hypnosis, suggestions and psychosomatic phenomena: a new look from the standpoint of recent experimental studies.' *Am. J. Clin. Hypnosis 21*, 13–17.

30. Fellows. B.J. (1986) *op. cit.*

31. Edelstein, E.J. and Edelstein, L. (1945) *Asclepius: A Collection and Interpretation of the Testimonies.* Baltimore, MD: Johns Hopkins University Press.

32. Webster, C. (1988) 'The nineteenth century after-life of Paracelsus.' In R. Cooter (ed) *Studies in the History of Alternative Medicine.* London: MacMillan, pp.79–88.

33. Inglis, B. (1990) *Trance: A Natural History of Altered States of Mind.* London: Paladin.

34. Hearnshaw, L.S. (1989) *The Shaping of Modern Psychology: An Historical Introduction.* London: Routledge.

35. Lovelock, J.E. (1979) *Gaia.* London: Oxford University Press.

36. Hearnshaw, L.S. (1989) *op. cit.* p.152.

37. Hearnshaw, L.S. (1989) *op. cit.* p.120.

38. Chertok, L. (1981) *op. cit.*

39. Jameson, R.M. (1963) cited in A. Borthwick Clarke (1981) 'Hypnosis in general practice.' *Practitioner 1225*, 1355, 746ff.

40. Fayronville, M.E. *at al.* (1995) 'Hypnosis as an adjunct therapy in conscious sedation for plastic surgery.' *Regional Anaesthesia 20*, 2, 145–151.

41. Schulz-Slubner, S. (1996) 'Hypnosis – a side effect-free alternative to medical sedation in regional anesthesia.' *Anaesthetist 45*, 10, 965–969.

42. Finlay, I.G. and Jones, O.L. (1996) 'Hypnotherapy in palliative care.' *Journal of Research in Social Medicine, 89*, 9, 493–496.

43. Moon, T. and Moon, H. (1984) 'Hypnosis and childbirth: self-report and comment.' *Hypnosis 1*, 49–52.

44. Taugher, V.T. (1958) 'Hypno-anaesthesia.' *Wisconsin Medicine Journal* 57, 95.

45. Hilgard, E.R. (1973) 'A neodissociation theory of pain reduction in hypnosis.' *Psychological Review 80*, 396–411.

46. Stern, J.A. *et al.* (1977) 'A comparison of hypnosis, acupuncture, morphine, valium, aspirin and placebos in the management of experimentally induced pain.' *Annals of the New York Academy of Sciences 296*, 175–193.

47. Stephenson, J.B.P. (1978) 'Reversal of hypnosis-induced analgesia by naloxone.' *Lancet 11*, 991–992.

48. Finer, B. (1982) 'Endorphins under hypnosis in chronic pain patients: some experimental findings.' Paper given at Ninth Congress of Hypnosis and Psychosomatic Medicine, Montréal.

49. Erikson, M.H. (1959) 'Hypnosis in painful terminal illness.' *American Journal of Clinical Hypnosis 2*, 117, 122.

50. Hilgard, E.R. (1973) *ibid.*

51. Hilgard, E.R. and Hilgard, J.R. (1975) 'Hypnosis in the relief of pain.' Los Altos, CA: W. Kaufman.

52. Sacerdote, P. (1982) 'Techniques of hypnotic intervention with pain patients.' *Annals of the New York Academy of Sciences 125*, 3, 101–19.

53. Zeltzer, L.K. (1980) 'The adolescent with cancer.' In J. Kellerman (ed) *Psychological Aspects of Childhood Cancer.* Springfield, IL: Chas. C Thomas.

54. Redd, W.H., Andersen, G.V. and Minagawa, R.Y. (1982) 'Hypnotic control of anticipatory emesis in patients receiving cancer chemotherapy.' *Journal of Consulting and Clinical Psychology 50*, 1, 14–19.

55. Hall, H.R. (1985) 'Hypnosis and the immune system: a review with implications for cancer and the psychology of healing.' *American Journal of Clinical Hypnosis 25*, 92–103.

56. Finlay, I.G. and Jones, O.L. (1966) *op.cit.*

57. Enqvist, B. and Fisher, K. (1977) 'Preoperative hypnotic techniques reduce consumption of anelgesics after surgical removal of third mandibular molars: a brief communication.' *International Journal of Clinical and Experimental Hypnosis 45*, 2, 102–108.

58. Houghton, L.A. *et al.* (1996) 'Symptomatology, quality of life and economic features of irritable bowel syndrome – the effect of hypnotherapy.' *Alimentary Pharmacology and Therapeutics 10*, 1, 91–95.

59. Roet, B. (1987) *All in The Mind.* London: MacDonald, Optima.

60. Dempster, C.R., Batson, P. and Whalen, B.Y. (1976) 'Supportive hypnotherapy during the radical treatment of malignancies.' *Journal of Clinical and Experimental Hypnosis 21*, 1–9.

61. Wagstaff, G.F. (1986) *op. cit.*

62. Spanos, N.P. (1986) *op. cit.*

63. Orne, M.T. (1959) 'The nature of hypnosis: artifact and essence.' *Journal of Abnormal and Social Psychology 58*, 277–299.

64. Sarbin, T.R. (1962) 'Attempts to understand hypnotic pheneomena.' In L. Postman (ed) *Psychology in the Making*, New York: Knopf, pp.98–103.

65. Chertok, L. (1969) *The Evolution of Research Into Hypotheses in Psychophysiological Mechanisms of Hypnosis.* New York: Springer Verlag.

66. Chertok, L. (1981) *op. cit.*

67. Ellenberger, H.H. (1970) *The Discovery of the Unconscious*. New York: Basic Books.

68. Barber, T.X. (1969) *op. cit.*

69. Barber, T.X. (1978) *op. cit.*

70. Barber, T.X., Spanos, N.P and Chaves, J.P. (1974) *op. cit.*

71. Wagstaff, G.F. (1981) *op. cit.*

72. Spanos, N.P. (1982) *op. cit.*

73. Naish, P.L.N. (1986) *op. cit.*

74. Bertrand, L.D. and Spanos, N.P. (1989) 'Hypnosis: historical and social psychological aspects.' In A.A. Shiekh and K.S. Sheikh (eds) *Eastern and Western Approaches to Healing: Ancient Wisdom and Modern Knowledge*. New York: Wiley, pp.237–263.

75. Milgram, S. (1974) *Obedience to Authority: An Experimental View*. New York: Harper and Row.

76. Zimbardo, P.G. (1969) *The Cognitive Control of Motivation*. New York: Scott Foresman.

77. Hunt, S.M. (1979) 'Hypnosis as obedience behaviour.' *British Journal of Social and Clinical Psychology 18*, 21–27.

78. Wagstaff, G.F. (1977) *op. cit.*

79. Schacter, S. and Singer, J.E. (1962) 'Cognitive, social and physiological determinants of emotional states.' *Psychological Review 69*, 379.

80. Bem. D.J. (1972) 'Self perception theory.' In L. Berkowitz (ed) *Advances in Experimental Social Psychology*. Vol. 6. New York: Academic Press.

81. Valins, S. (1966) 'Cognitive effects of false heart-rate feedback.' *Journal of Personality and Social Psychology 4*, 400–408.

82. Valins, S. and Ray, A.A. (1967) 'Effects of cognitive sensitization of avoidance behaviour.' *Journal of Personality and Social Psychology 4*, 7, 345–350.

83. Wagstaff, G.F. (1986) 'Hypnosis as compliance and belief: A sociocognitive view.' In P.L. Naish (ed) *What is Hypnosis? Current Theories and Research*. Milton Keynes: Open University Press, p.66.

84. Wagstaff, G.F. (1986) *ibid.* p.87.

85. Spanos, N.P. (1986) *op. cit.* p.111–112.

86. Hariman, J. (1981) *How to Use the Power of Self-Hypnosis*. Wellingborough, Northamptonshire: Thorsons.

87. Bertrand, A. (1823) *Traite du Somnambulism*. Paris.

88. Blythe, P. (1979) 'Auto-suggestion.' In A. Hill (ed) *A Visual Encyclopaedia of Unconventional Medicine*. London: New English Library, pp.186–187.

89. Schultz, J.R. (1932) *Das Autogene Training*. Stuttgart: Geegthieme Verlag.

90. Luthe, W. (1969) 'Autogenic Training: methods, research and applications in medicine.' In C.T. Tart (ed) *Altered States of Consciousness*. New York: Wiley, pp.309–319.

91. Pelletier, K.R. (1978) *Mind as Healer, Mind as Slayer*. London: George Allen, pp.229–251.

92. Day, H. (1953) *The Study and Practice of Yoga*. London: Thorsons, p.25.

93. Pelletier, K.R. (1978) *op. cit.* p.244.

94. Gorton, B. (1959) 'Autogenic Training.' *American Journal of Clinical Hypnosis 2*, 31–41.

95. Kamiya, J. (1969) 'Operant control of the EEG alpha rhythm and some of its reported effects on consciousness.' In C.T. Tart (ed) *Altered States of Consciousness*. Third edition. New York: Wiley, pp.600–611.

96. Pelletier, K.R. (1978) *op. cit.* p.248.

97. Luthe, W. (1969) *op. cit.*

98. Binswanger, H. (1929) 'Beobachtungen an entspanntern und versenken Versuchpersonen Ein Beitrag zu Moglichen Mechanismen der Konversionhysterie.' *Nervenartz 4*, 193.

99. Stovkis, B., Renes, B. and Landemann, H. (1961) 'Skin temperature under experimental stress and during Autogenic Training.' International Proceedings of the Third Conference of Psychiatry, Montréal. Cited in K.R. Pelletier (1978) *op.cit.*

100. Polzein, P. (1961) 'Electrocardiographic changes during the first standard exercise.' International Proceedings of the Third Conference of Psychiatry, Montréal. Cited in K.R. Pelletier (1978) *op.cit.*

101. Polzein, P. (1961) 'Respiratory changes during passive concentration.' International Proceedings of the Third Conference of Psychiatry, Montréal. Cited in K.R. Pelletier (1978) *op.cit.*

102. Polzein, P. (1961) 'Therapeutic Possibilities of Autogenic Training in hyperthyroid conditions.' International Proceedings of the Third Conference of Psychiatry, Montréal. Cited in K.R. Pelletier (1978) *op.cit.*

103. Marchand, H. (1956) 'Die suggestionder warme im oberbauch und ihr einfluss auf blutzucker und leukozytem.' *Psychotherapie 3,* 154.

104. Marchand, H. (1961) 'Das verhallen vonblutzucker und leukozyten wahrend des autogenen trainings. International Proceedings of the Third Conference of Psychiatry, Montréal. Cited in K.R. Pelletier (1978) *ibid.*

105. Schultz, G. and Luthe, W. (1959) *op. cit.*

106. Kelly, C.R. (1961) 'Psychological factors in myopia.' In *Proceedings of American Psychological Association,* 31 August.

107. Lewis, J.H. and Sarbin, T.R. (1943) 'Studies in Psychosomatics.' *Psychosomatic Medicine 5,* 125.

108. Gorton, B. (1959) *op. cit.*

109. Medik, L. and Fursland, A. (1984) 'Maximising scarce resources. Autogenic relaxation classes at a health centre.' *British Journal of Medical Psychology 57,* 181–185.

110. Horn, S. (1987) *Relaxation: Modern Techniques for Stress Management.* Wellingborough: Thorsons.

111. Prosser, G.V., Carson, P. and Phillips, R. (1985) 'Exercise after myocardial infarction: Long-term rehabilitation effects.' *Journal of Psychosomatic Research 29,* 5, 535–540.

112. Wilson, V.S. (1989) 'Autogenic Training in the context of yoga.' In M.I. Gharote and M. Lockhart (eds) *The Art of Survival: A Guide to Yoga Therapy.* London: Unwin Hyman, p.116.

113. Luthe, W. (1969) *op. cit.* p.317.

114. Linden, W. (1994) 'Autogenic Training: a narrative and qualitative review of clinical outcome.' *Biofeedback Self Regul 19,* 3, 227–264.

115. Watanabe, Y. *et al.* (1996) 'Chronobiometric assessment of Autogenic Training effects upon blood pressure and heart rate.' *Perception and Motor Skills 83* (3 Part 2) 1395–1410.

116. Labbe, E.E. (1995) 'Treatment of childhood migraine with Autogenic training and skin temperature biofeedback: a component analysis.' *Headache 35,* 1, 3–10.

117. Carruthers, M. (1984) 'Health promotion by mental and physical training.' *British Journal of Holistic Medicine 1,* 2, 142–147.

118. Kermani, K. (1987) 'Stress, emotions, Autogenic Training and AIDS: a holistic approach to the management of HIV-infected individuals.' *Holistic Medicine 2,* 203–215.

119. Sakai, M. (1977) 'Application of autogenic training for anxiety disorders: a clinical study in a psychiatric setting.' *Fukuoka Igaku Zasshi 56–64,* March.

Chapter 9: Relaxation

1. Jacobsen, E. (1938) *Progressive Relaxation.* Chicago: University of Chicago Press.

2. Cousins, N. (1981) *Anatomy of an Illness as Perceived by a Patient: Reflections on Healing and Regeneration.* London: Bantam.

3. Bell, C. (1847) *The Anatomy and Philosophy of Expression as Connected with the Fine Arts.* Fourth Edition. London: John Murray.

4. Jacobsen, E. (1938) *op. cit.* p.183.

5. Jacobsen, E. (1938) *ibid.* p.184.

6. Wolpe, J. (1977) 'Systematic desensitization based on relaxation.' In S.J. Morse and R.I. Watson (eds) *Psychotherapies: A Comparative Casebook.* New York: Holt, Rinehart, Winston, pp.298–306.

7. Blows, M. (1987) 'Relaxation and meditation.' In M.I. Gharote and M. Lockhart (eds) *The Art of Survival: A Guide to Yoga Therapy.* New York: Unwin Hyman Ltd.

8. Carlson, C.R. and Curran, S.L. (1994) 'Stretch-based relaxation training.' *Patient Education 23*, 1, 5–12 April.

9. Meares, A. (1977) 'Atavistic regression as a factor in the remission of cancer.' *Medical Journal of Australia 2*, 132–133.

10. Good, M. (1997) 'Effects of relaxation and music on post-operative pain: a review.' *Journal of Advances in Nursing 24*, 5, 9–5. 14 November.

11. Benson, H.B. with Zlipper, M.Z. (1975) *The Relaxation Response.* London: Collins, p.123.

12. Maupin, E.W. (1969) 'On meditation.' In C. Tart (ed.) *Altered States of Consciousness.* London: John Wiley.

13. Benson, H.B. with Zlipper, M.Z. (1975) *op. cit.*

14. Benson, H.B. with Zlipper, M.Z. (1975) *ibid.*

15. Saxena, R.P. and Saxena, U. (1978) 'Psychotherapeutic approach in the treatment of asthma.' *Journal of Chronic Disease and Therapeutic Research 1*, 25.

16. Erskine, M.J. and Schonell, M. (1981) 'Relaxation therapy in asthma: a critical review.' *Psychosomatic Medicine 43*, 365–372.

17. Meares, A. (1981) 'Regression or recurrence of carcinoma of the breast at mastectomy site associated with intensive meditation.' *Australian Family Physician 10*, 218–219.

18. Burish, T.G. and Lyles, J.N. (1981) 'Effectiveness of relaxation training in reducing adverse reactions to cancer chemotherapy.' *Journal of Behavioural Medicine 4*, 65–78.

19. Bindemann, S. *et al.* (1986) 'Enhancement of quality of life with relaxation training in cancer patients attending a chemotherapy unit.' In M. Watson and S. Greer (eds) *Psychosocial Issues in Malignant Disease.* Oxford: Pergamon.

20. Kiecolt-Glaser, J. and Glaser, R. (1985) 'Psychosocial enhancement of immuno-competence in a geriatric population.' *Psychology Today 4*, 24–41.

21. Boryshenko, J. cited in Siegel, B.S. (1986) *Love, Medicine, Miracles.* London: Rider.

22. Tello-Bernabe, M.E. *et al.* (1977) 'Group techniques and relaxation in the treatment of several subtypes of anxiety: a non-randomised controlled trial.' *Aten Primaria19*, 2, 67–71.

23. Skinner, P.T. (1984) 'Skills not pills: learning to cope with anxiety symptoms.' *Journal of Royal College of Practitioners,* May, 258–259.

24. Rowden, R. (1984) 'Relaxation and visualisation techniques in patients with breast cancer.' *Nursing Times,* September 12, 42–44.

25. Turner, J.A. and Chapman, C.P. (1981) 'Psychological intervention in chronic pain: a critical review. I. Relaxation and Biofeedback. *Pain 12*, 1, 21.

26. Good, M. (1997) *op. cit.*

27. Larsson, B. and Carlsson, J. (1996) 'School-based nurse-administered relaxation training for children with chronic tension-type headache.' *Journal of Pediatrics 4*, 21, 5, 603–614.

28. Horn, S. (1986) *Relaxation: Modern Techniques for Stress Management.* Wellingborough: Thorsons.

29. Libo, L.M. and Arnold, G.E. (1983) 'Relaxation practice after biofeedback therapy: a long-term follow-up study of ultilization and effectiveness.' *Biofeedback and Self-Regulation 8*, 2.

30. Achterberg, J. Collerain, I. and Craig, P. (1978) 'A possible relationship between cancer, mental retardation and mental disorders.' *Journal of Social Science and Medicine,* 12 May, 135–139.

31. Greer, S. (1983) 'Cancer and the mind.' *British Journal of Psychiatry 143*, 535–543.

32. Greer, S. (1983) *ibid.*

33. Miller, F.R. and Jones, H.W. (1948) 'The possibility of precipitating the leukaemia state by emotional factors.' *Blood 8*, 880–885.

34. Muslin, H.L., Gyarfas, K. and Pieper, W.J. (1966) 'Separation experience and cancer of the breast.' *Annals of New York Academy of Sciences 125*, 802–806.

35. LeShan, L. (1966) 'An emotional life-history pattern associated with neoplastic disease.' *Annals of New York Academy of Sciences 125*, 780–793.

36. Priestman, T.J., Priestman, S.G., and Bradshaw, C. (1985) 'Stress and breast cancer.' *British Journal of Cancer 51*, 493–498.

37. Blumberg, E.M., West, P.M. and Ellis, F.W. (1954) 'A possible relationship between psychological factors and human cancer.' *Psychosomatic Medicine 16*, 4, 277–286.

38. Greer, S, and Morris, T. (1975) 'Psychological attributes of women who develop breast cancer: a controlled study.' *Journal of Psychosomatic Research 19*, 147–153.

39. Schonfield, J. (1975) 'Psychological and life experience differences between Israeli women with benign and cancerous breast lesions.' *Journal of Psychosomatic Research 19*, 229–234.

40. Stoll, B.A. (1979) 'Restraint of growth and spontaneous regression of cancer'. In B.A. Stoll (ed) *Mind and Cancer Prognosis.* Chichester: Wiley.

41. Shekelle, R.B. *et al.* (1981) 'Psychological depression and 17 year risk of death from cancer.' *Psychosomatic Medicine 43*, 117–125.

42. Alvarez, A. (1989) 'Stressful life events and the recurrence of breast cancer in women.' Reported in *Medicine Now*, BBC Radio 4, 15 February.

43. Cooper, C. (1984) *Stress and Cancer.* Chichester: Wiley.

44. Cooper, C., Cooper, R. and Eaker, L. (1988) *Living With Stress.* Harmondsworth: Penguin.

45. Editorial (anonymous) (1987) 'Depression, stress and immunity.' *Lancet*, 27 June, 1467–1468.

46. Glaser, R. and Kiecolt-Glaser, J. (eds) (1994) *Handbook of Human Stress and Immunity.* San Diego: Academic Press, p.xxi.

47. Moynihan, J.A. *et al.* (1994) 'Stress-induced modulation of immune function in mice.' In R. Glaser and J. Kiecolt-Glaser (eds) (1994) *Handbook of Human Stress and Immunity.* San Diego: Academic Press, p.1.

48. Glaser, R. and Kiecolt-Glaser, J. (1994) *op. cit.*

49. Whitacre, C.C., Cummings, S.O. and Griffin, A.C. (1994) 'The effects of stress on autoimmune disease.' In R. Glaser and J. Kiecolt-Glaser (eds) (1994) *Handbook of Human Stress and Immunity.* San Diego: Academic Press, p.77.

50. Whitacre, C.C. *et al.* (1994) *ibid.* p.78.

51. Whitacre, C.C. *et al.* (1994) *ibid.* p.79.

52. Whitacre, C.C. *et al.* (1994) *ibid.* p.79.

53. Whitacre, C.C. *et al.* (1994) *ibid.* p.80.

54. Kissen, D.M. and Eysenck, H.J. (1962) 'Personality in male lung cancer patients.' *British Journal of Medical Psychology 36*, 123–127.

55. Kissen, D.M. and Eysenck, H.J. (1963) 'Personality characteristics in males conducive to lung cancer.' *British Journal of Medical Psychology 36*, 27–36.

56. Kissen, D.M. and Eysenck, H.J. (1964) 'Relationship between lung cancer, cigarette smoking, inhalation and personality.' *British Journal of Medical Psychology 37*, 203–216.

57. Kissen, D.M. and Eysenck, H.J. (1967) 'Psychosocial factors, personality and lung cancer in men aged 55–64.' *British Journal of Medical Psychology 40*, 29–43.

58. LeShan, L. (1966) *op. cit.*

59. Solomon, G.F. (1969) 'Emotions, stress, the CNS and immunity.' Second Conference on Psychophysiological Aspects of Cancer. *Annals of the New York Academy of Sciences,* 335–342.

60. Abse, D.W. *et al.* (1974) 'Personality and behavioural characteristics of lung cancer patients.' *Journal of Psychosomatic Research* 1001–1113.

61. Achterberg, J., Simonton, S.M. and Simonton, O.C. (1977) 'Psychology of the exceptional cancer patient: a description of patients who outlive predicted life expectancies.' *Psychotherapy: Theory, Research and Practice14*, 4, Winter, 416–422.

62. Reich, W. (1975) *Reich Speaks of Freud.* Harmondsworth: Penguin.

63. Manning, M. (1988) Seminar on Self-healing, Holistic Health Workshop, Farnham Holistic Health Centre, 30 April.

64. Greer, S., Morris, T. and Pettingale, K.W. (1979) 'Psychological response to breast cancer: effect and outcome.' *Lancet 2*, 785–787.

65. Derogatis, L., Abeloff, M. and Melisaratos, N. (1979) 'Psychological coping mechanisms and survival time in metastatic breast cancer.' *Journal of the American Medical Association 242*, 1504–1508.

66. Temoshok, L. and Heller, B.W. (1985) 'Biopsychosocial studies on cutaneous malignant melonoma; psychosocial factors associated with prognostic indicators, progression, psychophysiology and tumor-host response.' *Social Science and Medicine* 20, 8, 833–840.

67. Meares, A. (1979) 'Meditation: a psychological approach to cancer treatment.' *Practitioner, 222*, 119–122.

68. Simonton, O.C. and Matthews-Simonton, S. (1975) 'Belief systems and management of the emotional aspects of malignancy.' *Journal of Transpersonal Psychology 8*, 29–47.

69. Hughes, J. (1987) *Cancer and Emotion: Psychological Preludes and Reactions to Cancer.* Chichester: J. Wiley.

70. Blumberg, J. (1954) *op. cit.*

71. LeShan, L. (1966) *op. cit.*

72. Stoll, B.A. (1979) *op. cit.*

73. Solomon, G.F. (1969) *op. cit.*

74. Jacobs, T.J. and Charles, E. (1980) 'Life events and the occurrence of cancer in children.' *Psychosomatic Medicine 42*, 1–24.

75. Greer. S. and Watson, M. (1985) 'Towards a Psychological Model of cancer: psychological considerations.' *Social Science and Medicine 20*, 8, 773–777.

76. Rosch, P.J. (1984) 'Stress and cancer.' In C.L. Cooper (ed) *Stress and Cancer.* Chichester: Wiley.

77. Temoshok, L. and Heller, B.W. (1981) 'Stress and "Type C" versus epidemiological risk factors in melanoma.' Paper presented at 89th Annual Convention of the American Psychological Association, Los Angeles, California, reported in Temoshok (1985) *op. cit.*

78. Riley, V. (1981) 'Psychoneuroendocrine influences on immunocompetence and neoplasma.' *Science 212*, 1100–1109.

79. Shekelle, R.B. *et al.* (1981) *op. cit.*

80. Greer, S. and Watson, M. (1985) Towards a psychological model of cancer: Psychological consideration.' *Social Science and Medicine 20*, 8, 773–7.

81. Dattore, P.J., Schontz, F.C. and Coyne, L. (1980) 'Premorbid personality differentiation of cancer and non-cancer groups: a test of the hypothesis of cancer proneness.' *Journal of Consulting and Clinical Psychology 48*, 388–394.

82. Schmale, A. and Iker, S.H. (1991) 'Hopelessness as a predictor of cervical cancer.' *Social Science and Medicine 5*, 95–100.

83. Samuels, A. (1984) 'Beyond the relaxation response: self-regulation mechanisms and clinical strategies.' LA, California UCLA Extension, cited Achterberg, J. (1985) *Imagery in Healing.* Boston: Shambhala.

84. Moos, R.H. (1964) 'Personality factors associated with rheumatoid arthritis: review.' *Journal of Chronic Disorders 17*, 41.

85. Moos, R.H. and Solomon, G.F. (1965) 'Psychological comparisons between women with rheumatoid arthritis and their non-arthritic sisters. I. Personality tests and interview rating data.' *Psychosomatic Medicine 27*, 135.

86. Moos, R.H. and Solomon, G.F. (1965) 'Psychological comparisons between women with rheumatoid arthritis and their non-arthritic sisters. II Content analysis of interviews.' *Psychosomatic Medicine 27*, 150.

87. Canter, A. (1972) 'Changes in mood during incubation of acute febrile disease and the effect of pre-exposure psychological status.' *Psychosomatic Medicine 34*, 424–425.

88. Kasl, V.S., Evans, A.S. and Neiderman, J.C. (1979) 'Psychological risk factors in the development of infectious mononucleosis.' *Psychosomatic Medicine 412*, 444–466.

89. Kleiger, J.H. and Kinsman, R.A. (1980) 'The development of the MMPI alexithymia scale.' *Psychotherapy and Psychosomatics 31*, 1, 17–24.

90. Dirks, J.F., Robinson, S.K. and Dirks, D.L. (1981) 'Alexithymia and the psychomaintenance of bronchial asthma.' *Psychotherapy and Psychosomatics 36*, 63–71.

91. Mason, J.W. (1968) 'Organisation of psychoendocrine mechanisms.' *Psychosomatic Medicine 30*, 365–408.

92. Solomon, G.F. (1969) *op. cit.*

93. Curtis, G.C. (1979) 'Psychoendocrine stress response: steroid and peptide hormones.' In B.A. Stoll (ed) *Mind and Cancer.* Chichester: Wiley.

94. Rose, R.M. (1980) 'Endocrine responses to stressful psychological events.' *Psychiatric Clinics of North America 3*, 251–276.

95. Ader, R. and Cohen, N. (1975) 'Behaviourally conditioned immunosuppression.' *Psychosomatic Medicine 37*, 333–340.

96. Rogers, M.P., Dubey, D. and Reich, P. (1979) 'The influence of the psyche and the brain on immunity and disease susceptibility: a critical review.' *Psychosomatic Medicine 41*, 147–161.

97. McClelland, D.C. *et al.* (1980) 'Stressed power motivation, sympathetic activation, immune function and illness.' *Journal of Human Stress 6*, 11–19.

98. McClelland, D.C. and Jemmot, J.B. (1980) 'Power motivation, stress and physical illness.' *Journal of Human Stress 6*, 6–15.

99. Editorial (anonymous) (1985) 'Emotion and immunity.' *Lancet 21*, 2, 133–134.

100. Editorial (anonymous) (1989) 'Depression, stress and immunity.' *Lancet*, 27 June, 1467–1468.

101. Nicholas, R.S. *et al.* (1994) 'Stress and immunity in humans: modifying variables.' In R. Glaser and J. Kiecolt-Glaser (eds) *Handbook of Human Stress and Immunity.* San Diego: Academic Press.

102. Ward, S.E., Leventhal, H. and Love, R. (1988) 'Repression revisited: Tactics used in coping with a severe health threat.' *Personality and Social Psychology Bulletin 14*, 4, 735–746.

103. Nicholas, R.S. *et al.* (1994) *op. cit.*

104. Reported in above.

105. Bresnitz, S. (ed) (1983) *The Denial of Stress.* New York: International Universities Press.

106. Rossi, E.L. (1986) *The Psychobiology of Mind-body Healing: New Concepts of Therapeutic Hypnosis.* New York: W.W. Norton.

107. Cousins, N. (1981) *Human Options.* New York: W.W. Norton.

108. Cousins, N. (1981) *ibid.* pp.56–57.

109. Kanner, A.D. *et al.* (1981) 'Comparisons of two modes of stress measurement. Daily hassles and upsets versus major life events.' *Journal of Behavioural Medicine, 1–39.*

110. Lazarus, R.S. (1981) 'Little hassles can be hazardous to health.' *Psychology Today 15*, 58–62.

111. Lazarus, R.S. (1984) 'Puzzles in the study of daily hassles.' *Journal of Behavioural Medicine, 7*, 375–389.

112. Cooper, C. *et al.* (1988) *op. cit.*

113. Harrison, J. (1984) *Love Your Disease: It's Keeping You Healthy.* London: Angus and Robertson, p.172.

114. Ecker, R. (1989) *The Stress Myth.* Tring: Lion Publishing.

115. Kobasa, S.C., Maddi, S. and Kahn, S. (1982) 'Hardiness and health: a prospective study.' *Journal of Personality and Social Science 42*, 168–177.

116. Ornstein, R.E. and Sobel, D. (1988) *The Healing Brain: A Radical New Approach to Health Care.* London: MacMillan, p.213.

117. Achterberg, J., Simonton, O.C. and Simonton, S.M. (1977) 'Psychology of the exceptional cancer patient: A description of patients who outlive predicted life expectancies. *Psychotherapy: Theory, Research and Practice 14*, 416–422.

118. Greer, S., Morris, T. and Pettingale, K.W. (1979) 'Psychological response to breast cancer: a controlled study.' *Lancet 2*, 785–787.

119. Achterberg, J. *et al.* (1977) *op. cit.*

120. Graham, H. (1997) *Make Stress Work For You.* Dublin: Gill and MacMillan, pp.31–2.

121. Bradley, B. and McCanne, T. (1981) 'Autonomic responses to stress: the effects of progressive relaxation, the relaxation response and the expectancy of relief.' *Biofeedback and Self-Regulation 6*, 235–251.

122. Cousins, N. (1981) *op. cit.*

123. Jampolsky, G.G. (1979) *Love Is Letting Go Of Fear.* Berkeley, CA: Celestial Arts.

124. Jeffries, S. (1991) *Feel the Fear and Do It Anyway.* London: Arrow.

125. Manning, M. (1988) *op. cit.*

126. Cousins, N. (1981) *op. cit.*

127. Freud, S. (1960) *Jokes and Their Relation to the Unconscious.* New York: W.W. Norton and Co.

128. Thurber, J. citing Lord Boothby in J. Levine 'Humour as a form of therapy.' In A.J. Chapman and H.C. Foot (eds) (1977) *It's a Funny Thing, Humor.* Oxford: Pergamon, pp.127–139.

129. Cousins, N. (1981) *op. cit.*

130. Fowzy, F.I. and Fowzy, N.W. (1994) 'Psychoeducational interventions and health outcomes.' In R. Glaser and J. Kiecolt-Glaser (eds) *Handbook of Human Stress and Immunity.* San Diego: Academic Press, p.387.

131. Saper, B. (1988) 'Humor in psychiatric healing.' *Psychiatric Quarterly 59*, 4, Winter, 306–319.

132. Adams, E.R. and McGuire, F.A. (1986) 'Is laughter the best medicine?' *Activities, Adaptation, Ageing 8*, 3–4, 167–175.

133. Dillon, K.M. *et al.* (1985) 'Positive emotional states and the enhancement of the immune system.' *International Journal of Psychiatric Medicine 15*, 13–17.

134. Cousins, N. (1981) *op. cit.* p.138.

135. Berk, L.S. *et al.* (1989) 'Neuroendocrine and stress hormone changes during mirthful laughter.' *American Journal of the Medical Sciences 298*, 390–396.

136. Rabin, B.S. *et al.* (1994) 'Mechanistic aspects of stressor-induced immune alleviation.' In R. Glaser and J. Kiecolt-Glaser (eds) *Handbook of Human Stress and Immunity.* San Diego: Academic Press.

137. Achterberg, J. *et al.* (1977) *op. cit.*

138. Simonton, O.C., Matthews-Simonton, S. and Creighton, J. (1978) *Getting Well Again.* New York: Bantam.

139. Fiore, N. (1974) 'Fighting cancer: one patient's perspective.' *New England Journal of Medicine, 300*, 284.

140. Meares, A. (1981) *op. cit.*

141. Bindemann, S. *et al.* (1986) *op. cit.*

142. Newton, B.W. (1980) 'The use of hypnosis in the treatment of cancer patients: a five year report.' Presented at the Annual Science Progress of the American Society of Clinical Hypnosis, Minneapolis.

143. Hegarty, J.R. (1989) 'Psychologists, doctors and cancer patients.' In J. Hartley and J.A. Branthwaite (eds) *The Applied Psychologist.* Milton Keynes: Open University Press.

144. Feinstein, A.D. (1983) 'Interventions in treatment of cancer.' *Clinical Psychology Review 3*, 1–14.

Chapter 10: Visualisation

1. Trechmann, E.J. (trans) (1927) *The Essays of Montaigne.* Oxford: Oxford University Press, pp.91–92.

2. Trechmann, E.J. (1927) *ibid.*

3. Siegel, B.S. (1990) *Peace, Love and Healing: Bodymind Communication and the Path to Self Healing.* London: Rider, p.96.

4. Dossey, L. (1982) *Space, Time and Medicine.* Boston: Shambhala.

5. Shapiro, A.K. (1960) 'Contribution to a history of the placebo effect.' *Behaviour Science 5*, 109–135.

6. Beecher, H.K. (1955) 'The powerful placebo.' *Journal of the American Medical Association 159*, 1602–1606.

7. Rossi, E.L. (1986) *The Psychobiology of Mind-Body Healing: New Concepts in Therapeutic Hypnosis.* New York: W.W. Norton.

8. Cousins, N. (1981) *Human Options.* New York: W.W. Norton.

9. Wagstaff, G.F. (1987) 'Is hypnotherapy a placebo?' *British Journal of Experimental and Clinical Hypnosis 4,* 3, 135–140.

10. Bowers, K.S. (1976) *Hypnosis for the Seriously Curious.* Monterey, CA: Brooks/Cole, p.152.

11. Siegel, B.S. (1986) *Love, Medicine and Miracles.* London: Rider.

12. Shapiro, A.K. and Morris, L.A. (1978) 'The placebo effect in medical and psychological therapies.' In S.L. Garfield and A.E. Bergin (eds) *A Handbook of Psychotherapy and Behaviour Change.* New York: Wiley.

13. Rossi, E.L. (1986) *op. cit.*

14. Rossi, E.L. (1986) *ibid.*

15. Barber, T.X. (1987) 'On not beating dead horses.' *British Journal of Experimental and Clinical Hypnosis ,* 156–157.

16. Barber, T.X. (1961) 'Psychological aspects of hypnosis.' *Psychological Bulletin 58,* 390–419.

17. Achterberg, J. (1985) *Imagery in Healing: Shamanism and Modern Medicine.* London: Routledge and Kegan Paul.

18. Achterberg, J. (1985) *ibid.* p.3.

19. Hunter, I.M.L. (1986) 'Exceptional memory skill.' In A Gellatly (ed) *The Skilful Mind.* Milton Keynes: Open University Press.

20. Jacobsen, E. (1929) 'Electrical measurement of neuromuscular states during mental activities: imagination of movement involving skeletal muscles.' *American Journal of Physiology 91,* 597–608.

21. Shaw, W.A. (1946) 'The relaxation of muscular action potentials to imaginal weightlifting.' *Archives of Psychology 247,* 250.

22. Bakker, F.C., Boschker, M.S.J. and Chung, T. (1996) 'Changes in muscular activity while imagining weight lifting using stimulus or response propositions.' *Journal of Sport and Exercise 18,* 313–324.

23. Barber, T.X., Chauncey, H.H. and Winer, R.A. (1964) 'Effects of hypnotic and non-hynotic suggestion on parotid gland responses to gustatory stimuli.' *Psychosomatic Medicine 26,* 374–380.

24. Barber, T.X. (1978) 'Hypnosis, suggestions and psychosomatic phenomena: a new look from the standpoint of recent experimental studies.' *American Journal of Clinical Hypnosis 21,* 13–27.

25. Laws, D.R. and Rubin, H.B. (1969) 'Instructional control of an autonomic response.' *Journal of Applied Behaviour Analysis 2,* 93–99.

26. Marks, I. *et al.* (1971) 'Physiological accompaniments of mental and phobic imagery.' *Psychological Medicine 1,* 299–307.

27. Marks, I. and Huson, J. (1973) 'Physiological aspects of neutral and phobic imagery: further observations.' *British Journal of Psychiatry 122,* 567–572.

28. Kazdin, A.E. and Wilcoxin, L.A. (1975) 'Systematic desensitization and non-specific treatment effects: a methodological evaluation.' *Psychological Bulletin 83,* 5.

29. Marzillier, J.J., Carroll, D. and Newland, J.R. (1979) 'Self-report and physiological changes accompanying repeated imaging of a phobic scene.' *Behaviour Research and Therapy 17,* 71–77.

30. Stock, W.E. and Geer, J.H. (1982) 'A study of fantasy-based sexual arousal in women.' *Archives of Sexual Behaviour 11,* 33–47.

31. Smith, D. and Over, R. (1987) 'Does fantasy-induced sexual behaviour habituate?' *Behaviour Research and Therapy 25,* 477–485.

32. Schwartz, G.E. (1973) 'Pros and cons of meditation: anxiety, self-control, drug abuse and creativity.' Paper delivered at the 81st Annual Convention of the American Psychological Association, Montréal.

33. Schwartz, G.E., Weinberger, D.A. and Singer, J.A. (1981) 'Cardiovascular differentiation of happiness, sadness, anger and fear following imagery and exercise. *Psychosomatic Medicine 43,* 343–364.

34. Schneider, J., Smith , C.W., Minning, C., Whitcher, S. and Humanson, J. (1988) 'Psychological factors influencing immune system function in normal subjects: a summary of research findings and implications for the use of guided imagery.' Paper presented at the 10th Annual Conference of the American Association for the Study of Mental Imagery, New Haven, CT, cited in Sheikh, A.A., Kunzendorf, R.G. and Sheikh K.S. (1989) 'Healing images: from ancient wisdom to modern science.' In A.A. Sheikh and K.S. Sheikh (eds) *Eastern and Western Approaches to Healing: Ancient Wisdom and Modern Knowledge.* New York: Wiley, pp.470–515.

35. Craig, K.D. (1968) 'Physiological arousal as a function of imagined, vicarious or direct stress experience.' *Journal of Abnormal Psychology 73*, 513–520.

36. Waters, W.F. and McDonald, D.G. (1973) 'Autonomic response to auditory, visual and imagined stimuli in a systematic desensitization context.' *Behaviour Research and Therapy 11*, 577–585.

37. Gottschalk, L.A. (1974) 'Self-induced visual imagery, affect arousal and autonomic correlates.' *Psychosomatics 15*, 166–169.

38. Bell, I.R. and Schwartz, G.E. (1975) 'Voluntary control and reactivity of human heart rate.' *Psychophysiology 12,* 339–348.

39. Blizard, D.A., Cowings, P. and Miller, N.E. (1975) 'Visceral responses to opposite types of autogenic training imagery.' *Biological Psychology, 4*, 49–55.

40. Jones, G.E. and Johnson, H.J. (1978) 'Physiological responding during self-generated imagery of contextually complete stimuli.' *Psychophysiology 15*, 449–446.

41. Jones, G.E. and Johnson, H.J. (1980) 'Heart rate and somatic concomitants of mental imagery.' *Psychophysiology 17*, 339–347.

42. Bauer, R.M. and Craighead, W.E. (1979) 'Psychophysiological responses to the imagination of fearful and neutral situations: the effects of imagery instructions.' *Behaviour Therapy 10*, 389–403.

43. Jordan, C.S. and Lenington, K.T. (1979) 'Physiological correlates of eidetic imagery and induced anxiety. *Journal of Mental Imagery 3*, 31–42.

44. Shea, J.D. (1985) 'Effects of absorption and instructions on heart rate control.' *Journal of Mental Imagery 9*, 87–100.

45. Bell, I.R. and Schwartz, G.E. (1975) *op.cit.*

46. Furedy, J.J. and Klajner, F. (1978) 'Imaginational Pavlovian conditioning of large-magnitude cardiac decelerations with tilt as UCS.' *Psychophysiology 15*, 538–548.

47. McCanne, T.R. and Ienerrella, R.S. (1980) 'Cognitive and somatic events associated with discriminate changes in heart rate.' *Psychophysiology 10*, 19–28.

48. Shea, J.D. (1985) *op. cit.*

49. Arabian, J.M. and Furedy, J.J. (1983) 'Individual differences in imagery ability and Pavlovian heart rate decelerative conditioning.' *Psychophysiology 20*, 325–331.

50. Stern, R.M. and Lewis, N.L. (1968) 'Ability of actors to control their GSRs and express emotion.' *Psychophysiology 4*, 2294–2299.

51. Marks, I. *et al.* (1971) *op. cit.*

52. Waters, W.F. and McDonald, D.G. (1973) *op. cit.*

53. Gottschalk, L.A. (1974) *op. cit.*

54. Yaremko, R.M. and Butler, M.C. (1975) 'Imaginal experience and attenuation of the galvanic skin response to shock.' *Bulletin of the Psychonomic Society 5*. 317–318.

55. Haney, J.N. and Euse, F.J. (1976) 'Skin conductance and heart rate responses to neutral, positive and negative imagery: implications for covert behaviour therapy procedures.' *Behaviour Therapy 7*, 494–503.

56. Drummond, P., White, K. and Ashton, R. (1978) 'Imagery vividness affects habituation rate.' *Psychophysiotherapy 15*, 193–195.

57. Bauer, R.M. and Craighead, W.E. (1979) *op. cit.*

58. Jordan, C.S. and Lenington, K.T. (1979) *op. cit.*

59. Passchier, J. and Helm-Hylkema, H. (1981) 'The effect of stress imagery on arousal and its implications for biofeedback of the frontalis muscles.' *Biofeedback Self Regulation 6*, 295–303.

60. Schwartz, G.E., Weinberger, D.A. and Singer, J.A. (1981) 'Cardiovascular differentiation of happiness, sadness, anger and fear following imagery and exercise.' *Psychosomatic Medicine 43*, 3–64.

61. Roberts, R.J. and Weerts, T.C. (1982) 'Cardiovascular responding during anger and fear imagery.' *Psychological Reports 50*, 219–230.

62. Dugan, M. and Sheridan, C. (1976) 'Effects of instructed imagery on temperature of the hands.' *Perceptual and Motor Skills 41*, 14.

63. Kunzendorf, R.G. (1981) 'Individual differences in imagery and autonomic control.' *Journal of Mental Imagery, 5*, 47–60.

64. Kunzendorf, R.G. (1984) 'Centrifugal effects of eidetic imagery on flash electroretinograms and autonomic responses. *Journal of Mental Imagery 8*, 67–76.

65. Okhuma, Y. (1985) 'Effects of evoking imagery on the control of peripheral skin temperature.' *Japanese Journal of Psychology 54*, 88–94 (English abstract).

66. Lucas, O. (1965) 'Dental extractions in the hemophiliac: control of the emotional factors by hypnosis.' *American Journal of Clinical Hypnosis 7*, 301–307.

67. Willard, R.D. (1977) 'Breast enlargement through visual imagery and hypnosis.' *Clinical Hypnosis 19*, 195–200.

68. Chaves, J.F. (1980) 'Hypnotic control of surgical bleeding.' Paper presented at the Annual Meeting of the American Psychological Association, Montréal. In A.A. Sheikh (ed) *Imagination and Healing.* New York: Baywood, pp.65–158.

69. Siegel, B.S. (1986) *op. cit.*

70. Hall, H.R., London, S. and Dixon, R. (1981) 'Hypnosis and the immune system: the effect of hypnosis on T and B cell function.' Paper presented at 33rd Annual Meeting of the Society for Clinical and Experimental Hypnosis, Portland, Oregon, reported by Hall, H.R. (1984) 'Imagery and Cancer.' In A.A. Sheikh (ed) *Imagination and Healing.* New York: Baywood, pp.159–169.

71. Rider, M.S., Floyd, J.W. and Kirkpatrick, J. (1985) 'The effect of music, imagery and relaxation on adrenal corticosteroids and the re-entrainment of circadian rhythms.' *Journal of Music Therapy 22*, 46–58.

72. Smith, G.R. *et al.* (1985) 'Psychologic modulation of the human response to varicella zoster.' *Archives of International Medicine 145*, 2110–2112.

73. Schneider, J. *et al.* (1988) *op. cit.*

74. Editorial (anonymous) (1987) 'Depression, stress and immunity.' *Lancet*, 27, 1467–1468.

75. Grossberg, J.M. and Wilson, K.M. (1968) 'Physiological changes accompanying the visualization of fearful and neutral situations.' *Journal of Personality and Social Psychology 10*, 124–133.

76. Revland, P. and Hirschman, R. (1976) 'Imagery training and visual biofeedback.' *Psychophysiology 13*, 186–187.

77. Carroll, D., Baker, J. and Preston, M. (1979) 'Individual differences in normal imaging and the voluntary control of heart rate. *British Journal of Psychology 670*, 39–49.

78. Carroll, D., Marzillier, J.S. and Merian, S. (1982) 'Psychophysiological changes accompanying different types of arousing and relaxing imagery.' *Psychophysiology 19*, 75–82.

79. Engel, B.T. (1979) 'Behavioural applications in the treatment of patients with cardiovascular disorders.' In J.V. Basmajian (ed) *Biofeedback: Principles and Practices for Clinicians.* Baltimore, MD: Williams and Wilkins.

80. Lang, P.J. *et al.* (1980) 'Emotional imagery: conceptual structure and pattern of somato-visceral response.' *Psychobiology 17*, 179–192.

81. Achterberg, J. (1985) *op. cit.*

82. Burish, T.G. and Lyles, J.N. (1981) 'Effects of relaxation training in reducing adverse reactions to cancer.' *Journal of Behavioural Medicine 4*, 65–78.

83. Ahsen, A. (1978) 'Eidetics: neural experiential growth potential for the treatment of accident traumas, debilitating stress conditions and chronic emotional blocking'. *Journal of Mental Imagery 2*, 1–22.

84. Crowther, J.H. (1983) 'Stress management training and relaxation imagery in the treatment of essential hypertension.' *Journal of Behavioural Medicine 6,* 169–187.

85. Fiore, N. (1974) 'Fighting cancer: one patient's perspective.' *New England Journal of Medicine 300,* 284.

86. Achterberg, J., Simonton, O.C. and Matthews-Simonton (1977) 'Psychology of the exceptional cancer patient: a description of patients who outlive predicted life expectancies.' *Psychotherapy, Theory, Research and Practice 14,* 416–422.

87. Simonton, O.C., Matthews-Simonton, S. and Creighton, J. (1978) *Getting Well Again.* New York: Bantam.

88. Simonton, O.C., Matthews-Simonton, S. and Sparks, T.F. (1980) 'Psychological interventions in the treatment of cancer.' *Psychosomatics 21,* 226–227.

89. Achterberg, J. and Lawlis, G.F. (1979) 'A canonical analysis of blood chemistry variables related to psychological measures of cancer patients.' *Multivariate Clinical Research 3,* 107–122.

90. Meares, N. (1977) 'Atavistic regression as a factor in the remission of cancer.' *Medical Journal of Australia 2,* 32–133.

91. Achterberg, J. (1984) 'Imagery and medicine: psychophysiological speculations.' *Journal of Mental Imagery 8,* 1–13.

92. Hall, H.R. (1984) 'Imagery and cancer.' In A.A. Sheikh (ed) *Imagination and Healing.* New York: Baywood, pp.157–169.

93. Pickett, E. (1987) 'Fibroid tumors: a response to guided imagery and music; two case studies.' *Imagination, Cognition and Personality 7,* 165–176.

94. Bradley, B. and McCanne, T. (1981) 'Autonomic responses to stress: the effects of progressive relaxation, the relaxation response and the expectancy of relief.' *Biofeedback Self Regulation 6,* 235–251.

95. Oldham, J. (1989) 'Psychological support for cancer patients.' *British Journal of Occupational Therapy 52,* 12, 463–465.

96. Donovan, M. (1980) 'Relaxation with guided imagery: a useful technique.' *Cancer Nursing 3,* 27–32.

97. Lyles, J. *et al.* (1982) 'Efficacy of relaxation and guided imagery in reducing the aversiveness of cancer chemotherapy.' *Journal of Consulting and Clinical Psychology 50,* 4, 509–524.

98. Galton, F. (1888) *Inquiries into Human Faculty and its Development.* London: Macmillan.

99. Russell, P. (1979) *Meditation: Paths to Tranquility.* London: BBC Publications, p.45.

100. Shepard, R.N. and Chipman, S. (1970) 'Second-order isomorphism of internal representations: shapes of states.' *Cognitive Psychology 1,* 1–17.

101. Shepard, R.N. (1975) 'Form, formation and transformation of internal representations.' In R. Solos (ed) *Information Processing and Cognition.* Hillsdale, NJ: Erlbaum.

102. Shepard, R.N. and Cooper, L.A. (1975) 'Representation of colors in normal, blind and color blind subjects.' Paper presented at the Annual Meeting of the America Psychological Association, Chicago, 2 September, reported in Shepard, R.N. (1977) 'The mental image.' *American Psychologist 33,* 125–137.

103. Shepard, R.N., Kilpatrick, D.W. and Cunningham, J.P. (1975) 'The internal representation of numbers.' *Cognitive Psychology 7,* 82–138.

104. Shepard, R.N. (1977) 'The mental Image.' *American Psychologist, 33,* 125–137.

105. Shepard, R.N. (1977) *ibid.*

106. Helmholtz, H. cited in Warren, R.M. and Warren, R.P. (1969) *Helmholtz on Perception: Its Physiology and Development.* New York: Wiley, pp.252–254.

107. Shepard, R.N. and Metzler, J. (1971) 'Mental rotation of three-dimensional objects.' *Science 171,* 701–703.

108. Cooper, L.A. and Shepard, R.N. (1973) 'Chronometric studies of the rotation of mental images.' In W.G. Chase (ed) *Visual Information Processing.* New York: Academic Press.

109. Metzler, J. and Shepard, R.N. (1974) 'Transformational studies of the internal representation of three-dimensional objects.' In R. Solos (ed) *Theories in Cognitive Psychology: The Loyola Symposium*. Potomac, MD: Erlbaum.

110. Cooper, R.N. (1975) 'Mental rotation of random two-dimensional shapes.' *Cognitive Psychology 7*, 20–43.

111. Shuttleworth, E.C., Syring, V. and Allen, V. (1982) 'Further observations on the nature of prosopagnosia.' *Brain Cognition 1*, 302–332.

112. Farah, M.J. (1984) 'The neurological basis of mental imagery: a componential analysis.' *Cognition 19*, 245–272.

113. Levine, D.N., Warach, J. and Farah, M.J. (1985) 'Two visual systems in mental imagery: disociation of "what" and "where" in imagery disorders due to bilateral posterior cerebral lesions.' *Neurology 35*, 1010–1018.

114. Farah, M.J. (1989) 'The neuropsychology of mental imagery.' In J.W. Brown (ed) *Neuropsychology of Visual Perception*. Hillsdale, NJ: Lawrence Erlbaum Associates, pp.183–201.

115. Reader, A.L. III (1995) 'The internal mystery plays: the role and physiology of the visual system in contemplative practices.' *Alternative Therapies*, September, 1, 4, 54–63.

116. Ornstein, R.E. *et al.* (1979) 'Differential right hemispheric involvement in two reading tasks.' *Psychophysiology 16*, 398–401.

117. Ley, R.G. and Bryden, M.P. (1983) 'Right hemispheric involvement in imagery and affect.' In E. Perecman (ed) *Cognitive Processing in the Right Hemisphere*. New York: Academic Press.

118. Ley, R.G. (1983) 'Cerebral laterality and imagery.' In A.A. Sheikh (ed) *Imagery: Current Theory, Research and Application*. New York: Wiley.

119. Tucker, D.M. *et al.* (1977) 'Right hemisphere activation during stress.' *Neuropsychologia 15*, 697–700.

120. Ley, R.G. and Bryden, M.P. (1983) *op. cit.*

121. Achterberg, J (1985) *op. cit.* p.126.

122. Achterberg, J. (1985) *ibid.* p.122.

123. Achterberg, J. (1985) *ibid.* p.127.

124. Aristotle *De Memoria* cited Hearnshaw, L.S. (1989) *The Shaping of Modern Psychology: An Historical Introduction*. London: Routledge, p. 25.

125. Paivio, A. (1989) 'A dual coding perspective on imagery and the brain.' In J.W. Brown (ed) *Neuropsychology of Visual Perception*. Hillsdale, NJ: Lawrence Erlbaum and Associates, pp.203–216.

126. Ley, R.G. (1983) *op. cit.*

127. Silberman, E.K. and Weingartner, H. (1986) 'Hemispheric lateralization of functions related to emotion.' *Brain Cognition 5*, 322–353.

128. Geschwind, N. and Behan, P. (1982) 'Left-handedness: association with immune disease, migraine and developmental learning disorder.' Proceedings of the National Academy of Science, USA 79, 5097–5100.

129. Wechsler, R. (1987) 'A new prescription: Mind over malady.' *Discover,* February, 51–61. Cited in Pelletier, K.R. and Herzing, D.L. (1989) 'Psychoneuroimmunology: towards a mind-body model.' In A.A. Sheikh and K.S. Sheikh (eds) *Eastern and Western Approaches to Healing: Ancient Wisdom and Modern Knowledge*. Chichester: Wiley, pp.344–394.

130. Pelletier, K.R. and Herzing, D.L. (1989) In A.A. Sheikh and K.S. Sheikh (eds) *Eastern and Western Approaches to Healing: Ancient Wisdom and Modern Knowledge*. Chichester: Wiley, p.371.

131. Ley, R.G. and Smilie, M. (1989) 'Cerebral laterality: implications for Eastern and Western therapies.' In In A.A. Sheikh and K.S. Sheikh (eds) *Eastern and Western Approaches to Healing: Ancient Wisdom and Modern Knowledge*. Chichester: Wiley, p.330.

132. Sargent, J. (1982) 'The cerebral balance of power: confrontation and cooperation.' *Journal of Experimental Psychology: Human Perception Performance 8,* 253–272.

133. Paivio, A. (1989) *op. cit.*, p.203.

134. Houston, J. (1982) *The Possible Human.* Los Angeles: J.P. Tarcher, p.135.

135. Achterberg, J. (1985) *op. cit.*

136. Pangioutou, N. and Sheikh, A.A. (1977) 'The image and the unconscious.' *International Journal of Social Psychiatry 23,* 169–186.

137. Sheikh, A.A., Kunzendorf, R.G. and Sheikh, K.S. (1989) 'Healing images: from ancient wisdom to modern science.' In A.A. Sheikh and K.S. Sheikh (eds) *Eastern and Western Approaches to Healing: Ancient Wisdom and Modern Knowledge.* New York: Wiley, pp.470–515, p.493.

138. Achterberg, J. (1985) *op. cit.* p.56.

139. Achterberg, J. (1985) *ibid.* p.64.

140. Achterberg, J. (1985) *ibid.* pp.65–66.

141. Hartman, F. (1973) *Paracelsus: Life and Prophecies.* New York: Blauveit.

142. Clifford, T. (1984) *Tibetan Buddhist Medicine and Psychiatry.* New York: Samuel Weiser.

143. Evans-Wentz, W.Y. (1967) *Tibetan Yoga and Secret Doctrines.* London: Oxford University Press.

144. Norris, P. (1989) 'Current conceptual trends in biofeedback and self-regulation.' In A.A. Sheikh and K.S. Sheikh (eds) *Eastern and Western Approaches to Healing: Ancient Wisdom and Modern Knowledge.* New York: Wiley, pp.264–295, p.279.

145. Achterberg, J. (1985) *op. cit.*

146. Mangan, G.L. (1974) 'Personality and conditioning: some personality, cognitive and psychophysiological parameters of classical (appetitive) sexual GSR conditioning.' *Pavlovian Journal of Behavioural Science 9,* 125–135.

147. Arabian, J.M. and Furedy, J.J. (1983) *op. cit.*

148. Sheikh, A.A. *et al.* (1989) *op. cit.*

149. Hirschman, R. and Favaro, L. (1986) 'Individual differences in imagery vividness and voluntary heart rate control.' *Personality and Individual Diffs. 1,* 129–133.

150. Okeda, Y. and Hirai, T. (1976) 'Voluntary control of electrodermal activity in relation to imagery and internal perception sources.' *Psychophysiology 13,* 330–333.

151. Kunzendorf, R.G. and Bradbury, J.L. (1983) 'Better liars have better imaginations.' *Psychological Reports 52,* 634.

152. Roberts, A.H., Kewman, D.G. and MacDonald, H. (1973) 'Voluntary control of skin temperatures: unilateral changes using hypnosis and feedback.' *Journal of Abnormal Psychology 82,* 163–168.

153. Schwartz, G.E. (1975) 'Biofeedback, self-regulation and the patterning of physiological responses.' *American Scientist 63,* 314–324.

154. Bell, I.R. and Schwartz, G.E. (1975) 'Voluntary control and reactivity of human heart rate.' *Psychophysiology 12,* 339–348.

155. White, T., Holmes, D. and Bennett, D. (1977) 'Effects of instructions, biofeedback and cognitive activities on heart rate control.' *Journal of Experimental Psychology: Human Learning Memory 3,* 477–484.

156. Takahashi, H. (1984) 'Experimental study of self-control of heart rate: experiment for a biofeedback treatment of anxiety state.' *Journal of Mental Health 31,* 109–125.

157. LeBoeuf, A. and Wilson, C. (1978) 'The importance of imagery in maintenance of feedback-assisted relaxation over extinction trials.' *Perceptual Motor Skills 47,* 824–826.

158. Qualls, P.J. and Sheehan, P.W. (1979) 'Capacity for absorption and relaxation during electromyograph biofeedback and no feedback conditions.' *Journal of Abnormal Psychology 88,* 652–662.

159. Herzfield, G.M. and Taub, E. (1980) 'Effect of slide projections and tape recorded suggestions on thermal biofeedback training.' *Biofeedback and Individual Differences 1,* 129–33.

160. Okhuma, Y. (1985) 'Effects of evoking imagery on the control of peripheral skin temperature.' *Japanese Journal of Psychology 54,* 88–94. (English abstract.)

161. Qualls, P.J. and Sheehan, P.W. (1981a) 'Imagery encouragement, absorption capacity and relaxation during electomyograph biofeedback and no feedback conditions.' *Journal of Personality Social Psychology 41,* 370–379.

162. Qualls, P.J. and Sheehan, P.W. (1981b) 'Imagery encouragement, absorption capacity and relaxation during electromyograph biofeedback.' *Journal of Experimental Psychology: General 110*, 204–216.

163. Shea, J.D. (1985) *op. cit.*

164. Sheikh, A.A. *et al.* (1989) *op. cit.* p.496.

165. Bertrand, L.D. and Spanos, N.P. (1989) 'Hypnosis: historical and social psychological aspects.' In A.A. Sheikh and K.S. Sheikh (eds) *Eastern and Western Approaches to Healing: Ancient Wisdom and Modern Knowledge.* New York: Wiley, pp.237–263.

166. Barber, T.X. (1961) *op. cit.*

167. Pelletier, K.R. (1978) *Mind as Healer; Mind as Slayer: A Holistic Approach to Preventing Stress Disorders.* London: George Allen and Unwin, p.244.

168. Gorton, B. (1959) 'Autogenic Training.' *American Journal of Clinical Hypnosis 2*, 31–41.

169. Pelletier, K.R. (1978) *op. cit.* p.248.

170. Sheikh, A.A. *et al.* (1989) *op. cit.*

171. Singer, J.L. (1974) *Imagery and Daydream Methods in Psychotherapy and Behaviour Modification.* New York: Academic Press.

172. Meichenbaum, D. (1978) 'Why does using imagery in psychotherapy lead to change?' In J.L. Singer and K.S. Pope (eds) *The Power of the Human Imagination.* New York: Plenum.

173. Sheikh, A.A. and Jordan, C.S. (1983) 'Clinical uses of mental imagery.' In A.A. Sheikh (ed) *Imagery: Current Theory, Research and Applications.* New York: Wiley.

174. Sheikh, A.A. and Panagioutou, N.C. (1975) 'Use of mental imagery in psychotherapy: a critical review.' *Perceptual Motor Skills 41*, 55–85.

175. Kepecs, J.G. (1954) 'Observations on screens and barriers in the mind.' *Psychoanalytical Quarterly 23*, 63–77.

176. Singer, J.L. (1979) 'Imagery and affect in psychotherapy: elaborating private scripts and generating contexts.' In A.A. Sheikh and J.T. Shaffer (eds) *The Potential of Fantasy and Imagination.* New York: Brandon House.

177. Klinger, E. (1971) *The Structure of Fantasy.* New York: Wiley.

178. Reyher, J. (1963) 'Free imagery: an uncovering procedure.' *Journal of Clinical Psychology, 19*, 454–459.

179. Singer, J.L. (1974) *op. cit.*

180. Sheikh, A.A. and Jordan, C.S. (1983) *op. cit.*

181. Happich, C. (1932) 'Das Bildenwusstein als Ansatztelle Psychischer Behandlung.' *Zentralblat für Psychoanalyse und Psychotherapie 5*, 663–667.

182. Happich, C. (1939) 'Symbolic consciousness and the creative situation.' *Deutsche Medizinische Wochenschrift 2.*

183. Happich, C. (1948) *Introduction to Meditation.* Third edition. Darmstadt: E. Rother.

184. Desoille, R. (1945) *The Waking Dream in Psychotherapy: An Essay on the Regulatory Function of the Unconscious.* (La reveille eveille en psychotherapie.) Paris: Universitaire.

185. Desoille, R. (1965) *The Directed Daydream.* New York: Psychosynthesis Research Foundation.

186. Frederking, W. (1948) 'Deep relaxation and symbolism.' *Psyche 2.*

187. Kretschmer, W. (1969) 'Meditative techniques in psychotherapy.' In C. Tart (ed) *Altered States of Consciousness: A Book of Readings.* New York: Wiley, pp.219–231.

188. Mauz, F. (1948) 'The psychotic man.' *Archiv für Psychiatrie.*

189. Leuner, H. (1969) 'Guided Affective Imagery.' *American Journal of Psychotherapy.*

190. Leuner, H. (1977) 'Guided Affective Imagery: an account of its development.' *Journal of Mental Imagery 1*, 73–92.

191. Leuner, H. (1978) 'Basic principles in therapeutic efficacy of Guided Affected Imagery. In J.L. Singer and K.S. Pope (eds) *The Power of the Human Imagination.* New York: Plenum.

192. Leuner, H. (1984) *Guided Affective Imagery.* New York: Thieme-Stratton.

193. Fretigny, R. and Virel, A. (1968) *L'Imagerie Mentale.* Geneva: Mont Blanc.

194. Fretigny, R. and Virel, A. (1968) *ibid.*

195. Sheikh, A.A. and Jordan, C.S. (1983) *op. cit.*

196. Bandler, R. and Grinder, J. (1975) *The Structure of Magic, Vol. 1. Science and Behaviour.* Palo Alto, California: California Press.

197. Stevens, J.O. (1971) *Awareness: Exploring, Experimenting, Experiencing.* Moab, Utah: Real People Press.

198. Krystal, P. (1982) *Cutting The Ties That Bind: How To Achieve Liberation From False Security and Negative Conditioning.* Shaftesbury: Element.

199. Krystal, P. (1990) *Cutting More Ties That Bind: Educating Children and Reprogramming Adults.* Shaftesbury: Element.

200. Kubler-Ross, E. (1982) *Working It Through.* New York: MacMillan.

201. Gawain, S. (1985) *Creative Visualisation.* New York: Bantam.

202. Gawain, G. and King, L. (1988) *Living In The Light.* London: Eden Grove.

203. Hay, L.L. (1988) *You Can Heal Your Life.* London: Eden Grove.

204. Glouberman, D. (1989) *Life Choices and Life Changes Through Imagework.* London: Mandala.

205. Edwards, G. (1991) *Living Magically: A New Vision of Reality.* London: Piatkus.

206. Graham, H. (1992) *The Magic Shop: An Imaginative Guide to Self-Healing.* London: Rider.

207. Graham, H. (1995) *A Picture of Health: How To Use Guided Imagery for Self-Healing and Personal Growth.* London: Piatkus.

208. Graham H. (1996) *Visualisation.* London: Piatkus.

209. Graham, H. (1997) *Make Stress Work For You.* Dublin: Gill and MacMillan.

210. Assagioli, R. (1965) *Psychosynthesis: A Collection of Basic Writings.* New York: Viking.

211. Assagioli, R. (1967) *Jung and Psychosynthesis.* New York: Psychosynthesis Foundation.

212. Assagioli, R. (1975) *Psychosynthesis.* Wellingborough: Turnstone Press.

213. Assagioli, R. (1991a) *Transpersonal Development.* London: Crucible.

214. Assagioli, R. (1991b) 'Psychosynthesis.' In W. Bloom (ed) *The New Age: An Anthology of Essential Writings.* London: Rider, pp.118–124.

215. Wolpe, J. (1969) *The Practice of Behaviour Therapy.* New York: Pergamon.

216. Wolpe, J. 'Systematic desensitization based on relaxation.' In S.J. Morse and R.I. Watson (eds) *Psychotherapies: A Comprehensive Casebook.* New York: Holt, Rhinehart, Winston, pp.198–206.

217. Lazarus, R.S. (1966) *Psychological Stress and the Coping Process.* New York: McGraw Hill.

218. Singer, J.L. (1975) *Daydreaming and Fantasy.* London: George Allen and Unwin, p.223.

219. Cautela, J.R. (1967) 'Covert desensitization.' *Psychological Reports 20,* 459–468.

220. Cautela, J.R. (1993) *Covert Conditioning Casebook.* New York: Brooks Cole.

221. Kolvin, I. (1967) 'Adverse imagery treatment in adolescents.' *Behavioural Research Therapy, 5,* 245–248.

222. Marks, I. and Gelder, M.G. (1967) 'Transvestitism and fetishism: clinical and psychological changes during faradic aversion.' *British Journal of Psychiatry 113,* 711–729.

223. Stampfl, T.G. and Lewis, D.J. (1967) 'Essentials of Implosive Therapy: a learning theory based on psychodynamic behavioural therapy.' *Abnormal Psychology 72,* 496–503.

224. Perls, F.S. (1976) *The Gestalt Approach and Eye Witness to Therapy.* New York: Bantam, p.86.

225. Routledge, P. (1998) *Parkinson.* BBC Television, 31 January.

226. Perls, F.S. (1976) *op. cit.* p.86.

227. Liebmann, M. (1990) *Art Therapy in Practice.* London: Jessica Kingsley Publishers.

228. Simonton, O.C. *et al.* (1978) *op. cit.*

229. Kubler-Ross, E. (1982) *op. cit.*

230. Siegel, B.S. (1986) *op. cit.*

231. Siegel, B.S. (1990) *Peace, Love and Healing.* London: Rider.

232. Samuels, M. (1995) 'Art as a healing force.' *Alternative Therapies 1*, 4, 38–40.

233. Samuels, M. (1995) *ibid.*

234. Samuels, M. (1995) *ibid.* pp.38–39.

235. McNiff, S. (1992) *Art As Medicine: Creating a Therapy of the Imagination.* London: Piatkus, p.5.

236. Oaklander, V. (1978) *Windows To Our Children: A Gestalt Therapy Approach to Children and Adolescents.* Moab, Utah: Real People Press.

237. McNiff, S. (1992) *op. cit.* p.18.

238. Ferrini, V. (1991) *This Other Ocean, Books VI and VII of Know Fish.* Storrs, University of Connecticut Library.

239. Green, B. with Gallwey, W.T. (1986) *The Inner Game of Music.* New York: Anchor Press, Doubleday, p.154.

240. Green, B. and Gallwey, T.W. (1986) *ibid.*

241. Lambert, H. (1997) 'Music as medicine.' *Positive Health 20*, 12–14.

242. Lambert, H. (1997) *ibid.*

243. Augustin, P. and Hains, A.A. (1996) 'Effect of music on ambulatory surgery patients' preoperative anxiety.' Abstract. *Positive Health 15*, 62.

244. Lambert, H. (1997) *op. cit.* p.13.

245. Rouget, G. (1988) *Music and Trance.* Chicago: University of Chicago Press.

246. Samuels, M. and Samuels, N. (1975) *Seeing with the Mind's Eye.* New York: Random House.

247. Skaggs, R. (1990) 'Music centred psychotherapy: Shamanism in a contemporary therapeutic setting.' *Theta*, Fall, West Georgia College, 19–23.

248. Harner, M. (1988) 'Shamanic counselling.' In G. Doore (ed) *Shaman's Path: Healing, Personal Growth and Empowerment.* Boston: Shambhala, pp.179–188.

249. Champman, L. (1997) 'Bang a gong.' *Sunday Times* Style, 10 August, p.35.

250. For a review of music and sound therapies, including drumming and chanting, see *Sound Healing Caduceus*, Issue 23, 1994, and Gale, D. (1977) 'Osteopathy and voice.' *Positive Health 20*, 15–17.

251. Bonny, H. and Savary, L.M. (1990) *Music and Your Mind: Listening With a New Consciousness.* New York: Station Hill Press.

252. Skaggs, R. (1990) *op. cit.* p.20.

253. Schwarz, J. (1978) *Voluntary Controls: Exercises in Creative Meditation for the Activation of the Potential of the Chakras.* New York: The Aletheia Foundation.

254. Gunther, B. (1979) *Energy Ecstasy and Your Seven Vital Chakras. Second Edition.* Los Angeles, CA: Guild of Tutors' Press.

255. Harner, M. (1990) *The Way of the Shaman: A Guide to Power and Healing.* New York: Harper and Row.

256. Gallegos, E.S. (1983) 'Animal imagery, the chakra system and psychotherapy.' *Journal of Transpersonal Psychology 15*, 2, 125–136.

257. Gallegos, E.S. (1989) *The Personal Totem Pole: Animal Imagery, the Chakras and Psychotherapy.* Santa Fe: Moon Bear Press.

258. Gallegos, E.S (1993) *Animals of the Psychological Windows: Integrating, Sensing, Feeling and Imagery.* Santa Fe: Bear and Co.

259. Harner, M. (1988) *op. cit.*

260. Storm, H. (1972) *Seven Arrows.* New York: Ballantine.

261. Andrews, L. (1981) *Medicine Woman.* San Francisco: Harper and Row.

262. Roth, G. (1991) 'An urban shaman.' *Kindred Spirit 2*, 1, 33–37.

263. Jamal, M. (1987) *Shape Shifters.* London: Arkana.

264. Krippner, S. (1988) 'The first healers.' In G. Doore (ed) *Shaman's Path: Healing, Personal Growth and Empowerment.* Boston: Shambhala, pp.101–114.

265. Drury, N. (1991) *The Elements of Shamanism.* Shaftesbury: Element Books.

266. Money, M. (1992) 'The shamanic path to mental health.' Paper presented at the Second Annual Conference for the Promotion of Mental Health, Keele University, September.

267. Money, M. (1997) 'Shamans in complementary therapy.' *Complementary Therapies in Nursing and Midwifery 3*, 5, 131–135.

268. Buckley, L. (1993) 'The shamanic path to mental health.' Paper presented at the Third Annual Conference, the Promotion of Mental Health European Conference, Botanical Gardens, Birmingham, England. 6–8 September.

269. Harner, M. (1990) *op. cit.*

270. Simonton, O.C. and Matthews-Simonton, S. (1975) *op. cit.*

271. Simonton, O.C. *et al.* (1978) *op. cit.*

272. Gillespie, J. (1989) *Brave Heart.* London: Century.

273. Borysenko, M. (1987) 'Area review: psychoneuroimmunology.' *Annals of Behavioral Medicine 9*, 3–10.

274. Fiore, N. (1974) *op. cit.*

275. Meares, A. (1981) *op. cit.*

276. Donovan, M. (1980) *op. cit.*

277. Bradley, B. and McCanne, T. (1981) *op. cit.*

278. Walker, cited in Harley, G. (1989) 'Mind over body in cancer care.' *Sunday Times*, 30 April.

279. Lyles, J. *et al.* (1982), *op. cit.*

280. Achterberg, J. (1985) *op. cit.*

281. Achterberg, J. (1985) *ibid.* pp.101–102.

282. Kiecolt-Glaser, J.K. *et al.* (1985) 'Psychosocial enhancement of immunocompetence in a geriatric population.' *Health Psychology 4*, 25–41.

283. Walker, L. (1997) 'Relaxing imagery improved mood in women receiving treatment for locally advanced breast cancer.' *European Journal of Social Oncology 23*, 93–95.

284. Walker, L. and Eremin, O. (1996) 'Psychological assessment and intervention. Future prospects for women with breast cancer.' *Seminars in Surgical Oncology 12*, 76–83.

285. Walker, L. *et al.* (1977) *op. cit.*

286. Geissner *et al.* (1994) 'Psychological treatment approaches in pain. A comparative study of therapies in patients whith chronic polyarthritis.' *Zeitschrift für Klinische Psychologie und Psychopathologie 42*, 4, 319–338.

287. Cousins, N. (1981) *Anatomy of an Illness as Perceived by the Patient: Reflections on Healing and Regeneration.* London: Bantam.

288. Minchoff, K.M., Baker, B. and Dillon, K.H. (1985) 'Positive emotional states and enhancement of the immune system.' *International Journal of Psychiatric Medicine 15*, 13–17.

289. McClelland, D. and Kirschnit, C. (1984) 'The effect of motivational arousal through films on salivary immune function.' Unpublished paper, Harvard University Department of Psychology and Social Relations, Cambridge, MA cited in Pelletier and Herzing (1989) *op. cit.*

290. Hall, H.R. (1985) 'Hypnosis and the immune system: a review with implications for the psychology of healing.' *American Journal of Clinical Hypnosis 25*, 92–103.

291. Coates, T.J. and Greenblatt, R.M. (1986) 'Behavioural change using intervention at the community level.' In K.K. Holmes (ed) *Sexually Transmitted Disease.* New York: McGraw Hill.

292. Asistent, N.M. with Duffy, P. (1991) *Why I Survive AIDS.* New York: Simon and Schuster.

293. Smith, G.R. *et al.* (1985) *op. cit.*

294. Pelletier, K.M. and Peper, E. (1977) 'Alpha EEG feedback as a means of pain control.' *Journal of Clinical Experimental Hypnosis 25*, 4, 361–371.

295. Gordon, R. (1962) 'Stereotyping of image and belief.' *British Journal of Psychology Monograph Supplements.* Cambridge: Cambridge University Press.

296. Kemple, cited in Rosenman (1986).

297. Dossey, L. (1982) *op. cit.*

298. Siegel, B.S. (1986) (1990) *op. cit.*

299. Dossey, L. (1982) *op. cit.*

300. Dossey, L. (1982) *op. cit.*

Chapter 11: Energetic Treatments

1. Franz, von, M.L. (1985) 'Synchronicity and the I Ching.' In C. Rawlence (ed) *About Time.* London: Jonathan Cape, p.135.

2. Franz, von, M.L. (1974) *Number and Time: Reflections Leading Towards a Unification of Psychology and Physics.* London: Rider and Co, p.259.

3. Piaget, J. (1969) *The Child's Conception of Time.* London: Routledge and Kegan Paul, p.25.

4. Ornstein, R.E. (1969) *On the Experience of Time.* New York: Penguin.

5. Jacobsen, E. (1977) *You Must Relax.* London: Souvenir Press.

6. Pierrakos, J.C. (1990) *Core Energetics.* Mendocino, CA: Life Rhythm.

7. Franz, von, M.L. (1974) *op. cit.* p.157.

8. Schwarz. J. (1980) *Human Energy Systems.* Hillsdale, NJ: Erlbaum, p.21.

9. Gallegos, E.S. (1983) 'Animal imagery: the chakra system and psychotherapy.' *Journal of Transpersonal Psychology 15,* 2, 125. T. 136.

10. Leadbetter, C.W. (1927) *The Chakras: A Monologue.* Adyar, Madras, India: Theosophical Publishing House.

11. Avalon, A. *The Serpent Power,* a translation of the Shatchakra Nirupana, cited in Leadbetter, C.W. (1927) *The Chakras: A Monologue.* Adyar, Madras, India: Theosophical Publishing House.

12. Leadbetter, C.W. (1927) *op. cit.* p.48.

13. Butler, W.E. (1987) *How To Read The Aura.* Wellingborough: Aquarian Press.

14. *Corinthians,* 15, v.44.

15. Karagulla, S. (1967) *Breakthrough to Creativity.* Santa Monica, CA: Ade Vorss.

16. Pierrakos, J.C. (1990) *op. cit.*

17. Brennan, B. (1988) *Hands of Light: A Guide to Healing Through the Human Energy Field.* New York: Bantam, p.89.

18. Ivanov, J. (1965) 'Soviet experiments in eyeless vision.' *International Journal of Parapsychology 6,* 15–22.

19. Novomeiski, I. *et al.* (1965) reported in Ostrander, S. and Shroeder, L.S. (1973) *Psychic Discoveries Behind the Iron Curtain.* London: Sphere Books.

20. Vilenskaya, L. (1982) 'Studies in skin vision.' *Applied Psi Newsletter.* 1 Issue 2 May/June.

21. Davidson, J. (1987) *Subtle Energy.* Saffron Walden: C.W. Daniels Co.

22. Bell, A.H. (ed) (1965) *Practical Dowsing: A Symposium.* London: G. Bell and Sons.

23. Westlake, A.T. (1977) *The Origins and History of Psionic Medicine.* London: Psionic Medical Society.

24. Brennan, B. (1988) *op. cit.*

25. Kenyon, J.J. (1993) 'Human energy fields: a doctor's view from science and medicine.' Part III. *Caduceus 21,* 14–15, p.14.

26. Watson, M. (1988) 'Vital force and electricity.' *Caduceus 5,* Autumn, 24–26

27. Adamenko, V. (1990) 'Kirlian photography.' *Caduceus 12,* 18–21.

28. Inyushin, V.M. *et al.* (1968) 'On the biological essence of the Kirlian effect.' Kazach State University Alma-Ata.

29. Tomkins, P. and Bird. C. (1973) *The Secret Life of Plants.* London: Penguin.

30. Adamenko, V.G. 1990 *op. cit.*

31. Adamenko, V.G. *et al.* (1988) 'Kirlian photography – a tool in the diagnosing of psychopathy.' *Journal of Biological Photography 56,* 385–388.

32. Marangoni, V., Evangelopolou, T., and Yfantapoulos, J. (1988) 'Kirlian photography: a tool in the diagnosis of psychopathology.' *Journal of Biological Photography 56,* 3.

33. Adamenko, V.G. 'Enigmas of high frequency bioelectronics.' *Teknika-molodiojiss*, No. 10, cited in Adamenko (1990) *op. cit.*

34. Adamenko, V. (1990) *ibid.* p.21.

35. Nagl, N.W. and Popp, F.A. (1987) In *Energy Transfer Dynamics* (eds T.W. Barrett, and H.A. Pohl) pp.248–256 cited Ho, M.W. and Popp, F.A. 'On the coherent lightness of being.' *Caduceus 13*, 28–31 (1991).

36. Ho, M.W. and Popp, F.A. (1991) 'On the coherent lightness of being.' *Caduceus 13*, 28–31, p.28.

37. Ho, M.W. and Popp, F.A. (1991) *ibid.* pp.27–31.

38. Rubik, B. (1995) 'Can western science provide a foundation for acupuncture?' *Alternative Therapies*, September 1, 4, 41–47.

39. Ho, M.W. and Popp, F.A. (1991) *op. cit.* p.28.

40. Rubik, B. (1995) *op. cit.* p.44.

41. Kenyon, J.J. (1993) *op. cit.* p.15.

42. Konikiewicz, L.W. (1977) 'Kirlian photography in theory and clinical application.' *J. Biol Photog. Assoc. 45*, 3, 115–137.

43. Chouhan, P.S. (1989) 'Biolectrographic images in normal subjects and patients with cervical cancer.' Thesis submitted to International Institute of Integral Human Sciences, Montréal, Quebec, cited Kenyon, J.J. (1993) *op. cit.*

44. Adamenko, V. (1990) *op. cit.* p.20.

45. Motoyama, H. (1988) *Theories of the Chakras: Bridge To Higher Consciousness.* Wheaton, IL: Theosophical Publishing House, p.257.

46. Motoyama, H. (1985) 'Prepolarization resistance of the skin as determined by the single square voltage pulse method.' *Psychophysiology 21*, 5.

47. Motoyama, H. (1986) 'Before polarization current and the acupuncture meridians.' *J. Holistic Medicine 8*, 1–2.

48. Rubik, B. (1995) *op. cit.* p.41.

49. Rubik, B. (1995) *op. cit.*

50. Pomeranz, B. and Stux, G. (eds) (1989) *Scientific Bases of Acupuncture.* Berlin, Germany: Springer Verlag.

51. Rubik, B. (1995) *op. cit.* p.43.

52. Hopwood, V. (1996) 'Acupuncture in stroke recovery: a literature review.' *Complementary Therapies in Medicine, 4*, 258–263.

53. Staebler, F.E. *et al.* (1994) 'Why research into Traditional Chinese Acupuncture has proved difficult. Strategies of the Council for Acupuncture, U.K. to overcome the problem.' *Complementary Therapies in Medicine 2*, 86–92.

54. Wu, B. *et al.* (1996) 'Effect of acupuncture on immunomodulation in patients with malignant tumours.' *Chung Kuo Chung Hsi I Chien Ho Stsa Chi 16* (3) 139–4 March. Abstract in *Positive Health* (1998) 25, p.50.

55. Vincent, C. and Tsutani, K. (1994) 'Integrating acupuncture and Western medicine: report of the WFAS Third World Conference of Acupuncture.' November 1993, Kyoto, Japan. *Complementary Therapies in Medicine 2*, 169–171.

56. Hodgkinson, N. (1989) 'Doctors see the point in pins.' *Sunday Times*, 8 January.

57. Saks, M. (1991) 'The flight from science? The reporting of acupuncture in mainstream British medical journals from 1800–1990.' *Complementary Medicine Research 5*, 3, 178–182.

58. Bensoussan, A. (1994) 'Acupuncture meridians – myth or reality? Part 2.' *Complementary Therapies in Medicine 2*, 80–85, p.81.

59. Bensoussan, A. (1994) *ibid.*

60. Zhang, C.L. and Popp, F.A. (1992) 'Standing wave superposition hypothesis of acupuncture.' Unpublished manuscript. cited in Rubik, B. (1995) *op. cit.* 44–45.

61. Lovesay, M. (1994) 'Acupuncture and physiotherapy: an international perspective.' *Complementary Therapies in Medicine 2*, 99–103.

62. Hobbs, B. (1994) 'The application of electricity to acupuncture needles: a review of current literature and research with a brief outline of principles involved.' *Complementary Therapies in Medicine 2*, 36–40.

63. Phillips, K. and Gill, L. (1994) 'The use of simple acupressure bands reduces post-operative nausea.' *Complementary Therapies in Medicine 2*, 3, 158–160.

64. Bayreuther, J., Lewith, G.T. and Pickering, R. (1994) 'A double-blind cross-over study to evaluate the effectiveness of acupressure at pericardium 6 (P6) in the treatment of early morning sickness (EMS).' *Complementary Therapies in Medicine 2*, 70–76.

65. Ingham, E. (1938) *Stories the Feet Can Tell.* St. Petersburg, FL: Ingham Publishing Inc.

66. Bayley, D.E. (1982) *Reflexology Today.* Wellingborough: Thorsons.

67. Byers, D.C. (1983) *Foot Reflexology: The Original Ingham Method.* St. Petersburg, FL: Ingham Publishing Inc..

68. St. Pierre, G. and Boater, D. (1982) *The Metamorphic Technique: Principles and Practice.* Bodmin, Cornwall: Robert Hartol Ltd.

69. Askenazi, R. (1993) 'Multidimensional reflexology.' *International Journal of Alternative and Complementary Medicine 11*, 6, 8–12.

70. Griffiths, P. (1996) 'Reflexology.' *Complementary Therapies in Nursing and Midwifery 2*, 13–16.

71. Goodwin, H. (1992) 'Reflex Zone Therapy.' In D. Rankin-Box (ed) *Complementary Health Therapies: A Guide for Nurses and the Caring Professions.* London: Chapman and Hall.

72. Dougans, T. and Ellis, S. (1992) *The Art of Reflexology.* Shaftesbury: Element.

73. Adamson, S. (1994) 'Best feet foremost.' *Health Visitor 67*, 261.

74. Barron, H. (1990) 'Towards better health with reflexology.' *Nursing Standard 4*, 32–33.

75. Crowther, D. (1991) 'Complementary therapy in practice.' *Nursing Standard 5*, 23, 25–27.

76. Evans, M. (1990) 'Reflex Zone Therapy for mothers.' *Nursing Times 86*, 4, 229–232.

77. Levin, S. (1992) 'Why homeopathy, wherefore reflexology?' *Nursing (South Africa) 7*, 8, 38–39.

78. Lockett, J. (1992) 'Reflexology – a nurse's tool?' *Australian Nurses' Journal 22*, 1, 14–15.

79. Wynn, S. (1988) 'Reflex Zone Therapy.' *Nursing Standard 2*, 17, 28.

80. Askenazi, R. (1993) *op. cit.*

81. Aschendorf (1995) cited in Botting, D. (1997) 'Review of literature on the effectiveness of reflexology.' *Complementary Therapies in Nursing and Midwifery 3*, 123–130.

82. Shaw, J. (1987) 'Reflexology.' *Health Visitor 60*, 11, 367.

83. Wilson, A. (1995) 'A case of feet.' *Australian College of Midwives Inc. 8*, 1, 17–18.

84. Tiran, D. (1996) 'The uses of complementary therapies in midwifery practice; a focus on reflexology.' *Complementary Therapies in Nursing and Midwifery 2*, 32–37.

85. Lafuente, A. *et al.* (1990) cited in D. Tiran (1996) 'The uses of complementary therapies in midwifery practice; a focus on reflexology.' *Complementary Therapies in Nursing and Midwifery 2*, 32–37.

86. Flocco, B. (1992) 'Reflexology and premenstrual syndrome research study.' *Reflections*, 6–9.

87. Oleson, T. and Flocco, B. (1993) 'Study of premenstrual symptoms treated with ear, hand and foot reflexology.' *Obstetrics and Gynaecology 82*, 6, 906–911.

88. Griffiths, P. (1996) *op. cit.*

89. Berker, L. (1994) 'Is chest pain affected by reflexology intervention?' Reflexology Research Reports (Second Edition). Association of Reflexologists, London. cited in Botting, D. (1997) 'Review of literature on the effectiveness of reflexology.' *Complementary Therapies in Nursing and Midwifery 3*, 123–130.

90. Bosiger, C. (1989) 'Vacuflex reflexology study shows the system is successful in clearing back pain.' *Journal of Alternative and Complementary Medicine 7*, 8, 25–26.

91. Kovacs, F.M., Abraira, V., Lopez-Abente, G. and Pozo, F. (1993) 'Neuro-reflexology intervention in the treatment of non-specified low back pain.' Reflexology Research Reports. Association of Reflexologists (1994) cited in Botting, D. (1997) 'Review of literature on the effectiveness of reflexology.' *Complementary Therapies in Nursing and Midwifery 3*, 123–130.

92. Wang, Y. (1993) 'Treating type II diabetes mellitus with foot reflexotherapy.' *Chung-Kuo Chung Hsi I Chien Ho Tsa Chih 13* (0 536–538) cited in Botting, D. (1997) 'Review of literature on the effectiveness of reflexology.' *Complementary Therapies in Nursing and Midwifery 3,* 123–130.

93. Thomas, M. (1989) 'Fancy footwork.' *Nursing Times 85,* 41, 42–44.

94. Botting, D. (1997) 'Review of literature on the effectiveness of reflexology.' *Complementary Therapies in Nursing and Midwifery 3,* 123–130.

95. Capra, F.J. (1982) *The Turning Point: Science, Society and the Rising Culture.* London: Wildwood House, p.377.

96. Fisher, P. (1995) 'The development of research methodology in homeopathy.' *Complementary Therapies in Nursing and Midwifery 1,* 168–174.

97. Fisher, P. (1995) *ibid.* p.170.

98. Kliejnem, J., Knipschild, P. and ter Riet, G. (1991) 'Clinical trials of homeopathy.' *British Medical Journal 302,* 316–323.

99. Katz, T. (1995) 'Homeopathic treatment of premenstrual symptoms.' *Complementary Therapies in Nursing and Midwifery 1,* 133–137.

100. Katz, T. (1997) 'Homeopathic treatment during menopause.' *Complementary Therapies in Nursing and Midwifery 3,* 46–50.

101. Rogers, J. (1997) 'Homeopathy and the treatment of alcohol-related problems.' *Complementary Therapies in Nursing and Midwifery 3,* 21–28.

102. Katz, T. (1995) 'Management of pregnancy and labour with homeopathy.' *Complementary Therapies in Nursing and Midwifery 1,* 159–164.

103. Goodman, S. (1995) Editorial comment on Reilly, D. *et al.* (1994) 'Is evidence for homeopathy reproducible?' *Lancet 344,* b. 937, 1601–1606, in *Positive Health* May (1995), p.36.

Chapter 12: Psychosomatic Treatments

1. Reich, W. (1950) *Character Analysis.* London: Vision Press.

2. Pierrakos, J. (1990) *Core Energetics.* Mendocino, CA: Liferhythm.

3. Brennan, B.A. (1987) *Light Emerging: A Guide to Healing Through the Human Energy Field.* New York: Bantam.

4. Brennan, B.A. (1993) *Light Emerging: The Journey of Personal Healing.* New York: Bantam.

5. Lowen, A. (1975) *Bioenergetics.* London: Penguin.

6. Lowen, A. (1981) *Fear of Life.* New York: Collier MacMillan.

7. Boadella, D. (1987) *Lifestreams: An Introduction to Biosynthesis.* London: Routledge and Kegan Paul.

8. Boyeson, G. (1995) 'Biodynamic Psychology.' *Positive Health 6,* 31–33.

9. Rolf, I. (1995) 'Personal views from Ida Rolf.' *Positive Health 6,* 23–24, p.24.

10. Hunt, V. *et al.* (1977) 'Project: A Study of Structural Integration from neuromuscular energy field and emotional approaches.' UCLA.

11. Subjective impressions of the above study reported in Bruyere, R.L. (edited by J. Farrens) *Wheels of Light.* New York: Simon and Schuster.

12. Pavek, R. (1995) 'The re-emergence of biofield therapeutics within complementary medicine.' *Caduceus 30,* 36–38.

13. Jacobsen, C.F. (1929) 'Measurements of neuromuscular states during mental activities: imagination of movement involving skeletal muscle.' *American Journal of Physiology 91,* 597–608.

14. Barlow. W. (1975) *The Alexander Principle: How To Use Your Body.* London: Arrow.

15. Feldenkrais, M. (1980) *Awareness Through Movement: Health Exercises for Personal Growth.* Harmondsworth: Penguin.

16. Steiner, R. (1969) *Occult Science: An Outline.* Trans. by G. Adams and M. Adams. London: R. Steiner Press.

17. Davis and Rawls, (1979) cited in Davidson, J. (1987) *Subtle Energy.* Saffron Walden: C.W. Daniel and Co.

18. Davidson, J. (1987) *Subtle Energy.* Saffron Walden: C.W. Daniels and Co.

19. Taylor, A.S. (1902) *The Philosophical and Mechanical Principles of Osteopathy.* Self-published. USA: Hudson Kimberley.

20. Magoun, H.I. (1976) *Osteopathy in the Cranial Field.* Third Edition.

21. Goodman, J. (1997) 'Cranial osteopathy.' *Positive Health 18,* 55–58.

22. Attlee, T. (1994) 'Craniosacral therapy and the treatment of common childhood conditions.' *Health Visit 67,* 7, 232–234.

23. Upledger, J. E. and Vredevoorgd, J.D. (1983) *Craniosacral Therapy.* Seattle, WA: Eastland Press.

24. DeJanette, M.B. (1978–80) *Cranial Technique* series. Nebraska: self-published.

25. Maslak, R.A. (1987) 'Yoga and osteopathy: health care for the year 2000.' In M.I. Gharote and M. Lockhart (eds) *The Art of Survival: A Guide to Yoga Therapy.* London: Unwin Hyman Ltd., pp.162–168.

26. Upledger, J.E. (1983) *Craniosacral Therapy.* Chicago: Eastland.

27. Krieger, D. (1979) *The Therapeutic Touch: How To Use Your Hands to Help and Heal.* Englewood Cliffs, NJ: Prentice Hall.

28. Krieger, D. (1979) *ibid.* p.69.

29. Wirth, D.P. *et al.* (1992) 'The effect of alternative healing therapy on the regeneration rate of salamander forelimbs.' *Journal of Scientific Exploration 6,* 375–391.

30. Krieger, D. (1975) 'The imprimatur of nursing.' *American Journal of Nursing 5,* 484–487.

31. Wirth, D.P. and Cram, J.R. (1993) 'Multi-site surface electromyographic analysis of non-contact Therapeutic Touch.' *International Journal of Psychomatics 40,* 45–55.

32. Heidt, P. (1981) 'The effect of Therapeutic Touch on anxiety level of hospitalised patients.' *Nursing Research 30,* 1, 32–37.

33. Keller, E. and Bzdek, U.M. (1986) 'Effect of Therapeutic Touch on tension headache pain.' *Nursing Research 35,* 101–105.

34. Wirth, D.P. (1990) 'The effect of non-contact Therapeutic Touch on the healing rate of full thickness dermal wounds.' *Subtle Energies 1,* 1–2.

35. Wirth, D.P. *et al.* (1993) 'Full thickness dermal wounds treated with non-contact Therapeutic Touch: a replication and extension.' *Complementary Therapies in Medicine 1,* 3, 127–132.

36. Randolph, G.L. (1984) 'Therapeutic and physical touch: physiological responses to stressful stimulation.' *Nursing Research 33,* 133–136.

37. Meehan, M.T.C. (1985) 'The effects of Therapeutic Touch on the experience of acute pain in post-operative patients.' *Doctoral Dissertions.* New York: University Dissertation. Abstracts International 46, 01, 795.

38. Quinn, J. (1982) 'The effects of Therapeutic Touch done without physical contact on state anxiety of hospital cardiovascular patients.' Doc. Diss N.Y. Univ. Diss. Abstracts Int. 4606 1797B.

39. Quinn, J. (1984) 'Therapeutic Touch as energy exchange.' *Advances in Nursing Science 1,* January, 42–49.

40. Wirth, D.P. *et al.* (1996) 'Non-contact Therapeutic Touch intervention and full-thickness cutaneous wounds: a replication.' *Complementary Therapy Research 4,* 237–240.

41. Turton, P. (1988) 'Healing: Therapeutic Touch.' In D.F. Rankin-Box (ed) *Complementary Health Therapies: A Guide for Nurses and The Caring Professions.* London: Croom Helm, pp.148–162.

42. Sayre-Adams, J. (1994) 'Therapeutic Touch in health visiting practice.' *Health Visit 67,* 9, 304–305, September.

43. Nicoll, L.L. (1996) 'Pathfinders in Therapeutic Touch.' *Complementary Therapies in Medicine 4,* 264–267, p.266.

44. MacKereth, P. and Wright, J. (1997) 'Therapeutic Touch: a nursing activity or a form of spiritual activity?' *Complementary Therapies in Nursing and Midwifery 3,* 106–110.

45. Gennis, F. (1992) 'Alternative roads to hell?' *Nursing Standard 6,* 44, 42–43.

46. Benor, D.J. (1984) 'Psychic Healing: research evidence and potential for improving medical care.' In S.W. Salmon (ed) *Alternative Medicines: Popular and Policy Perspectives.* London: Tavistock.

47. Benor, D.J. (1990) 'Survey of spiritual healing research.' *Complementary Medicine Research 4,* 3, 9–33.

48. Weatherhead, L.D. (1951) *Psychology, Religion and Healing.* London: Hodder and Stoughton, p.50.

49. *Acts of the Apostles* 8 v 7; 3 v 10; 9 v 32–4; 9 v 17; 14 v 8; 28 v 7–8.

50. Edwards, H. (1987) *A Guide to Spirit Healing.* Tenth impression. London: The Harry Edwards Spiritual Healing Sanctuary Trust.

51. LeShan, L. (1982) *Clairvoyant Reality: Towards a General Theory of the Paranormal.* Wellingborough, Northants: Turnstone Press, p.102.

52. Grad, B. (1963) 'A telekinetic effect on plant growth.' *International Journal of Paranormal Psychology 5,* 117–134.

53. Grad, B, Cadoret, R.J. and Paul, G.J. (1961) 'The influence of an unorthodox method of treatment on wound healing of mice.' *International Journal of Parapsychology 3,* 5.

54. Barry, J. (1968) 'General and comparative study of the psychokinetic effect on a fungus culture.' *Journal of Parapsychology 32,* 237–243.

55. Grad, B. (1965) 'Some biological effects of the "laying on of hands": A review of experiments with animals and plants.' *Journal of the American Society for Psychical Research 59,* 95–129.

56. Grad, B. (1967) 'The "laying on of hands": implications for psychotherapy, gentling and the placebo effect.' *International Journal for the Society for Psychical Research 61,* 286–305.

57. Miller, R.N. (1972) 'The positive effect of prayer on plants.' *Psychic 22,* April.

58. Holmes, E. (1975) 'Thought as energy.' *Science of Mind Annual,* cited in D.J. Benor (1990) *op. cit.*

59. Krieger, D. (1975) *op. cit.*

60. Krieger, D. (1981) *The Renaissance Nurse.* Philadelphia: J.B. Lippinicott.

61. Krieger, D. (1982) 'Therapeutic Touch mediscope.' *Manchester Medical Gazette 61,* 1, 10–12 Manchester University.

62. Benor, D.J. (1990) *op. cit.*

63. Krippner, A. (1973) *Galaxies of Life: Human Aura in Acupuncture and Kirlian Photography.* New York: Gordon and Breach.

64. Adamenko, V. (1990) 'Kirlian photography.' *Caduceus 12,* 18–21.

65. Cade, C.M. and Coxhead, N. (1979) *The Awakened Mind: Biofeedback and the Development of Higher States of Awareness.* Shaftesbury: Wildwood House.

66. Gerber, R. (1988) *Vibrational Medicine: New Choices for Healing Ourselves.* Sante Fe, NM: Bear and Co, p.306.

67. LeShan, L. (1982) *op. cit.*

68. Edwards, H. (1987) *op. cit.*

69. Hall, A.G. (1950) *Primal Healing: A Discussion of the Newest Approach to Scientific Spiritual Healing.* London: Pearson Foundation, p.40.

70. LeShan, L. (1982) *op. cit.*

71. Edwards, H. (1987) *op. cit.*

72. Ouseley, S.G.J. (1981) *The Power of the Rays: The Science of Colour-Healing.* Eleventh impression. London: L.N. Fowler and Co Ltd, p.84.

73. Edwards, H. (1987) *op. cit.*

Chapter 13: Psychoenergetic Treatments

1. LeShan, L. (1982) *Clairvoyant Reality: Towards a General Theory of the Paranormal.* Wellingborough: Turnstone Press.

2. LeShan. L. (1982) *ibid.* p.148.

3. LeShan. L. (1982) *ibid.* p.150.

4. LeShan. L. (1982) *ibid.* p.150.

5. Puharich, A. (1962) *Beyond Telepathy.* London: Pan.

6. Watson, L. (1974) *The Romeo Error: A Matter of Life and Death.* London: Hodder and Stoughton.

7. Playfair, G.L. (1977) *The Unknown Power: Research into Paranormal Phenomena in the World's Most Psychic Country*. Frogmore, St. Albans: Granada.

8. Coxhead, N. (1977) *Mindpower*. Harmondsworth: Penguin.

9. Dooley, A. (1973) *Every Wall A Door: Exploring Psychic Surgery and Healing*. London: Transworld.

10. Chapman, G. and Stemman, R. (1978) *Surgeon From Another World*. London: Black Swan.

11. Taylor. A. (1987) *I Fly Out With Bright Feathers: The Quest of Novice Healer*. London: Fontana.

12. McCausland, M. (1979) 'Psychic Surgery.' In A. Hill (ed) *A Visual Encyclopedia of Unconventional Medicine*. London: New English Library, pp.180–182.

13. McCausland, M. (1979) *ibid.*

14. McCausland, M. (1979) *ibid.*

15. Blair, L. (1975) *Rhythms of Vision*. London: Croom Helm.

16. Blair, L. (1975) *ibid.*

17. LeShan, L. (1982) *op. cit.* p.165.

18. LeShan, L. (1982) *ibid.* p.166.

19. LeShan, L. (1982) *ibid.* p.166.

20. LeShan, L. (1982) *ibid.* pp.166–167.

21. Edwards, H. (1987) *A Guide to Spirit Healing*. Tenth impression. London: Psychic Press Ltd.

22. Edwards, H. (1987) *ibid.*

23. Hall, A.G. (1950) *Primal Healing: A Discussion of the Newest Approach to Scientific Spiritual Healing*. London: Pearson Foundation.

24. Carrington, H. (1920) *Your Psychic Powers and How To Develop Them*. London: K. Paul, Trench, Trubner and Co. Ltd.

25. Hall, A.G. (1950) *op. cit.*

26. Shealy, N.S. and Myss, C.M. (1988) *The Creation of Health: Merging Traditional Medicine with Intuitive Diagnosis*. Walpole, NH: Stillpoint International, pp.69–70.

27. Shealy, N.S. and Myss, C.M. (1988) *ibid.*

28. Shealy, N.S. and Myss, C.M. (1988) *ibid.*

29. Benor, D.J. (1989) 'Science looks at healing.' *Caduceus* 6, 18–20.

30. Playfair, G.L. (1977) *op. cit.*

31. McGarey, W. (1983) *The Edgar Cayce Remedies*. London: Bantam.

32. Hall, A.G. (1950) *op. cit.*

33. Edwards, H. (1987) *op. cit.*

34. Hall, A.G. (1950) *op. cit.*

35. Cade, C.M. and Coxhead, N. (1979) *The Awakened Mind: Biofeedback and the Development of Higher States of Awareness*. Shaftesbury: Wildwood House.

36. Holmes, E. (1975) 'Thought as energy.' *Science of Mind Annual*, cited in D.J. Benor (1990) 'Survey of spiritual healing research.' *Complementary Therapies in Medicine 4,* 3, 9–33.

37. Anonymous (1988) 'What is radionics?' *Radionics Quarterly*, March (rear cover).

38. Smith, J. (1995) 'The medical science of energy.' *Positive Health* June/July 6, 44–45, p.44.

39. Abrams, A. (1916) *New Concepts in Diagnosis and Treatment*. San Francisco, CA: The Philopolis Press.

40. Day, L. and Warr, de la, G. (1956) *New Worlds Beyond The Atom*. London: Vincent Stuart Ltd.

41. Day, L. and Warr, de la, G. (1966) *Matter in the Making*. London: Vincent Stuart Ltd.

42. Tansley, D. (1972) *Radionics and the Subtle Anatomy of Man*. Saffron Walden, Essex: Health Science Press.

43. Tansley, D., Rae, M. and Westlake, A. (1977) *Dimensions of Radionics: New Techniques of Instrumental Distant Healing*. Saffron Walden, Essex: C.W. Daniels and Co.

44. Anonymous (1988) *op. cit.*

45. Gerber, R. (1988) *Vibrational Medicine: New Choices for Healing Ourselves*. Santa Fe, NM: Bear and Co.

46. Gerber, R. (1988) *ibid.* p.227.

47. Gerber, R. (1988) *ibid.* p.233.

48. Gerber, R. (1988) *ibid.* p.224.

49. Franz, von, M.L. (1974) *Number and Time: Reflections Leading Towards a Unification of Psychology and Physics*. London: Rider and Co, p.155.

50. Franz, von, M.L. (1974) *ibid.*

51. Jung, C.G. (1967) *Symbols of Transformation, Collected Works Vol. 2*. Second edition. London: Routledge.

52. Franz, von, M.L. (1974) *op. cit.* p.157.

53. Jung, C.G. (1967) *op. cit.*

54. Franz, von, M.L. (1974) p.158.

55. White, K.D. (1954) *Accent on Form*. New York: World Perspectives.

56. Franz, von, M.L. (1974) *op. cit.*

57. Jung, C.G. (1967) *op. cit.*

58. Edwards, H. (1987) *op. cit.*

59. Manning, M. (1988) Seminar on Self-healing, Holistic Health Workshop. Farnham Holistic Health Centre, 30 April.

60. Schwarz, J. (1980) *Human Energy Systems*. Hillsdale, NJ: Erlbaum.

61. Worrall, O. cited in Miller, R.N. (1975) Taped talk with Olga Worrall. 'Scientific methods for the detection and measurement of healing energies.' *Science of Mind Symposium, Thought is Energy*. Los Angeles, California.

62. LeShan, L. (1982) *op. cit.*

63. Miller, R.N. (1975) Taped talk with Olga Worrall, *op. cit.*

64. LeShan, L. (1982) *op. cit.* pp.199–200.

65. Gawain, S. (1985) *Creative Visualization*. New York: Bantam, p.6.

66. Jacobi, J. (1962) *The Psychology of C.G. Jung*. London: Routledge and Kegan Paul.

67. Needleman, J. (1972) *The New Religions*. London: Penguin, Allen Lane, p.139.

68. Wright, P.A. (1995) 'The interconnectivity of mind, brain and behaviour in altered states of consciousness: focus on shamanism.' *Alternative Therapies*, July, 1, no. 3, 50–56.

69. Jelik, W. (1982) 'Altered states of consciousness in North American Indian ceremonials.' *Ethos 10*, 4, 326–343.

70. Laughlin, C.D., McManus, J. and d'Aquili, E.G. (1990) *Symbol and Experience: Towards a Neurophenomenology of Human Consciousness*. Boston: Shambhala.

71. Bourguignon, E. (1989) 'Trance and shamanism: what's in a name?' *Journal of Psychoactive Drugs*. 21, 9–15.

72. Needleman, J. (1972) *op. cit.* p.139.

73. Needlemen, J. (1972) *ibid.* p.139.

74. Epes Brown, J. (1985) 'North American Indian Religions.' In J.R. Hinnells (ed) *A Handbook of Living Religions*. Harmondsworth: Penguin, pp.392–411.

75. Watson, L. (1973) *Supernature: The Natural History of the Supernatural*. London: Hodder and Stoughton, p.105.

76. Stanway, A. (1982) *Alternative Medicine: A Guide to Natural Therapies*. Harmondsworth: Penguin.

77. Blair, L. (1975) *op. cit.*

78. Watson, L. (1973) *op. cit.* p.101.

79. Jenny, H. (1966) *Cymatics*. Basle: Basilius Press.

80. Jenny, H. (1968) 'Visualising sound.' *Science Journal*, June. Cited in L. Blair (1975) *op. cit.*

81. Blair, L. (1975) *op. cit.* p.114.

82. Blair, L. (1975) *op. cit.* p.114.

83. Blair, L. (1975) *op. cit.* p.116.

84. Rogers, S.L. (1982) *The Shaman: His Symbols and His Healing Power.* Springfield, IL: Chas. C. Thomas, pp.7–26.

85. Blair, L. (1975) *op. cit.* p.116.

86. Blair, L. (1975) *ibid.* pp.106–107.

87. Aldridge, D. (1994) 'An overview of music therapy research.' *Complementary Therapies in Medicine 2,* 204–216.

88. Aldridge, D. (1994) *ibid.*

89. Pleasanton, A.J. (1876) *Blue and Sun-lights.* Philadelphia: Claxton, Remsein and Haffelfinger.

90. Pancoast, S. (1877) *Blue and Red Lights.* Philadelphia: J.M. Stoddart and Co.

91. Babbitt, E. (1978) *Principles of Light and Color: The Healing Power of Color.* Secaucus, NJ: Citadel Press. Reprint, originally self-published 1876.

92. Steiner, R. (1982) *Colour.* London: Rudolf Steiner Press.

93. Gimbel, T. (1978) *Healing Through Colour.* Saffron Walden, Essex: C.W. Daniels and Co.

94. Gimbel, T. (1987) *Form, Sound, Colour and Healing.* Saffron Walden, Essex: C.W. Daniels and Co.

95. Gimbel. T. (1994) *The Book of Colour Healing.* London: Gaia Books.

96. Luscher, M. (1969) *The Luscher Colour Test.* New York: Washington Square Press.

97. Krakov, S.V. (1942) 'Color vision and the nervous system.' *Journal of the Optical Society of America,* June. Cited in J. Libermann (1971) *op. cit.* p.42.

98. Gerard, R.M. (1958) 'Differential effects of colored lights on psychophysiological functions.' PhD. Thesis UCLA.

99. Wolhfarth, H. (1958) 'Psychological evaluation of experiments to assert the effects of color-stimuli upon the autonomic nervous system.' *Excerpta Medica, Neurology and Psychiatry 2,* 4.

100. Ott, J. (1985) 'Color and light: their effects on plants, animals and people.' *Journal of Biosocial Research 7,* Part 1.

101. Ott, J. (1973) *Health and Light: The Effects of Natural and Artificial Light on Man and Other Living Things.* Greenwich, CT: Devin-Adair Co.

102. Cremer, R.J., Perrman, P.W. and Richards, D.H. (1958) 'Influence of light on hyperbilirubinemia in infants.' *Lancet 1,* 1094.

103. Lucey, J.R. (1972) 'Neonatal jaundice and phototherapy.' *Pediatric Clinics of North America 19,* 4, 1–7.

104. Liberman, J. (1991) *Light: Medicine of the Future.* Santa Fe, NM: Bear and Co.

105. McDonald, S.F. (1982) 'Effects of visible light waves on arthritis pain: a controlled study.' *International Journal of Biosocial Research 3,* 249–254.

106. Liberman, J. (1992) 'Light, medicine of the future.' *Caduceus,* Summer, 22–25.

107. Anderson, J, cited in Liberman, J. (1991) *op. cit.*

108. Oren, D.A. and Brainard, G.C. (1991) 'Treatment of Seasonal Affective Disorder with green and red light.' *American Journal of Psychiatry* 148, April.

109. Dougherty, T.J. (1980) 'Photosensititisation of malignant tumors.' In S. Ecomon (ed) *Adjuncts to Cancer Therapy.* Philadelphia: Lea and Febinger.

110. Dougherty, T.J. *et al.* (1978) 'Photoradiation therapy for the treatment of malignant tumors.' *Cancer Research 38,* 2628–2635.

111. Dougherty, T.J. (1989) 'Photoradiation therapy: New Approaches.' *Seminars in Surgical Oncology 5,* 6–16.

112. Pelligrini, R.J., Schauss, A.G. and Birk, T.J. (1980) 'Leg strength as a function of exposure to visual stimuli of different hues.' *Bulletin of the Psychonomic Society 16,* 2, 111–112.

113. Legwold, G. (1988) 'Color-boosted energy: how lights effects muscle action.' *American Health,* May. Cited in J. Libermann (1991) *op. cit.*

114. Schauss, A.G. (1985) 'The physiological effect of color on the suppression of human aggression: research on Baker-Miller pink.' *International Journal of Biosocial Research 72*, 55–64.

115. Schauss, A.G. (1974) 'Tranquillising effect of color reduces aggressive behaviour and potential violence.' *Journal of Orthomolecular Psychiatry 8*, 4, 218–221.

116. Aaronson, B.S. (1971) 'Color perception and affect.' *American Journal of Clinical Hypnosis 14*, 38–42.

117. Irlen, H. (1983) 'Successful treatment of learning disabilities.' Paper presented at 91st Annual Convention of the American psychological Association, Anaheim, CA, reported in Liberman, J. (1991) *op. cit.*

118. Ivanov, A, (1965) 'Soviet experiments in eyeless vision.' *International Journal of Parapsychology 1*, 1, 5–22.

119. Novomeiski *et al.* cited in Ostrander, S. and Schroeder, L.S. (1973) *Psychic Discoveries Behind The Iron Curtain.* London: Sphere Books.

120. Gimbel, T. (1994) *op. cit.*

121. Gimbel, T. (1994) *ibid.*

122. Graham, H. (1996) *Healing With Colour.* Dublin: Gill and MacMillan.

123. Wright, M.S. (1988) *Flower Essences.* Warrenton, VA: Perelandra Ltd.

124. Kaminski, P. and Katz, K. (1994) *Flower Essence Repertory.* Nevada, CA: Flower Essence Society.

125. Pelletier, K.R. and Herzing, D.L. (1989) 'Psychoneuroimmunology: a mind-body model.' In A.S. Sheikh and K.S. Sheikh (eds) *Eastern and Western Approaches to Healing: Ancient Wisdom and Modern Knowledge.* New York: Wiley, pp.344–394.

126. Bach, E. (1931) *Heal Thyself: An Exploration of the Real Cause and Effect of Disease.* Saffron Walden, Essex: C.W. Daniel and Co.

127. Bach, E. (1936) *The Twelve Healers and Other Remedies.* 19th Imprint. Frome, Somerset: Hillman Ltd (1986).

128. Bach, E. (1931) *op. cit.* p.6.

129. Bach, E. cited in Ramsall, J. and Murray, N. (1987) *Questions and Answers: Clarifying the Basic Principles of Bach Flower Remedies.* Mount Vernon: Bach Centre, p.12.

130. Kaminski, P. and Katz, R. (1994) *op. cit.*

131. Gurudas (1988) *Flower Essences and Vibrational Healing.* San Rafael, CA: Cassandra Press.

132. Davis , P. (1990) *Subtle Aromatherapy.* Saffron Walden, Essex: C.W. Daniel and Co.

Time, Energy and Healing

1. British Medical Association (1986) 'Report of the Board of Science and Education in Alternative Therapy.' In M. Saks (ed) *Alternative Medicine in Britain.* Oxford: Clarendon Press (1992), pp.211–231, p.229.

2. Prigogine, I. and Stengers, I. (1985) *Order Out Of Chaos: Man's New Dialogue With Nature.* London: Fontana, p.xxviii.

3. Kuhn, T.S. (1962) *The Structure of Scientific Revolutions.* (Second edition). International Encyclopaedia of Unified Science, 2, 11. London and Chicago: University of Chicago Press, reprinted 1970.

4. Tart, C.T. (ed) (1975) *Transpersonal Psychologies.* London: Routledge and Kegan Paul.

5. Ferguson, M. (1983) *The Aquarian Conspiracy: Personal and Social Transformation in the 1980s.* London: Paladin.

6. Kuhn, T.S. (1962) *op. cit.*

7. Kuhn, T.S. (1962) *ibid.*

8. Sahtouris, E. (1990) 'The brink of maturity: towards a scientific myth of our times.' *Leading Edge* 1 July, 12–22, p.12.

9. Sahtouris, E. (1990) *ibid.* p.13.

10. Schröedinger, E. (1957) *Science Theory and Man.* New York: Dover.

11. Holden, R. (1988) 'Modern cardiology: the biophysical approach to heart disease.' *Caduceus 4,* 6–9.

12. Cousins, N. (1988) 'Intangibles in medicine: an attempt at a balancing perspective.' *Journal of American Medical Association 260,* 11, September 16, 1610–1612, p.1610

13. Cousins, N. (1988) *ibid.* p.1612.

Index

Printed in the United Kingdom
by Lightning Source UK Ltd.
114740UKS00001B/85-102